Extreme Right Wing Political Violence and Terrorism

NEW DIRECTIONS IN TERRORISM STUDIES

A series edited by

Max Taylor
Professor in International Relations (retired), University of St Andrews, Scotland where he was formerly Director of the Centre for the Study of Terrorism and Political Violence

PM Currie
Senior Visiting Fellow at the School of International Relations at the University of St Andrews, Scotland

John Horgan
Associate Professor of Science, Technology and Society and Director of the International Centre for the Study of Terrorism at Pennsylvania State University, USA

New Directions in Terrorism Studies aims to introduce new and innovative approaches to understanding terrorism and the terrorist. It does this by bringing forward innovative ideas and concepts to assist the practitioner, analyst and academic to better understand and respond to the threat of terrorism, challenging existing assumptions and moving the debate forward into new areas.

The approach is characterised by an emphasis on intellectual quality and rigour, interdisciplinary perspectives, and a drawing together of theory and practice. The key qualities of the series are contemporary relevance, accessibility and innovation.

Extreme Right Wing Political Violence and Terrorism

Edited by

**MAX TAYLOR,
DONALD HOLBROOK
AND
P.M. CURRIE**

New Directions in Terrorism Studies

BLOOMSBURY
LONDON • NEW DELHI • NEW YORK • SYDNEY

Bloomsbury Academic
An imprint of Bloomsbury Publishing Plc

175 Fifth Avenue	50 Bedford Square
New York	London
NY 10010	WC1B 3DP
USA	UK

www.bloomsbury.com

First published 2013

© Max Taylor, Donald Holbrook and P. M. Currie, 2013

All rights reserved. No part of this publication may be reproduced or transmitted in any form or by any means, electronic or mechanical, including photocopying, recording, or any information storage or retrieval system, without prior permission in writing from the publishers.

No responsibility for loss caused to any individual or organization acting on or refraining from action as a result of the material in this publication can be accepted by Bloomsbury Academic or the author.

Library of Congress Cataloging-in-Publication Data
Extreme right wing political violence and terrorism / edited by Max Taylor, Donald Holbrook and PM Currie.
p. cm.– (New directions in terrorism studies)
Includes bibliographical references and index.
ISBN 978-1-4411-5162-9 (pbk. : alk. paper)– ISBN 978-1-4411-5012-7 (hardcover : alk. paper)
1. Right-wing extremists. 2. Political violence. 3. Terrorism I. Taylor, Max. II. Holbrook, Donald. III. Currie, P. M.
HN17.5.E985 2013
303.6–dc23
2012028553

ISBN: HB: 978-1-4411-5012-7
PB: 978-1-4411-5162-9
PDF: 978-1-4411-4087-6
ePub: 978-1-4411-0183-9

Typeset by Fakenham Prepress Solutions, Fakenham, Norfolk NR21 8NN
Printed and bound in the United States of America

Contents

Contributors vii
Acknowledgements xi

1 Introduction
   Donald Holbrook and Max Taylor 1

2 Violence by the Far Right: The American Experience
   Leonard Weinberg 15

3 Anti-Muslim Violence in the UK: Extremist Nationalist Involvement and Influence
   Robert Lambert 31

4 Grassroots Activism in the English Defence League: Discourse and Public (Dis)order
   Joel Busher 65

5 Ulster Loyalism and Extreme Right Wing Politics
   James W. McAuley 85

6 The Dutch Far Right: From 'Classical Outsiders' to 'Modern Insiders'
   Rob Witte 105

7 Youth Engagement in Right Wing Extremism: Comparative Cases from the Netherlands
Ineke van der Valk 129

8 Right Wing Political Violence in France: Stock Take and Perspectives
Michel Gandilhon 149

9 Breivik's Mindset: The Counterjihad and the New Transatlantic Anti-Muslim Right
Toby Archer 169

10 Still Blind in the Right Eye? A Comparison of German Responses to Political Violence from the Extreme Left and the Extreme Right
Peter Lehr 187

11 Far Right and Islamist Extremist Discourses: Shifting Patterns of Enmity
Donald Holbrook 215

12 Conclusion
PM Currie 239

Bibliography 253
Index 271

Contributors

Toby Archer is a freelance writer and researcher specializing in security politics, with a particular interest in political radicalization and violence. From 2002 to 2010 he was a researcher at the Finnish Institute of International Affairs covering terrorism and the politics around immigration in Europe. He has followed the formation of the counter-jihad movement since the mid–2000s and was one of the first academic researchers to write about it both for the academic audience and also in the wider media. He holds a PhD from Manchester Metropolitan University on post-Cold War Finnish security policy.

Joel Busher is a Research Fellow at the University of Huddersfield in the School of Human and Health Sciences. During 2011–12, he conducted ethnographic and narrative research with English Defence League (EDL) activists in Southeast England. His research examines the organizational, ideological and affective structures that operate at the grass roots of the EDL. His other research interests include public responses to the narratives and mobilizations of the EDL, and the local delivery of counter-terrorism. Prior to joining Huddersfield, Dr Busher worked at the University of East London, which kindly funded his ethnography of EDL activism, and as an analyst with the Defence Science Technology Laboratory (DSTL), part of the Ministry of Defence. He holds a PhD in International Development from the University of East Anglia.

P. M. Currie is a Senior Visiting Fellow at the School of International Relations, St Andrews University. He co-edited and contributed to *Dissident Irish Republicanism* (2011) and *Terrorism and Affordance* (2012), both published by Continuum. He is a contributor to the new edition of *The Encyclopedia of Islam* published by Brill. He holds degrees from Cambridge and Oxford universities. His doctorate on Islam in India was published as *The Shrine and Cult of Muin al-din Chishti of Ajmer* (OUP 1989; reissued 1993, 2006, 2012).

Michel Gandilhon is head of study in the French monitoring centre for drugs, where he works in particular on drug geopolicy. In 2011, he published a book about the FARC in Colombia, *La Guerre des paysans en Colombie, de l'autodéfense agraire aux FARC* (éditions Les Nuits rouges). He collaborates with the Department of Research on Contemporary Criminal Threats of the Institute of Criminology at Panthéon-Assas University (Paris 2).

Donald Holbrook is a Research Fellow at the Centre for the Study of Terrorism and Political Violence, University of St Andrews. He holds postgraduate degrees from the Universities of Cambridge and St Andrews and completed his PhD from the latter in 2012. His research has focused primarily on Al-Qa'ida leadership communiqués, extremist ideologies and the discourses of militant Islamist and far-right movements. In addition to publishing academic papers on these topics, his work focuses on conducting research and presenting results tailored for the UK and US practitioner communities.

Robert Lambert lectures on responses to threats of terrorism and political violence at the Centre for the Study of Terrorism and Political Violence (CSTPV) at the University of St Andrews. He has written and teaches a module on far-right terrorism and political violence that pays close attention to a rise in anti-Muslim bigotry and violence. Lambert first monitored far-right political violence when he joined Metropolitan Police Special Branch (MPSB) in 1980. In *Countering al-Qaeda in London: Police and Muslims in Partnership* (London: Hurst, September 2011) Lambert reflects on his final MPSB role as head of the Muslim Contact Unit (MCU) from January 2002 to December 2007. In 2010 he co-authored two reports on *Islamophobia and Anti-Muslim Hate Crimes* in London and the UK (published by the European Muslim Research Centre at the University of Exeter).

Peter Lehr is lecturer in terrorism studies at the Centre for the Study of Terrorism and Political Violence (CSTPV), University of St Andrews, Scotland/UK. He has published on issues including political Islam in South and Southeast Asia, critical infrastructure protection and extreme right- and left-wing terrorism, as well as on Indian Ocean maritime security issues. He is the editor of *Violence at Sea: Piracy in the Age of Global Terrorism* (New York: Routledge, 2007), and the co-editor (together with Rupert Herbert-Burns and Sam Bateman) of *Lloyd's MIU Handbook of Maritime Security* (Boca Raton: Taylor & Francis, 2009). He is the co-author (with Anthony Richards) of *Terrorism: A Comprehensive Reader* (Oxford: Oxford University Press, Autumn 2013). He earned his PhD from the University of Heidelberg, Germany.

James McAuley is Professor of Political Sociology and Irish Studies and Associate Dean for Research at the University of Huddersfield, UK. He has written extensively on Northern Irish politics and on issues around conflict, division and peace processes. He has a particular interest in the construction of political identities in Ireland. His latest book is *Ulster's Last Stand?* (Irish Academic Press 2010).

Max Taylor retired as Professor in International Relations at the University of St Andrews in 2012. Prior to that, he was Professor and Head of the Department of Applied Psychology at University College Cork, Ireland from 1983 to 2006. He is a Legal and Forensic Psychologist with wide international experience of research and consultancy in the area of terrorism and terrorist behaviour. He is editor of the journal *Terrorism and Political Violence*.

Ineke van der Valk is a researcher who specializes in racism, extremism, ethnic relations and diversity in multicultural societies. Until recently she worked as a senior researcher in the Research Department of the Anne Frank House, Monitor Racism & Extremism project where she studied processes of (de)radicalization of right-wing extremists, Islamic extremism and Islamophobia. She has a background in educational studies and ethnic studies, and obtained her doctorate focusing on the interplay between social sciences and discourse analysis with a comparative study of the perception of ethnic issues in the political discourse of the Netherlands and France, paying special attention to the extreme right. The title of the thesis was: *Difference, Deviance, Threat*. She also worked at the University of Amsterdam, where she participated in a joint research project with the University of Vienna on racism in European countries. She has published on issues relating to racism, representation of ethnic issues in politics and the media, citizenship and integration, the post-war history of immigrants in the Netherlands, human rights in Morocco and intercultural education.

Leonard Weinberg is Foundation Professor emeritus of Political Science at the University of Nevada and a senior fellow at the National Memorial Institute for the Prevention of Terrorism in Oklahoma City and at the National Security Studies Centre at the University of Haifa (Israel). Over the course of his career he has been a Fulbright senior research fellow for Italy, a visiting scholar at UCLA, a guest professor at the University of Florence, and the recipient of an H. F. Guggenheim Foundation grant for the study of political violence. He has also served as a consultant to the United Nations Office for the Prevention of Terrorism (Agency for Crime Control and Drug Prevention). For his work in promoting Christian-Jewish reconciliation Weinberg was a recipient of the 1999 Thornton Peace Prize. His books include *The End of Terrorism* (2011), *Democratic Responses to Terrorism* (2007, (ed.), *Global*

Terrorism (2005), *Political Parties and Terrorist Groups* (2003, with Ami Pedahzur), *Right-Wing Extremism in the Twenty-First Century* (2003, (ed.) with Peter Merkl), *Religious Fundamentalism and Political Extremism* (2003, (ed.) with Ami Pedahzur) *The Democratic Experience and Political Violence* (2001, (ed.) with David Rapoport), *The Emergence of a Euro-American Radical Right* (1998, with Jeffrey Kaplan). His articles have appeared in such journals as *The British Journal of Political Science, Comparative Politics,* and *Party Politics*. He is the senior editor of the journal *Democracy and Security*.

Rob Witte is senior researcher and consultant at IVA Beleidsonderzoek affiliated with Tilburg University. He works as a researcher and consultant in the field of interethnic relations, racism, radicalization, (social) crisis management as well as youth and security. Recent research projects include a study of polarization and social tensions in the city of The Hague (2012), the ENAR-report on racist violence in the Netherlands (2011), a study of far-right extremism in the city of Rotterdam (2011) and a comparative study of the processes of animal rights, asylum policies and far-right and Islamic radicalization (2010). He is author of *Racist violence and the State: A Comparative Analysis of State Responses to Racist Violence in Britain, France and the Netherlands* (1995) and co-editor of *Racist Violence in Europe* (1993). In a recent publication, '*Al eeuwenlang een gastvrij volk. Racistisch geweld en overheidsreacties in Nederland 1950–2009*' *(A tolerant people for centuries. Racist violence and state responses in the Netherlands 1950–2009)*, he updated the Netherlands section of the 1995 publication in Dutch. He examined various local case studies of racist and/of interethnic violence and led experimental projects of de-radicalization of far-right youths and the development of the so-called 'social calamities' approach and of signalizing networks among professionals involved in youth work, law enforcement, municipal and local authorities, social housing-related fields.

Acknowledgements

The Editors wish to thank all the contributors to this volume and to Peter Currie for his excellent translation from the French of Michel Gandilhon's chapter.

1

Introduction

Donald Holbrook and Max Taylor

*Three plagues, three contagions, threaten the world.
The first is the plague of nationalism.
The second is the plague of racism.
The third is the plague of religious fundamentalism. [...]
A mind touched by such a contagion is a closed mind,
one-dimensional, monothematic, spinning round one subject only
– its enemy.*

RYSZARD KAPUŚCIŃSKI (1992) *IMPERIUM*

The political extreme right wing: dissecting conceptual ambiguities

The extreme right political milieu is not a holistic entity. As with all generalizations, this descriptive label ties together a host of heterogeneous strands of diffuse political activities and divergent justificatory narratives. Moreover, people who are attracted to movements and political discourse associated with the extreme right (as might equally be said of the extreme left) do not share common or universal identities, cultures and grievances. 'Right-wing extremism', as Knoope (unpublished) noted, 'is a moving target. It is ever changing and evolving whilst being studied.'

The terms right and left wing are generally identified as having their origins in late eighteenth-century France and the early stages of the French Revolution, where they referred to the seating order of the French legislature. In the 1789 National Assembly, the 'President' or chairman of the legislature had on his right in the position of honour the representatives of the aristocracy and the church (the First Estate), whereas on his left sat the commoners (the Third Estate). Sitting on the right therefore broadly implied support for the aristocratic and royal interests, whereas the left implied republicanism, civil liberties and secularism. This broad sense of usage has persisted, in the sense that right-wing views are still generally associated with being socially conservative and holding on to the status quo, where as left-wing views are frequently characterised as embracing change and novelty. However, in the contemporary world the legacy of the Second World War, and the Nazi atrocities, further colour our view of extreme right-wing views, and complicate our analysis.

As a broad generalization, we might say that extreme right-wing political violence and terrorism constitutes an umbrella term that is applied to cluster together extremist and violent political activity that targets specific communities and actors who are blamed for the failed aspirations and grievances of belligerents. These targets can include Jews and the 'ZOG' (Zionist Occupation Government), Muslims, 'elites' and government or law-enforcement officials, non-white races, left-wing and liberal political activists and proponents of multiculturalism, immigrants, gays and 'traitors' (potential constituents who have failed to support the particular 'vanguard' in question). Belligerents, meanwhile, include diffuse youth gangs, nationalist movements, religious and millenarian movements, racist, neo-Nazi and anti-Semitic groups and other activist groups.

Some far-right extremist groups purport to adhere to religious doctrine and principles, including those that advocate vehemently millenarian goals and worldviews. Others are non-religious or even anti-religious. Elements of the far-right extremist fringe, meanwhile, continue to identify with historical fascist or Nazi traditions, whilst other strands dismiss or condemn this legacy (Bjørgo 1995). Furthermore, levels of organization, control and cohesion differ from case to case. Some forms of extreme right-wing violence might include isolated individuals acting on behalf of perceived common beliefs and sources of identity whilst other types of violent activity could be carried out by hierarchical groups seeking to emulate the rigid command and control structures of the Third Reich.

By extension, membership of far-right extremist groups is not uniform. As this volume explores, the English Defence League, for instance, purports to welcome non-whites and Jews even though these constitute targets in the actions and discourse of more 'traditional' extreme right-wing operatives. As Archer explores in Chapter Nine of this volume, moreover, Anders Behring Breivik's 'European Declaration of Independence' and his 'Vienna School' of thought did not condone racism, fascism or Nazi totalitarianism. Indeed, the logo Breivik devised for the 'Justiciar Knights' depicted a red cross piercing through a skull bearing the symbols of the Islamic half-crescent, a Swastika and a hammer and sickle.

Membership of other groups, movements and ideational strands associated with the extreme right may be more rigid. Many neo-Nazi and white supremacist groups, for example, include only a handful of activists united in their common goal of defending the white race against 'Zionist' and government conspiracies. Indeed, many of these groupings see their membership numbers dwindle as mutual distrust and paranoia cause groups to split, fragment and implode.

Conceptual ambiguities and definitional conundrums are exacerbated by the fact that extreme right-wing activists rarely recognise or operate under this label that has been defined by others to describe their activities. Unlike Islamist militants and 'jihadists', for example, far-right violent extremists tend not to describe their efforts and methods of political involvement as extreme. Rather than members of the 'extreme right', activists will refer to themselves as Aryans, Creators, white patriots, 'Justiciar knights' and 'cultural conservatives', members of the 'counter-jihad', specific militia members, national defenders, national socialists, racial holy warriors, racial volunteers, Klansmen or any other names linking them to their particular gangs, movements and ideational strands.

Activists may indeed all be intolerant and ignorant of that which they hate, but no common political denominator unites them all. There is no single common enemy amongst those we label as right wing, although many diverse groupings will share similar hierarchies of enmity. 'The enemy of my enemy is not my friend' (Weinberg, Chapter 2 in this volume) seems appropriate when it comes to extreme right-wing political violence.

Furthermore, it is unclear where distinctions should be drawn between extreme, *violent* manifestations of the far-right and more moderate political platforms that sometimes espouse similar rhetoric. Explaining how these latter groupings emerged and operate can provide valuable context that shows how more extreme right-wing political activism and violence has evolved in a particular geographical setting. Several contributions in this volume explore this wider political context in relation to the development of more violent and terrorist strands of the extreme right.

The heterogeneity of our focus of analysis, however, means that groupings under review are not only disunited when it comes to identifying enemies.

Many, as the earlier noted examples from Breivik's manifesto and the English Defence League (EDL) illustrate, are in clear opposition to each other. One prominent white-supremacist group, for example, declared EDL activists to be traitors and disseminated buttons that read 'EDL GO–2-ELL 14 WORDS'.[1]

In psychological terms, many of the qualities we might identify as characterizing right-wing views have been associated with the authoritarian personality type. Exaggerated submission to authority, extreme levels of conformity to conventional standards of behaviour, self-righteousness associated with aggression, and punitive approaches to minorities and deviant groups (Adorno et al. 1950) all tend to be associated with both authoritarian and right-wing views. Adorno's early work had its origins in the post-Second World War period, and particularly focused on Nazi and anti-Semitic views as exemplars. Early approaches tended to locate the origins of these kinds of views in psychopathy, but more recent understanding emphasises the role of social learning from family and friends, and also on a lack of experience of groups against whom prejudice is shown.

In ideological terms, extreme right-wing views are often contrasted with extreme left-wing views, where the former tend to focus on support for social order, in contrast to challenge to authority rather than social stability predominantly found in the latter. However, in psychological terms there are grounds for supposing that there may be critical common links between right and left effects on behaviour that lie not in contrasting qualities of ideologies, but in the role of extremism. Both Eysenck (1954) and Rokeach (1960) were early researchers who pointed to commonalities in personality and cognitive qualities between extreme right and left-wing activists. If this is the case, then engagement with 'the extreme per se' rather than 'engagement with extreme qualities of ideology' may be the critical variable. However, this is further complicated by the way we label someone as 'extreme right wing' which tends to be not just a description of political perspective, but also a pejorative and condemnatory term (in much the same way left-wing extremist is used). It seems likely that what we are referring to (at least in psychological terms) are complex clusters of attitudes rather than specific qualities. The views of the contributors to this book seem to largely take this perspective.

The pejorative nature of the term 'extreme right wing' can be understood in relation to Goffman's (1986) notion of 'spoiled identity', when political positions are spoiled or have become politically incorrect or unacceptable following certain historic events. Knoope (unpublished) developed these ideas further in relation to far-right extremism and the role of violence:

> This phenomenon can be characterised by the changing attitudes towards anti-Semitic groups after the Second World War. The societal/political

position of individuals or groups that still adhered to anti-Semitic ideology changed dramatically due to events in World War II and became socially unacceptable.

Similarly, after the fall of the Berlin Wall in 1989 all those who admired or supported Communism suddenly became outcasts. Marxist intellectuals in Western Europe were suddenly on the defensive and needed to deny their past sympathies. One could argue that a similar development occurred in the aftermath of 9/11 in relation to political Islamists and perhaps even to Muslims in Western society at large. A conflict arose in contemporary societies between the ideas within a certain group (Islamists and their communities) and the environment that deemed these ideas as totally unacceptable (society at large).

Spoiled identity has the potential to lead to alienation and even exclusion – both in the individual and collective sense. In a rather complex and unpredictable way, this development underpins violent action.

The conflict between one's ideological, personal and moral convictions on the one hand and the political acceptance of these positions on the other determines the, what could be called, 'potential-for-violence-factor'. The attractiveness of this exclusion, however, is determined by other factors: one being the societal position of the individual. The risk of being maneuvered into the 'outsider' position should not be underestimated. Here the 'spoiled identity' plays an important role. If it leads to (known) followers of that identity being excluded from job opportunities or careers, he or she can channel this grievance in several ways, based on the individual's own calculation.

The aims of this book

The purpose of this volume is to highlight and explore different strands of violent political activity, attitudes and related discourses and contexts that have been grouped under 'extreme right wing' banner. This is done in recognition of the fact that many of these strands are contradictory and that the label applied is awkward, at times inconsistent and ambiguous.

For this reason, the contributors to this volume have all explored the specific ideational, definitional and political contexts from their own perspective. This is not to suggest that ideas, movements and events do not transcend temporal and geographical boundaries. Indeed, movements such as the English Defence League have influenced debates on Islam in the United States, as well as elsewhere in Europe. The Dutch politician Geert Wilders has become almost a global celebrity and spokesperson for anti-Islamic far right political discourse. Yet more extremist movements, such as British neo-Nazi groups and the US Creativity Church seek to expand their reach and influence through online forums, websites and regional 'representatives' or 'chapters.'

The contributions in this volume explore these linkages and influences whilst describing the ways in which the extreme right-wing label has been applied within the specific context and for the particular case under review. Given the ambiguity of the concept of extreme right-wing terrorism and political violence and the extent to which it is applied broadly, to describe diffuse movements and activities, the contributions in this volume thus collectively emphasise the importance of understanding context and the formative evolution of the phenomenon under review.

The chapters in this volume therefore explore the development of extreme right-wing discourses and movements within specific geographical settings. The emergence of new strands is compared with the type of activities that were traditionally categorized as extreme right-wing and different types of movements and discourses are compared and contrasted. The editors hope that through this, the reader will appreciate the complexity of the phenomenon, the importance of context and the variety of dispositions, ideas and motivations that inform extremist political activity that is often labelled 'extreme right-wing' in the public discourse.

In addition to exploring specific cases in their historic context, this volume has sought to be sensitive to what appears to be a more recent dynamic that has become increasingly prominent among movements associated with the extreme right. This pertains particularly to the identification of Muslim culture and immigration and the concept and manifestation of multicultural policies as a source of grievance. Traditional elements of the extreme right have altered or rearranged enemy hierarchies, focusing increasingly on the perceived threat to their core interests from Islam and multiculturalism. At the same time, new single-issue clusters and movements have emerged that have been grouped (rightly or wrongly) under the far-right banner. The majority of these channel their animosity squarely towards Islamist ideological strands, or Islamic culture more generally, as well as aspects of modern political representation and participation that are seen to facilitate the spread of such 'alien' cultures. The English Defence League (Chapter 4 in this volume), the 'counter-jihad' (Chapter 9 in this volume) and violence focused against Islamic centres and mosques (see Chapters 3 and 7 in this volume) form part of this on-going development.

Hostility towards immigrants and asylum-seekers is not, of course, a new or recent addition to the far-right extremist milieu. Nor is the greater mobilizing potential and appeal of such movements – compared to most other strands of the extreme far right – unprecedented. Willems, for instance, warned in 1995 of the

> emergence of new ethnic conflicts and [...] of xenophobic nationalist movements which reach far beyond the right-wing political margin into the centre of society as a whole. The conflict about asylum is only the prelude to a new fundamental conflict: the conflict over immigration and by extension over the future definition of our society as a multicultural and multi-ethnic society. (Willems 1995: 180–1)

'For the first time,' Willems argued, 'these groups can experience a new self-definition and collective meaning as representatives of general interests through the unspoken or open support of parts of the population' (ibid: 180). Nascent movements on the far-right targeting Islam, Islamism or multiculturalism do not, as noted above, always fit the conventional mould of ethno-nationalistic anti-immigrant groups. They do, however, provoke similar emotions relating to the protection of 'indigenous' cultures and sources of identity and have greater potential for garnering popular support than other more rigid and isolated elements such as neo-Nazi and millenarian groups.

These anti-Islamic/Islamist and counter-multiculturalist movements and groups convey threat perceptions that may have greater resonance than those targeting the 'ZOG' and are presented as defensive: protecting common cultural norms against the influx of traditions and practices that are seen to constitute an existential threat. This perceived threat consists not only of (Islamist-inspired) violence and terrorism, but also the implementation of Shari'ah law, overtly conservative Islamic practices and even completely unrelated crimes of gangs, as well as pluralist and inclusive political structures.

This 'changing terrain of far right and populist politics in the UK' (Busher in this volume) and elsewhere seems to be less, therefore, a result of new, proactive thinking on the extreme right fringe and more a reaction to the heightened profile of Islamist-inspired violence and radicalism. Given this, it seems likely that the extent to which far-right 'responses' gain credence and momentum within some facets of society will continue to be a focus of analysis and cause for concern. This relates also to the potential danger of reciprocal radicalization, where far-right extremist groups with anti-Islamic agendas emerge in response to Islamist-inspired violent extremism, triggering further radicalization within some Islamic communities. This volume is intended to shed light on these dynamics, within individual geographical and political contexts, in addition to the composition and development of more 'traditional' far-right extremist elements.

It should be stressed at this point that this collection of essays is not intended to be an exhaustive account of the development of the extreme right wing in each relevant geographic context. Several areas that have seen important and prominent developments within the extreme right-wing milieu – such as Italy, Eastern Europe and Russia – are not covered. Rather, the aim of this volume is both to give detailed examples of how this phenomenon has evolved and to help account for the nascent dynamism that has seen movements on the extreme right rise in prominence within public discourse in recent years.

The Editors hope that this volume can inform and contribute to an on-going debate concerning different strands of the extreme right wing, the way in which movements, individuals and actors become violent and the way in which different components have evolved.

Background

The editors and most of the contributors to this volume initially explored these issues together at a workshop hosted by the Centre for the Study of Terrorism and Political Violence, University of St Andrews, held in Oxfordshire in May 2011. Prior to the workshop five general questions were distributed to participants addressing themes concerning the composition of far-right extremism and processes of involvement were identified in order to structure the debate. These concerned: (1) elements that made up the extreme right wing in Europe and the US and their principal drivers; (2) processes of radicalization and engagement and potential points of comparison with other forms of violent extremist participation; (3) the risk of violence, potential tipping points and catalysts and the relationship between street gang violence and more ideological engagement; (4) the strands and foundations of far-right extremist ideology and propaganda and how this compared with Islamist extremist discourse; (5) disengagement from extreme right wing groups and movements, points of vulnerability and potentials for intervention.

These five themes were developed into a set of questions on which participants at the workshop were invited to reflect:

- What elements make up the extreme right wing in the UK, Europe and US and what drives it?

- Are more people being drawn to these groups than before? In this respect, is there a risk of reciprocal radicalization whereby extreme right-wing groups emerge in response to extreme Islamist movements?

- How and why does someone become radicalized and engaged with the extreme right wing?
- How big is the risk of violence, beyond rhetoric and assembly/collection of explosives or weapons, and is there an element of change in this respect within the UK or Europe?
- What does the historical record show about the nature and incidence of extreme right-wing violence?
- What are the strands, sources and foundations of extreme right-wing propaganda and how dynamic is the political narrative? How do these ideological foundations compare with those of militant Islamism?
- What do we know about disengagement from extreme right-wing groups and how do people disengage?

These topics and the arrangement of the workshop were informed by a much earlier initiative led by Tore Bjørgo and other leading academics in the field who gathered for a workshop in Berlin in August 1994 to tackle issues concerning extreme right-wing political violence, focusing particularly on processes leading to violent action. The period leading up to the Berlin workshop had seen a rise in this form of violent activity. Bjørgo noted how 'in several parts of the world, terrorism and political violence of the late 1980s and early 1990s have gravitated towards the extreme right' (1995: 1).

For the 1994 workshop, participants were asked to consider the following questions (ibid: 6):

- How, under which circumstances, and for what motives, extremists turn from radical right politics – or from just harbouring racist or right-wing attitudes – to violent action.
- What is the relationship between ideology/rhetoric and actual violence?
- Does the widely held notion that violence is intrinsic to racist and right-wing extremist movements hold against empirical evidence?
- Although many right-wing groups propagate violence and hate, what can account for the often noticeable gap between their extremely violent rhetoric and their actual behaviour in terms of violent acts? (In fact, most of the racist violence is carried out by individuals and small groups not affiliated to political organizations, although often influenced by their propaganda.)
- Under what circumstances do such movements and groups cross the threshold into actual violence and even fully fledged terrorism?

- Which factors may keep groups that advocate violence from actually carrying out terrorist violence?

The participants addressed these questions in research papers published in a special edition of *Terrorism and Political Violence* (vol. 7, issue 1, 1995). Eight months after the Berlin workshop, Timothy McVeigh detonated a truck bomb that devastated the Alfred P. Murrah federal office building in Oklahoma City, killing 168 people and injuring scores more. In a rather macabre coincidence, another major attack involving 'domestic extremism' associated with the extreme right wing (although, as Archer explores in this volume, not in a traditional sense) was carried out shortly after the May 2011 workshop. On 22 July, Anders Behring Breivik detonated a car bomb next to a government office complex in Oslo before going on a shooting rampage on the island of Utøya, close to the Norwegian capital, targeting participants at a summer camp organised by the youth division of the Labour Party. Seventy-seven people were killed and over 150 were injured in these attacks.

The May 2011 workshop which formed the basis of the papers in this volume took place during a period when academic and practitioner focus has primarily been on various facets of Islamist-inspired terrorism, the impact of the 9/11 attacks (and other subsequent Islamist terrorist attacks) and the way in which Al-Qa'ida and affiliated elements have evolved since then. Breivik (who ironically saw himself as a 'defender' against the Islamist threat) and the 22 July Norway attacks have partly shifted the focus to other forms of violent extremism, at least in the short term.

The debate on the future direction, appeal and impact of extreme right-wing sentiments and political violence necessarily needs to rest on a thorough empirical understanding and appreciation for historical, ideational and geographic contexts. The contributions in this volume are intended to enhance this knowledge and understanding. This volume begins with Weinberg's overview of the composition and evolution of movements, ideologies and individual forms of activism that together have been classified as right-wing extremist manifestations in the United States. Weinberg explores the emergence of the 'Euro-American revolutionary right', warning of the potential for a wave of terrorist activity provoked by tensions rising from anger toward minorities within Europe and the US and the perceived threat they pose to existing cultural or ethnic purity.

In Chapter 3, Lambert focuses on attacks against Muslim minorities within the UK context, presenting results from qualitative research into violence targeting Mosques and Islamic organizations. Lambert makes the case for these attacks to be classified as political violence, rather than simply hate crime, and explores linkages with far-right extremist motivations. Busher, in Chapter 4, presents results from his research into the English Defence League, the most prominent of the anti-Islamist movements that have been associated with the far right. Busher emphasises that the EDL is not a homogenous entity and describes divergent facets of the movement and sources of tension, which can partly be traced to efforts of leaders to disassociate the EDL from the traditional far right.

Synergies between Ulster Loyalists and extreme right-wing political violence and motivations are the focus of McAuley's analysis in Chapter Five. Northern Ireland is a largely underexplored geographic context in this respect, which has, in some areas, recently witnessed a rise in attacks against migrants and minorities. In his analysis, McAuley emphasises that Loyalist identity is not uniform or straightforward, but warns that the defensive and pro-British discourse of local far-right extremism might appeal to some Loyalist sympathizers who may perceive the influx of migrants as a threat.

Shifting the focus towards the European mainland, Witte's contribution in Chapter 6 traces the development of the Dutch far-right extremist scene, developing the dichotomy between 'classical outsiders' and 'modern insiders'. The former refers to traditional far-right extremist elements, especially Nazi sympathizers that were rejected by mainstream society. The far right in the Netherlands, Witte argues, has evolved and splintered into different facets. More violent manifestations can be witnessed in the activities of street gangs targeting minorities, whilst far right populist groups – especially that centred on Geert Wilders – have in some ways become part of the establishment (through parliamentary participation) with a prominent share of the mainstream discourse.

Staying within the Dutch geographical context, in Chapter 7 van der Valk examines new research into processes of engagement and disengagement in far-right groupings and movements, focusing in particular on approaches towards violence and recent increases in the targeting of Islamic communities and culture. Based on this research, van der Valk discusses potential opportunities for intervention, emphasizing that these need to target the individual early on in the engagement process and be sensitive to their social needs.

The case of France is the focus of analysis in Chapter 8. Here Gandilhon investigates the emergence of right-wing extremist political violence amid periodical surges of support for far-right electoral platforms. Current manifestations of right-wing extremist engagement are compared with historical developments at the dawn of the Fifth Republic and terrorist violence borne out of the struggle for French Algeria, 'which led to the greatest wave of terrorism that France has experienced throughout her history' (Chapter 8 in this volume). Gandilhon focuses on the question of Islam in France and

Europe which may, he argues, provide the context for new forms of violent opposition informed by far-right extremist sentiments.

Condemnation of Islamic culture and the progressive political ideas that allowed such a 'multicultural' society to flourish in Europe appear to have motivated Anders Behring Breivik to carry out mass murder in Norway on 22 July 2011. Archer dissects Breivik's justifications – and the wider context of the 'counterjihad' movement – in Chapter 9. Archer argues that this attack and the wider discourse of the counterjihad does not fit within conventional notions of far-right extremism and reminds us that Breivik was far from the first proponent of an ideology that continues to evolve.

Focusing on Germany, Lehr considers the way in which far-right extremism has developed in the country over the years, paying particular attention to recent cases of far-right violence targeting minorities that have pressed the issue back onto the political agenda. Lehr warns against underestimating the danger emanating from the political far right and considers whether German authorities continue to be 'blind in the right eye', unresponsive in the face of this threat.

Offering a different comparative perspective, Holbrook contrasts far-right and Islamist extremist discourses in the penultimate chapter of this volume. This review covers the core features of traditional far-right extremist discourses and focuses on points of comparison in terms of: convergence of issues; the usage of emotive language; and issues relating to strategy and the use of force. This review concludes with an exploration of cases revealing usage of Islamist discourse in far-right propaganda to vilify Muslims.

In the concluding chapter to this volume, Currie explores the common themes that are addressed in the contributions. These relate in particular to the emerging distinction between 'traditional' or 'classical' elements of far-right extremism and more nascent developments that have seen populist parties rising in prominence in recent years and the elevated profile of anti-Islamic and anti-multiculturalist movements and ideologies. These more recent developments are best appreciated if the historical context is understood. Right-wing extremism should be approached as a multifaceted and evolving phenomenon that can, in some forms, achieve a limited degree of popular support by appealing to core emotions of the communities from which they seek their membership. The frustrations, anxieties, grievances and intolerances that are associated with right-wing extremism have been linked to bloody acts of terrorism in the past and continue to motivate those who seek to prepare and orchestrate violent attacks in pursuit of perceived dangers and injustices. It seems clear, therefore, that this phenomenon should be a cause for concern and a focus of continued research and analysis.

Note

1 '14 words' refers to David Lane's battle cry: 'We must secure the existence of our people and a future for white children,' purportedly derived from his reading of Hitler's *Mein Kampf*. See also Weinberg, in this volume

References

Adorno, T. W., Frenkel-Brunswik, E., Levinson, D. J. and Sanford, R. N. (1950) *The Authoritarian Personality*, New York: Harper & Brothers.

Bjørgo, T. (1995) Introduction to 'Special issue on Terror from the Extreme Right' in *Terrorism and Political Violence* (vol. 7, issue 1, pp. 1–16).

Eysenck, H. J. (1954) *The Psychology of Politics*, London: Routledge & Kegan Paul.

Goffman, E. (1986) *Stigma: Notes on the Management of Spoiled Identity*, New York: Simon & Schuster.

Knoope, P. *Right Wing Extremism: A spoiled identity perspective* (unpublished).

Rokeach, M. (1960) *The Open and Closed Mind: Investigations into the nature of belief systems and personality systems*. New York: Basic Books.

Willems, H., (1995) 'Development, Patterns and Causes of Violence against Foreigners in Germany: Social and Biographical Characteristics of Perpetrators and the Process of Escalation,' in *Terrorism and Political Violence* (vol. 7, issue 1, pp. 162–81).

2

Violence by the Far Right: The American Experience

Leonard Weinberg

'The Allies won the war, but Hitler won our hearts'
VARG QUISLING VIGERNES

Currently the United States offers a virtual cornucopia of right-wing groups, organizations, websites, congressional representatives, tweeters, and cable television personalities. I know nothing is more likely to induce a reader to turn the page or to skip reading a paper altogether than by beginning it with an exercise in definition. Despite this probability, given the abundance and diversity of the phenomena it makes sense to devote some space to defining the American extreme right and its various components.

Many years ago (c. 1970) Seymour Lipset and Earl Rabb sought to identify the distinctive attributes of right-wing extremism.[1] Extremism in general or procedural extremism, they suggested, is the tendency to treat social and political differences as illegitimate (no shades of gray between black and white). They refer to this quality as 'monism'. By 'monism' they have in mind the belief that there is only one correct answer to any problem and that the powers that be ought to prevent competing views from being expressed. If these powers do not act accordingly, there is a reason: a conspiracy has taken charge. What Richard Hofstadter described as 'the paranoid style in American politics' is the view that there exists a hidden hand behind almost all social and political events. Nothing happens by accident. Rather, a small cabal (e.g. Chinese Communists, Illuminati, Jews, wealthy bankers, the Vatican, Insiders) controls these events.

So far, these views might just as well apply to left-wing extremism as the rightist outlook. What then is Right? In the American context Lipset and Raab maintained that 'The substantive ideology of the right is classically liberal in its stress on individualism and libertarianism.... These elements have comprised an inter-related web of stresses on individualism, egalitarianism, anti-elitism and moralism.'[2] They also refer to the concept of 'preservatism', the goal of preserving or restoring an imagined past.

The historian David Bennett captures the concept: 'America is a dream from the past imperiled; it needs protectors to preserve its promise for future generations. Only idealists who see themselves as supreme patriots are willing to rise to its defense.'[3]

A large number of extreme groups and organizations, past and present, articulate these sentiments: The John Birch Society, the anti-communist crusaders, sacred and secular, that were attracted to Senator Joe McCarthy's struggle of the 1950s, the 'New Right' of Richard Viguerie during the 1980s, Jerry Falwell and Pat Robertson's New Christian Right, the militia movement of the 1990s and beyond, and, arguably today's Tea Party Express.

None of these groups or movements currently expresses their understandings by reference to racial, religious or ethnic hatreds (opposition to illegal immigration might be an exception). This was not the case before the Second World War when the stock-in-trade of their pre-war predecessors was the expression of nativist hostility to Catholics, Jews, Asians, and African Americans. Since the war, modern far-right groups have tried to avoid open expressions of group bigotry.

Things may be changing however. Since the turn of the twenty-first century, spokespeople for far-right groups, ones either chosen or self-appointed, have been willing to condemn Islam and Muslims as subversive forces in American society. And in deploring illegal immigration, these spokespeople usually make little effort to disguise who they think the illegal immigrants are and where they are coming from.

The constellation of groups and movements I have sought to describe should be labeled as right-wing populist.[4] They claim to represent the people whose real interests and outlook has come to be ignored by a self-serving elite that corrupts and dominates government institutions. In comparative terms, America's right-wing populists bear a resemblance to such West European people's parties as have surged in voter support in Austria, Scandinavia, the Netherlands and Italy (the Northern League) in recent years.

The militia movement appears to straddle the divide and act as a bridge between right-wing populists and the revolutionary groups I discuss below. In the early 1990s, various localities throughout the country developed local militias, bands of armed men and boys engaging in paramilitary exercises, fearful that the government intended to impose restrictions on their constitutional right to bear arms. President Bush's reference to a 'New World Order' seemed to ignite fears that American sovereignty would be replaced by the UN or some other international body. Officially the various state militia spokesmen denied they were racist or anti-Semitic. In reality though, leaders of some of the state militias, the Militias of Michigan and Montana for example, had backgrounds in white supremacist groups.[5] Further, the militias attracted and became linked to the 'sovereign citizen' movement. For reasons having to do with their ancestry, some native-born Americans believed they could renounce their citizenship and declare themselves sovereign. This meant, at least in their minds, they were not bound by the laws of the land. They could not be required to abide by requirements to possess a driver's licence or a hunting permit, for instance. It also meant they were not obliged to pay income taxes or abide by the decisions of the courts. As may be imagined, these 'freemen' often came into conflict with local authorities.

Right-wing populism only represents one half of the spectrum of far-right extremism present in the United States. The other half consists of groups that the Southern Poverty Law Centre (SPLC) and other watchdog organizations call 'hate groups'. By using the term 'hate group' the SPLC and the others are trying to convince audiences that the groups so identified are beyond the pale of civilized discourse. And of course hatred in political life is hardly confined to groups on the right.

I think it makes sense to identify these groups as belonging to a revolutionary right. Before I describe what the outlook of these revolutionary right or 'hate groups' is and how it differs from that of the right-wing populists, it seems worthwhile to get some sense of the number of groups involved and the websites they sponsor.

The numbers reported in Table 1 below seem impressive, but they require some qualification. First, some of the groups have pretty meagre memberships, consisting of no more than a handful of individuals. Second, over the years far-right revolutionary groups have been exceptionally prone to factionalism and fragmentation, with various aspiring leaders splitting from the group if their aspirations are not met and then forming a rival one of their own. Recriminations are common, with leaders alleging their rivals are secretly Jewish or FBI agents. As a result, the sheer numbers may be a sign of weakness rather than strength. If this is the case, what do these groups have in common?

By and large these are not patriotic groups in the sense they hope to return the United States to its previous glory by cutting taxes, dismantling the federal government, preventing gun control or repealing some constitutional provisions. Nor unlike the right-wing populists do they claim to be acting on

Table 2.1. Far Right Revolutionary Groups in 2011*

Group	Number	Number of Websites
Neo-Nazi	170	67
Ku Klux Klan	221	49
White Nationalist	136	187
Racist Skinhead	136	24
Christian Identity	26	42
General Hate	122	214
	N = 811	583

* Southern Poverty Law Centre, *Intelligence Report* 141 (spring 2011) pp. 44–55. The criteria used to define each of these categories are included in the Report. Under the heading of 'General Hate' the Report refers to anti-gay, anti-immigrant, Holocaust denial, anti-Muslim, racist music and radical traditional Catholic groups. Readers should also be aware that some of the numbers include various local or subsidiary units of national groups, so that, for example, the Report lists the American National Socialist Party as having 13 chapters, each of which is counted separately. The Report mentions, but I did not include, two additional categories, Neo-Confederate (42) and Black Separatist (149) organizations, because they did not seem germane to the issues to be discussed in the balance of this chapter.

behalf of 'the people' against elites of power and privilege. If anything, they hold 'the people' in contempt as really 'sheeple' in need of guidance and control. To quote David Lane, one of the key figures in hate group circles: '... the masses are selfish, greedy asses. They have always been and always will be. They will either follow us or follow them. They will worship and adore whoever is the greater tyrant. That's the nature of the masses.'[6]

It is race not nationalism that is the organising principle for these groups. Lane, among other things, is the author of the '14 Words', the creed by which adherents are supposed to act. 'We must secure the existence of our people and a future for white children.' (Lane communicated this whilst in prison serving a life term for murder.)

The world-view of the revolutionary right is that Aryans or whites are a beleaguered race both in the United States and on a worldwide basis. Aryans are the exclusive source of human invention and creativity. North America, Europe, South Africa and Australia/New Zealand are the natural habitats of

Aryans. Other regions of the world have fallen into the hands of inferior dark-skinned 'mud races', incapable of achieving a high level of civilization. To make matters worse, the 'mud races' have now invaded the natural homeland of the white race. And thanks to the satanic manipulations of the Jews, these inferior races have come to dominate the United States and will shortly come to dominate the remaining Aryan domains.

Oftentimes, the revolutionary right in the United States has been dominated by a variety of religious doctrines. Typically, conventional Christian views are rejected out of hand. Christianity, for those on the revolutionary right, is a slave religion for the weak, foisted on Aryans by Jews for the purpose of achieving their subordination. If not Christianity, what?

Most of the 'new' or revived religions involved are of European origins. An exception is Creativity, itself the creation of the late Ben Klassen, a Ukrainian immigrant. Klassen founded the Church of Creativity in 1982. Naming himself Pontifex Maximus and using the slogan 'our race is our religion', he scorned all forms of revealed religion and replaced them with a doctrine of white racial supremacy and a correlative call for violence to restore it.[7]

There is also an attraction to paganism and the pre-Christian Norse gods, Odin or Wotan especially. As Mattias Gardell writes, 'As an iron-willed warrior God, Wotan is said to instill in the white race the determination and heroic qualities necessary for them (sic) to arise victoriously in the ongoing struggle for Aryan survival and prosperity.'[8] Various rural communities and compounds around the United States have been founded by people devoted to the worship of Wotan as either Odinism or the related religion of Asatru.

Many on the revolutionary right have adopted Identity Christianity as their religion of choice. An American offshoot of nineteenth-century British Israelism, this doctrine posits the existence of a dual Creation. God's first attempt at creating human beings failed because its result was the dark-skinned 'mud people'. Recognizing the error, God then formed whites (people able to exhibit 'blood in the face') or Aryans. Jews or people who claim to be Israelites are the literal descendants of Satan ('seeds of Satan'), the result of a relation between Eve and the devil.[9] Identity preachers emphasise the Aryan origins of Christ and the demonic character of the so-called Jews. One outgrowth of Identity theology is the Phineas Priesthood. Derived from a passage in the Book of Numbers, which describes the slaying by Phineas of an Israelite man and his Midianite bride, the incident has been understood to justify the slaying of inter-racial couples. Contemporary Phineas priests who kill such couples are following the biblical example, or so they believe.

Nazism or neo-Nazism in the United States has also taken on religious-like qualities. Leaving aside the strong propensity of neo-Nazis to simulate what they consider to be authentic attributes and symbols of the German original, replete with 'Sieg Heils', stiff-armed salutes and SS lightning bolts, some neo-Nazi groups celebrate a Rudolf Hess Day (much as their European counterparts do). Others light votive candles to express their worship of the Fuhrer on his birthday and venerate pictures of Hitler on a year around basis.

What is it that the revolutionary right hopes to achieve? There is of course a strong element of fantasy involved, but the revolutionary right would like to spark a Racial Holy War (RAHOWA) which would restore white racial supremacy in the United States – and perhaps beyond. Jews would be annihilated and Israel destroyed by an atomic bomb. If possible 'mud people' would be returned to their countries of origin.

There is also a less ambitious alternative that receives some commentary. Since the American Northwest (Oregon, Washington, Idaho and perhaps the Canadian province of British Columbia) bears a resemblance to Scandinavia, some revolutionary rightists would be satisfied with a 'Nordland', a separate white bastion in a physical environment natural to Aryan yeomen. Some attempts along these lines have already been made. Until it was seized as the result of a court settlement, the Aryan Nations compound of the late 'Reverend' Richard Butler in Hayden Lake Idaho served as a model of things to come.

How is RAHOWA to be ignited? The late William Pierce, head of the neo-Nazi National Alliance offered two solutions as expressed in his two widely read novels: *Turner Diaries* and *Hunter*. The former depicted RAHOWA as the result of a terrorist campaign launched by a small group (the Brotherhood) that begins by assassinating prominent public figures and bombing FBI headquarters in Washington. (Here it is worth noting that Timothy McVeigh, who set off the bomb at the Murrah Federal Building in Oklahoma City in 1995, had sold copies of the novel at gun shows around the country.) *Hunter* offers an alternative: the 'lone wolf'. RAHOWA will be the outcome of a wave of assassinations, beginning with inter-racial couples carried out by single individuals better able to avoid detection than organised groups.

Pierce's fictional account of lone-wolf assassins was not completely original. Louis Beam, another key figure on the revolutionary right, had disseminated his ideas about 'leaderless resistance' years earlier than *Hunter*'s publication. Beam, an ex-Klansman who had been prosecuted for sedition, argued that the formation of revolutionary right organizations was a futile enterprise. These organizations were easily penetrated by the FBI or local law-enforcement agencies. Members of the organizations (and this must have been based on his experiences in the KKK) were easily bribed into disclosing whatever the authorities wished to know. Instead Beam urged those individuals committed to the cause to act spontaneously. Rather than receiving instructions from some group leader, lone wolves should simply react to events going on in the country, e.g. the election of Barack Obama to the American presidency, and carry out assassinations and bombings accordingly.

An example: on 10 August 1999 Buford Furrow, a former member of Aryan Nations, walked into a Jewish community centre in a Los Angeles suburb and opened fire on a group of boys and girls attending a summer camp. Later he drove to the San Fernando Valley and shot dead a Filipino-American mailman, for no obvious reason other than the victim's race. When he surrendered to authorities, Furrow said he wanted to send a 'wake-up call to Americans to kill Jews.'[10]

Aside from the 9/11 attacks, the most lethal act of terrorism in American history was the attack on the Murrah Federal Building in Oklahoma City on 19 April 1995. The explosion killed 168 people. The bomber, Timothy McVeigh, had had a loose tie to a Michigan militia group and spent some time at Elohim City, a Christian Identity compound in Oklahoma. McVeigh and his collaborators (e.g. Terry Nichols) were seeking revenge for a government assault on a family of right-wing extremists (the Weaver family) at Ruby Ridge in Idaho in 1992 and its invasion of the Branch Davidian religious compound at Waco Texas the following year.

The Oklahoma City bombing calls our attention to the fact that right-wing extremism in the United States has often served as a breeding ground for serious political violence. Before examining this violence though, I think we are best served if we get some sense of the size of the problem.

One way of measuring the magnitude of right-wing violence is by the FBI's reports on what the agency labels as 'hate crimes'.

Since 1990 the US Justice Department has been required by law to compile data on crimes committed because of the victim's race, religion, disability, sexual orientation or ethnicity (28 U.S.C. 534,2). These data have been published on annual basis ever since. According to the 2007 Report, there were a total 9,006 offenses that met the relevant criteria. Slightly more than 50 per cent of these crimes were motivated by racial bias. The remaining were crimes almost equally distributed among acts motivated by religious bias (18.4 per cent), sexual orientation (16.6 per cent), and ethnicity/national origins (13.2 per cent). [11]

These figures reflect how widespread the willingness to use violence as a means of showing hatred for the groups mentioned above. According to the Anti-Defamation League most of hate crimes, though, were carried out by individuals unaffiliated with an organised right-wing group. Most often they were carried out by young people on a lark who found it amusing to attack relatively helpless individuals.

What about organised right-wing violence? In *Understanding Terrorism in America* Christopher Hewitt sought to evaluate terrorist activity in the United

States between 1954 and 2000, that is before the 9/11 attacks. The years encompass the desegregation struggles of the 1950s and 1960s. Using a legal definition of terrorism, Hewitt reports the following frequency distribution of incidents and fatalities (see Table 2).

What the data suggest are that prior to Al Qaeda's attacks on the World Trade Centre and Pentagon, terrorist violence in the United States was significantly a right-wing activity measured both in terms of the frequency of incidents and the fatalities inflicted. If anything, Hewitt's distribution underestimates the role of the far right. Not all but certainly many of those engaged in anti-abortion violence had backgrounds in far-right organizations. For instance, Erich Rudolph, a man who attacked a women's health clinic in Alabama, was the same person who set off a bomb at the site of the 1996 Olympic Games in Atlanta. Previously Rudolph had spent time at a Christian Identity compound in Missouri before embarking on his spree.

Table 2.2. Terrorist incidents and fatalities by those responsible, 1954–2000 (per cent)

Type of terrorism	Incidents	Fatalities
Foreign		
Cuban émigré	5.2	1.5
Puerto Rican	11.9	4.3
Islamic	1.1	1.7
Other foreign	2.1	4.1
Domestic terrorism		
White racist/Rightist	31.2	51.6
Revolutionary Left	21.2	2.0
Black militant	14.7	25.0
Anti-abortionist	6.2	0.9
Jewish	3.6	0.8
Other domestic/unknown	2.8	8.1
Total N	(3,228)	(661)

Christopher Hewitt, *Understanding Terrorism in America* (London: Routledge, 2003) p. 15.

The most spectacular episode of right-wing violence prior to the Oklahoma City attack was the terrorist campaign carried out by Robert Mathews and members of his Silent Brotherhood or Order band in the period 1983–4. Mathews and some of his approximately two dozen followers had been members of the Aryan Nations compound in Hayden Lake Idaho. Mathews reached the conclusion that the latter was almost all talk with very little action. He issued a 'Declaration of War' which read, in part: 'It is now a dark and dismal time in the history of our race. All about us lie the green graves of our sires, yet in a land once ours we have become a people dispossessed.... By the millions, those not of our blood violate our borders and mock our claim to sovereignty. Yet our people only react with lethargy.'[12] Mathews came to believe that he and his followers would be able to spark a racist revolution in the US by killing prominent Jews, individuals he believed were part of ZOG. In practice, members of the order assassinated Alan Berg, a Denver talk-radio host, and staged a number of holdups in the Northwest. Most members of the Silent Brotherhood were arrested in 1984. Mathews chose to shoot it out with the FBI at his refuge on Whidbey Island in Puget Sound – with the predictable outcome.[13]

The SPLC has sought to chronicle more recent terrorist operations planned or carried out by the far right between 1995 and the middle of 2009.[14] The SPLC records a total of 75 incidents. Some of the incidents reported were simply plots that were not carried out because those involved were arrested before they could act. The other events were about evenly divided between group operations and lone-wolf attacks. Here are three illustrations:

'January 18, 1996 – Peter Kevin Langan, the pseudonymous 'Commander Pedro' who leads the underground Aryan Republican Party, is arrested after a shootout with the FBI in Ohio. Along with six other suspects arrested around the same time, Langan is charged in connection with a string of 22 bank robberies in seven Midwestern states between 1994 and 1996.'

'April 1, 2004 – Neo-Nazi Skinhead Sean Gillespie videotapes himself as he firebombs Temple B'nai Israel, an Oklahoma City synagogue, as part of a film he is preparing to inspire other racists to violent revolution.' (Mr Gillespie apparently did not anticipate that his videotape would be used in a court proceeding.)

'January 21, 2009 – On the day after Barack Obama is inaugurated as the nation's first black president, Keith Luke of Brockton Mass. is arrested for allegedly shooting three black immigrants from Cape Verde, killing two of them, as part of a racially motivated killing spree. The two murders are apparently only part of Luke's plan to kill black, Latino, and Jewish people.... Luke charged with murder, kidnapping and aggravated rape, has etched a swastika into his own forehead, apparently using a jail razor.'

I think it is worthwhile to point out that we are dealing with two types of 'lone wolves'. Mr Luke evidently became a violent racial supremacist as the result of prolonged exposure to racist websites, of which there is a large number. Mr Gillespie and Mr Furrow (see earlier) were also lone wolves but they were essentially spin-offs of right-wing revolutionary bands to which they belonged for some period.

The next question we should pose is, where do these revolutionaries come from? We should resist the temptation to respond immediately by saying 'mental health facilities', although that is true in a few cases, e.g. Buford Furrow. It seems a trap to think that people with exotic and extreme beliefs are themselves exotic or deranged. Some of the key figures on the revolutionary right have been successful at other endeavours. Richard Butler, late head of Aryan Nations, was an aircraft engineer who held several patents. David Duke, the personable Klansman and former national socialist ('gas the Chicago seven'), was elected to the Louisiana legislature. William Pierce, late head of the National Alliance, held a Ph.D. in physics. Tom Metzger, leader of the White Aryan Resistance (WAR) and former Klansman, owns a TV repair shop. Harold Covington, once a key figure in the National White People's Party, came from a wealthy family. Serta Mattress was identified as a 'gifted student' and awarded a college scholarship in North Carolina.

These biographical accounts are worth reporting because they help to dispel the stereotype that right-wing revolutionaries are necessarily of limited accomplishment and intelligence – and therefore not to be taken seriously.

If we consider things in the aggregate and repeat the question 'where do they come from?', a number of milieu are involved and require descriptions.

Prisons, both federal and state, provide fertile territory for the conversion and recruitment of right-wing revolutionaries. Inmates typically divide themselves along racial and ethnic lines. Black and Hispanic gangs often dominate inmates' lives. Whites have reacted correspondingly by forming their own gangs to protect themselves. Known variously as the Aryan Brotherhood, Aryan Warriors, the European Kindred and other names, these gangs were first formed in the late 1960s when previously segregated prison populations were racially integrated. Members typically wear tattoos (Nazi symbols are favorites) that identify them as belonging to a particular gang or sub-group.

Following their release from prison, Aryan gang members often pursue or continue to pursue criminal activities. Drug trafficking is an especially lucrative pursuit for such gangs as the southern California Nazi Low Riders.

A subset of these Aryan inmates become politicized whilst in prison: Gary Yarborough, a key figure in the Silent Brotherhood, became politically aware whilst serving a prison sentence. Yarborough and others were the beneficiaries of prison ministries. Such Identity congregations as the Church of Jesus Christian and a number of Odinist groups have outreach programs involving letter-writing and personal visits.

Music may have charms to sooth the savage beast, but at least in the case of potential neo-Nazis it seems to have the opposite effect. White Power or Hate Music (whose origins are in the UK with the band Skrewdriver) is a common way by which young white youths in the big cities become attracted to the Aryan cause.[15] Such groups as Hate Train and Max Resist perform at music festivals where naïve teenagers may be transformed into 'freshcuts' (novice neo-Nazis). The latter may then be invited to 'crashpads' (shared flats in rundown neighbourhoods) and Aryan parties where they are inducted into neo-Nazism through a series of ceremonies and rituals.

Then there are the compound dwellers. If neo-Nazi groups are an essentially urban phenomenon, followers of Identity and the various neo-pagan religions often retreat to rural encampments, sanctuaries for Aryans. Over the last few decades religiously inspired revolutionary rightists have established such compounds as the Covenant, Sword and Arm of the Lord (CSA), Elohim City, Cosmotheism Community Church, Aryan Nations, the Holy Order of the Phineas Priesthood, WOTANSVOLK, JUSTUS Township and others.[16]

These retreats not only provide an opportunity for religious worship, but often become centres from which revolutionary violence emerges. In the case of the CSA, members were discovered to have stockpiled chemicals to be used to poison the water supply of a major American city – before the FBI intervened. Paramilitary training and target practice are common, but so is the scrutiny of the police and undercover agents of the Watchdog groups.

'Lone wolves', of whom Timothy McVeigh was the most prominent, have emerged from these compounds from time to time. And of course there is the case of Robert J. Mathews and his Silent Brotherhood band of right-wing terrorists. Another consideration is the fact that it is much easier to obtain guns and other weapons in the United States.

Compounds based on Identity theology frequently attract members with apocalyptic views; these individuals believe the end of the world is imminent, and, on occasion at least, do what they can to 'force the end'. Over the years, the retreats have also provided locales for white power festivals at which Aryans from Australia, Great Britain, Canada, Sweden and other 'white' nations participate.

In recent years the Internet has provided an important source of recruits for the revolutionary right. Virtually all the relevant groups have their own websites, some quite sophisticated in their appeals to a wide spectrum of people from children (Aryan cartoons) to adults, both men and women. The first white supremacist to take advantage of the new medium was Don Black.

A former Grand Dragon of the KKK and national socialist, in 1981 Black and nine like-minded individuals were arrested in New Orleans (they were storing weapons aboard a boat) whilst preparing to invade the Caribbean island of Dominica where they hoped to establish a white bastion and tourist resort.

After his release from prison, Black created Stormfront in 1995 which is, even today, one of the most popular websites of its kind. According to Jeff Kaplan, 'Stormfront offers files from a number of racialist groups, hypertext links to a number of others, and several email discussion and news lists that allow the white nationalist community to discuss issues of interest.'[17]

Since Black's initiative a long list of revolutionary right groups and luminaries have taken advantage of the Internet. The now numerous websites provide a useful recruiting tool. The youthful background of many Internet users – they are often college students – permit right-wing webmasters to reach a wider pool of potential recruits than was previously the case.

To what extent, if any, is the revolutionary right in the United States linked to similar-minded groups in Great Britain and the rest of Europe? And to what extent does this hypothesised linkage pose a threat of terrorism and less dramatic types of violence? In other words, is there an emerging Euro-American revolutionary right that poses a challenge to democratic governments on both sides of the Atlantic?

On this point, I think it best to call attention to common conditions. These circumstances were best defined years ago by Donald Clerkin, head of the Euro-American Alliance:

'Whites are beginning to feel the pressure of dispossession. Amerika (sic) is beginning to look like images in National Geographic, its cities resembling Mexico City and Calcutta. The U.S. Armed Services are turning Black, Brown and Yellow .... Hi Tech jobs are going overseas. The universities fill up with Asians .... Media preach a steady stream of minority rights propaganda, telling young Whites that they must share their country with the refuse of the entire world. The same message is spread into each and every White country in the world.'[18]

If we changed a few names, addresses and epithets, Clerkin's comment could also be applied to the situations in a number of West European countries. But does a similarity of situation lead to a commonality of purpose and action?

For analysts of political conflict, the answer is 'no'. The ingredients that seem to be missing are a common web of organizations to tie the affected White populations together and a group of 'movement entrepreneurs' to mobilise them into protest and violent action.

These ingredients have been present in the not too distant past but did not spark much violence. In the 1950s an American lawyer, Francis Parker Yockey, formed the European Liberation Front. Further, during the 1960s George Lincoln Rockwell, the founder of the American Nazi party, and his English counterpart, Colin Jordan (along with Swedish representatives) signed the Cotswold Agreement which led to the establishment of the World Union of National Socialists (WUNS). Neither organization though amounted to very much.

Post-war American and European history has not lacked would-be revolutionary right entrepreneurs. Over the decades such revolutionary rightists as Manfred Roeder, Gary Rex Lauck, William Pierce, Don Black, David Irving, Roy Godenau, and a substantial list of others have crossed the Atlantic in both directions in efforts to forge bonds, without much success.

Have things changed? Is there some prospect of an 'Aryan spring' to go along with an Arab one?

As in the latter case, there are the new social media with which to contend. Cyberspace now offers the media by which revolutionary right groups on both sides of the Atlantic can circumvent older means of mass communication. Legal limits on 'hate speech' (e.g. prohibitions on Holocaust denial in Germany) may be avoided. Thanks to the First Amendment to the US Constitution, messages and symbols of racial and religious bigotry articulated by European groups may be redirected and transmitted via American-based servers.[19]

Then there are the Nazi skinheads and their 'hate rock' music to contemplate. Skinhead gangs or the skinhead sub-culture first appeared in England during the 1970s. Since those years these gangs have spread to other countries in Europe – Sweden, Germany, Poland, Hungary – and have crossed the Atlantic where skinheads may be found throughout the United States and Canada (beginning in the 1980s). As I understand it, not all skinhead gangs are Nazi or neo-Nazi, but enough of them are to warrant their inclusion under the revolutionary right heading. Despite the Nazi ideology, skinhead gangs do not resemble the original storm troopers or brown shirts. There is too little discipline for them to constitute paramilitary formations along the lines of the inter-war groups in Germany and the successor states. Furthermore, in the American case neo-Nazi skinheads need not be of Nordic background in order to join, being white is sufficient. So we find such historical curiosities as Polish and other Slavic background skinheads. In recent years there has been a proliferation of Nazi skinhead gangs in Russia as well; a country and a people after all that would have disappeared if Hitler had won his war.[20]

The neo-Nazi skinheads do not constitute an international group so much as a 'scene'. These loosely connected gangs are linked to one another by the music which they enjoy and the violence they commit. So far as the former is concerned, the Swedish social scientist Helené Lööw reports some of the lyrics from the song Ukklavaek as performed by the band Division S:

'Anarchist, anarchist we're going to make you bleed
Race war, race war! That's what we're heading for
Communist, communist! Gonna break your neck
White Power, White Power! We're gonna save our race
Fuck you, fuck you! Kill yourself
You boy, you boy waste of space
Democracy, democracy, fucking hypocrisy
Niggative, niggative, you smell like a pig
Media man, media man, you're gonna die in pain....'[21]

The sentiments expressed in these lyrics are of course invitations to violence directed against members of the public. In fact, over the years, skinhead gangs in Europe and America have carried out a long list of attacks on vulnerable members of racial minorities. Gays are also favorite targets. Jewish cemeteries and places of worship have been desecrated with some frequency. Skinhead gang leaders have bought in to the ZOG discourse. Further, at least in some countries – Germany and nations farther to its east – skinhead gangs have developed ties to far-right political parties, e.g. the National Democrats (NPD) in eastern Germany.

Where does all this leave us? I think it is fair to say that the emergent Euro-American revolutionary right – no matter how much attention it manages to attract and how enticing its message becomes to increasingly threatened, economically and socially, white populations – is unlikely to induce a race war, holy or otherwise. It does share a common hatred of Jews and the state of Israel with growing Muslim populations and their leadership(s) in Europe and elsewhere. The common hatred, though, seems unlikely to produce more than temporary cooperation. In this instance, the enemy of my enemy is not my friend. Because it is precisely the growing Muslim populations, in Western Europe especially, that are likely to be the targets of intensifying 'white power' backlash.

If not RAHOWA within one or more of the Western democracies, the potential certainly exists for a wave of terrorist activity. For revolutionary right terrorism to occur, the late Israeli political scientist Ehud Sprinzak identified two indispensable elements.[22] First, a racial or religious minority group(s) must be present that appears to be making illegitimate demands for political and social equality with the dominant white population. Right-wing groups form to protect this population from the minorities' claims to legitimacy and recognition. In turn, these groups seek the assistance of governments to prevent the minorities from achieving their aims. If the governments are unresponsive or, worse, appear to side with the white populations' racial or religious enemies, then the conditions are present for a terrorist campaign directed not only at members of the minority groups, but also at the governments that now appear to constitute the 'enemy' as well. It seems difficult to deny these elements are currently present in a number of the Western democracies.

Notes

1 Seymour Lipset and Earl Raab (1970), *The Politics of Unreason* New York: Harper & Row, pp. 3–31.
2 Lipset and Raab, p. 8, 24.
3 David Bennett (1995), *The Party of Fear* 2nd edn New York: Vintage Books, p. 3.
4 For a discussion see Chip Berlet and Mathew Lyons (2000), *Right-Wing Populism in America* New York: The Guilford Press, pp. 4–18.
5 For a review of the militia groups see Morris Dees (1996), *Gathering Storm* New York: HarperCollins, and Kenneth Stern (1996), *A Force upon the Plain* New York: Simon and Schuster.
6 Quoted in Mattias Gardell (2003), *Gods of the Blood* Durham, NC: Duke University Press, p. 201.
7 Jeffrey Kaplan (ed.) (n.d.), *Encyclopedia of White Power* Walnut Creek, CA: Alta Mira Press, pp. 54–7.
8 Gardell, p. 208.
9 For a discussion see Michael Barkun (1994), *Religion and the Racist Right* Chapel Hill, NC: University of North Carolina Press.
10 Intelligence Project (2009), *Terror from the Right* Montgomery, AL: SPLC, p. 16.
11 U.S. Department of Justice – Federal Bureau of Investigation, *Hate Crime Statistics, 2007* (released October 2008).
12 Quoted in Kaplan, p. 523.
13 For an account see Kevin Flynn and Gary Gerhardt (1990), *The Silent Brotherhood* New York: Signet.
14 *Terror from the Right* (2009) Montgomery AL: Southern Poverty Law Centre.
15 Pete Simi and Robert Futrell (2010), *American Swastika* Lanham Maryland: Rowman and Littlefield, pp. 59–82.
16 James Coates, *Armed and Dangerous* (1987) New York: Hill and Wang, pp. 123–56.
17 Kaplan, p. 24.
18 Maj. D. V. Clerkin, 'Who we really are' *The Talon* (1989) pp. 2–3.
19 This writer's interview with Agent Klaus Schmidt, German Federal Criminal Police, Bonn, June 1997.
20 See, for example, Irwin Suall (1995), *The Skinhead International* New York: Anti-Defamation League, pp. 5–9.

21 Helené Lööw (1998), 'White Power Rock 'n' Roll: A Growing Industry' in Jeffrey Kaplan and Tore Bjørgo (eds), *Nation and Race* Boston: Northeastern University Press, p. 128.

22 Ehud Sprinzak (1995), 'Right-Wing Terrorism in Comparative Perspective' in Tore Bjørgo (ed.), *Terror from the Extreme Right* London: Frank Cass, pp. 17–43.

3

Anti-Muslim Violence in the UK: Extremist Nationalist Involvement and Influence

Robert Lambert

Given the clear evidence of extremist nationalist involvement in racist violence in the UK in the last 50 years[1], it is reasonable to enquire whether there is evidence of the same milieu being involved in anti-Muslim violence during the last ten years in which it has become prevalent. To be sure, the evidence that extremist nationalist organizations have spent the last decade campaigning against Muslims and Islam is clear enough. Equally clear is the growth of anti-Muslim violence during the same post 9/11 period. Less clear, and providing a basis for the research analysed in this chapter, is a connection between the two new phenomena. By examining anti-Muslim violence and especially violence aimed at mosques, Islamic institutions and Muslim organizations, it is intended to illuminate the role of extremist nationalists and to place it in a political and community context. This chapter therefore consists of a preliminary analysis of qualitative research conducted into the nature and impact of anti-Muslim violence, in particular violence against mosques, Islamic centres and Muslim organizations in the UK. In doing so it does not always cast a direct light on the question of extremist nationalist involvement in the violence that is the subject of analysis. It does however shed sufficient light on the question so as to establish a prima facie case for both extremist nationalist involvement and influence.

Terms of reference

Research data that relates specifically to attacks on mosques, Islamic institutions and Muslim organizations is utilised whilst research data that deals with more general violence against Muslim communities and Muslim individuals in the street is also acknowledged and referenced so as to provide context.[2] It should also be mentioned that the desecration of Muslim graves in public cemeteries is an important and familiar category that discloses a clear anti-Muslim motivation on the part of perpetrators. The research is based on interviews with victims, witnesses and investigators of this kind of violence and is supported by responses to a questionnaire sent to over 1,000 mosques, Islamic centres and Muslim organizations.[3] Secondary sources such as reports in local newspapers and the monitoring work of bodies including the Institute of Race Relations, Islamophobia Watch and Engage have also been used to corroborate and triangulate the research findings. Far from offering definitive findings, this preliminary analysis does however provide a clear indication that extremist nationalist organizations including the British National Party (BNP) and the English Defence League (EDL) have played a key role in fostering a climate in which anti-Muslim or Islamophobic violence has become an established feature of British life since 9/11. This is not to argue that leaders of the BNP or the EDL have been involved in criminal conspiracies to attack Muslims or their places of worship or congregation, but rather to provide evidence that their campaigning activities against Muslims have provided motivation and a rationale for many of the criminal attacks that have taken place. In consequence it becomes clear that many Muslim communities have, since 9/11, faced a double jeopardy of becoming victims of violence aimed at them because of their religion as well as by virtue of their ethnic origins.

By focusing primarily on what might be perceived as violence against buildings and their occupants and against institutions and organizations rather than violence against individuals, there is no intention to prioritise one kind of anti-Muslim violence over the other. On the contrary, both areas of research are assessed to be equally important and complementary.[4] The complementary and cumulative nature of the violence and intimidation being analysed becomes more clearly defined when approached from the perspective of victims – a vantage point that has been adopted by academics and practitioners in relation to racist violence and extremist nationalist participation in it.[5] Necessarily tentative research findings nonetheless add substance to the notion that an established extremist nationalist milieu has contributed to specifically anti-Muslim violence since 9/11 in the same way that it has contributed to more general and more widely researched racist violence before and since.

Anti-Muslim campaigning

Violence against Muslims is generally considered under the rubric of Islamophobia.[6] However, rather like a study of racism, a study of Islamophobia invariably involves an analysis of non-violent activity such as discrimination alongside violent behaviour.[7] By analysing violent conduct towards Muslims it is not intended to ignore the wider experience of Muslims as victims of Islamophobic discrimination or bigotry.[8] On the contrary, by acknowledging a victim's perspective every effort is made to contextualize the lived experience of Muslims in the UK.[9] For the same reason it seems that the terms *anti-Muslim bigotry*[10] and *anti-Muslim racism*[11] better describe the experience of Muslims than the term Islamophobia, which is also used to describe criticism or fear of Islam. Suffice to say there is an obvious overlap between the notion of anti-Muslim bigotry and the notion of Islamophobia and academic preferences for one or the other term should not hinder the kind of analysis undertaken in this chapter.

Where preference for the term anti-Muslim bigotry may have some special value is when considering violent and intimidating demonstrations against Muslim communities and organizations that are widely (although wrongly in the view of the researcher[12]) held to be extremist. This kind of demonstration allows protesters to challenge the allegation that they are Islamophobic. Instead, by repeating the arguments of mainstream politicians and media commentators, they can claim plausibly to be opposed to 'Muslim extremists' and to have a concomitant respect for Islam and its 'moderate' adherents. To illustrate, in June 2010 EDL members and supporters started to visit Tower Hamlets in the days leading up to a planned demonstration against so-called 'Muslim extremists'. For Reverend Alan Green who was closely involved in organising opposition to the EDL this was a clear attempt by the EDL to provoke a reaction:

> ... there were still fears that the EDL were coming and that in particular that they were going to attempt to demonstrate outside the ELM [East London Mosque] or attack it, and that was fuelled by a visit Tuesday before by a group of fifteen or so EDL who had been in Barking for the day and decided it would be a good wheeze to get off the underground at Whitechapel and have a beer and make themselves known, and that produced a group of 200 young people [Muslim youths] within quarter of an hour.[13]

Fortunately police in Tower Hamlets had built a close working partnership with the East London Mosque (ELM), the London Muslim Centre (LMC), the

Islamic Forum of Europe (IFE), the Muslim Council of Britain (MCB) and other Muslim organizations based locally over a long period of time. As a result police and purportedly 'extreme' Muslim organizations worked hand in glove to defeat attempts by the EDL to provoke fear and anger in the run-up to a planned demonstration. Although the EDL eventually decided to cancel their demonstration, they were able to do so in the knowledge that their claim to be opposing 'radical' and 'subversive' Muslims in Tower Hamlets was one that received daily endorsements in the national and local media. The same Muslim 'extremists' were defended as reasonable and responsible citizens by their partners in the police, by Neil Jameson, director of London Citizens,[14] by Reverend Alan Green, chair of the Tower Hamlets Interfaith Forum,[15] and many other local partners. In interview Reverend Green highlights the value of the close partnership he has established with the ELM and London Muslim Centre (LMC) over a long period, especially with Dilwar Hussain, director of the ELM:

> We can work at big problems together, and I recognise you need to stay awake and astute to things, but in the end it is simply those practical moments, and if people are coming and supporting you, then they're people I can work with. And when the bombs went off in London [7/7], I got the bishop down to the ELM so that there could be immediate joint statements, and Dilwar on the Sunday was here in St. John's preaching with me about our opposition to bombers. Now that was entirely unnecessary, that wasn't before TV screens, it wasn't to get anything out of it...[16]

Green was at the forefront of partnership work with ELM, IFE, LMC and others to tackle the EDL threat:

> ... it was important that we had a clear public statement of opposition to the EDL, that they might have achieved what they had set out to do in stopping this conference, but they needed to know, and we needed the general population to know, that Tower Hamlets was not going to put up with the sort of tactics that the EDL use.[17]

In research in other towns and cities in the UK where the EDL have held demonstrations there is a similar paucity of evidence to support the notion that the EDL is genuinely campaigning against Muslim extremists who threaten public safety, security and social cohesion.[18] More generally, to illustrate the extent to which it has become commonplace to adopt a different standard when discussing Muslims, the novelist Ronan Bennett asks what we are we to make of the following statement:

Asians are gaining on us demographically at a huge rate. A quarter of humanity now and by 2025 they'll be a third. Italy's down to 1.1 child per woman. We're just going to be outnumbered. whilst we're at it, what do you think of this, incidentally from the same speaker: 'The Black community will have to suffer until it gets its house in order.' Or this, the same speaker again: 'I just don't hear from moderate Judaism, do you?' And (yes, same speaker): 'Strip-searching Irish people. Discriminatory stuff, until it hurts the whole Irish community and they start getting tough with their children'.[19]

The speaker was fellow novelist Martin Amis and Bennett has modified the quotations, with Asians, Blacks and Irish substituting for Muslims, and Judaism for Islam – 'though, it should be stressed', Bennett adds, 'these are the only amendments'.[20] Bennett is right to claim that 'Amis's views are symptomatic of a much wider and deeper hostility to Islam and intolerance of otherness'.[21] To illustrate the point he refers to a debate *Is Islam good for London* sponsored by the London Evening Standard. It is worth accepting his invitation to 'do another substitution here and imagine the reaction had Judaism been the subject':[22]

As Rabbi Pete Tobias noted [...], the so-called debate was sinisterly reminiscent of the paper's campaign a century ago to alert its readers to the 'problem of the alien', namely the eastern European Jews fleeing persecution who had found refuge in the capital[23]. In this context, Rod Liddle's contribution to proceedings – 'Islamophobia? Count me in' – sounds neither brave, brash nor provocatively outrageous, merely racist. Those who claim that Islamophobia can't be racist, because Islam is a religion not a race, are fooling themselves: religion is not only about faith but also about identity, background and culture, and Muslims are overwhelmingly non-white. Islamophobia is racist, and so is anti-Semitism.[24]

It would certainly be naïve to discount the possibility that the articulate, sometimes sophisticated views of Amis, Liddle and other similarly powerful voices translate into street violence in the hands of less articulate thugs who target Muslims and mosques for attack in their preferred way. At the very least this provides evidence that the self-censorship which commentators employ when discussing minority ethnic communities generally does not apply in the case of Muslims. Moreover, it is widely accepted that the concept and major typologies of racism accurately conceptualise defining experiences of minority ethnic communities in the UK. This is particularly applicable to black and Asian victims of violence, bigotry, hostility, suspicion and discrimination inflicted by members of majority communities. In fact, sociologists and other academics and researchers have produced a voluminous literature on the topic of racism that has helped shape anti-racism policies during the last four decades.[25] However, the notion of institutional racism enshrined in the body politic by Lord Macpherson[26] does not translate easily to a notion of institutional Islamophobia. In fact, the concept of Islamophobia *per se* enjoys none of the academic and policy-maker status attached to the concept of racism.

Hate crimes

Another important typological issue concerns the notion of hate crime. This is a term that has been imported from the US that does not fit neatly into pre-existing criminal law and practice. The term *Islamophobia* as well as the associated terms *Islamophobic hate crime, Islamophobic incident,* as well as *religiously aggravated crime* and *racist hate crime* posit the need for an anti-religious or racist motivation on the part of an assailant that is often lacking or not immediately apparent from an evidential point of view. Indeed, according to this research, several cases where a suspect might have been successfully charged and prosecuted for a religiously aggravated offence or racially aggravated offence[27] have been lost because the investigators failed to discern an anti-Muslim motivation. In many other cases clear anti-Muslim sentiment has been ignored by investigators in favour of a less apparent racist motivation.[28] Whether such outcomes are legislative or investigative failings is unclear and probably varies on a case-by-case basis. Muslim interviewees who have been physically injured in the course of violent assaults by unknown assailants – assailants who have expressed their antipathy to their victims as 'terrorists' or in related terms during the course of the assaults – are best described as being victims of *anti-Muslim hate crime*. In a majority of cases the victims know why they were attacked, having been told by their assailants in no uncertain terms. It is, moreover, highly plausible and logically consistent that their attackers are motivated by a negative view of Muslims as 'terrorists' or 'terrorist sympathizers' in a way that has become common coinage since 9/11. It is less clear that motivation in cases of this kind involves hatred or fear of Islam *per se* in the way that Islamophobia was seminally conceived by the Runnymede Trust.[29]

Albeit provisional, the research findings are sufficiently clear that the full extent of anti-Muslim violence that has taken place during the last decade is significant in volume and impact yet will never be fully quantified and analysed. There are three main reasons for this lack of information: a lack of police data in respect of attacks on Muslims; a reticence to report attacks by Muslim victims; and a failure by Muslim community organizations to implement procedures to encourage and facilitate reporting. This last failing stands in marked contrast to the impressive level of rigour and efficiency that surrounds the reporting and investigation of anti-Semitic violence by the voluntary Jewish community organization, the Community Security Trust (CST). In the ten years that have elapsed since 9/11 Muslim communities have failed to emulate the CST in this regard and despite some praiseworthy efforts by the Muslim Safety Forum (MSF) and the MCB there is no national programme third-party reporting of support for victims of anti-Muslim hate crime. The lack of police data is being remedied in the Metropolitan Police but not all police forces, and improvements will not be able to remedy earlier deficits throughout the decade. Many victims of anti-Muslim hate crime and Muslim victims of crime more generally do not report the incidents to police. Fear, suspicion and alienation are amongst a complex set of reasons for this. Equally disturbing, the research reveals instances where mosque managements and community elders are in denial about violence and intimidation – even when presented with evidence of attacks that have been committed against them. To date, government has not encouraged police to mount a nationwide campaign to address the problem in the same way it has in respect of underreporting of racist attacks and other hate crimes.

As in the case of racist violence aimed at minority ethnic communities, the contribution of extremist nationalists to anti-Muslim violence is found to be both direct and indirect. Direct contributions include cases where known members and associates of extremist nationalist organizations or groups have been convicted of criminal attacks on Muslims, mosques, Islamic institutions or Muslim organizations. Indirect contributions include cases where the same attacks have been carried out by individuals who express extremist nationalist sentiments. Contributions that appear to be both direct and indirect include cases where violence against Muslim targets occurs in the immediate aftermath of provocative and intimidating anti-Muslim demonstrations staged by extremist nationalist organizations. Consequently, reference is made to specific extremist nationalist organizations – most notably the well-established BNP and the more recent and evolving EDL – and their shared preoccupation with a perceived Muslim threat. Reference to an extremist nationalist milieu serves to distinguish formally structured organizations like the BNP and loosely structured ones like the EDL from a surrounding milieu that contains a wide range of individuals in terms of levels of commitment but which includes a hard core of individuals preoccupied with street violence. whilst it is wholly explicable that many of these individuals have come initially to police and subsequently to media and academic attention as sole actors rather than conspirators or members of a discernable movement, it is worth noting that the UK (in common with other Western countries) has for half a century witnessed a phenomenon of racist violence to which an extremist nationalist milieu has made a significant contribution. Paying particular attention to more serious examples of racist violence perpetrated by sole actors such as the 'nailbomber' David Copeland, researchers at the University of Northampton have found the notion of 'lone wolves' (like Copeland) to be misleading and sometimes negligently applied.[30] Instead they review evidence to suggest that the BNP and other extremist nationalist organizations have had a considerable influence in promoting racist violence carried out by 'lone wolves'.

It is instructive that two individuals are at the time of writing facing trial for the racist murder of Stephen Lawrence in 1993.[31] Interviews with former members of an extremist nationalist milieu suggest that there has been a clear shift in focus from the period when Lawrence was murdered by a racist gang away from street violence aimed at minority ethnic communities in general and towards Muslims in particular.[32] This is not to suggest that racist violence or violence aimed at immigrant communities has ceased to be of interest to members of an extremist nationalist milieu. Rather, a picture emerges of Muslims becoming prime targets for attack in the period since 9/11. In addition, the fact that the trial of two suspects for the murder of Stephen Lawrence is front page news and a major focus of editorial comment in 2011 serves to illustrate the success of a decade-long campaign by Lawrence's parents which culminated in a finding of 'institutional racism' against the Metropolitan Police and a major shift in police resources in support of victims of racist violence.

In respect of both direct and indirect contributions to anti-Muslim violence from an extremist nationalist milieu, it is often far easier to discern and establish a specific anti-Muslim motivation (as opposed to a more general racist or anti-immigrant motivation) when the target is a mosque, Islamic institution or Muslim organization. This is to recognise that in the case of violent attacks in the street on individual Muslims it has sometimes been more difficult to discern and establish the perpetrator's motivation. For example, in a common kind of case where a Muslim taxi driver is assaulted by a drunken and abusive customer, it is often not immediately clear to the victim, witnesses and investigators if the violence is motivated by a specific anti-Muslim sentiment, more general racist or anti-immigrant sentiment or is simply a case of random, drunken violence. However, when a mosque is subjected to an ongoing campaign of violence and intimidation, evidence of clear anti-Muslim motivation becomes easier to establish. It has also been a reasonable research strategy to send questionnaires to mosques to help examine the extent and nature of the problem.

History of racism

Anti-Muslim violence is therefore a new phenomenon and one that needs to be located and assessed within the context of racist violence and extremist nationalist politics that first came to police and public attention in the 1950s and 1960s. Post-Macpherson, much of this history of racism has entered the police training curriculum and more than one Muslim police officer has referred to it in the course of this research. Thus, when Kelso Cochrane became the first unofficial murder victim of racist violence in contemporary Britain, it was likely that his undetected young white assailants had the same pejorative views of their black victim's community as they read in some of the newspapers at the time.[33] Similarly, just as gangs who have more recently attacked Muslims in the UK may have found inspirational mainstream anti-Muslim bigotry in the media amplified on the websites of the BNP and the EDL, so too did Cochrane's murderers locate mainstream anti-black bigotry in the nearby Notting Hill bookshop of the White Defence League (WDL), a forerunner of the BNP. It is salutary to recall how Detective Superintendent Ian Forbes-Leith, leading the hunt for Cochrane's killers in 1959, told a newspaper: 'We are satisfied that it was the work of a group of about six anti-law white teenagers who had only one motive in view – robbery or attempted robbery.'[34] Significantly, the murder of Kelso Cochrane would have been investigated vigorously as a serious racist incident had it taken place in identical circumstances in London after the Stephen Lawrence Inquiry forty years later.

Several Muslim interviewees with experience of working with the police have pointed to the difficulty of translating this post-Lawrence learning into a Muslim community context. The murder of Kamal Raza Butt will illustrate the point. Shortly after the 7/7 London bombings Butt was beaten to death outside a corner shop by a gang of youths who shouted anti-Muslim abuse at him: 'Butt, 48, from Pakistan, was visiting Britain to see friends and family. On Sunday afternoon he went to a shop in Nottingham to buy cigarettes and was first called "Taliban" by the youths and then set upon'.[35] Nottinghamshire police described the incident as racially aggravated, not Islamophobic. Azad Ali, who chaired the Muslim Safety Forum, argued 'there was no racist abuse shouted at him, it was Islamophobic ... It is good the police have made arrests. We are disappointed that they have misclassified it, especially after all the advice to be more alert to Islamophobic hate crime.'[36]

By the 1970s many black and Asian residents in towns and cities in the UK (primarily in England) had grown used to being victims of racist attacks in which their attackers often expressed the sentiments of extremist nationalists – perhaps most frequently in the admonition to leave Britain and 'return home'. When racist thugs threw a brick through the window of a house in a Medway town in Kent it nearly struck the mother of a hard-working Muslim family from Bangladesh. Luckily it just missed her head and she was not injured, just badly shaken physically and emotionally. Her teenage son was so incensed that very soon after he threw a brick through the window of the home belonging to a local racist thug who he reasonably suspected of carrying out the attack. That response took place in the late 1980s and serves to mark a turning point in what had become a widespread phenomenon in the UK since the late 1960s – violent racism or 'Paki bashing', as both perpetrators and victims understood it.[37] For two decades 'Paki-bashers' had come to perceive their victims as docile and passive, unable or unwilling to fight back. The change was led by teenage sons like the one described who had grown up with neighbourhood and classroom racism in UK towns and schools and had grown frustrated by their parents' unreasonable passivity and forbearance.

Nowhere is that change from passive victimhood to active resistance more pronounced than in Tower Hamlets in the East End of London where the NF and allied racist thugs were eventually forced to abandon their violent intimidation of a burgeoning Muslim Bangladeshi community in the mid–1990s.[38] The stoic resignation and forbearance of immigrant parents was gradually replaced by the active resolve and resistance of a second generation born and brought up in the UK.[39] Not all active resistance to violent racism in the East End and around the UK was as violent as that meted out by racist attackers, but some of it was.[40] In that respect community resistance resembled an earlier local model provided by Jewish community activists who fought violent anti-Semites on the same streets for the same reason.[41] Significantly, in both instances, the two immigrant communities in the East End of London were not always sure that politicians and police were sufficiently supportive so as to allow them to rely solely on legal responses to the daily violence and intimidation they faced.[42] To a large extent both minority communities felt compelled to respond directly and violently towards their attackers because of a failure by politicians and police to protect and support them.[43] Notably, in both cases influential sections of the national and local media did little to highlight the violence against minority immigrant communities and much to exacerbate it.[44] Suffice to say there have been many instances since 9/11 when sections of the media have fanned the flames of anti-Muslim sentiment[45] with little apparent regard for history that shows how readily racist comment or bigotry can foster a climate in which racist violence or violence against vulnerable minorities gains licence and tacit approval.[46]

A lack of confidence in political and police support against racist violence has also been evident in other immigrant communities around the UK.

Eventually in 1999 politicians and police responded positively and pro-actively to the issue, largely as a result of the Stephen Lawrence Inquiry.[47] In addition to providing a clear imperative to protect and support victims of racist violence, it followed logically out of Lord Macpherson's famous findings that victims of racist violence would be less likely to take the law into their own hands if they received fair and equitable treatment from the police and the criminal justice system.[48] Notwithstanding major improvements in the support offered to victims of racist violence in the new millennium, a number of cases documented by the Institute of Race Relations[49] serve to caution against complacency and the erroneous notion that racism and racist violence are things of the past.[50] To the contrary, minority ethnic communities continue to face the threat of racism and racist hate crimes in many towns and cities in the UK.[51] One of the most telling aspects of the research is the discovery that several UK citizens who, because of their ethnicity, faced daily threats of racist violence and intimidation in the last century now face a repeat of the same violent threat because of their visible attachment to Islam. Belatedly, and largely due to the pressure of grass-roots campaigners including Doreen and Neville Lawrence,[52] the first threat began to be taken seriously just as the second threat emerged.

Ajmal is just one of a number of Muslim interviewees who has been a victim of serious racist violence – 'Paki-bashing' – in the 1980s and a victim of violent anti-Muslim hate crime in the last decade.[53] In the 20 years that separated the two serious assaults carried out against him he helped tackle violent racism in his local community and felt much satisfaction and relief that his children would not have to face the daily violence and intimidation that he and his friends endured growing up with NF supporters for neighbours and classmates at school.[54] That relief, he says in interview, was relatively short-lived. whilst he felt confident that large, established Muslim communities in the UK were now much safer than their fledgling counterparts had been in the last millennium, he was equally concerned that smaller Muslim communities and their mosques and community centres were extremely vulnerable to violence and intimidation in 2010, especially in towns where BNP, EDL and other anti-Muslim influence was present and tangible.

Inception and growth of anti-Muslim violence post–9/11

Shortly before 9/11 a burgeoning BNP and an ailing NF played key roles in fomenting community tensions that led to rioting by largely Asian-Muslim gangs in the Northern English towns of Bradford, Oldham and Burnley.[55] This experience provided Nick Griffin, the BNP leader, with the material for his widely circulated BNP recording: *The Truth about Islam*. Circulation and promotion of this Islamophobic text was greatly boosted by the 9/11 terrorist attack and the popular notion that Muslims were all complicit in terrorism, either actively or by acquiescence. Therefore, 9/11 serves as a marker for the inception and growth of anti-Muslim violence in the UK. Several interviewees note that whilst Islamophobia was not unknown before 9/11 it was only afterwards that violence against mosques became widespread. Several interviewees talk about one of the most immediate indicators of a change in attitudes towards Muslims in the aftermath of 9/11: suspicion and hostility. In and of themselves suspicion and hostility do not constitute hate crimes or even matters for civil complaint, although in many instances they serve as precursors to threatening behaviour, abuse, intimidation and violence. Moreover, although suspicion is often accompanied by discernable hostility, it is not always the case and so the two responses warrant separate as well as dual consideration. Suspicion is not unreasonable or problematic in most day-to-day situations. However, the kind of suspicion that many Muslims experienced for the first time after 9/11 is clearly both unreasonable and problematic. As this typical Muslim experience illustrates:

> I had been travelling on the train to Moorgate [from Harrow-on-the Hill] every day for eighteen years and no one ever said bad things or gave me bad looks. Then all they [fellow commuters from the suburbs of Metro-land[56]] were reading was Muslim terrorist this, Muslim terrorist that, and threats to London, and suicide bombs and everything and all of a sudden they see you as bad person, dangerous person ... bad looks, don't sit next to me even when it's only seat ... yes small things only but when you travel every day with these people you know straight away when things change for the worse.[57]

For Muslims who had lived in the UK for several years prior to 9/11 the emergence of suspicion from strangers towards them for the first time was uncomfortable and disconcerting. For some this negative experience would be compounded when they overheard conversations in public places or in the workplace that highlighted this new adverse perception of Muslims as a security threat.[58] This negative experience might be compounded further still when overhearing the same kind of negative comments from colleagues or associates in the workplace or in other social settings.[59] Muslim interviewees with experience of life in the UK before and after 9/11 do not suggest that a terrorist incident in a foreign country in 2001 signalled a negative change of behaviour from all of their non-Muslim neighbours and fellow citizens, but they do suggest that a negative change of attitude towards them was sufficiently widespread as to make a discernable and adverse impact on their lives. whilst some interviewees highlight the significance of 9/11, others identify an increase in hostility against Muslims after 7/7. To a certain extent this reflects what is widely known as 'backlash' – an immediate response to an event such as 7/7 in which an increase in violence is discernable. The phenomenon of backlash was especially marked across the UK in the weeks after 7/7. However, for some of our interviewees 7/7 also serves to mark a change in attitudes and behaviour towards Muslims that would become more profound and long-lasting.

Since 9/11 arson, criminal damage, violence and intimidation against mosques, Islamic institutions and Muslim organizations has become commonplace.[60] Many mosques in isolated Muslim communities have become especially vulnerable. Violent attacks on mosques, Islamic institutions and Muslim organizations invariably provide prima facie evidence of an anti-Muslim motive. When a multi-ethnic or minority-ethnic gang attack a mosque and its worshippers it should be sufficient to appreciate that the existing paradigms and typologies of racist hate crime are sometimes inappropriate and misleading. At the same time it is equally true that these kinds of attack impact on a particular faith community that is overwhelmingly made up of minority ethnic communities who are amongst the most socially and economically deprived in the UK. To a large extent the difficulties that sometimes militate against establishing a clear anti-Muslim motive in connection with attacks in which individual Muslims are victims dissolve when analysing attacks on mosques, Islamic centres and Muslim organizations. Just as an attack on a vivisection laboratory provides prima facie evidence of an anti-vivisection motive or an attack on a synagogue is considered prima facie evidence of an anti-Semitic motive, so too does an attack on a mosque – or, as in the case that follows, a Muslim prayer room used by Muslim students – offer prime facie evidence of an anti-Muslim motive.

City University attack: an example

On Thursday 5 November 2009, three Muslim students were stabbed in an attack by a multi-ethnic gang in a street near City University in the London Borough of Islington.[61] These serious assaults were the culmination of a sustained campaign of violent intimidation by the same gang against Muslim students at City University that started on Monday 2 November.[62] The focus of this campaign of violent intimidation were two Muslim prayer rooms (male and female) which are situated in the basement of City University's Gloucester Building in Whiskin Street, a short walk from the main campus building in Northampton Square. The gang appeared to be aware of the regular presence of Muslim students at this venue and laid siege to it. On Monday 2 November the gang attacked Muslim students as they left the Gloucester Building after prayers, shouting 'get those Muslims'. Three students required hospital treatment for facial and head injuries after the gang attacked them with bricks and other projectiles. Although representatives of the City University Islamic Society reported the incident to the University and police immediately they did not receive pro-active support until after the second attacks on Thursday 5 November.

Between 2 and 5 November the Muslim prayer rooms at City University became the focus of attack for a local gang.[63] All the available evidence indicates that the motivation for the gang's violent actions was hatred towards Muslims in general, whom they regarded as terrorists or supporters of terrorism, not antipathy towards any individual Muslim students.[64] According to English criminal law, even if the Muslim victims had been convicted or suspected of terrorism, such facts would not have afforded the gang any basis for defence. Instead, the victims sustained injuries and hurt that was inflicted on a totally false premise. Thus, one of the key features of this kind of attack is that victims are wrongly targeted as having some specific or general association with terrorists such as the London tube bombers. It is also worth noting that the gang was made up of members from different majority and minority ethnic backgrounds who expressed their antipathy towards Muslims in the clearest possible terms. The Muslim students were themselves equally diverse in their ethnic origins and appearance. Anyone witnessing the attack would have observed only one visible difference between the assailants and their victims: both male and female victims were dressed in a way that signified they were Muslims. Observers would also have noted that the attackers had targeted the Gloucester Building because it housed the Muslim student prayer room. Our interviewee describes the attack outside the Gloucester Building:

> A lot of the students, the Muslim students ... because these people who attacked them weren't students from the university. So a lot of the students kind of ran and a few of them were attacked ... quite severely injured. One of them ... they all pretty much had bricks across their faces and things like that. One of the students had severe swelling to his knee ... was hit on the knee with a baton. He was walking with a limp for several weeks. Another student received quite a lot of head injuries, to the extent

that when he went to the hospital for a check-up, they told him: 'had you received another head blow, it could have caused paralysis.' All of them went to the hospital after the attack; one of them was OK pretty much, just a lot of cuts and bruises. The other two ... like I said, one of them with the knee, the other one with the bruising to the head. And then they were released the same evening, the same night.[65]

Not surprisingly our interviewee was upset when recounting this episode. He said he is British through and through, has many non-Muslim friends and he loves studying in London. To be confronted, he explained, by a gang that hates you and wants to harm you because you are a Muslim is extremely troubling. Like many other young Muslims, this kind of incident makes him question whether the country and the city he loves is any longer a place he can call home. Fortunately, he recounts, a neighbour came to their aid:

The fight only stopped when a local man ... maybe he was Irish ... he shouted: 'I've called the police, the police are coming.' And then the youths just ran. They live local, because we see them around; we've seen them around quite a lot. So, obviously, they'll know how to get away from the scene and stuff like that. So they ran and they shouted things: 'Oh, the terrorists are going to get it; you're going to get it, this isn't over.' And things like that. So we told the police everything that happened, and they said they'd increase the patrols in the area. We told the university; they said as well that they'd increase security in the area.[66]

Early indications suggests that between 40 and 60 per cent of over 1,600 mosques, Islamic centres and Muslim organizations in the UK have suffered at least one attack that has or could have been reported to police as a hate crime since 9/11. Interestingly, whilst a significant number of mosques, Islamic centres and Muslim organizations have suffered no violence since 9/11, it is already clear that an equally significant number have suffered repeated attacks and ongoing vandalism and anti-social behaviour that amounts to intimidation. Attacks include petrol bombs thrown into mosques, serious physical assaults on imams and staff, bricks thrown through mosque windows, pigs' heads being fixed prominently to mosque entrances and minarets, death threats, other threatening and abusive messages – sometimes verbal sometimes written – and vandalism.[67]

It is too early to describe year-on-year patterns but it is safe to say that a significant number of attacks and incidents have taken place in each year since 9/11 and that there is no sign of the problem diminishing. There is also already clear evidence that more attacks have taken place in the aftermath of high-profile terrorist and related incidents. Most notably, for instance, the 7/7 bombings in London prompted a pronounced spate of attacks on mosques, Islamic centres and Muslim organizations. Most disturbingly and less well known, several attacks have not been reported to the police. Moreover, in some instances a failure to report attacks to police is prompted by a desire not to draw attention to the problem by trustees and staff at mosques and Islamic centres. In the last two years a number of mosques, Islamic centres and Muslim organizations have also been subjected to intimidatory demonstrations and campaigns by violent protestors belonging to or associated with the English Defence League and other Islamophobic groups.

Victims' perspectives

In interviews several imams at mosques in the UK have expressed deep sorrow when asked to recount the circumstances in which their own masjid[67] had been attacked and damaged. One imam in particular spoke movingly about the tangible hurt Muslims felt when the 'House of Allah' they attended every day was attacked by a petrol bomb or desecrated in some other way. Over and above the damage, disruption and fear that is documented below is a profound sense of violation and religious sacrilege which devout members of other faiths will readily comprehend but which may require an empathetic effort from non-believers. Throughout the last four decades the overwhelming majority of first-generation Muslims in the UK have devoted themselves to working tirelessly in low-paid jobs to provide homes and better futures for their families. For many, their precious spare time has been spent converting buildings for use as mosques and prayer rooms. After an attack there is an adverse impact on the morale of the local Muslim community that uses the mosque. Ongoing intimidation of a public place of congregation is a defining feature of a breakdown of law and order. It was only when the National Front was finally forced to abandon its provocative and intimidatory paper sales in Brick Lane in the early 1990s that the local Bangladeshi Muslim community was able to experience safe passage and congregation for the first time in their own neighbourhood. Today, a significant number of Muslims in different parts of the UK are once again being put in fear of attack, abuse and harassment when attending their mosques to pray and socialize.[68]

Arson is an especially serious form of attack and consists of setting a building ablaze with criminal intent. Most cases of arson we have investigated reveal a callous disregard for the safety of Muslims who are, or who might reasonably be expected to be, inside the building being attacked. Mohamed

Koheeallee, the caretaker of the Greenwich Islamic Centre was injured defending the mosque and rescuing a copy of the Qur'an.[69] The mosque was petrol bombed twice in one week in 2009:

> Mohamed Koheeallee, 62, raced to tackle 7ft flames at the Greenwich Islamic Centre in Plumstead Road at 12.15am on Tuesday. Grabbing a bucket of water, he extinguished the fire as it spread inside but when he opened a fire exit, he was engulfed by flames burning his arm and his face. Choking with smoke inhalation and despite his injuries, he carried on dousing the fire until the mosque was safe but when he tried to tackle the source of the blaze he was pushed back by its intensity.[70]

In interview it emerged that Mr Koheeallee's bravery extended beyond his heroics in tackling the blaze but also in maintaining a 24 hour presence inside the building ever since. In other venues we have visited, arson attacks have left their mark both physically and psychologically. Not all victims show the same courage as Mr Koheeallee but all show a degree of stoicism and resignation.

At the present time it is impossible to estimate how many arson attacks against mosques, Islamic institutions and Muslim organizations have taken place in the UK in the last decade, still less how many deserve to be classified as political violence. Most victims of this kind of attack reported petrol bombs being thrown into mosques in the hours of darkness, as in a case reported by a mosque official in Edinburgh. In many mosques worshippers and staff can be inside the building at such a time, but thankfully in this case the building was empty. This particular attack received national media attention because it was the first of its kind after 9/11. It is also one of the few cases where the culprit was arrested and convicted. Since then most arson attacks on mosques have generally only received attention in the local media. A mosque representative showed us the residual damage to a petrol bomb attack at a mosque in Nottingham. We have encountered several cases where loss of life and serious harm was narrowly avoided. Whereas most mosque representatives we have interviewed have been unable to comment authoritatively about the identity and political affiliations of perpetrators of petrol bombings of their mosques, Abdal Qadir Baksh, a spokesman for the Masjid al Ghurabaa, a salafi mosque in Luton, was far more insightful. The mosque was firebombed in the aftermath of extremist political activity in Luton organised by the EDL in response to a provocative demonstration against returning British troops by an affiliate of extremist group al-Muhajiroun.[71]

One potential indicator that a petrol bomb attack has been carried out by violent extremist nationalists or others with an extremist political motive is the presence of an accelerant. Baksh has strong links in the community and claims to have reliable local information that the attack was connected to these protests. 'We had a major incident where our Mosque was firebombed ... but those who did this act actually used some form of accelerant [...] which made the bomb really bigger than a normal fire bomb.' He explained the impact: 'it actually blew down a whole wall, collapsed it onto another wall, and that is not normal of normal fire bombs. Forensics came back and told us that something was used in there,' he continues, 'and we knew they couldn't get hold of these accelerants except from professional people, people who know what they're doing. So it was organised. They knew what they were doing.'[72] Once again the attack occurred at night, yet with real potential to cause fatalities. Baksh explains: 'About 2 o'clock in the morning, I think, smashed the window, threw the bombs in and ran off. Fortunately there was nobody there at the time, at 2 o'clock in the morning; however, our morning prayer was about 4 o'clock at that time and only two hours away from somebody actually being there.'[73] As in many other interviews, Baksh expresses satisfaction with the emergency services, the fire brigade and the police responses to the incident itself but less satisfaction with the subsequent investigation. 'The fire brigade had to be called to extinguish the fire and then our members got here as quickly as possible. The place was cordoned off. Loads of forensic tests.' He was less enthusiastic about the investigation: 'but nobody was caught. I don't believe enough effort was put into finding out the arsonists anyway.'[74] This is also a typical case where a mosque experienced prior hate crimes. 'It was clear that it was an attack on Islam and was a planned for attack [because] ... prior to that attack we were threatened a number of times. About half a dozen times, through letters, through hate mail. And the hate mail was really, really bad, against Islam, against our Prophet Mohammad, against Allah, against us, threatened to kill us, wipe us off Bury Park.'[75] Baksh explains the nature and extent of the impact of a firebombing:

> For a good three weeks we weren't allowed access to the mosque, not allowed to pray there. You know, we're Muslims, we pray five times a day. No classes there, all education had ceased. All the classes for the kids, the Qu'ran, all Arabic, had ceased. And then, after that, once we had access, we had limited access. So again, we got the space back but we weren't able to continue the classes. And then we had to wait for insurance and everything for all that to get in place. And only then were we able to get working on it, and that took quite a long time, but eventually, about February the following year, everything had finished.[76]

We have recorded similar accounts at mosques, Islamic centres and Muslim organizations in different parts of the UK. In Luton the firebombing of the mosque combined with the impact of a violent EDL demonstration to cause fear in the community:

> Yeah, psychologically. Muslims now walking in the streets ... raise their eyebrows in fear, especially if they're walking in town. Walking in the streets, women covered up ... it's created dislike and hatred, you know, between Muslims and non-Muslims in general. And we found when Muslims now speak to non-Muslims, we're always, 'well what's his real opinion behind this', 'what does he really think of me'. Whereas previously it wouldn't have been there ... We haven't found not one English organisation condemns the acts and when it happened no one ever speaks.[77]

What begins as occasional anti-social behaviour and vandalism can become harassment and intimidation when it is purposefully pursued over a sustained period. In such circumstances it can have a serious negative impact that is far greater than the individual acts themselves would suggest. This is just one example from Bishops Stortford where a mosque has endured ongoing vandalism, attacks and assaults over a long period at three separate venues in the town. The mosque representative is describing the state of siege that is evoked by boarding up windows that are constantly being broken by acts of vandalism:

> We had just boarded stuff all around. It looked like it's not a mosque; it's not a holy place. It's like a vandalised building or somewhere in the middle of nowhere. It wasn't like a building in the centre of the town. Well, I think the majority of the people ... because kids used to walk around there from school; and later on they used to get into bunches and into little mini-gangs. And they used to come and attack and throw stones and they [would] just abuse sometimes ... people. And chase them.[78]

We have so far documented 42 cases where pigs' heads, bacon and pork have been used in a variety of ways to signal anti-Muslim hatred at mosques, Islamic institutions and Muslim organizations since 9/11. The intimidation at the Bishops Stortford mosque has also suffered this form of attack, placing a pig's head over the CCTV camera. In other cases a pig's head has been displayed prominently on the mosque, even on the minaret. In addition bacon and pork are sometimes shoved through letter boxes at mosques and even sent by post. In the same way copies of the Qur'an will often be defaced with obscenities and delivered to a mosque. Many mosque officials have explained how these kinds of attack cause additional offence. 'I don't mind being called Paki,' one imam explained, 'but the Qur'an is the word of Allah'.[79] The most common kind of attack we have encountered involve missiles, sometimes bricks and stones, sometimes eggs, being thrown through or at mosque windows and doors. Very often this will be done by gangs who do not attempt to hide. At other times it will be carried out by gangs and individuals when the mosque is empty and the damage is discovered later. At several mosques we have visited windows are no longer replaced because they are so regularly broken. Instead windows and doors are boarded up and the building often looks as the worshippers feel: under siege. For instance, in Harlow the mosque has had every single window smashed 'even though [they] were reinforced, double glazed and had a metal cage around them'. The mosque representative explained that as soon as they put in a fresh pane of glass it got smashed straight away.[80]

Involvement and influence of BNP and EDL

Harlow has a strong BNP and extremist nationalist presence that adds to the sense of siege for the small Muslim community.[81] Building on Nick Griffin's 2001 seminal audio recording *The Truth about Islam*, the BNP developed a decade-long campaign against Muslims. In fact Griffin's trenchant analysis – especially regarding terrorism and the Bradford and Northern riots of 2001 – has become embedded in BNP culture and far beyond. This moral outrage against Muslims and against Islam was illustrated in March 2009 when the BNP responded to what it called 'the shocking anti-British army protest by a group of Muslims in central Luton earlier today' and described it as 'a portent of what is to come unless the Islamification of this country is halted.'[82] Peter Mullins, the BNP defence spokesman warned:

> The disgraceful sight of Muslim protestors carrying posters saying 'Anglian Soldiers Go to Hell' whilst parading through town after tours of duty risking their lives is the inevitable consequence of the colonisation of this country by Third Worlders. Luton is well known as a heavily Muslim colonised town, and it is little wonder that there was nearly a confrontation between indigenous British people watching the parade and the Muslim protestors. Only the BNP will bring an end to this madness.[83]

The same event sparked the mobilization and expansion of the EDL. Throughout the decade since 9/11 the BNP campaigned passionately and angrily against Islam and Muslims. For the last two years it was joined and then overtaken by the EDL as the most vocal critic of 'Muslim extremists' and 'the Islamification of Europe'. In consequence Muslims in many UK towns and cities faced an increased threat of intimidation, including verbal and physical threats. Experienced investigators of extremist nationalist political violence confirm that the BNP and allied groups have enjoyed pockets of tight support in key locations in most parts of the country.[84] Often these venues can be discerned in higher levels of BNP votes in general and local elections. Dave Allport, project manager for a local community initiative aimed at curbing racism, explains how BNP strongholds have deep roots in parts of the West Midlands: 'In Sandwell, I think, historically – I always quote this, and it's true – I've been to meetings in the council house, and they talk about "hotspots", where they need to engage white people and so on ...' He continues: 'So areas like Tipton, per se, generally Tipton, not the whole of Tipton, but probably certain areas: Prince's End, Tivington Estate, within Tipton, Friar Park, in Wednesbury, and Newbury Estate, which is just on the Walsall border ...'. All of which has a local history. 'In the '70s there was National Front activity, and KKK activity in Newbury Estate, for a time that they had to report. Because they were actually burning crosses. And that's not that long ago. Probably about ten years ago. Probably less. So the [far] right has been active for years.'[85]

Long-time analyst of the extremist nationalist scene in the UK, Nigel Copsey cautions that 'the EDL is not the street fighting wing of the BNP' but that it has emerged instead from 'several ultra-patriotic anti-Jihadist groups with origins in the football casual subculture'.[86] For Copsey the EDL is 'best understood as an Islamophobic, new social movement, born of a particularly unattractive and intolerant strand of English nationalism'.[87] In June 2010 an unnamed 16-year-old youth, together with Jason Cunningham, aged 27 from Tamworth, became the latest in a growing list of UK citizens convicted of manufacturing improvized explosive devices (particularly nail bombs) or explosive substances where there is evidence of allegiance to extreme nationalism, in this case to the EDL, BNP and neo-Nazism.[88] It is also clearly the kind of case where access to prosecution and court files will be needed to conduct the detailed research needed to ascertain precise information about motivation and targeting.

Mehdi Hasan, editor of the *New Statesman*, reported that 'Robert Cottage, a former BNP candidate jailed in July 2007 for possessing explosive chemicals in his home – described by police at the time of his arrest as the largest amount of chemical explosive of its type ever found in this country.' Hasan notes that Martyn Gilleard, a Nazi sympathizer, was 'jailed in June 2008 after police found nail bombs, bullets, swords, axes and knives in his flat;

Nathan Worrell, a neo-Nazi, described by police as a "dangerous individual", who hoarded bomb-making materials in his home, and was found guilty in December 2008 of possessing material for terrorist purposes and for racially aggravated harassment'. Another case in this category is 'Neil MacGregor, who pleaded guilty to "threatening to blow up Glasgow Central Mosque and behead a Muslim every week until every mosque in Scotland was closed"'.[89]

These criminal cases are qualitatively different from violent and intimidatory demonstrations by extremist nationalist groups such as the NF, BNP and EDL. It follows that to demonstrate adherence to the ideology of the EDL by taking part in its protests against Muslim 'extremists' is to provide necessary evidence of commitment to a cause but insufficient evidence of the different kind of commitment required to take part in a conspiracy to murder or seriously injure Muslims.[90] Motivation for political violence requires a criminal *mens rea* as well as a commitment to an ideology.[91] The reticence of most extremist nationalists to take the risks inherent in political violence is often used by recruiters and facilitators of political violence to galvanize new recruits to leave the 'comfort zone' of 'armchair revolutionaries' who are to be despised for being 'all talk and no action'.[92] This is the point Martin Gilleard, a violent extremist nationalist convicted of manufacturing nail bombs in 2008, makes when he explains his motivation and exhorts others to follow his example:

> Be under no illusion, we are at war. And it is a war we are losing badly … I am so sick and tired of hearing nationalists talk of killing Muslims, of blowing up mosques, of fighting back … the time has come to stop the talk and start to act … [93]

Gilleard is one of a small number of UK extremist nationalists who have been arrested and convicted before their terrorist plans came to fruition. On 15 January 2010 Terence Gavan, a former BNP member and soldier, was convicted of manufacturing nail bombs and an array of explosives, firearms and weapons that Mr Justice Calvert-Smith described as the largest find of its kind in the UK in modern history. Gavan had previously pleaded guilty to 22 charges at Woolwich Crown Court, a case in which police discovered 12 firearms and 54 improvized explosive devices, which included nail bombs and a booby-trapped cigarette packet. After the case, head of the North East Counter Terrorism Unit David Buxton said Gavan used his extensive knowledge to manufacture and accumulate devices capable of causing significant injury or harm and posed a significant risk to public safety.[94] Gavan was reported as having specifically Muslim targets in mind; in particular he is reported to have planned to 'target an address he had seen on a television programme that he believed was linked to the 7 July bomb attacks in London'.[95] In one hand-written note Gavan explains: 'the patriot must always be ready to defend his country against enemies and their governments'.[96] whilst the explanations and rationalizations of those who commit acts of terrorism and political violence should never be taken at face value, still less should they be disregarded in favour of analyses that propose an unrealistic and opposing interpretation of their actions.

Prior to 9/11 and the war on terror that the available evidence suggests, Muslims in the UK shared the same threats of violence as many other minority immigrant communities. A significant majority of Muslims in the UK have family backgrounds in Pakistan, Bangladesh and India and their arrival in the UK in the second half of the last century coincided with the arrival of their Hindu and Sikh neighbours from the Indian sub-continent. For the perpetrators of racist violence that became known as 'Paki-bashing' it did not matter if their victim was Muslim, Hindu or Sikh. In 1979 a racist teenage gang resident in Kentish Town committed grievous bodily harm against a Sikh man resident in Southall and advised him to 'fuck off home, you fucking Paki' without realising or caring that their victim had no connection with Pakistan.[97] 'Paki-bashing' and other kinds of racist violence reached a peak at this time when the NF and the BNP reflected and exploited widespread racist sentiment in political campaigns that aimed to intimidate and remove black and Asian immigrants from the UK. In contrast, since 9/11 an enlarged BNP and a much reduced NF have focused their campaigns almost exclusively on Muslims, often ignoring opportunities to campaign against former targets in other minority communities. This focus on 'the Muslim threat' reflects much comment in the mainstream media and goes some way to explaining a significant shift away from 'Paki-bashing' and towards anti-Muslim violence instead. Racist and anti-immigrant violence still occurs in the UK but since 9/11 Muslims have increasingly been singled out for attack, often by gangs and individuals who themselves belong to minority ethnic communities. Similarly, since 2009, the EDL has campaigned exclusively against Muslim targets and, although predominantly white working-class, the movement also attracts a handful of members from minority ethnic communities. Like the BNP and NF, the EDL seeks and fails to distance itself from the street violence it fosters.

Motivations for violence

Investigators of violence, predominantly police officers who have trained as detectives, often display a keen awareness of the motivation for violence. Intriguingly, some Muslim police officers charged with the task of investigating violent crime have themselves been the victims of random, racist or anti-Muslim violence either before or during their police careers. Suffice to say from victim, witness and investigator vantage points a sufficiently clear picture emerges of Muslims facing a cumulative threat of random, racist and specifically anti-Muslim violence. Often clarity about motive arises simply from the direct communication of intent and purpose from an assailant. For instance, many victims, witnesses and investigators of hate crimes are familiar with cases where a violent assault is accompanied by threats and language that elucidate motive and leave no room for equivocation. Random street violence has a greater impact on poorer communities than on others and therefore Muslims suffer disproportionately from it. Poverty, unemployment and low pay adversely affect more Muslims than other minority faith or ethnic communities in the UK. Consequently, a majority of Muslims reside in neighbourhoods where violent street crime and anti-social behaviour is most prevalent. Typically, in towns and cities across the UK, Muslims walk streets where random alcohol or drug-fuelled violence puts pedestrians at greater risk than in other more affluent and secure neighbourhoods. By the same token, Muslims living in poor neighbourhoods share with their poor non-Muslim neighbours the problem of being unable to buy cars or hire taxis so as to reduce the risk of encountering random violence that often arises on the streets, on trains and buses and in other places of public congress, especially late at night.

To illustrate, in June 2005, Ahmed, a Muslim with a family background in Bangladesh, was hit over the head with a bottle whilst walking home after a long day working in an Indian restaurant in North London.[98] Ahmed's assailant was drunk and appeared incapable of forming any coherent thought yet was still able to muster violence towards a passerby. Police arrested him for the assault on Ahmed and for another assault on another pedestrian in the same locality that occurred five minutes earlier. Cursory police enquiries suggested that the assailant – a middle-aged man with a family background in Strathclyde – was an habitual drunk with a propensity to inflict violence randomly on strangers. Ahmed was taken to the accident and emergency department at a nearby hospital where he received six stitches to a head wound. Later, Ahmed explained how during the course of 15 years working in Bangladeshi-owned restaurants he had been the victim of racist abuse and violence on a number of occasions. This kind of violence is common yet generally unreported and unacknowledged. Indeed, the Institute of Race Relations is the only body to pay any sustained attention to racist and random violence towards low-paid workers in restaurants and other businesses.[99] Many of Ahmed's Muslim friends were taxi drivers and they too suffered the same combination of random and racist violence. In one case that Ahmed recalled, the perpetrators of racist insults towards Muslim restaurant staff subsequently assaulted a Muslim taxi driver when he drove them from the restaurant to a residential address. Although Ahmed is able to illustrate how much racist violence and abuse has developed specific anti-Muslim features since 9/11, he is also a strong witness in support of the continuity of racist and random violence faced and shared by low-paid workers in vulnerable jobs including restaurant work and taxi or mini-cab driving.

Conclusion

While it is important to acknowledge the threats of racist and random violence that Muslims share with fellow citizens, this chapter has highlighted violence that is specifically aimed at Muslims and which has become prevalent since 9/11. When the violence is motivated by violent extremist nationalism – whether linked to groups like the BNP, NF, EDL or not – it seems reasonable to classify it as political violence rather than hate crime. Self-evidently, anti-Muslim sentiment and motivation is most easily detected in cases where mosques, Islamic centres and Muslim organizations are attacked. To a large extent the difficulties that sometimes militate against establishing a clear anti-Muslim motive in connection with attacks in which individual Muslims are victims dissolve when analysing attacks on mosques, Islamic centres and Muslim organizations. Just as an attack on a vivisection laboratory provides *prima facie* evidence of an anti-vivisection motive or an attack on a synagogue is considered *prima facie* evidence of an anti-Semitic motive, so too does an attack on a mosque offer *prima facie* evidence of an anti-Muslim motive. In many instances perpetrators will underline the basis for their violence by daubing a message on a mosque wall, posting abusive messages to the mosque, and most symbolically and commonly by sticking a pig's head to the mosque building itself.

Typologically and notwithstanding overlaps, Muslims in the UK may be said to face the threat of two kinds of post–9/11 violence: political violence committed by a small number of extremist nationalists, generally referred to as 'lone wolves'; and widespread anti-Muslim violence committed by individuals and gangs. Both categories are new and neither has purchase in policing and political circles where the official language of racist and religiously motivated hate crime remains intact. It is therefore important to make a case for adopting the terms – political violence and anti-Muslim violence – as part of a new typology of violence faced by Muslims in the UK. By doing so it will help to ensure that adequate and commensurate resources are devoted to the threat. To be sure, Muslims also face a threat of ongoing racist, anti-immigrant violence – a threat they share with other minorities in the UK. In this respect there is continuity with the threat of violence Muslims faced before 9/11. In addition, Muslims face the same threat of random violence as other members of the general public. Cumulatively, therefore, Muslims in the UK now face a combination of violent threats to their safety that is not shared by other minority communities: extremist nationalist political violence targeted against Muslims; anti-Muslim violence; racist and anti-immigrant violence; and random street violence.

Notes

1 Gable, Gerry and Paul Jackson (2011). Lone wolves: myth or reality? London: Searchlight Publications.
2 Lambert, Robert and Jonathan Githens-Mazer (2010). *Islamophobia and Anti-Muslim Hate Crime: UK case studies*. Exeter: European Muslim Research Centre, University of Exeter; Githens-Mazer, Jonathan and Robert Lambert, 2010. *Islamophobia and Anti-Muslim Hate Crime: a London case study*. Exeter: European Muslim Research Centre, University of Exeter.
3 Ibid.
4 Ibid.
5 Souhami, A. (2007). Understanding Institutional Racism: the Stephen Lawrence Inquiry and the police service reaction, in: Policing beyond Macpherson: Issues in policing, race and society. Devon: Willan, pp. 66–87.
6 Islamophobia was first defined by the Runnymede Trust in expansive terms: '1) Islam is seen as a monolithic bloc, static and unresponsive to change; 2) Islam is seen as separate and "other". It does not have values in common with other cultures, is not affected by them and does not influence them; 3) Islam is seen as inferior to the West. It is seen as barbaric, irrational, primitive and sexist; 4) Islam is seen as violent, aggressive, threatening, supportive of terrorism and engaged in a "clash of civilizations"; 5) Islam is seen as a political ideology and is used for political or military advantage; 6) Criticisms made of the West by Islam are rejected out of hand; 7) Hostility towards Islam is used to justify discriminatory practices towards Muslims and exclusion of Muslims from mainstream society; 8) Anti-Muslim hostility is seen as natural or normal' – Richardson, Robin, (ed.), 1997. Commission on British Muslims and Islamophobia: Islamophobia: a challenge for us all. London: Runnymede Trust.
7 Allen, Chris (2010). *Islamophobia*. Aldershot: Ashgate.
8 Lambert and Githens-Mazer (2010). op. cit.
9 Ibid.
10 'Anti-Muslim bigotry', a term adopted by Bob Pitt, editor of Islamophobia Watch. http://www.islamophobia-watch.com/islamophobia-a-definition/

[accessed 12 November 2011]; see also Malek, Maleiha (ed.) 2010. *Anti-Muslim Prejudice*. London: Routledge.

11 'Anti-Muslim Racism', a typology advanced by Liz Fekete and other researchers at the Institute of Race Relations; see for example Fekete, Liz, (2004). Anti-Muslim racism and the European security state. Race & Class. 46 (1), pp. 3–29; Fekete, Liz, 2008. Integration, Islamophobia and Civil Rights in Europe. London: Institute of Race Relations; Fekete, Liz, (2009). A Suitable Enemy: Racism, Migration and Islamophobia in Europe. London: Pluto Press.

12 Lambert and Githens-Mazer (2010), op. cit. pp. 11–12.

13 Ibid.

14 London Citizens http://www.citizensuk.org/ [accessed 1 October 2010].

15 Tower Hamlets Inter Faith Forum. http://www.faithintowerhamlets.com/default/1000.home/index.htm [accessed 1 October 2010]; see also Green, Alan and Leon Silver, 2009. Letter to editor: response to Martin Bright. Jewish Chronicle. 27 November.

16 Lambert and Githens-Mazer (2010), op. cit.

17 Ibid.

18 Ibid.

19 Bennett, Ronan (2007), Shame on us. Guardian. 19 November. http://www.guardian.co.uk/uk/2007/nov/19/race.bookscomment [accessed 20 August 2010].

20 Ibid.

21 Ibid.

22 Ibid.

23 Tobias, Rabbi Pete (2007), Undesirable debate. Guardian – comment is free. http://www.guardian.co.uk/commentisfree/2007/nov/14/undesirablesdebate [accessed 20 August 2010].

24 Bennett, Ronan (2007), op. cit.

25 See for example Modood, Tariq (1988), 'Black', Racial Equality and Asian Identity. New Community. 14 (3), pp. 297–404; Bonnett, Alistair, 1993. Radicalism, Anti-Racism and Representation. London: Routledge.

26 Macpherson, Lord (1999), *The Stephen Lawrence Inquiry: Report*, Cm. 4262–1.

27 The Racial and Religious Hatred Act 2006 enacts that 'threatening words and behaviour' may constitute an act 'intended to stir up religious hatred' and hence a criminal offence of 'religious incitement'. Police interviewees have explained how this presents investigative hurdles in respect of anti-Muslim hate crimes that are not present in respect of similar cases where 'stirring up racial hatred' is the point at issue. In other words, the burden of proof in an investigation of anti-Muslim hate crime is set higher than in a comparable investigation of racist violence.

28 See for example a case study of a serious anti-Muslim gang attack on Muslim students at City University, London in Githens-Mazer,and Lambert, 2010, pp. 26–32.

29 Richardson, Robin (ed.) (1997), op. cit.
30 Gable, Gerry and Paul Jackson (2011). Lone wolves: myth or reality? London: Searchlight publications.
31 Dodd, Vikram (2011). Stephen Lawrence murder suspects to stand trial. Guardian. http://www.guardian.co.uk/uk/2011/may/18/stephen-lawrence-suspects-stand-trial [accessed 12 September 2011].
32 Lambert and Githens-Mazer (2010), op. cit.
33 Rowe, Raphael, 2006. Who killed Kelso Cochrane? 7 April. http://news.bbc.co.uk/1/hi/programmes/4871898.stm [accessed 20 August 2010].
34 Ibid.
35 Dodd, Vikram (2005). Islamophobia blamed for attack. Guardian. 13 July.http://www.guardian.co.uk/uk/2005/jul/13/race.july7 [accessed 10 August 2010].
36 Ibid.
37 See for example Pearson, Geoff (1976). 'Paki-Bashing' in a North East Lancashire Cotton Town: A case study and its history. In G. Mungham and G. Pearson (eds), Working Class Youth Culture London: Routledge & Kegan Paul.
38 Lambert and Githens-Mazer (2010), op. cit.
39 Ibid.
40 Ibid.
41 Catterall, Peter (1994). The Battle of Cable Street. *Contemporary British History*. 8 (1), pp. 105–32.
42 Lambert and Githens-Mazer (2010), op. cit.
43 Meer, Nasar and Noorani, Tehseen (2008). A sociological comparison of anti-Semitism and anti-Muslim sentiment in Britain. The Sociological Review. 56 (2). pp. 195–219; Malik, Maleiha (2006). Muslims are now getting the same treatment Jews had a century ago. Comment is Free: Guardian Online 2 February. http://www.guardian.co.uk/commentisfree/story/0,,2004258,00.html [accessed 2 November 2011], Meer, Nasar (2008). The politics of voluntary and involuntary identities: are Muslims in Britain an ethnic, racial or religious minority? Patterns of Prejudice, 42 (1), pp. 61–81.
44 Ibid.
45 See for example Poole, Elizabeth (2006). The Effects of September 11 and the War in Iraq on British Newspaper Coverage. In Poole, Elizabeth and John E. Richardson (eds), Muslims and the News Media. London: I.B. Taurus, pp. 96–7.
46 Malik, Maleiha (2006), op. cit.
47 Macpherson, Lord (1999), op. cit.
48 An observation also made in the Scarman Inquiry into the Brixton riots in 1981 – Scarman, Lord (1982), The Scarman Report: The Brixton Disorders 10–12 April, 1981. London: Pelican.
49 Athwal, Harmit, Jenny Bourne and Rebecca Wood, (2010). Racial Violence: The Buried Issue. IRR briefing paper no. 6. London: Institute of Race Relations. http://www.irr.org.uk/pdf2/IRR_Briefing_No.6.pdf [accessed 6

August 2010]; IRR News Team, (2010). Racial violence laid bare. 5 August. http://www.irr.org.uk/2010/august/ms000008.html [accessed 6 August 2010].

50 Straw, Jack, (2009). Stephen Lawrence Inquiry: Ten years on. London: Ministry of Justice. http://www.justice.gov.uk/news/speech240209a.htm [accessed 10 September 2010].
51 Athwal, Bourne and Wood, (2010), op. cit.
52 Pendlebury, Richard and Stephen Wright, (2010). Could this finally be the year for justice for Stephen Lawrence? Daily Mail. 5 January. http://www.dailymail.co.uk/news/article-1239768/Could-finally-year-justice-Stephen-Lawrence.html [accessed 8 January 2010].
53 'Ajmal', an assumed name for anonymous interviewee, EMRC 34/10.
54 Ibid.
55 Allen, Chris, (2003). Fair Justice: The Bradford Disturbances, the sentencing and impact. London: FAIR.
56 Amersham, Chorleywood, Rickmansworth, Moor Park, Northwood, Pinner and Harrow.
57 Lambert and Githens-Mazer, (2010), op. cit.
58 Ibid.
59 Ibid.
60 Ibid.
61 Ibid.
62 Ibid.
63 Ibid.
64 Ibid.
65 Ibid.
66 Ibid.
67 Formal and correct name of the building used by many practicing Muslims in preference to the word 'mosque'.
68 Lambert and Githens-Mazer, (2010), op. cit.
69 Githens-Mazer and Lambert, (2010), op. cit. p. 37.
70 Bexley Times, (2009). Greenwich Islamic Centre petrol bombed twice in a week. 17 June.
71 Ibid.
72 Lambert and Githens-Mazer, (2010), op. cit.
73 Ibid.
74 Ibid.
75 Ibid.
76 Ibid.
77 Ibid.

78 Ibid.
79 Ibid.
80 Ibid.
81 Ibid.
82 BBC News, (2004). BNP activists admit to race crime. 15 July. http://news.bbc.co.uk/1/hi/uk/3894529.stm [accessed 13 August 2011].
83 Ibid.
84 Lambert and Githens-Mazer, (2010).
85 Ibid.
86 Copsey, Nigel, (2010). *The English Defence League: Challenging our country and our values of social inclusion, fairness and equality.* London: Faith Matters, p. 5.
87 Ibid.
88 Britten, Nick, (2010). Youth supporter of EDL and BNP manufactured gunpowder and nail bomb. Daily Telegraph. 26 June. http://www.telegraph.co.uk/news/uknews/crime/7855025/Boy-made-nailbombs-with-chemicals-bought-on-eBay.html [accessed 6 October 2011].
89 Hasan, Mehdi, 2009. Know your enemy. *New Statesman.* 9 July. http://www.newstatesman.com/2009/07/mehdi-hasan-muslim-terrorism-white-british [accessed 6 October 2011].
90 Githens-Mazer and Lambert, (2010), op. cit, pp. 20–6.
91 Ibid.
92 The example of Abu Hamza in this regard is discussed in Lambert, Robert, (2011), op. cit.
93 Hasan, Mehdi, (2009), op. cit.
94 Ibid.
95 Githens-Mazer and Lambert, (2010), op. cit.; see also Guardian, 2010. BNP member given 11 years for making bombs and guns. 15 January. http://www.guardian.co.uk/uk/2010/jan/15/bnp-member-jailed-guns-bombs [accessed 12 August 2011].
96 Ibid.
97 Author interview.
98 Lambert and Githens-Mazer, (2010), op. cit.
99 Athwal, Bourne and Wood, (2010), op. cit.

References

Allen, Chris (2010). *Islamophobia.* Aldershot: Ashgate.
—(2009). *The Rise of the British National Party: Anti-Muslim Policies and the Politics of Fear.* University of Birmingham: Institute of Applied Social Studies.

—(2003). Fair Justice: The Bradford Disturbances, the sentencing and impact. London: FAIR.
Allen, Chris and Jorgen Nielsen (2002). Summary report on Islamophobia in the EU after 11 September 2001, European Monitoring Centre on Racism and Xenophobia (EUMC), Vienna.
Athwal, Harmit, Jenny Bourne and Rebecca Wood (2010). Racial Violence: The Buried Issue. IRR briefing paper no. 6. London: Institute of Race Relations.
BBC News (2004). BNP activists admit to race crime. 15 July. http://news.bbc.co.uk/1/hi/uk/3894529.stm [accessed 13 August 2011].
—(2002). Islamophobia 'explosion' in UK. 24 May. http://news.bbc.co.uk/1/hi/uk/2005943.stm accessed 13.8.11.Bennett, Ronan, 2007. Shame on us. Guardian. 19 November. http://www.guardian.co.uk/uk/2007/nov/19/race.bookscomment [accessed 20 August 2010].
Bexley Times (2009). *Greenwich Islamic Centre petrol bombed twice in a week.* 17 June.
Birt, Yahya (2009). Defining Islamophobia today: the state of the art. Musings on the Britannic Crescent blog. 15 September. http://www.yahyabirt.com/?p=175 [accessed 29 December 2009].
Bonnett, Alistair (1993). Radicalism, Anti-Racism and Representation. London: Routledge.
Britten, Nick (2010). Youth supporter of EDL and BNP manufactured gunpowder and nail bomb. Daily Telegraph. 26 June. http://www.telegraph.co.uk/news/uknews/crime/7855025/Boy-made-nailbombs-with-chemicals-bought-on-eBay.html [accessed 17 October 2010].
Catterall, Peter (1994). The Battle of Cable Street. Contemporary British History. 8 (1), pp. 105–32.
Copsey, Nigel, 2010. *The English Defence League: Challenging our country and our values of social inclusion, fairness and equality.* London: Faith Matters.
—(2010). *The English Defence League: Challenging our country and our values of social inclusion, fairness and equality.* London: Faith Matters.
Dodd, Vikram (2011). Stephen Lawrence murder suspects to stand trial. Guardian. http://www.guardian.co.uk/uk/2011/may/18/stephen-lawrence-suspects-stand-trial [accessed 12 September 2011].
—(2005). Islamophobia blamed for attack. Guardian. 13 July. http://www.guardian.co.uk/uk/2005/jul/13/race.july7 [accessed 10 August 2010].
Guardian (2010). BNP member given 11 years for making bombs and guns. 15 January. http://www.guardian.co.uk/uk/2010/jan/15/bnp-member-jailed-guns-bombs [accessed 12 August 2011].
Fekete, Liz (2009). A Suitable Enemy: Racism, Migration and Islamophobia in Europe. London: Pluto Press.
—(2008). Integration, Islamophobia and Civil Rights in Europe. London: Institute of Race Relations.
—(2004). Anti-Muslim racism and the European security state. Race & Class. 46 (1), pp. 3–29.
Gable, Gerry and Paul Jackson (2011). Lone wolves: myth or reality? London: Searchlight publications.

Githens-Mazer, Jonathan and Robert Lambert (2010). *Islamophobia and Anti-Muslim Hate Crime: a London case study.* Exeter: European Muslim Research Centre, University of Exeter.

Grieve, John G. D and Julie French (2000). Does Institutional Racism Exist In the Metropolitan Police Service? In David G. Green (ed.) *Institutional Racism and the Police: Fact or Fiction?* London: Institute for the Study of Civil Society (Civitas).

Griffin, Nick (2007). Islamization of Europe, Clemson University, 24 October 2007, Part 2, http://www.youtube.com/watch?v= 916qkfhT8DU [accessed 21 November 2009].

—(2008). By their fruits (or lack of them) shall you know them. BNP website. http://web.archive.org/web/20071014195717/ http://www.bnp.org.uk/columnists/chairman2.php?ngId=30 [accessed 3 April 2009].

Hasan, Mehdi (2009). Know your enemy. *New Statesman.* 9 July. http://www.newstatesman.com/2009/07/mehdi-hasan-muslim-terrorism-white-british [accessed 12 August 2011].

IRR News (2010). Racial violence laid bare. 5 August. http://www.irr.org.uk/2010/august/ms000008.html [accessed 6 August 2010].

—(2005). The anti-Muslim backlash goes on. 4 August. London: IRR.

—(2005). The anti-Muslim backlash continues. 21 July. London: IRR http://www.irr.org.uk/2005/july/ha000013.html [accessed 21 August 2010].

—(2005). The anti-Muslim backlash begins. 14 July. London: IRR http://www.irr.org.uk/2005/july/ak000008.html [accessed 21 August 2010].

Jenkins, Simon (2011). *The last thing Norway needs is illiberal Britain's patronising. The Guardian.* 26 July.

Lambert, Robert (2011). *Countering al-Qaeda in London: Police and Muslims in Partnership.* London: Hurst.

Lambert, Robert and Jonathan Githens-Mazer (2010). *Islamophobia and Anti-Muslim Hate Crime: UK case studies.* Exeter: EMRC, University of Exeter. http://centres.exeter.ac.uk/emrc/publications/Islamophobia_and_Anti-Muslim_Hate_Crime.pdf [accessed 12 August 2011].

Macpherson, Lord (1999). The Stephen Lawrence Inquiry: Report, Cm. 4262–1.

Malek, Maleiha (ed.) (2010). *Anti-Muslim Prejudice.* London: Routledge.

—(2006). Muslims are now getting the same treatment Jews had a century ago. Comment is Free: Guardian Online 2 February. http://www.guardian.co.uk/commentisfree/story/0,,2004258,00.html [accessed 2 November 2011].

Meer, Nasar (2008). The politics of voluntary and involuntary identities: are Muslims in Britain an ethnic, racial or religious minority? Patterns of Prejudice, 42 (1), pp. 61–81.

Meer, Nasar and Noorani, Tehseen (2008). A sociological comparison of anti-Semitism and anti-Muslim sentiment in Britain. The Sociological Review. 56 (2). pp. 195–219;

Modood, Tariq (1988). 'Black', Racial Equality and Asian Identity. New Community. 14 (3), pp. 297–404.

Muslim Safety Forum, (2007). Islamophobia: the Impact on London. London: MSF. http://muslimsafetyforum.org/docs/Islamophobia&ImpactonLondon.pdf [accessed 3 November 2009].

Pearson, Geoff (1976). 'Paki-Bashing' in a North East Lancashire Cotton Town: A case study and its history. In G. Mungham and G. Pearson (eds), Working Class Youth Culture London: Routledge & Kegan Paul.

Pendlebury, Richard and Stephen Wright (2010). Could this finally be the year for justice for Stephen Lawrence? *Daily Mail*. 5 January. http://www.dailymail.co.uk/news/article-1239768/Could-finally-year-justice-Stephen-Lawrence.html [accessed 8 January 2010].

Poole, Elizabeth (2006). The Effects of September 11 and the War in Iraq on British Newspaper Coverage. In Poole, Elizabeth and John E. Richardson (eds), Muslims and the News Media. London: I.B. Taurus, pp. 96–97.

Richardson, Robin (ed.), 1997 Commission on British Muslims and Islamophobia: Islamophobia: a challenge for us all. London: Runnymede Trust

Scarman, Lord (1982). The Scarman Report: The Brixton Disorders 10–12 April, 1981. London: Pelican.

Schmid, Alex P. (2004). Frameworks for Conceptualising Terrorism. *Terrorism and Political Violence*. 16 (2) pp. 197–221.

Souhami, A. (2007). Understanding Institutional Racism: the Stephen Lawrence Inquiry and the police service reaction, in: Policing beyond Macpherson: Issues in policing, race and society. Devon: Willan, pp. 66–87.

Straw, Jack (2009). Stephen Lawrence Inquiry: Ten years on. London: Ministry of Justice. http://www.justice.gov.uk/news/speech240209a.htm [accessed 10 September 2010].

Tobias, Rabbi Pete (2007). Undesirable debate. Guardian–comment is free. http://www.guardian.co.uk/commentisfree/2007/nov/14/undesirablesdebate [accessed 20 August 2010].

Werbner, Pnina (2005). Islamophobia: Incitement to religious hatred – legislating for a new fear? Anthropology Today. 21 (1) pp. 5–9.

4

Grassroots Activism in the English Defence League: Discourse and Public (Dis)order

Joel Busher

In Luton on 10 March 2009, there was a homecoming parade to mark the return of soldiers from the Royal Anglian Regiment after a six-month tour of duty in Iraq. On the day of the parade, a small number of activists from a group called *Ahlus Sunnah wal Jamaah* staged a protest, shouting abuse at the soldiers and calling them 'baby killers' and 'butchers of Basra' (Copsey 2010). There was an immediate and hostile reaction from some of the people who had gathered to support the soldiers, and police officers intervened to prevent the activists from being attacked. It was in the aftermath of this incident, and in an environment of public outrage about the protest (see *Daily Mail*, 14/3/09), that a network of small and already existing street movements started to come together to form the English Defence League (EDL). The movement was mobilised around a core narrative about the threat posed by 'militant Islam' to the UK and more generally to the West, and initially drew much of its support from the English and Welsh football casuals community (part of the football hooligan culture), as well as from a variety of other 'nationalist' or 'ultra-patriotic' groups (Copsey 2010; Jackson 2011a; Marsh 2010). The first major street demonstrations took place in Birmingham during the summer of 2009 (Jackson 2011). At the time, many public order police officers expected that 'it would all blow over when the new football season kicked off' (Personal communication with public order police officer), but that didn't happen. EDL activists have continued to organise frequent local and national demonstrations. In the 12 months from June 2010 to May 2011, there were

11 major EDL demonstrations (>300 supporters) and a further 73 smaller demonstrations (<300 supporters). Whilst there are ongoing rumblings about infighting within the EDL (see Collins 2011), since the movement first emerged it has drawn support from members of established Zionist groups and networks, started to form relations with similar movements elsewhere in Europe – France, Scandinavia, Germany and the Netherlands – and won admirers in the USA and in Canada.

After its formation, the EDL quickly became one of the most controversial social movements in the UK. The rise of the EDL has prompted widespread fears both about a re-emergence of far-right street violence, and about broader processes of 'cumulative extremism' (Eatwell 2006) or 'tit for tat radicalization' (Jackson 2011a) – a spiral of hostility between opposing social movements as groups associated with the 'far right' and with 'radical Islam' antagonize one another and stir up prejudice and hatred in the communities from which they draw their support. In light of such fears, it is perhaps unsurprising that the groups that have led campaigns against the EDL, such as Unite Against Fascism (UAF), the Socialist Workers Party and *Searchlight* Magazine, have mobilised supporters around claims that the EDL is an 'extreme right-wing', 'racist' or 'fascist' organization, often highlighting the links of some of the EDL's members to the British National Party (BNP) and to other extreme right-wing groups (cf. UAF 2011) – such concepts are after all rich in their emotive potential. Calls from these groups for the EDL to be officially identified by the UK government and police as an 'extremist' organization have intensified recently amidst allegations about links between EDL activists and Anders Behring Breivik, the Norwegian man who killed 77 people in Norway on 22 July 2011 (see Lowles August 2011).

However, the EDL leadership and many of its activists have repeatedly sought to distance themselves from Britain's 'traditional' far right, such as the BNP and the National Front (NF). And whilst opposition groups have tended to view such claims as a cynical attempt by the EDL to make itself more respectable, these claims by the EDL and the way in which activists have mobilised around them have also provoked reflection on the changing terrain of far-right and populist politics in the UK. It has been argued, for example, that the rise of the EDL points both to a shift away from party politics and conventional channels of political organization (Jackson 2011a; Jackson 2011b), and to the way that 'culture' has replaced 'race' and 'indigeneity' as the core concept around which far-right or populist social movements are able to construct identities and mobilise support (Copsey 2010; Jackson 2011a).

It is hoped that this chapter can contribute to these reflections, although it perhaps does so only obliquely. Here, rather than attempt to describe or define the ideology of the EDL as a movement, I instead set out only to elaborate on the discourse and practices of a small number of EDL activists from London and the Southeast. The chapter starts by outlining five prominent themes within activists' discourse. In the second part of this chapter I consider how elements within this discourse have shaped the dynamics of public order and disorder in the context of EDL demonstrations. In doing so, the chapter starts to sketch out some of the tensions and contradictions that have come to characterise grassroots activism in the EDL and, I argue, it is these points of friction that must be further explored if we are to gain a more nuanced understanding of EDL activism and its implications for community cohesion and public order.

The account presented here is based on overt qualitative research, which has been carried out with EDL activists from London and the Southeast of England over a period of nine months between February and October 2011. Observation has been carried out at nine demonstrations in the Southeast, the West Midlands and the Northwest of England, as well as at divisional and regional meetings in and around London. The research also makes use of life history interviews carried out with eight activists from London and the Southeast, and many informal conversations with activists in the same area. Contrary to the expectations of some fellow researchers, although I aroused some suspicion when I first started attending EDL demonstrations, activists have for the most part been quite willing to allow me to attend demonstrations and divisional meetings – 'we have nothing to hide, and we've got police infiltrators anyway; why should we care if you come [to meetings] too, feel free' (Respondent 4, EDL national leadership, 18/8/11). Having said that, it is important to acknowledge that my research encounters with EDL activists are likely to have been shaped to some extent by activists' efforts at 'impression management' (Goffman 1969). Before proceeding with this account, it is also important to stress that I do not claim that this research is representative of the movement as a whole. There are differences between EDL divisions in different parts of the country, as indeed there are within local divisions in terms of activists' political backgrounds and interests.

The discourse of EDL activists in London and the Southeast

At EDL demonstrations and meetings in London and the Southeast, it is not uncommon to meet people who have a history of support for the far right in Britain – such as voting for the BNP or supporting the NF – but it is also not uncommon to meet, among others, seasoned campaigners from counter-jihad and Zionist networks; people who have had little involvement in political organizations but have been part of the football casuals milieu; people with a history of participation in various popular or political patriotic movements like March for England or the English Democrats; former and now disenchanted left-wing activists and union representatives; people campaigning about the persecution of Christians in majority Muslim countries; or activists who became involved in the EDL after just going along to a demonstration 'to see what it was all about' (Respondents 1 and 9). As with other contemporary protest movements from across the political spectrum, part of what enables these activists with diverse backgrounds and interests to coalesce as a movement is a shared discourse through which activists are able to construct and articulate shared grievances and their sense of identification with one another (Jackson 2011a; Jasper 2007; Melucci 1980) – the discourse of a movement provides its supporters with a set of concepts with which they are able to construct themselves as a collectivity, and with which they are able to produce or reconfigure notions of inclusion and exclusion (Pratt 2003). Here, I outline five themes that are prominent in the discourse of the EDL activists with whom I have spoken, and that have provided the core concepts around which the activists have mobilised.

'Not racist, not violent ...': The EDL as 'a human rights organisation'

> We're not racist, we're not violent; we're just no longer silent
>
> (Kevin Carroll, speech to a demonstration in Dagenham, 18 June 2011)

Since it was formed, efforts to distance the EDL from the 'traditional' far right and to reject claims that the movement is either racist or violent have emanated from the national leadership (Copsey 2010; Jackson 2011), and these claims are frequently reproduced by grassroots activists. Activists often stress the EDL's non-BNP credentials, and local leaders in and around London have been keen to ensure that there have been no EDL events at which there has been an official BNP presence. A popular anecdote among London activists is about an EDL London meeting in 2010 when Richard Barnbrooke, for some time one of the leading lights of the BNP, attended the meeting only to be told by EDL activists that they wanted nothing to do with him or the BNP. Activists also draw attention to the fact that there are members of the EDL from black and other minority ethnic populations, and to the fact that the EDL has a Jewish Division. In addition, all except one respondent in this research has been keen to display their own personal non-racist credentials. For example, during life history interviews, seven of the eight respondents have spoken about family members and/or close friends who are from black and minority ethnic groups.

Rather than adopt the language of the traditional far right, with its emphasis on concepts such as race, ethnicity and indigeneity, EDL activists have instead sought to adopt a more contemporary and politically acceptable language that is based around concepts such as 'human rights' and 'freedom of expression' (Jackson 2011a). The claim made in the EDL mission statement that the EDL is 'a human rights organization' (see EDL 2011) is often repeated by grassroots activists, and the use of this universal claims-making language, as opposed to the more particularized language of claims based on racial and ethnic identities, appears to have been particularly important in enabling the EDL to appeal to many of the activists in London and the Southeast who are proud of their immigrant heritage (Respondents 3, 5, 8 and 9).

Most activists also continue to maintain that the EDL is a peaceful protest movement, with violent behaviour presented very much as the exception rather than the rule. Activists point to examples of demonstrations with a relatively small police presence at which there have not been instances of violence or public disorder, and also cite other occasions when people who have caused trouble have been told to leave the demonstration, or even to leave the EDL. When pressed about public disorder during demonstrations, the activists argue that such incidents usually occur only when EDL activists come into contact with counter-demonstrations.

The threat of (militant) Islam[1]

The efforts to distance themselves from the traditional far right and from racial politics have led many activists in London and the Southeast to describe the EDL as a 'single issue group', with that single issue being the threat of what activists refer to as 'militant Islam'.

Activists who have taken part in this research express differing views about the extent to which a distinction should be made between 'militant Islam' and 'Islam', or between 'Muslim extremists' and 'Muslims'. However, there is sufficient malleability in these categories for EDL activism to cohere around a broad narrative about an overarching and existential threat posed to the UK and the West by the expansion of (militant) Islam. Around this central theme, activists elaborate and articulate a set of issues and anxieties that may encompass concerns about security, perceived attempts by (militant) Muslim groups to seize political power, and about attempts to impose legal and cultural change on the UK. In doing so, they often weave local and particular concerns – about how their neighbourhoods are changing, or how their children and elderly relatives feel like outsiders in their communities – together with much broader narratives about social, cultural and political change.

It is in these broader narratives that some activists make use of concepts such as a 'clash of civilizations' between Islam and the West (see Huntingdon 1993) or make reference to 'Eurabia' theories (see Ye'or 2005) and the ongoing 'Islamification' of Europe through immigration and through higher birth rates among Europe's Muslim populations. Indeed, activists make reference to a wide range of written and audio-visual materials from beyond the parameters of the EDL, much of which is shared via online forums and social media (Jackson 2011b) – a common theme in activists' life histories is about how they have become more avid readers and more interested in debates about Islam and the West since becoming involved with the movement. Popular commentators and public figures among the activists that I have met include Geert Wilders, Robert Spencer, Melanie Philips, Andrew Gilligan, Douglas Murray, Pat Condell, and some of the commentators who contribute to forums like Alan Lake's Four Freedoms website. Also often referenced are materials from the websites of some of the most overtly anti-Western Muslim groups such as Muslims Against Crusades (MAC), Islam4UK and Hizb-ut Tahrir, usually as evidence to support claims about the threat posed by (militant) Islam.

The threat narrative is also built around a series of important symbolic events that can span the local, national and international levels and that have come to constitute an accumulated body of shared experiences among EDL activists. Recent events often cited by EDL activists in the Southeast of England during the course of this research include the burning of a remembrance poppy by a member of MAC at the Armistice Day memorial on 11 November 2010 (see *Daily Telegraph* 11/11/10); a march by members of MAC and Islam4UK in support of Osama bin Laden after he was killed in May 2011 (see *Daily Mail* 7/5/11); the annual demonstration by members of groups like Islam4UK outside the American embassy on the anniversary of 9/11 (see *Daily Telegraph* 11/9/11); and attacks on Christian communities during the uprisings in North Africa and the Middle East during 2011 (see BBC 10/10/11).

In the most acute form of this threat narrative, some activists have spoken of their fears about an impending civil war as this 'clash of civilizations' eventually reaches a crisis point. One of the most intriguing elements of EDL activists' narrative and their self-image is how they situate themselves in relation to this looming threat. EDL activists spoken to during the course of this research have echoed Tommy Robinson's comments on *Newsnight*

(25/7/11), warning that if things continue as they are at present, then a violent backlash by the far right will become increasingly likely (a view given particular salience by Anders Breivik's attack in Norway). However, in keeping with their claims not to comprise part of the far right, activists have argued that it is precisely to avoid this kind of backlash that the EDL is campaigning for action to be taken now to prevent the expansion of (militant) Islam.

The threat of 'the left'

As Hewitt (2005) describes in some detail, within what might broadly be conceived of as the 'backlash' against multicultural politics that has taken place in recent decades, a recurring theme has been the collusion, or at least an imagined symbiotic relationship, between 'the left' and the 'dangerous Other' (Douglas 1991), whether that Other be black people, Muslims or any other group conceived of as the relevant outsiders. It is unsurprising therefore that activists' comments about the threat posed by (militant) Islam are often situated alongside observations about how 'the left' has undermined the ability of Western states, and in particular of the UK government, to take action against (militant) Islam. Much of the blame is attributed either to the policies of 'the left', in particular to its multicultural policies, or to the wider political and media influence of the 'the left'. Activists often complain 'for example' that the mainstream media in Britain has a 'left-wing bias', that it promotes multiculturalism, and that it censors stories that might show the EDL in a positive light – 85 per cent of 1,295 EDL activists report that they tend not to trust the press (Bartlett 2011).These concerns can then be linked into a wide array of complaints that touch on issues ranging from a perceived decline in national pride, to mass immigration, or to what are perceived as the insidious effects of 'political correctness'.

Animosity towards 'the left' is also personalised, because it is grounded in EDL activists' everyday lives. Many activists have first-hand experience of confrontations (either verbal or physical) with 'lefties' during demonstrations and in online forums. In addition, a number of EDL activists have been the subject of exposé-style reports by publications such as *Searchlight Magazine* (cf. King 2011) or by documentary programmes such as *Unmasked: The Welsh Defence League* on BBC1 in December 2010.

Victimisation: 'We're treated like second-class citizens'

Following on from the issue of media bias, a fourth prominent theme is EDL activists' sense of being victimized by state authorities – especially by politicians, the courts and the police – a theme which again resonates with previous studies on the backlash against multiculturalism in Britain (Hewitt 2005).

Activists' comments about victimization often centre on claims that they are treated differently to other protest groups – and in particular (militant) Muslim protest groups. For example, in recent months activists' sense of outrage has often focused on the discrepancy between the £50 fine given to Emdadur Choudhury for burning a remembrance poppy on 11 November 2010, and the much larger fines awarded to EDL activists for their parts in confrontations between these opposing groups of activists. Activists make similar claims about being unfairly treated by the police during demonstrations. They claim for example that they are searched more often than members of groups like MAC and Islam4UK, and that the police are far more disposed to use force on EDL activists than they are on these other groups. Such claims are repeated after most EDL events, and have become integral to activists' narrative about institutionalized bias against them and in favour of (militant) Islam – once again reinforcing their belief that there are people within the state who are colluding with Muslim (extremists). For example, on 11 September 2011 activists from MAC and Islam4UK held a protest outside the US embassy in London. EDL activists who went there to counter-demonstrate were forcibly moved on by the police in order to prevent violent confrontation between the two groups. After the event one activist posted on Facebook:

> It was refreshing yesterday chatting to a Welsh plod [policeman] who admitted we had a lot of support within their ranks but can't show it. He also let it out that the guidelines they receive from above tell them not to engage with Muslims causing trouble as it may inflame community relations. Fair play for his honesty.
> (Reference not cited to preserve anonymity)

For the purposes of this chapter, the veracity or otherwise of this kind of rumour is largely immaterial. What is important is the way this kind of anecdote circulates after most demonstrations and is used to normalize the belief among EDL activists that they are victimized and treated differently to their opponents.

The EDL as a vanguard

The activist's comments about the Welsh policeman introduce the fifth theme, which relates in part to claims by activists about growing public support for the EDL, or at least growing support for the ideas that it expresses, and is in part about the construction of activists' 'heroic narrative' (Treadwell and Garland 2011).

Linked to the EDL leadership's and activists' claims that the EDL is not an 'extremist' movement, is another set of claims about how the EDL articulates the fears and concerns of many 'ordinary English people', and enjoys a breadth of tacit support from outside the movement. Activists in London and the Southeast often point out that during demonstrations they do receive support and encouragement from members of the public. At each of the four demonstrations in Dagenham, whilst there has been some organised opposition to the demonstration and whilst some residents have peered nervously from behind net curtains whilst the EDL activists have marched by, there have also been onlookers who have waved St George's flags, hooted their car horns in support or applauded and cheered. Activists also share anecdotes about clandestine support or sympathy for the EDL from people whose professional position would prevent them from being able to support the EDL more overtly. It is common after demonstrations, for example, to hear stories about police officers who are 'on our side', such as the anecdote above about the Welsh policeman. Also popular among activists are stories about support for the EDL from politicians, members of the legal profession and people in the armed forces – 'I've got loads of mates in the army, they all love us' (Respondent 4 18/8/11). Whether or not there is any truth in these rumours, they reinforce among activists the belief that they are part of a much larger community that extends beyond the 1,000–3,000 EDL activists who will turn up at demonstrations.

Linked to this sense of being part of a larger community is the heroic narrative that activists construct around the movement and around their own actions. There is a powerful tension that runs through EDL activists' discourse between on the one hand a deep pessimism about the threat of (militant) Islam and failure of Western states to resist its advance, and on the other an image of themselves as the leaders of a growing resistance to this threat. Activists' discourse is thick with references to protecting the nation, as well as with the use of war and military metaphors – the EDL is formed in 'divisions'; activists have been referred to in a number of speeches as 'warriors'; and Facebook messages are often signed off 'no surrender'. Activists construct this heroic narrative around their (often verbal) confrontations with the opposition

– whether they be Muslim (extremists) or 'lefties' – and around decisions taken by local and national authorities that, EDL activists claim, reflect their growing influence: cancelled planning permission for a new mosque; a ban on a particular anti-Western Muslim cleric entering the country; the cancellation of a Muslim conference at the Troxy Centre in East London in 2010 (see Marsh 2010); and any hardening of the UK government's rhetoric on 'Islamic extremism'.

EDL demonstrations and the threat of street violence

Although the EDL leadership and most of the activists spoken to in the course of this research often reiterate the claim that the EDL is a peaceful protest movement and that it does not support violence, instances of violence and public disorder have occurred at many demonstrations, and there have been several cases of anti-Muslim assaults and property damage associated with people who identify as EDL activists (see Lambert, this volume). In the remainder of this chapter, I start to sketch out some of the ways in which the prominent themes in this discourse have shaped the dynamics of violence and non-violence in the context of EDL demonstrations. In doing so, I start also to elaborate on the tensions that the issues of violence and public disorder have generated and highlighted within the EDL activist community with which I have been carrying out research.

During EDL demonstrations, instances of public disorder are usually concentrated around emotionally charged confrontations between EDL activists and counter-demonstrators (see Amis 2009). However, for the most part, police are able to keep opposing groups of activists at sufficient distance to minimise the risk of physical confrontation. During the demonstrations observed as part of this research, the instances of violence that have taken place have tended to occur when EDL activists have been confronted by unofficial opposition, i.e. not by organised and policed counter-demonstrations by groups such as UAF. For example, during a demonstration in Dagenham on 18 June 2011, there was a fight between EDL activists and two Muslim men. As the EDL activists left the muster point at the beginning of their march, they were accompanied by just one community support officer. The activists made their way to Chadwell Heath station where they held a minute of silence for a fellow activist who had passed away, and then proceeded towards the demonstration site. On the way there, two young Muslim men came out of a side road, and were involved in a brief and heated verbal exchange with some of the EDL activists. It is alleged by EDL activists that one of them then spat at the EDL (I was 15 metres further back and my view of this was obstructed). As the two men tried to run away, some of the EDL activists managed to grab one of them and knocked him to the floor. Other EDL activists and stewards sought to restrain their fellow activists, but by the time they managed to do so, the man had sustained several facial injuries.

Similarly, outside West London Magistrates' Court in Hammersmith on 11 May 2011, violence broke out when EDL activists clashed with local youths, at least some of whom were Muslim, but who were not there as part of an organised counter-demonstration by a known opposition group (see *Fulham & Hammersmith Chronicle* 11/05/11). A group of approximately 100 EDL activists had gathered outside the court in support of Tommy Robinson (aka Stephen Yaxley-Lennon), the EDL's main spokesperson, who was appearing there. There was a very light police presence, and activists spent most of the afternoon talking amongst themselves or waving flags and cheering passing motorists who hooted their horns in support. Later in the afternoon there was a verbal altercation between a couple of local youths and some of the EDL activists. A group of youths then started to gather around the side of the court. Some of these youths shouted at the EDL, and although the police officers and some of the EDL activists tried to diffuse the situation, it quickly escalated into a brawl involving about 15–20 youths and a slightly greater number of the EDL activists. Within 15 minutes there was a large police presence; the EDL activists were held in a police kettle; two of the youths were held in the court building by the police and the other youths were also held in a police kettle whilst EDL activists were removed from the area under Section 27 of the Violent Crime Reduction Act 2006.

There have also been a number of instances of violence and public disorder that have taken place after demonstrations when activists have been dispersing, and when many of the EDL activists had already consumed a large quantity of alcohol. On 11 September 2011, for example, rival activists from MAC and the EDL clashed after the demonstration and counter-demonstration outside the US embassy, resulting in beer glasses being thrown by EDL activists and two EDL activists being stabbed by their opponents (see *Independent* 12/9/11); after the demonstration in Telford on 13 August 2011, 46 EDL activists were arrested when fights broke out with groups of local residents (see *Shropshire Star* 15/8/11). In much the same way, after the demonstration in Tower Hamlets on 3 September 2011, a bus carrying EDL supporters went the wrong way as it was leaving London and ended up driving through Stepney Green, East London, where a fight ensued between EDL activists and local residents (BBC 4/9/11).

Such instances of violence and public disorder would seem to support concerns that have been articulated by anti-EDL campaigners about the threat of street violence associated with the EDL. As Treadwell and Garland (2011) have argued, for some activists at least, EDL demonstrations seem to provide an outlet for violence, and an opportunity for marginalized (often young) men to enact an aggressive masculinity directed towards (militant) Muslims as the 'dangerous Other'. Although the national and local EDL leadership officially discourage activists from violence and repeatedly call for protests to be peaceful, violence still provides some activists a way of achieving status among their peers – indeed, it might be argued that Tommy Robinson's standing among some EDL activists has remained as high as it has due in part to his involvement in high-profile physical confrontations with MAC activists. Certainly, there are activists in London and the Southeast who have gained considerable kudos among their peers for their part in physical confrontations. Some of these have even entered into EDL activist folklore as the stories are told and retold by other activists at EDL events and meetings.

Furthermore, by grounding descriptions of these confrontations within the discourse about the threat of (militant) Islam and the alleged failure of the UK and other Western governments to take action, EDL activists are able to fit these confrontations within their heroic self-representation. Even when these confrontations do not appear to be with known opposition groups, it seems that the category 'Muslim extremists' is sufficiently flexible as to be extended to accommodate many new opponents. At the fight in Hammersmith, for example, even though some activists initially criticised their peers for getting in a fight with what one activist described as 'just local lads' (Respondent 9 11/5/11), in subsequent Facebook discussions about the event, the 'local lads' were soon being referred to as 'Muslim extremists'.

As such, it seems that the discourse of EDL activists can in some cases direct violence towards (militant) Muslims and towards others whom activists identify as part of their opposition, and can also provide a discursive framework within which some activists feel able to justify their participation in violence and public disorder.

Maintaining order and non-violence: EDL and the performance of political protest

Yet whilst there has been at least one violent incident at all except one of the demonstrations observed during the course of this research, these incidents have often been isolated and short-lived. Certainly, an account of EDL demonstrations that centres only on instances of violence and public disorder would fail to capture the demonstration experiences of many EDL activists. For some activists, demonstrations are an enjoyable day out, a chance to catch up with friends; and there are always activists who strive to ensure that EDL events reinforce rather than undermine their claims that the EDL is a legitimate and peaceful movement.

The actions performed by many activists during official demonstrations conform largely to the standard 'repertoire' (Tilly 2008) of street-level protest in the UK. Where permitted, demonstrations begin with a march. Many activists proceed in an orderly if sometimes noisy manner from the muster points to the demonstration site, usually waving banners and singing as they go. Demonstrations centre on a number of collective performances. There are speeches, usually made by national or local leaders of the movement, during which they articulate their grievances and specify their claims. At seven of the nine demonstrations observed during this research there have also been collective acts of commemoration in the form of a minute of silence – often, although not always, to remember a recently deceased 'fellow patriot', usually a member of the EDL. Throughout the event, some activists try to engage in wider public outreach, handing out leaflets to and speaking with passers-by, journalists, photographers and the occasional researcher.

While there have been incidents when some EDL activists have clashed with police officers, as happened at Tower Hamlets on 3 September 2011 (BBC 3/9/11), during the course of this research the majority of activists have complied with the instructions given to them by the police. It has become part of the ritual of EDL demonstrations for one of the speakers to express thanks to the police officers for doing their job and to call on activists to be respectful to the police. Outside of a few flashpoints, rapport between EDL activists and police officers has largely been non-confrontational, and sometimes even relaxed. The frequent complaints made by activists about unfair treatment at the hands of 'Old Bill' are rarely framed as complaints about front line police officers themselves, but as complaints about the instructions given to these officers 'from above' or by the 'powers that be'.

Considerable effort is also made by event organisers to avoid instances of public disorder. Prior to official demonstrations, organisers apply for permission to hold the demonstration and liaise with police to establish a route for the march. They identify suitable muster points and pubs in the area where the EDL activists will be able to gather prior to and after the demonstration. They also ensure that there will be sufficient numbers of stewards for the event.

On the day of the demonstration, organisers liaise with public order police officers, whilst event stewards don fluorescent vests and direct other activists. Most of the stewards' role involves keeping activists on the allocated route of the march, but during the demonstrations observed as part of this research I have also seen stewards ushering nervous-looking women of black and minority ethnic backgrounds through the crowd, intervening to stop racist taunts and attempting (with varying degrees of success) to maintain order when violence has started to escalate. During demonstrations, most activists are respectful towards the stewards and broadly comply with their instructions, although as some stewards have observed, as the day progresses and more alcohol – and in some cases also cocaine – is consumed, their job becomes harder and demonstrations can more easily spiral out of control.

For some activists, their sense of carrying out peaceful protests and of maintaining order during demonstrations has been integral to their identity construction, and therefore to their continued involvement in the movement. Their belief that they are not part of the racist and violent far right is to some extent contingent on the way that they and other EDL activists conduct themselves during demonstrations: clamping down on any Nazi salutes – for example, a recent incident of an alleged Nazi salute at a demonstration in London on 8 October 2011 has provoked anger and discord among activists; showing respect towards police officers; cleaning up litter after static demonstrations; and continuing to reiterate that they are opposed only to (militant) Islam. It is this need to maintain the narrative of the EDL as a peaceful protest movement – both for the viability of the movement as a whole, and for the self-image of many individuals within the movement – that has meant that incidents of violence and public disorder have at times provided a focus for tensions and friction within the EDL activist community.

Violence and public disorder as a focus for discord and possible fragmentation

During the attack on the Muslim man in Dagenham on 18 June described above, Kevin Carroll, one of the leaders of the EDL, bellowed from the back of the march, 'You're a disgrace! You're behaving like animals!' whilst a steward stormed away from the incident grumbling that 'it's a fucking waste of time' (Respondent 10 18/6/11). Similarly, in Hammersmith on 11 May, two activists fumed about the fight that had broken out, complaining that the people who had got involved with this were 'stupid' and had 'given them [the youths they were fighting with] and the photographers exactly what they wanted' (Respondent 9 11/5/11).

Instances of violence and disorder are often played down by EDL activists, and attributed to a minority of (usually younger) activists who have drunk too much or who don't 'have a head on them' (Respondent 5 21/09/11). However, for a number of current and former activists, these instances of violence and disorder have become a focus for fallings-out and rancour within the EDL activist community. Some former activists have cited them as a reason for leaving the movement (Respondent 11 2/4/11), and there are several current activists who have repeatedly expressed frustration at the lack of discipline within the movement. There have been a number of complaints, for example, about the heavy drinking and cocaine use by some activists as well as how this undermines efforts to carry out orderly protests – 'this is too serious for that, they think it's a jolly. It's not a jolly' (Respondent 7 15/9/11). There are even some activists who, pointing to Tommy Robinson's court cases for violent conduct (see BBC 15/6/2011; BBC 25/7/11), have argued that ill discipline is an issue that goes right to the top of the movement.

Activists relate these concerns about violence and public disorder both to strategic and personal issues. Activists, and particularly those involved as divisional leaders and event organisers, are well aware that the instances of violence and public disorder that take place during demonstrations make it harder for the movement to gain public support and distance itself from the image of the EDL as a group of violent and racist thugs. Discussing the public disorder that had marked the Tower Hamlets demonstration on 3 September, one activist remarked that 'we just don't need people like that, we're better off without them' (Respondent 7 15/9/11). Other activists have described how incidents of violence and public disorder have led them to question their own future involvement in the movement. For example, one activist, reflecting on what he called the 'element of thuggery' in the EDL, spoke about how he found it increasingly difficult to identify with the football hooligan element within the EDL activist community (Respondent 9 2/9/11). In the months that followed he has ceased to attend EDL demonstrations.

Conclusions

Social movements, and in particular those associated with populist or far-right politics, tend to be unstable organizations (Merkl 2003), and attempts to explain how they might expand or fragment require that we look closely at the competing pressures within these movements (Kriesi et al. 1995). The EDL is certainly not a homogenous block, and there are ongoing tensions and fallings-out within the EDL both nationally and within local divisions, some of which are related to issues around violence and public disorder. If we are to understand the changes that are taking place within this movement and recognise their possible implications in terms of community cohesion and public order, then it would seem incumbent on observers of the EDL from within academic and practitioner communities to acknowledge and attempt to further unpick these competing pressures, rather than falling back on crude categorizations of EDL activists as 'fascists', 'racists' or 'hooligans'.

I started this chapter by outlining some of the prominent themes in the discourse of the EDL activists who have taken part in this research. Based on what I have described, I would argue that activists' discourse can be broadly situated within the series of backlashes against multicultural politics that have taken place in the UK in recent decades (see Hewitt 2005). Whilst the narrative about the threat of (militant) Islam has provided the focal point around which the movement has been able to cohere, woven into this are a series of other themes about the collusion of 'the left' with (militant) Islam, and the victimization of EDL activists as 'ordinary English people'. The breadth of this narrative enables the EDL to operate as a vehicle through which activists can express an array of grievances that extend from everyday anxieties about how their neighbourhoods are changing, to the future of Britain and the decline of Western civilization and democracy.

Also integral to EDL activists' discourse and identities has been the way that they have distanced themselves from the traditional far right, such as the NF or BNP, and sought instead to situate themselves within a much wider imagined popular uprising against the advance of (militant) Islam. Indeed, among the activists who have taken part in this research, much of the appeal of the EDL lies in the attempts of the EDL leadership and other activists to distinguish the movement from the overtly racial politics of the traditional far right. Yet, whilst this has enabled the movement to expand and survive for much longer than many people initially anticipated, it has also laid the foundation for a number of tensions that run through the movement and that are an important part of the dynamics of EDL activism.

As other accounts of the EDL have described, the discourse of EDL activists, and in particular the construction of Muslim (extremists) as a 'dangerous Other', has channelled anger towards Muslims and Muslim communities. The EDL and EDL demonstrations have provided an outlet for hostility and in some instances for violence, and have enabled some activists to legitimize this violence by situating it within a heroic narrative about how they are protecting their community, country and/or culture from the advance of (militant) Islam. However, I have also described another aspect of EDL activism, which is the effort made by some activists to stage peaceful protests and to prevent public disorder and violence. This, I would argue, is just as much a part of EDL activism as the occasional instances of violence and disorder, and it is this aspect of EDL activism that sets up the tension within the EDL activist community that Copsey (2010) observed in his early report on the movement. On the one hand, the EDL's momentum derives at least in part from the energy produced by activists' anger, hostility and on occasion from their confrontations with the 'opposition'. Yet on the other hand, the broad appeal that has sustained the EDL is contingent on the movement and on EDL activists being able to construct a narrative in which the EDL is a legitimate single-issue protest group that is not part of the traditional, racist and violent far right.

Note

1 Throughout this chapter I use '(militant) Islam' and 'Muslim (extremists)' to reflect the fact that there is some variation among activists in terms of the extent to which they make a distinction between 'Islam' and 'militant Islam' and between 'Muslims' and 'Muslim extremists'.

References

Amis, L. (2009, November). In league with the extreme right? *Standpoint*. http://www.standpointmag.co.uk/ [accessed 18 March 2011]. in-league-with-the-extreme-right-features-louis-amis-english-defence-league

BBC (2011, June 15). EDL leader Stephen Lennon faces Blackburn assault charge. http://www.bbc.co.uk/news/uk-england-lancashire–13784285 [accessed 13 October 2011].

—(2011, July 25). EDL founder Stephen Lennon guilty over football brawl. from http://www.bbc.co.uk/news/uk-england-suffolk–14278957 [accessed 13 October 2011].

—(2011, September 3). Scuffles break out at EDL protest in east London. http://www.bbc.co.uk/news/uk-england-london–14775154 [accessed 13 October 2011].

—(2011, September 4). English Defence League coach attacked in east London. http://www.bbc.co.uk/news/uk-england-london–14779772 [accessed 13 October 2011].

—(2011, October 10). Cairo clashes leave 24 dead after Coptic church protest. from http://www.bbc.co.uk/news/world-middle-east–15235212[accessed 13 October 2011].

Bartlett, J. (2011). *Inside the English Defence League* (draught copy). A report by Demos. London: Demos.

Collins, M., (2011, May). War breaks out between EDL and 'Infidels,' *Searchlight*, 431, 8–10.

Copsey, N., (2010). *The English Defence League: Challenging our country and our values of social inclusion, fairness and equality*, London: Faith Matters.

Daily Mail (2009, March 14). Britons who HATE Britain: The Muslim extremists hell-bent on segregation rather than integration. http://www.dailymail.co.uk/

news/article-1161855/Britons-HATE-Britain-The-Muslim-extremists-hell-bent-segregation-integration.html [accessed 13 October 2011].

—(2011, May 7). On this day of all days! Hundreds of militant Muslims stage mock funeral for Bin Laden outside U.S. embassy in London... as relatives of 7/7 terror attack victims weep at inquest just three miles away. http://www.dailymail.co.uk/news/article-1384353/Osama-bin-Laden-mock-funeral-Fury-erupts-outside-US-Embassy-London.html [accessed 13 October 2011].

Daily Telegraph (2010, November 11). Armistice Day: Protesters burn poppy. from http://www.telegraph.co.uk/news/uknews/8125674/Armistice-Day-protesters-burn-poppy.html [accessed 13 October 2011].

—(2011, September 11). 9/11 anniversary: Muslim protesters burn US flag outside embassy in London. http://www.telegraph.co.uk/news/worldnews/september-11-attacks/8755834/911-anniversary-Muslim-protesters-burn-US-flag-outside-embassy-in-London.html [accessed 13 October 2011].

Douglas, M. (1984). *Purity and Danger*. Abingdon: Routledge.

Eatwell, R. (2006). Community cohesion and cumulative extremism in contemporary Britain. *The Political Quarterly*, 77(2) 204–16.

EDL (2011). Mission Statement. http://englishdefenceleague.org/about-us/mission-statement/ [accessed 7 October 2011].

Fulham & Hammersmith Chronicle (2011, May 11). More arrests after EDL clashes: Two women taken to hospital. http://www.fulhamchronicle.co.uk/fulham-and-hammersmith-news/2011/05/11/helicopter-circling-as-edl-thugs-descend-on-hammersmith-82029-28677660/ [accessed 13 October 2011].

Goffman, E. (1969). *Strategic interaction*. Philadelphia, PA: University of Pennsylvania Press.

Hewitt, R. (2005). *White backlash and the politics of multiculturalism*. Cambridge: Cambridge University Press.

Huntingdon, S. (1993). *The clash of civilizations and the remaking of world order*. London: Simon and Schuster.

Independent (2011, September 12). Extremists groups clash as London honours the victims of New York. http://www.independent.co.uk/news/uk/home-news/extremists-groups-clash-as-london-honours-the-victims-of-new-york-2353150.html [accessed 13 October 2011].

Jackson, P. (2011a). *The EDL: Britain's 'new far right' movement*. Northampton: RNM Publications.

—(2011b). English Defence League: Anti-Muslim politics online. In P. Jackson & G. Gable (eds) *Far-right.com: Nationalist extremism on the internet*. Northampton: RNM Publications.

Jasper, J. M. (2007). *The Art of Moral Protest: Culture, Biography and Creativity in Social Movements*. Chicago, IL: University of Chicago Press.

King, S. (2011, July). The EDL's supergrass. *Searchlight*, 433.

Kriesi, H., R. Koopmans, J. W. Duyvendak and M. G. Giugni (eds) (1995). *New social movements in Western Europe: A comparative analysis*. London: UCL Press.

Lowles, N. (2011, August). It's time to act against the EDL. *Searchlight*, 434, 14.

Marsh, J. (2010). *From Seasiders to Casuals United*. Mashed Swede Project.

Melucci, A. (1980). The new social movements: A theoretical approach. *Social Science Information* 19, (2), 199–226.

Merkl, P. H. (2003). Introduction. In P. H. Merkl and L. Weinberg (eds) *Right-wing extremism in the twenty-first century*. Oxon: Routledge.
Pratt, J. (2003). *Class, nation and identity: The anthropology of political movements*. London: Pluto Press.
Shropshire Star (2011, August 15). Forty six arrests after EDL protest in Telford. from http://www.shropshirestar.com/news/2011/08/15/forty-six-arrests-after-edl-protest-in-telford/ [accessed 13 October 2011].
Tilly, C. (2008). *Contentious performances*. Cambridge: Cambridge University Press.
Treadwell, J. and Garland, J. (2011) Masculinity, marginalization and violence: A case study of the English Defence League. *British Journal of Criminology* 51, 621–34.
UAF (2011, February). EDL's links to BNP exposed as antifascists march in Barnsley. [accessed 13 October 2011]. http://uaf.org.uk/2011/02/barnsley-antifascists-march-as-edls-links-to-bnp-exposed/
Ye'or, B. (2005). *Eurabia: The Euro-Arab axis*. New Jersey: Farleigh Dickinson University Press.

5

Ulster Loyalism and Extreme Right Wing Politics

James W. McAuley

They chant 'No surrender to the IRA' at England internationals and fly the Ulster flag, the symbol of Protestant loyalism, alongside the Cross of St George. They even come on 'solidarity tours' during the Northern Ireland marching season ... But now the far-Right neo-Nazis of Britain are being told they are not welcome in the staunchest loyalist town in Ulster and capital of Ian Paisley's Bible belt – Ballymena.

Henry McDonald, *The Observer*, 25 May 2003

Introduction

Despite the common images of ranks of Ulster Loyalists waving Union flags and displaying overt expressions of their sense of 'Britishness', alongside well-known photographs of a youthful Johnny Adair (the notorious Loyalist paramilitary leader) in neo-Nazi regalia, and much more recent incidents involving open hostility and violence toward migrant workers living in predominantly Loyalist areas of Northern Ireland (BBC 2009; NICEM 2009), the claim that there is a natural synergy between Ulster Loyalism and extreme Right politics merits careful examination and exploration.

Ulster Loyalists have most certainly engaged in pro-state politics and violence, and whilst there is evidence of engagement by some from Loyalist backgrounds in racist violence, this remains far from central to Loyalist ideology or political action. This is not to deny the significance of the social dynamics and politics of inclusion and exclusion in Northern Ireland, nor the possibility of particular social groups being racialized within that society. However, the notions that there is unison in the goals of Loyalism and the aims of British extreme Right, or that synergy exists because both groups overtly display their strong affiliation to their sense of Britishness needs to be approached with some prudence.

Those identifying as Loyalists hold a wide spectrum of political views, including those who would claim to be both avowedly loyal to the Crown, alongside being anti-fascist and anti-racist. Further, any understanding of the relations between Loyalism and the extreme Right in Northern Ireland is complicated by the need to consider not only the social forces of racism, but also the central importance of sectarianism in the social organization of that society (Brewer 1992). Looked at from across a variety of social science perspectives, both racism and sectarianism clearly show the strength and development of strong common communal values, used in the development of 'in-groups', set in opposition to the construction of 'out-groups' and the notion of 'the Other'.

Readings of the Other and the social constructions of both racism and sectarianism (and the politics that arise from them) must, however, be categorized meticulously. As Brewer (1991) points out, it is important not to collapse these into any common category of mere prejudice, nor to seek to harness these under some universal notion of gratuitous intolerance (McAuley 2010a).

Undeniably the reaction of some Loyalists to contemporary events has been to turn inward, reflecting the reinforcement of defensive ideological positions and the buttressing of physical and social definitions of territory (McAuley 2009). The result, however, has not been the emergence of an extreme Right organization or political dynamic found throughout much of the rest of United Kingdom or in the rest of Western Europe. Indeed, no overtly 'racist or fascistic organization has garnered serious electoral support in either part of Ireland' (Millar 2010).

Overall, this chapter considers the politics of the extreme Right in Northern Ireland, the attempts of British extreme Right to organise there, and the broad relationships between extreme Right politics and Ulster Loyalism. It further suggests ways in which the contemporary politics of Loyalism has developed in relation to issues of race and ethnicity. Finally, the chapter identifies the formation of contemporary views concerning race and ethnicity across unionism, as that section of the population repositions in relation to changed political, economic, social and cultural circumstances.

Defining the extreme Right

Recent decades have seen the rise of extreme Right and populist movements and parties across Europe (Kopeček 2007; Lubbers, Gijsberts and Scheepers 2002). Despite the ample contemporary evidence of the rise of right-wing extremism (Carter 2005; Norris 2005; Rydgren 2004) there remains much debate as to what actually constitutes such activism, its ideological composition and how it is best defined (Mudde 2000).

The extreme Right parties that have emerged have largely mobilised around two key dynamics (Rydgren 2005). Either they have direct links with, or are linked to 'traditional' fascist parties, such as the Social Movement (MSI) in Italy and the National Democratic Party in Germany, or they seek to distance themselves from such roots, through the construction of a new 'populist Right' (Rydgren, 2004).

Across Europe, populist extreme Right parties have made political advances in France (through the *Front National*), in Italy (by way of *Alleanza Nazionale*) and in Belgium (through the Flemish party *Vlaams Belang*) as well as through the Swedish Democrats, and progressive parties in Denmark and Norway. Extreme Right parties are now active in a large number of other European States, including the Netherlands, Switzerland, Denmark and the United Kingdom, and 'have made use of differing economic theories, political goals … usage of the media and the collection of financial means' (COT Institute 2008: 25).

The extreme Right is involved in a range of actions, including parliamentary and extra-parliamentary activities, street politics and political violence (Caiani and della Porta 2010), as they have sought to organise largely 'around places of intense economic deprivation and social breakdown' (Meleagrou-Hitchens and Standing 2010). Indeed, it is in the urban areas that 'Europe's immigrants disproportionately live [and] where poverty and unemployment are highest … that xenophobic parties have been successful' (Biswas 2011: 16–17).

Mudde (2000: 5) suggests, the 'rise of Right-wing extremists parties comes in waves'. If this is true, recent years have seen much of Europe on a crest of right-wing extremism. This often seeks to present the presence of ethnic minorities in any given society in apocalyptic terms, and the authoritarian Right as offering the only solution to the resulting social problems. Such views have found electoral support. In the most recent European Parliamentary elections, the Austrian Freedom Party (FPÖ) doubled its support to 12.7 per cent of the vote, whilst the BZÖ (another extreme right-wing party in Austria) fell just short of the five per cent cut-off point to elect an MEP.

Elsewhere, the Hungarian Jobbik party, standing on overtly anti-Semitic and anti-Roma policies (and with its own openly paramilitary section), drew 15 per cent of the vote. Even perceived bastions of social liberalism and cultural diversity such as Sweden and the Netherlands have seen the election of members of the extreme Right political representatives.

Extreme Right parties have also drawn heavily on populist and anti-establishment rhetoric, focusing on those social, economic and political areas that they claim are ignored by established political parties. They highlight what they see as threats to localized cultures through the promotion of slogans such as 'Germany First' [*Deutschland Zuerst*], or 'Austria First' [*Österreich Zuerst*]. Taken together, such perspectives represent a broad ideological position reflecting populist and racist beliefs about who is to be considered as a 'real Austrian' or 'real German', or other similar claims to made by other extreme Right parties across Europe to symbolize and protect 'indigenous' identity (Carter 2005).

In the case of the UK, a core organising principle for the British National Party (BNP) has been the promotion of the notion that they represent those who are truly 'British', expressed through hostility to all those seen as threatening what is perceived as the native British cultures. Support for such ideas manifested in the 2010 European Parliamentary election (Meleagrou-Hitchens and Standing 2010), when the BNP drew 943,598 votes from across the United Kingdom (having two MEPs elected with 6.2 per cent of the total vote) relying, in part at least, on the support of many white working-class former Labour Party voters located in deprived urban areas (Ford and Goodwin 2010).

While recognizing, as Mudde (2000: 10) indicates, that extreme Right ideology 'is constituted of a combination of several different features', within Northern Ireland the BNP also promotes the nativism common across the European extreme Right. Compared with some of the other regions highlighted above, however, support for the extreme Right in Northern Ireland is extremely limited. Leaked membership lists show that in 2008 the BNP had 39 members in Northern Ireland (Kennedy and Hines 2008), whilst in 2009 this had only risen to a membership of 49 (*Belfast Telegraph* 2009).

Electoral support for the extreme Right in Northern Ireland is both fleeting and peripheral. In 2011 the BNP stood candidates for the first time in Northern Ireland under a ticket of localism under the slogan 'Putting local people first' (see material in Copsey and Virchow [eds] 2011). It did pitifully badly in the May 2011 elections in Northern Ireland. At the local council level in Belfast their candidate standing in Castlereagh East polled 205 votes (some 2.8 per cent of the overall vote). Elsewhere, those standing for the BNP in the Larne Coast Road and in Larne Town constituencies polled 89 votes (2.7 per cent) and 93 votes (2.7 per cent of the vote) respectively. The BNP's final candidate in Newtownabbey fared even worse, polling only 1.3 per cent of the poll (104 votes).

The Party did no better in the Northern Ireland Assembly vote held on the same day. In East Belfast the BNP secured a mere 337 votes (around one per cent of the vote), in East Antrim, Steven Moore achieved 511 votes (1.8 per cent), and in South Antrim, the Party won the support of 404 voters (1.3 per cent of the total vote). Results in Northern Ireland and across the UK heralded the fragmentation of the BNP which remained dependent on white 'older working-class men who lack educational qualifications and are deeply pessimistic about their economic prospects' (Goodwin 2011: 6) for its base support.

Loyalism and the extreme Right in Northern Ireland

So what overlaps, if any, exist between the British extreme Right and Ulster Loyalism? Some suggest that because of deeply engrained intolerance many Loyalists may well slip seamlessly from the politics of sectarianism to racism (Lewis 2010; Rolston 2004) and that young Loyalists in particular will find an outlet for expression through racism and the extreme Right (*South Belfast News* 2002).

The real position is perhaps not so straightforward. Despite its centrality to the politics of the region, Loyalism remains under-researched and in particular, under-theorised (for some notable exceptions see Bruce 1992, 1994; McAuley 2010; Nelson 1984; Spencer 2008; and various material in Shirlow and McGovern [eds] 1997, and McAuley and Spencer [eds] 2011). whilst populist accounts continue to project an image of Loyalism deeply located in mindless bigotry (of which racism may be a part), apolitical criminality (McDowell 2008), and individualism (Adair 2007; Caldwell and Robinson 2006), such views do not begin to encompass the full spectrum of Loyalist political action or thought.

Certainly some Loyalists or Loyalist groups have sought to make contact with the extreme Right. In recent times, for example, some sections of the Ulster Defence Association (UDA) and – whilst it existed – the Loyalist Volunteer Force have explored establishing connections with the neo-Nazi organizations in Britain (Collins 2011a). Moreover, several extreme Right groupings, including the BNP, the National Front (NF) and the White Nationalist Party (WNP), have sought to organise and undertake recruitment in Northern Ireland and have actively promoted the Loyalist cause on the 'mainland'.

In the contemporary period, the British extreme Right has continued in its attempts to establish a bulkhead in Northern Ireland. There is evidence of some, often highly localized, support. The WNP, for example, has a presence in and around Ballymena, whilst the BNP is more prominent in parts of Belfast. Such groups draw heavily on anti-Irish Republican rhetoric and advance an agenda emphasizing the strength of the United Kingdom. This from the NF is typical:

> The National Front recognises that Northern Ireland is part of the United Kingdom and will be for all time. A National Front government would integrate Ulster into the rest of the UK. Any attack on Ulster and its people would be seen as an attack on the people of Britain as a whole. IRA supporters would be removed from the UK and the border with the Irish Republic would be sealed – all persons living in Ulster will be required to swear an oath of allegiance to the UK or revert to the status of a foreign national. The Irish Republic will be treated as any other nation such as France or Holland. (National Front 2011)

The immediate aftermath of the Ulster Workers' Council strike in 1974 saw the first serious attempt by the extreme Right to organise in Northern Ireland. It met with little support. There was another coherent attempt by the NF to organise in the mid–1980s following widespread unionist opposition to the Anglo-Irish Agreement (*Searchlight*, 1986). During this period, the NF sent a member of its National Directorate to work full-time in Northern Ireland. They also sought to establish an information centre in East Belfast, whilst one leading local NF activist, David Kerr, contested a council seat for the party.

Kerr, however, secured only a handful of votes (*Searchlight* 1989) and the information centre was forced to close in the face of local opposition and open hostility from sections of the Loyalist paramilitaries (Cusack and McDonald 1997). All attempts by the extreme Right to organise met with direct challenges from the Loyalist paramilitary leadership; witness a series of unfavourable articles in *Combat* – the 'in-house' magazine of the Ulster Volunteer Force (UVF) and general hostility from that organization (Cusack and McDonald 1997).

Throughout the 1980s, the mainstream NF supported those Loyalists promoting the notion of an independent Ulster, but the issue of Northern Ireland came to be less and less significant to the central politics of NF as it fragmented following a series of internal power struggles and personality clashes. By the early 1990s, however, the extreme Right again had Northern Ireland in its sights, the BNP in particular trying hard to establish political traction in Northern Ireland, seen again by them as fertile ground because of growing ethnic populations.

Despite regular appeals to, and claimed support of Loyalist paramilitaries, success of the extreme Right in forging any viable links with Ulster Loyalism has been limited (Collins 2011a; 2011b). Sharrock (2009) summarises the situation correctly as follows, when he suggests that in Northern Ireland attempts by the extreme Right groups to recruit

> '… have largely failed. Combat 18, which attempted to recruit a chapter of the Ulster Freedom Fighters in the 1990s, has no real presence in the Province although its name was chanted by thugs during attacks on Romanians.'

Minority populations in Northern Ireland

The area that now makes up Northern Ireland has had small minority ethnic populations for well over a century (largely located in and around Belfast). Importantly, Connolly (2002) has provided an overview of the histories of the main minority ethnic groups in Northern Ireland, including: the Irish Travellers; the Chinese community; the Vietnamese community; Indian, Pakistani and Bangladeshi communities; Latin American and Jewish communities; alongside refugees and asylum seekers. Each ethnic community, of course, has a distinct social structure and history, and there has been a significant growth in inward migration to Northern Ireland since 2001 (Gilligan 2008), from both the rest of the UK and elsewhere, alongside asylum seekers and refugees (NCB and ARK YLT 2010).

In recent times, as the levels of ethno-nationalist political violence has diminished and employment opportunities increased, and the composition of Northern Ireland population has become more ethnically diverse, migrant workers became a rapidly expanding pool for employment (Bell, Jarman and Lefebvre 2004). Specific numbers for both migrant workers and asylum seekers remain contested but it is generally accepted that the minority ethnic population of Northern Ireland stands at around 45,000 – about 3 per cent of the overall population (Beatty, Fagan and Marshall 2006; Jarman 2003; Jarman and Monaghan 2004; NISRA 2010).

Many of Northern Ireland's more recent migrants have come from the A8 countries (those East European states that joined the EU in 2004). Other notable groups of migrant workers now include a sizeable number of Portuguese nationals, many of whom have located in rural areas such as Dungannon and Portadown, where employment opportunities exist in large food processing plants (Suarez 2002). Suarez further suggests the major social characteristic of Northern Ireland's Portuguese population is that they are young, single, male, under the age of 35. Further it is highly transient, with just over three-quarters (77 per cent) staying for around six months, and two-thirds having worked in other countries across Europe before they arrived.

Elsewhere, migrant workers (largely from South Asia and the Philippines) are increasing found across the health care industry, whilst Northern Ireland's African communities are now recognizable, numbering around 2,500, of which between 30–40 per cent are concentrated in Belfast. In addition, there are probably around 2,000 refugees living in Northern Ireland (McVeigh 2002), from countries including the former Yugoslavia, China, Latin America, Africa, Romania, Nigeria and China (Geraghty et al. 2010).

Geoghegan (2008a; 2008b) suggests not only that the expanding size and impact of minority ethnic communities in Northern Irish society is a positive development but that this has been marked by a growing 'concern for minority ethnic communities' and a growing awareness of cultural pluralism in the devolved government (Geoghegan 2008a: 175). Elsewhere, McGarry et al. (2009) note the growing political awareness and prominence given to ethnic minority issues in the manifestos of all the major political parties in Northern Ireland.

But not all responses to a more culturally diverse population in Northern Ireland can be seen in such progressive terms. whilst there has been a positive decline in ethno-nationalist political violence emerging from the conflict over the legitimacy of the state, Northern Ireland has seen an increase in often violent hate crime. Thus, recorded homophobic incidents increased by 17 per cent between 2004/05 and 2005/06, whilst the same period witnessed a 10 per cent increase in domestic violence. As Table 1 below indicates, violence aimed at ethnic minority populations has become commonplace in Northern Ireland (PSNI 2006; 2011).

Indeed, some have even claimed, because of the dramatic increase in tensions and violence surrounding the social relations of race and ethnicity (BBC News 2000), that racism should now be seen as the 'new sectarianism' (Chrisafis 2004; Sharrock 2009), that Northern Ireland has become 'the race hate capital of Europe' (Knox 2011), or even that racist attacks should be regarded as 'the new terrorism' (McKittrick 2004).

Racism and attitudes in Northern Ireland

Paul Connolly is surely correct to point to how quickly in Northern Ireland issues of 'race relations' have 'emerged from almost complete obscurity to one of considerable legislative and political concern' (Connolly, 2002: 11). The current picture surrounding racist attitudes in Northern Ireland is complex (see material in Hainsworth [ed.] 1998; Martynowicz and Jarman 2009; McVeigh and Rolston 2007). Between 1994 and 2005, surveys indicate a clear increase in the number of respondents who hold prejudice against people from minority ethnic communities, from around 10 per cent of respondents in 1994, to one in four respondents in 2004 (Gilligan and Lloyd 2006). Other survey evidence indicates widespread opposition, or at best resistance, to developing multicultural themes (Connolly 2002).

How such views manifest in everyday politics is less clear, but there are some common themes that emerge from the prejudice of the political Right. One commonly held view, for example, is that migrants drain scarce resources, and, in the UK context, that a key driver for population movement is availability to migrants of social and welfare benefits – thus, the direct calls from the extreme Right for immigration to be halted instantly (Goodwin 2011).

Within Northern Ireland, however, as Gilligan (2008) points out, such views are widely rejected by large sections of the population, with almost half (some 47 per cent) either disagreeing or strongly disagreeing with such a proposition. Gilligan further suggests overall views towards migrants remain ambivalent, some 48 per cent believing that migrant workers take jobs away from those born in Northern Ireland, but a much greater number (80 per cent) thought that migrants largely take up jobs that Northern Irish workers don't wish to do.

That said, Northern Ireland has witnessed a significant rise in reports of racist violence. Police Service of Northern Ireland (PSNI) reports indicate that such incidents increased from 453 cases in 2003/04, to 813 in 2004/05, an increase of 79 per cent. This figure increased further to 936 in 2005/06 (PSNI 2006). Whilst these figures may in part reflect an increase in the number of people being prepared to report such incidents, as well as a growing awareness and improved forms of recording by the PSNI, they also undoubtedly reflect a real increase in the number of racist incidents (see Table 1), leading one journalist to highlight what is seen as 'Ulster disturbing descent into racism,' (*Belfast Telegraph* 2006).

In the most contemporary period it is no coincidence that the areas of largest representation for the extreme Right in Northern Ireland include districts such as Larne and Dungannon, which contain areas amongst the most economically and socially deprived in the Province (NIDETI 2006). In rural Portadown, for example, the White Nationalist Party (a split from the National Front) has targeted the town's extremely small Muslim community, issuing race hate leaflets entitled: 'This is Ulster not Islamabad'. Migrant workers in Portadown have also been subjected to a series of racist attacks.

Table 5.1. Racial and Sectarian Incidents and Crimes, 2005–2010

	2005/06	2006/07	2007/08	2008/09	2009/10
Racial incidents	936	1047	976	990	1038
Racial crimes	746	861	757	771	712
Sectarian incidents	1701	1695	1584	1595	1840
Sectarian crimes	1470	1217	1056	1017	1264

Source: Compiled from PSNI 2006; 2011.

Elsewhere, Hickman et al. (2008) and the NIHE (2009) demonstrate that in Dungannon (another large rural town) there is clear evidence of day-to-day hostility between existing residents and new arrivals (mostly from Poland, Lithuania and other East European nationals), who have mostly been recruited to employment in local food-processing plants.

Loyalism, racism, and anti-racism

While racist attacks occur throughout Northern Ireland, the 'majority ... have been recorded in predominately Protestant working class areas' (Jarman and Monaghan 2004). Further, between 1994 and 2005, Gilligan reports that the proportion of Catholics who saw themselves as racially prejudiced doubled (from 9 to 18 per cent). Moreover, the Northern Ireland Life and Times Survey for 2005 indicates that Protestant respondents were almost twice as likely as Catholics to *say* they were prejudiced against people from minority ethnic communities.

This, alongside the high level of racist incidents in Protestant areas, raises the question of whether Protestants are more likely to be racially prejudiced than Catholics (Coulter 2003; 2004). Given the social structure of Northern Irish society, this raises further questions concerning structured Loyalist paramilitary involvement in racist violence and racist crime.

All racist sub-cultures, of course, exist within a particular context. Ulster Loyalism draws on its own reference points and is perhaps most clearly understood as the political countenance of unionism after it is refined by the experiences of the everyday realities and marginalized economic position that is the Protestant working-class life (McAuley 2010). Over the past four decades the socio-economic standing of many Protestant working-class communities has declined dramatically (particularly with the loss of heavy industry) and direct patronage from the ruling Unionist group.

Many within such communities now see themselves as increasingly marginalized across the interconnected arenas of politics, culture and physical space. Feelings of political and cultural alienation are now deeply engrained within loyalist consciousness (Southern 2007). Moreover, Pehrson et al. (2012) argue that Protestant and unionist communities strongly believe that they have experienced higher measures of cultural threat than Catholic and nationalist communities since 1998.

In their analysis Pehrson et al. (2012) suggest that cultural threat can best be understood as a response to broader changes in Northern Irish society that have challenged the dominant status enjoyed by Protestants and unionists in the past. Further, many also believe that they have lost out economically, socially and politically in the period following the peace process manifest in a growing disconnect between working-class Loyalism and the political representatives of mainstream unionism (Kane 2011).

As such, some of the classic motivators are in place for a turn to extreme Right politics to take place (Balent 2011; Marsdal 2008). whilst making clear that racism 'is not related to the Loyalist ideology per se', one report highlighted how these factors can come together to produce certain political circumstances prevalent in an area of Belfast called 'the Village':

> Historically, [this] area of Belfast has been the choice of residence for Protestant people working in the nearby shipyards and other industrial sites. Due to the area's lack of investment and regeneration, private developer moved in buying those houses and renovated for the purpose private renting. As this area is close to the centre of Belfast, it tends to equally be the choice of residence for minority ethnic people, particularly the new migrants. Unfortunately the visibility of the diverse migrants living in the areas seems as a threat. Therefore, [this] area is a fertile ground for racial tension. (NICEM 2009)

However, any evidence that working-class Protestants have turned to the extreme Right is limited. Importantly, as Graham (2004) points out, Loyalism finds expression in a range of perspectives, from those who promote extreme right-wing politics, religious fundamentalism, the combination of religion and politics still expressed by sections of the Democratic Unionist Party (DUP) and the left of centre views found in the leadership of the Progressive Unionist Party (PUP), emerging as it did from sections of the UVF. Admittedly for some, at the heart of Loyalism remains the protection of old political certainties and the possibility of reinforcing existing social relationships. Others, however, see Loyalism as a much more dynamic social and political force.

Hence, for example, the leadership of major Loyalist paramilitary groups have consistently condemned racist attacks, although often admitting that 'rogue' Loyalists were responsible (BBC 2003), whilst others have recognised that whilst some Loyalist paramilitary members have a history of inflaming racial tensions, such actions have not necessarily been sanctioned by their central command (NICEM 2009). Further, the political representatives of the Loyalist paramilitaries have actively campaigned against racism, claiming that they will ensure racist groups 'are ostracized within the Loyalist community' (BBC 2003).

Elsewhere, former Loyalist paramilitaries have taken part in, and helped organise anti-racism training (McAleese 2009), also claiming that it is the duty of all Loyalists to inform on all those involved in racist attacks to the Police (McDonald 2009a). Moreover, the PUP has actively supported a campaign for the introduction of effective race relations legislation for Northern Ireland, whilst organising a door-to-door leafleting campaign to warn people against joining racist organizations (McDonald 2003).

Beyond this, the Loyalist Commission (representing the major Loyalist paramilitary groups, alongside church and other community representatives) has conducted a widespread anti-racist campaign under the banner headline 'Loyalist or Racist – You Can't Be Both'. The broad message is that Loyalism and racism are both politically and ideologically incompatible. Central to the campaign was the production and circulation of high quality glossy brochures and posters, part of which declared:

> Over the years the Loyalist people have rightly said No to those things that are a threat to our culture and tradition. But now there is something that threatens from within – Racism. Again it is time to say No – to racism. For British Loyalty is not to the national tribe or people – but to the crown. Therefore we welcome all who want to make our home their home – who gladly join us in working hard for a better future for the British people. (Loyalist Commission, c. 2005)

These publications by the Loyalist Commission seek to set the notion of anti-racism firmly within a broader Loyalist narrative. For example, one key passage reads as follows:

> As Loyal British subjects we are part of one of the greatest stories of world history. The world owes much to the British Empire – freedom of political choice, thought and religious belief. International trade and many global institutions are the positive result of British influence in the world. The great movements of Africa and Asia towards self-government and

independence were nurtured in the schools of Empire. What was a Right for us was offered as a Right for all.

(Loyalist Commission, c. 2005)

Under the further slogan 'Ensuring Civil and Religious Liberties for All', the Loyalist Commission publications also focus on images of the Orange Order. Despite its reduced membership and political influence in recent times, the Orange Order remains an important part of Protestant-Unionist-British life for many in Northern Ireland (McAuley, Tonge and Mycock 2011). With a membership of still around 40,000, the Order continues to offer distinctive social, religious and cultural traditions, which continue to impact upon the day-to-day life of many Protestants in Northern Ireland.

The Order also has an international presence, especially in Scotland and parts of England, and more widely where historical connections developed through military and Empire connections in dominions such as Australia, New Zealand and Canada and former colonies such as India, the West Indies and African possessions (McAuley, Tonge and Mycock 2011). One photograph in the 'Loyalist or Racist – You Can't Be Both' campaign shows what we can only assume are black members of African Lodges of the Orange Order marching in an Orange parade somewhere in Northern Ireland, no doubt reflecting the Order's claims to be upholders of universal civil and religious liberty.

The aim of these references is to persuade Loyalists of the merits of anti-racism by drawing directly on familiar narratives and senses of history and identity that are already firmly grounded within Ulster Loyalism. Such an approach may seem somewhat strange to outsiders, but it rests within the remit of 'single identity' work, as part of the matrix of conflict resolution and transformation. Within conflict situations single identity work is aimed at increasing confidence within one community in the hope that this will allow cross-community work to eventually develop (Church, Visser and Johnson 2004; Hughes 2002).

Conclusions

Northern Ireland, despite the many tangible social and political changes brought about by the peace process, remains a highly stratified society. The responses of Loyalism to contemporary events remain multi-layered. Within this, the core sense of the Loyalist collective remains intense. Feelings of belonging are deeply developed at a personal level, and through often highly localized bonds that link individuals to their political community.

Given the strength and longevity of such ties (Bell 1987) and their reinforcement during three decades of overt conflict, the resistance offered within some sections of working-class Protestant communities to outsiders marks continuity rather than a break in the construction of Loyalism of which racism or sectarianism may be a part (BBC News 2004; 2011).

The use of violence against the growing number of immigrants to Northern Ireland marks a further inward turn by some towards an intensely defensive construction of Loyalism, especially as, to some, Loyalists extreme Right groups 'can sound attractive to young Loyalists because their rhetoric is so pro-British and pro-unionist' (former Loyalist paramilitary, quoted in McDonald 2003).

Loyalist identity is not uniform or straightforward. Rather, the construction of Loyalism is fluid and draws on a variety of reference points, which are used to construct a coherent sense of identity (McAuley 2010). A hostile response to the Other is far from universal within Loyalism. Chrissie Steenkamp, one of the few researchers to have conducted ethnographic research amongst Loyalists, notes, for example, that many such communities 'are generally welcoming to immigrants' (Steenkamp 2008).

While evidence of racist violence undertaken by those who would term themselves as Loyalists is readily available, substantiation of any structural involvement by Loyalist paramilitary groups is much less assured. Extreme Right groupings based on the mainland have failed to secure any electoral base in Northern Ireland. Indeed, the most prominent reaction of the Loyalist paramilitary leadership, and the politicians most closely associated with them, has been to openly condemn racist-motivated violence. That does not make such violence any more palatable or acceptable, but it should focus the resistance of those who seek to oppose it.

References

Adair, J. with McKendry, G. (2007). *Mad Dog*, London: John Blake.
Balent, M. (2011). 'Disquiet over Identity in Europe: Rising to the Challenge set by National Populism', *European Issue Policy Paper*, Number 205, Paris: Robert Schuman Foundation.
BBC News (2000). 'Racism growing in NI'. Available at: http://www.bbc.co.uk/1/hi/northern_ireland/712826.stm [accessed 10 November 2011].
—(2003). 'Loyalists hit out at racist attacks'. Available at: http://news.bbc.co.uk/1/hi/northern_ireland/3042246.stm [accessed 10 June 2005].
—(2004). 'Loyalist link to racist leaflets'. Available at: http://news.bbc.co.uk/1/hi/northern_ireland/3504262.stm [accessed 10 June 2005].
—(2009). 'Racism in Northern Ireland'. Available at: http://news.bbc.co.uk/1/hi/northern_ireland/8104978.stm [accessed 16 September 2009].

—(2011). 'Loyalists target foreign nationals' homes in Portadown'. Available at: http://www.bbc.co.uk/news/uk-northern-ireland-14128805.stm [accessed 10 November 2011].

Belfast Telegraph (2009). 'New "list" of BNP members in Northern Ireland is leaked online', 21 October.

Bell, D. (1987). *Acts of Union: Youth Culture and Sectarianism in Northern Ireland*, Basingstoke: Macmillan.

Bell, K., Jarman, N. and Lefebvre, T. (2004). *Migrant Workers in Northern Ireland*, Belfast: Institute for Conflict Research.

Biswas, K. (2011). 'Eyes to the far Right', *New Internationalist*, 443, June, pp. 14–17.

Brewer, J. (1991). 'The parallels between sectarianism and racism: the Northern Ireland experience', in *One small step toward racial justice,* London: Central Council for Education and Training in Social Work.

—(1992). 'Sectarianism and racism, and their parallels and differences', *Ethnic and Racial Studies*, Volume 15, Issue 3, pp. 352–64.

Bruce, S. (1986). *God Save Ulster: The Religion and Politics of Paisleyism*, Oxford: Oxford University Press.

—(1994). *The Edge of the Union: The Ulster Loyalist Political Vision*, Oxford: Oxford University Press.

Caiani, M. and della Porta, D. (2010). *Extreme Right and Populism. A Frame Analysis of Extreme Right Wing Discourses in Italy and Germany*, Vienna: Institute for Advanced Studies.

Caldwell, J. and Robinson, J. (2006). *In Love with a Mad Dog*, Dublin: Gill and Macmillan.

Carter (2005). *The Extreme Right in Western Europe – Success or Failure?* Manchester: Manchester University Press.

Chrisafis, A. (2004). 'Racist war of the Loyalist street gangs', *The Guardian*, 10 January.

Church, C., Visser, A. and Johnson, L. S. (2004). 'A path to peace or persistence? The 'single identity' approach to conflict resolution in Northern Ireland', *Conflict Resolution Quarterly*, Volume 21, Issue 3, pp. 273–93.

Collins, M. (2011). *Hate: My Life in the British Far Right*, London: Biteback Publishing.

—(2011). 'Far-Right party offers only return to a hate-filled past', *Belfast Telegraph*, 14 April.

Connolly, P. (2002). '"Race" and Racism in Northern Ireland: A Review of the Research Evidence', Belfast: Office of the First Minister and Deputy First Minister.

Copsey, N. and Macklin, G. (eds) (2011). *The British National Party; contemporary perspectives*, Abingdon: Routledge.

COT Institute (2008). '20th Century Right Wing Groups in Europe: Prone to extremism or terrorism?', European Commission Sixth Framework Programme: Case Study, Work Package 3.

Coulter, J. (2003). ' Ireland – The Orange Swastika: The rise of new millennium Loyalist Nazism', *Searchlight*, November.

Coulter, M. (2004). 'From bigotry to racism', *Searchlight*, February.

Cusack, J. and McDonald, H. (1997). *UVF*, Dublin: Poolbeg Press.

Ford, R. and Goodwin, M. (2010). 'Angry White Men: Individual and contextual predictors of support for the British National Party', *Political Studies*, Volume 58, Number 1, pp. 1–26.

Geraghty, T., McStravick, C. and Mitchell, S. (2010). New to Northern Ireland: A study of the issues faced by migrant, asylum seeking and refugee children in Northern Ireland, London: NCBNI.

Geoghegan P. (2008a). 'Beyond Orange and Green? The awkwardness of negotiating difference in Northern Ireland', *Irish Studies Review*, Volume 16, Issue 2, pp. 173–94.

—(2008b). 'Multiculturalism and Sectarianism in Post-agreement Northern Ireland', *Scottish Geographical Journal*, Volume 124, Numbers 2–3, pp. 185–91.

Gilligan, C. (2008). 'Migration and migrant workers in Northern Ireland', *ARK Research Update*, Number 53, February, pp. 1–4.

Gilligan, C., Hainsworth, P. and McGarry, A. (2011). 'Fractures, Foreigners and Fitting In: Exploring Attitudes towards Immigration and Integration in "Post-Conflict" Northern Ireland', *Ethnopolitics*, Volume 10, Number 2, pp. 253–69.

Gilligan C. and Lloyd, K. (2006). 'Racial prejudice in Northern Ireland,' *ARK Research Update*, Belfast & Londonderry: ARK.

Goodwin, M. (2011). 'Europe's Radical Right: Support and Potential', *Political Insight*, Volume 2, Number 3, pp. 4–7.

Graham, B. (2004). 'The Past in the Present: The Shaping of Identity in Loyalist Ulster', *Terrorism and Political Violence*, Volume 16, Number 3, pp. 483–500.

Hainsworth, P. (ed.) (1998). *Divided Society: Ethnic Minorities and Racism in Northern Ireland*, London: Pluto Press.

Hayes, B. C. and Dowds, L. (2006). 'Social Contact, Cultural Marginality or Economic Self-Interest? Attitudes Towards Immigrants in Northern Ireland', *Journal of Ethnic and Migration Studies*, Volume 32, Number 3, pp. 455–76.

Hickman, M. Crowley, H. and Mai, N. (2008). *Immigration and social cohesion in the UK. The rhythms and realities of everyday life.* York: Joseph Rowntree Foundation.

Hughes, J. (2002). 'Resolving community relations problems in Northern Ireland: an intra-community approach', in Patrick G. Coy (ed.) *Consensus Decision Making, Northern Ireland and Indigenous Movements, Research in Social Movements, Conflicts and Change, Volume 24*, London: Emerald Group Publishing Limited, pp. 257–82.

Jarman, N. (2003). 'Victims and Perpetrators, Racism and Young People in Northern Ireland', *Child Care in Practice*, Volume 9, Number 2, pp. 129–39.

Jarman N. and Monaghan, R. (2004). *Racist Harassment in Northern Ireland*, Belfast: Institute for Conflict Research.

Kane, A. (2011). 'No voice for Loyalist working-class', *Newsletter*, 4 July.

Kennedy, D. and Hines, N. (2008). 'Thousands in fear after BNP members list leak', *The Times*, 19 November.

Knox, C. (2011). 'Tackling Racism in Northern Ireland: "The Race Hate Capital of Europe"', *Journal of Social Policy*, Volume 40, Number 2, pp. 387–412.

Kopeček, L. (2007). 'The Far Right in Europe', *Central European Political Studies Review*, Volume IX, Part 4, pp. 280–93.

Lewis, H. (2010). 'Racism & Sectarianism: Two Sides of the Same Coin?: The Northern Ireland Experience', *International Journal of Diversity in Organisations, Communities and Nations*, Volume 6, Issue 3, pp. 27–36.

Loyalist Commission (c. 2005). 'Loyalist or Racist? You can't be Both', Belfast: Loyalist Commission.

Lubbers. M., Gijsberts, M. and Scheepers, P. (2002). 'Extreme Right-wing voting in Western Europe', *European Journal of Political Research*, Volume 41, pp. 345–78.

Marsdal, M (2008). 'Underdog politics', *Red Pepper*, June.

Martynowicz, A. and Jarman, N. (2009). *New Migration, Equality and Integration: Issues and Challenges for Northern Ireland*, Belfast: Equality Commission for Northern Ireland.

Meleagrou-Hitchens, A. and Standing, E. (2010). *Blood & Honour: Britain's Far-Right Militants*, London: The Centre for Social Cohesion.

McAleese, D. (2009). 'Loyalists get funds to oppose racists', *Independent*, 9 April.

—(2008). 'Conflict resolution in asymmetric and symmetric situations: Northern Ireland as a case study', (with Catherine McGlynn and Jonathan Tonge), *Dynamics of Asymmetric Conflict: Pathways toward Terrorism and Genocide*, Volume 1, Number 1, pp. 88–102.

—(2009). 'Conflict Transformation and Former Loyalist Paramilitary Prisoners in Northern Ireland', (with Jonathan Tonge and Peter Shirlow), *Terrorism and Political Violence*, Volume 22, Number 1, pp. 22–40.

McAuley, J. W. (2010a). *Ulster's Last Stand? (Re)Constructing Ulster Unionism After the Peace Process*, Dublin: Irish Academic Press.

—(2010b). 'Changing Senses of Britishness in Northern Ireland after the Good Friday Agreement', (with Jonathan Tonge), *Parliamentary Affairs*, Volume 63, Number 2, pp. 266–85.

McAuley, J. W. and Spencer, G. (eds) (2011). *Ulster Loyalism after the Good Friday Agreement: History, Identity and Change*, Basingstoke: Palgrave Macmillan.

McAuley, J. W., Tonge, J. and Mycock, A. (2011). *Loyal to the Core? Orangeism and Britishness in Northern Ireland*, Dublin: Irish Academic Press.

McDonald, H. (2003). 'PUP campaigns to drive racists out of Ballymena', *Observer*, 25 May.

—(2009a). 'UDA leader: Loyalists have a duty to inform if they know racist attackers', *Observer*, 5 July.

—(2009b). 'Northern Ireland at risk of 'race war' anti-fascist campaigner warns police', *Observer*, 6 September.

—(2011). 'How Loyalists got out of step with fascism', *Belfast Telegraph*, 15 September.

McGarry, A., Hainsworth, P. and Gilligan, C. (2009). 'Political Parties and Minority Ethnic Communities in Northern Ireland: Election Manifestos 1994–2007', *Translocations: The Irish Migration, Race and Social Transformation Review* [http://www.translocations.ie], Number: 2009–0420.

McKittrick, D. (2004). 'Racism "is the new terrorism" as attacks rise in Ulster', *Independent on Sunday*, 16 October.

McVeigh, R. (2002). *A Place of Refuge? Asylum Seekers and Refugees in Northern Ireland: A Needs Assessment.* Belfast: Refugee Action.

McVeigh, R. and Rolston, B. (2007). 'From Good Friday to Good Relations: sectarianism, racism and the Northern Ireland state', *Race and Class*, Volume 48, Number 4, pp. 1–23.

Meleagrou-Hitchens, A. and Standing, E. (2010). *Blood and Honour: Britain's Far-Right Militants*, London: The Centre for Social Cohesion.

Millar, S. (2010). 'Irish far Right groups remain on the margins of political life', *Irish Examiner*, 12 January.

Mudde, C. (2000). *The Ideology of the Extreme Right*, Manchester: Manchester University Press.

National Children's Bureau and ARK Young Life and Times (2010). *Attitudes to Difference: Young people's attitudes to and experiences of contact with people from different ethnic and minority communities in Northern Ireland*, London: National Children's Bureau.

National Front (2011). Statement of Policy – Northern Ireland. Available at: http://www.national-front.org.uk/policy.html [accessed 4 July 2011].

Nelson, S. (1984). *Ulster's Uncertain Defenders*, Belfast: Appletree Press.

Norris, P. (2005). *Radical Right Voters and Parties in the Electoral Market*, Cambridge: Cambridge University Press.

Northern Ireland Council for Ethnic Minorities (2009). Annual Report, 2008/2009, Belfast: NICEM.

Northern Ireland Department of Enterprise Trade and Investment (2006). 'New Disadvantaged Area Maps Published', *Press Release*, 25 September.

Northern Ireland Housing Executive (2009). 'Migrant Workers and the Housing Market: A Case Study of Dungannon', Belfast: NIHE Research Unit.

Northern Ireland Statistics and Research Agency (2010). 'Migration Statistics for Northern Ireland, 2009', Belfast: NISRA.

Pehrson, S., Gheorghiu, M. A. and Ireland, T. (2012). 'Cultural Threat and Anti-immigrant Prejudice: The Case of Protestants in Northern Ireland', *Journal of Community & Applied Social Psychology*, Volume 22, Issue 2, pp. 111–24.

Police Service of Northern Ireland (2006). 'Domestic incidents and crimes 2005–06'. Available at: http://www.psni.police.uk/2._domestic_incidents_and_crimes–3.pdf [accessed 4 July 2011].

—(2011). 'Hate Incidents and Crimes 2005–06'. Available at: http://www.psni.police.uk/3._hate_incidents_and_crimes–4.pdf [accessed 4 July 2011].

Rolston, B. (2004). 'Legacy of intolerance: racism and Unionism in South Belfast'. Available at: http://www.irr.org.uk/2004/february/ak000008.html [accessed 4 July 2011].

Rydgren, J. (2004). *The Populist Challenge, Political Protest and Ethno-Nationalist Mobilization in France*, Oxford: Berghanan Books.

—(2005). 'Is Extreme Right-Wing Populism Contagious?' Explaining the Emergence of a New Party Family', *European Journal of Political Research*, Volume 44, pp. 413–37.

Searchlight (1986). 'Front's 'Fixer' with Paramilitaries Moves Full Time to Northern Ireland', Issue 137, pp. 3–4.

—(1989). 'Wales and Northern Ireland NF Heads "Where the Terror Is"', Issue 163, pp. 9–11.

Sharrock, D. (2009). 'Northern Ireland has "culture of intolerance"', *The Times*, 18 June.

Shirlow, P. and McGovern, M. (eds) (1997). *Who are 'The People'? Unionism, Protestantism and Loyalism in Northern Ireland*, London: Pluto.

South Belfast News (2002). 'East Belfast Loyalist to Take Part in Neo-Nazi March', 20 September.

Southern, N. (2007). 'Protestant Alienation in Northern Ireland: A Political, Cultural and Geographical Examination', *Journal of Ethnic and Migration Studies*, Volume 33, Number 1, pp. 159–80.

Spencer, G. (2008). *The State of Loyalism in Northern Ireland*, Basingstoke: Palgrave Macmillan.

Steenkamp C. J. (2008). 'Loyalist paramilitary violence after the Belfast Agreement', *Ethnopolitics*, Volume 7, Number 1, pp. 159–76.

Suarez, A. (2002). *Relatório Sobre Trabalhadores*, Belfast: Multicultural Resource Centre.

6

The Dutch Far Right: From 'Classical Outsiders' to 'Modern Insiders'

Rob Witte

Since the Second World War, the Netherlands have always had a tolerant, non-radical self-image and been presented as such through the public discourse. There was certainly no place for right-wing extremism in this self-image. However, this image has changed in recent years, domestically as well as internationally, especially since the Freedom Party of Geert Wilders was established. Was this self-image always false and, if so, which elements were skewed? Alternatively, have the Netherlands undergone extensive societal changes since 2001 and how were these manifested? This chapter seeks to address these questions.

The Netherlands as a coalition state

The Netherlands has always relied on coalition governments. It is, according to many, 'a nation of minorities'. The state system traditionally relied on a so-called 'pillar system' in which separate pillars encompassed catholic, protestant, liberal and socialists groups (Lijphart 1979). The social midfield (organizations, sport clubs, newspapers, educational institutions, etc.) was also organised according to these pillars. No single pillar ever exerted majority control within the democratic political system. State power existed through coalitions of elites representing individual pillars and conflict resolution was based on negotiations and consensus. In this 'nation of minorities' real conflicts were a major risk for social cohesion and peace. Any signs of conflict, therefore, were tackled as early as possible with preventative measures focusing on resolving outstanding issues through consensus. Top-down hierarchies and normative control existed within individual pillars, tackling, repressing and fragmenting radicalization and extremism through internal consensus and pressure.

'Classical' right-wing extremism in the Netherlands

In the dominating Dutch discourse after 1945, anti-Semitism and racism have always been presented as atypical within Dutch society (Witte 2010). According to many, this relates to Second World War experiences whereby the Netherlands saw the largest percentage of national Jewish populations in Europe killed, after Poland. One of the indirect contributing factors to this genocide was the Dutch practice of maintaining detailed population records of registered citizens. The subsequent complex of guilt left no place for (further) utterances of anti-Semitism or racism. Any signs of right-wing extremism were therefore linked with Nazism and thus oppressed immediately – publicly, politically as well as judicially.

However, despite this public self-awareness, cases of anti-Semitic and racist outbursts were nonetheless recorded in the immediate post-war period. In the 1950s and 1960s, various anti-Semitic incidents were reported and a number of confrontations between the native Dutch population on the one hand and labour migrants from Spain, Italy and young repatriates from the former Dutch colony of Indonesia on the other took place. Various debates and governmental reports pointed towards the 'alien culture and origin' of labour migrants (and repatriates), referring to traits, such as work ethics and lifestyle, which were portrayed as different from Dutch perceptions in this regard.

By the early 1970s, the Netherlands witnessed a series of large-scale ethnic confrontations. In 1972, native youth clashed in the city of Rotterdam with Turkish migrants, with Turkish-owned shops and houses vandalized during the violence that lasted several days. In 1976, similar events occurred in the nearby city of Schiedam. These violent clashes, as well as more individual racist incidents, were not, however, perceived or portrayed as racist incidents, but rather as symptoms of social backlash, deprivation, inner-city problems, unemployment and related tensions. Many explanations, moreover, linked social deprivation with the presence and concentration of migrant populations. These assumed links led Rotterdam authorities to propose dispersal policies whereby no more than 5 per cent of individual neighbourhoods would consist of individuals with a migrant background. These proposals, however, were rejected in the Higher Courts (Witte 2010).

Extreme right-wing political radicalisation and violence in the 1970s and 1980s

During the 1970s, several violent incidents occurred in which the perpetrators or the symbols left behind suggested a clear right-wing extremist motive. In these instances, the violence involved was immediately and unambiguously condemned publicly. For instance, the involvement of the right-wing extremist *Nederlandse Volkunie* (Dutch Peoples Union) in the aforementioned Schiedam riots was vigorously condemned by the wider population and even led to parliamentary initiatives to ban the party involved. However, the connection between these violent incidents and the involvement of extreme right-wing organizations was hardly ever proven categorically. Racist violence in which this organizational linkage was unknown or unproven was mainly portrayed as exceptional and explained with references to real or alleged backgrounds of the perpetrators, when known. Increasingly, attempts were made to refute any potential implicit or explicit links between these violent attacks and racist and far-right motivations. Perpetrators were portrayed as youngsters from inner-city areas with a strong concentration of migrant populations, with low levels of intellect and self-esteem and little education. In many cases, alcohol abuse was presented as a contributing factor to the violence involved, with any racist or far-right dimensions played down.

In the early 1980s, this approach changed somewhat as a result of the 'race riots' in Brixton, London in April 1981. These riots led to questions being asked relating to the Dutch situation and whether such riots could and would be possible in the Netherlands. Confrontations in the southern city of Tilburg, six weeks after the Brixton riots, appeared to provide an answer. However, the magnitude of the violence and the duration of the Tilburg riots were of a very different kind. Approximately one hundred people attacked a family of Surinamese origin, wounding three of them. The family fled into a police station for safety, whilst the attackers stormed their home. At the end, the family were relocated elsewhere, prompting one Surinamese community leader to warn that 'when one doesn't want to have Surinamese people around, one only has to throw them out and they won't return' (*de Volkskrant* 9 May 1981).

The beginning of the 1980s witnessed a steady increase in support for right-wing extremist parties. To begin with, this support was insufficient to secure seats in Parliament. However, in the Parliamentary elections in the autumn of 1982, the far-right *Centrum Party* secured one seat. The emergence of the far right within the established political arena did increase the awareness and attention, including that of the authorities, of right-wing extremist and racist expressions and related violent attacks. Amid the rising profile of far-right activity of this kind, reports of discrimination and racism within media discourse became more prominent. An important catalyst in this respect was the racist murder of 16-year-old Kerwin Duinmeijer of Antillean origin on 20 August 1983. The perpetrator was identified as a so-called 'Nazi-skinhead' who stated, as he was being interviewed by the police, that 'blacks should not look at me in an ugly way' (A. Holtrop and U. den Tex 1984: 27). As a result of the attack, the mayor of Amsterdam, Ed. Van Thijn, launched an anti-racism campaign warning that the murder could be 'a sign of [changing] times' (Witte 2010), referring to the rise of the far-right. In an Amsterdam policy paper (City of Amsterdam 1983), the city authorities designed a new anti-racism strategy reflecting preceding events, but, again, placed the primary responsibility of combating racism and extreme right-wing activism in the hands of the general population. The policy paper, however, also emphasised the official stand against racism, presenting as supporting evidence observed increases in reported cases of racially motivated violent attacks, even though these were represented as extraordinary within the wider context. This response exemplified the general approach of the Dutch state towards racist violence, whereby the incidents themselves were condemned, especially where involvement of right-wing violent extremists was confirmed.

Evidence of increased support for far-right extremism as well as a proliferation in the rate of extreme right-wing violent attacks prompted the establishment of a set of local anti-racism and anti-discrimination initiatives in the form of the so-called anti-discrimination bureaus (ADBs). The ADBs focused both on judicial support for victims of discrimination or racial abuse, as well as functioning as local centres for anti-racist activities.

During the second half of the 1980s, the presence of the far right disappeared from Parliament, chiefly due to the fragmentation of the *Centrum Party*. As the party disintegrated, public interest in extreme right-wing violence also appeared to dissipate, even though several studies examining extreme right-wing violence showed incidents of racist violence and hate crimes continued throughout the late 1980s (see, for instance, Buis 1988; Witte 1995; 2010). However, racist and extreme right-wing violence was still not officially registered in the Netherlands, so quantitative, long-term analyses are difficult.

Political far right and violence in the 1990s

German reunification had a great impact on the political climate within the Netherlands during the early 1990s. Amidst the jubilation and turmoil, numerous racist confrontations and incidents were reported in cities such as Rostock, Hoyerswerda, Mölln and Solingen. On the one hand, these incidents prompted a grassroots response within the Netherlands whereby thousands wrote to the German authorities expressing collective Dutch revulsion over reports of racist violence on German soil. On the other hand, questions were again raised as to whether or not these scenes of extreme right-wing violence would be possible within Dutch society.

These questions became ever more prominent after numerous opinion polls showed renewed support for right-wing extremism. Indeed, right-wing extremist political parties did have considerable success in various elections in this period. In 1989, the former *Centrum Party* MP Hans Janmaat returned to Parliament for his new party, the *Centrum Democraten*. On 21 March 1990 (the International Day against Racism), far-right platforms gained unprecedented ground in local elections (15 seats in nine city councils). Some seats were even taken by well-known neo-Nazis.

This renewed rise of the political far right coincided with an increasing number of violent incidents (Van Donselaar 1993), culminating in an arson attack on a mosque in the city of Amersfoort on 26 January 1992. No one was injured during the incident and the Imam and his family, who lived in the mosque, were rescued, but the perpetrators painted a South African version of the swastika on the wall of the mosque before fleeing the scene. This incident provoked a considerable reaction in the Netherlands. The daily newspaper, *de Volkskrant* (28 January 1992) pondered the question whether this incident marked the beginning of 'German circumstances' in terms of widespread extreme right-wing violence within the Netherlands and through increased xenophobia in Europe.

The Minister of Justice, Hirsch Balin, was quick to condemn the Amersfoort attack and stated 'that it was fundamental that the devout were free to practice their religion' (*Alkmaarsche Courant* 27 January 1992). The Minister of Home Affairs organised a meeting with migrant organizations and registered her revulsion over the incident. After the meeting, she stressed in a letter to the Provincial Representatives of the Queen (chairs of the Provincial Councils) that the Amersfoort attacks and other less prominent incidents of violence against minorities appeared to be haphazard rather than well organised, consisting primarily of individual acts of vandalism (as cited in Provincial Representative of the Province of Northern Holland 29 January

1992). It should be noted that many of the incidents in the early 1990s, including the Amersfoort attack, were never resolved, with the police failing to identify the culprits.

Presenting instances of violent attack as random acts of violence became an increasingly prominent feature of the state response. By extension, perpetrators – who were rarely identified – were portrayed as marginalized individuals responding to the plight of their circumstance. This perception was tied to the apparent success of extreme right-wing platforms to respond to social and socioeconomic phenomena, such as increasing presence of migrants, unemployment, bad housing and other inner-city problems. Within the dominant discourse, the opinion gained traction that supporters of extremist parties were not 'racist', but rather affected by the presence of migrant populations. Although these political organizations remained outside 'mainstream' society, as 'outsiders', the supporters of these more traditional right-wing extremist groups became accepted in this way within mainstream society and perceived as 'insiders'.

Shifting approaches towards migrant populations

In the 1990s, the dominant perspective towards migrants in the Netherlands changed rapidly. Perceptions concerning policies towards minorities changed from a focus on integration intertwined with the retention of diverse cultures towards concepts of integration involving specific duties of migrants within wider society. Migrants, formerly portrayed as 'guest workers', 'cultural minorities' and 'ethnic minorities', became perceived as 'allochthonous people' and accordingly 'minority policies' were transformed into 'allochthonous policies'. Far from being merely cosmetic or superficial, this change impacted upon antidiscrimination policies and affected the rights of minorities in terms of duties to integrate and societal responsibilities (WRR 1989).

At the same time, a major debate regarding the integration of minorities was triggered in response to a speech by the People's Party for Freedom and Democracy (VVD) leader Frits Bolkestein (*de Volkskrant* 12 September 1991). In his speech, Bolkestein placed Christian history opposite Islamic history and European history opposite the history of the Middle East. He did so especially in relation to perspectives on democracy and human rights:

> After a long history with numerous black pages, rationalism, humanism and Christianity produced a number of fundamental political principles, such as the disestablishment between religion and state, the freedom of

speech, tolerance and non-discrimination. Liberalism claims universal legitimacy and value of these principles. This is its political stand. This means, according to liberalism, that a civilisation honouring these principles is of a higher stand as a civilisation that does not (*de Volkskrant*, 12 September 1991).

Ethnic minorities in Europe in general and in the Netherlands in particular, so Bolkestein argued, had to integrate and not dare to question European and Dutch basic structures and rights. 'One issue is indisputable. The aforementioned political principles are non-negotiable. Not even one little bit', he insisted.

The coalition government of Christian Democrats and Labour responded to this speech by launching the National Debate on the Integration of Minorities. Primarily, this debate took place outside the political arena, especially among newspaper columnists and on radio and television programmes. Bolkestein's speech as well as this National Debate sharpened and strengthened a new dominant discourse contributing to the marginalization and criminalization of minorities in the Netherlands, with members of minority groups even presented as fundamentalists.

Bolkestein was criticised for using stereotypes portraying 'the European and Dutch way of life' and the 'way of life of minorities' as well as for presenting Islamic 'minorities' as Islamic fundamentalists. Positive responses to Bolkestein's speech were mainly directed towards the fact that at last someone focused on the assumed problematic integration of ethnic minorities (primarily from majority Islamic countries) as perceived in a causal relationship with their Islamic background. This opinion became increasingly dominant and in 2011 the speech is still referred to as the point whereby the political establishment finally corrected past errors in this respect. Four major factors suggest that these developments ushered in a fundamental shift in public discourse concerning minorities within the Netherlands, with consequences for the development of the far right within the country (Witte 2010: 101):

1 For the first time a prominent politician from the Dutch political establishment had talked about real or perceived problems in relation to the integration of ethnic minorities in the Netherlands.

2 Bolkestein was known to be an intellectual. His relatively tough stance on the necessity for change, and that this change had to come from those who 'had to integrate', was perceived as a new phenomenon from within the Dutch intellectual elite. Before, this debate was perceived as monopolised by right-wing extremists.

3 Bolkestein's statements and perception paved the way for others to express their thoughts and criticisms concerning migration and the 'lack of integration' without being pulled or pushed into the 'classical' right-wing extremist or even neo-Nazi categories.

4 Increasingly, the linear causal linkage between Islam and perceived integration difficulties, if not the impossibility of integration altogether, became dominant within the established political discourse. From a historical point of view, the implicit relation was presented with the historic malicious image of Islam within the Christian Western world. The alleged bipolarisation between Islam and Christianity and between the Western and Islamic worlds shaped an image of incompatibility and insuperability that informed subsequent debates and the approach of far-right and domestic extremist groupings towards the matter.

At first, the National Debate did not decrease support for 'classical' right-wing extremism. In the 1994 elections the Centrum Democrats gained three seats in Parliament and in local elections the number of council seats won by extremist parties rose from 15 to 87. However, the next national and local elections (in 1998) saw a total disappearance of the 'classical' right-wing extremist parties from Parliament as well as from city councils (with only one seat remaining).

Amid these developments, attitudes towards racist and right-wing extremism clearly changed. At first, reactions towards racist violence were two-fold. The violence was publically condemned and, internally, the police and local authorities were instructed to take this violence seriously. However, at the same time, the role of racism and right-wing extremism as well as any references to the racist and right-wing extremist violence as a structural, social problem in the Netherlands was dismissed. Official and public preoccupation with racism and right-wing extremism diminished during the second half of the 1990s, in large part due to the disappearance of far-right parties from Parliament and local councils. This diminishing attention did, however, not coincide with a decrease in the number of violent incidents. The *Monitor on Racism and Extremism*, established in 1997, reported that discrimination as well as right-wing extremist and/or racist violence had increased consistently within the Netherlands during these last years of the twentieth century: from 298 violent incidents in 1997, 313 in 1998, 345 in 1999, up to 406 in 2000 (Van Donselaar 1979; 2000).

What changed with the dawn of a new century?

The 1990s witnessed a considerable change in the dominant discourse within the Netherlands. In previous decades, the 'classical' far-right groups had dominated the debate, discussing issues such as 'integration problems', 'misuse of asylum policies' and the assumed incompatibility of different cultures and pleas for halts on migration as well as tougher conditions for integration. From the early 1990s onwards, however, similar terminology and deliberations became increasingly prominent within the mainstream political and public discourse, prompted by the Bolkestein speech and the National Debate on integration that followed. Within this discourse, migration became ever more associated with causes of social problems and crime. A major catalyst in propelling these issues onto the mainstream political stage during this period was the publication of two separate documents focusing on these matters from within the 'leftist' (Social Democratic) side of the political elite.

In 1999, the national institute for multicultural development, FORUM, published an essay by Paul Schnabel, head of the Netherlands Institute for Social Research (SCP), titled *'The multicultural illusion'*. Culture, so Schnabel argued, stood for personal capital and the 'allochthonous cultures were faced with a very uniform and dominant Dutch culture. (...) Besides, the social stratification of allochthonous groups is not comparable with that of the Netherlands as a whole. The large majority of allochthonous people (...) belong to the lower social fractions of society', according to Schnabel (Schnabel 1999: 13, 15). Schnabel's perspective is important because 'herewith social backlash and discrimination are proof of cultural difference and incompatibility. (...) The inequalities [economic by nature] become signs of cultural difference and, *a forteriori*, submissiveness' (Schinkel 2008: 325).

One year later, Labour activist Paul Scheffer published his essay on *'The multicultural drama'* (*NRC Handelsblad* 29 January 2000). In this essay Scheffer focused on the supposed lax attitude of politics and policies towards the integration of minorities. This laxity was partly based, Scheffer argued, on a perception of civilization as a combination of cultures existing as independent entities. In this way, the refusal by government and Parliament to see and identify the problems concerning ethnic minorities in the Netherlands is contrasted with wider public perceptions that highlight these problems. Scheffer argued that Parliamentary scrutiny into migration and integration policies was necessary, given that various sections of society were put off in order not to provoke the cloak of tolerance. The present policies of broad entrance of migrants and limited 'integration' exacerbated inequality, according to the essay, and contributed to a feeling of estrangement within society. Voices of tolerance were under threat due to the fact that social cohesion had been badly maintained and the issues of migration and integration insufficiently harmonized. This developing 'multicultural drama' was thus seen as the gravest threat to social peace.

In his essay, Scheffer emphasised the alleged linkage between 'allochthonous cultures' and economic and social backlash. Schinkel argued that both these essays stood for a 'new scientific multicultural realism' ('multiculturalism' as opposed to the 'multiculturalism' perceived by both authors as the cause of failing integration policies). This 'multiculturealism' was characteristic, Schinkel argued, of the culturist phase of the integration debate. 'It is this culturist paradigm that made it possible to associate "integration problems" with cultural issues' (2008: 149). In the years to come, this dominant discourse would evolve much further in terms of content as well as in the public and policy arenas.

9/11

For 2001, the aforementioned *Monitor on Racism and Extremism* reported the number of racist violent incidents in the Netherlands was decreasing compared to previous years. However, 60 per cent of the incidents cited took place after the 11 September (9/11) attacks. Many of these violent incidents involved the targeting of mosques and Islamic schools. For instance, mosques in the cities of Alkmaar, The Hague, Amersfoort, Vlissingen, Ijmuiden, Eindhoven, Zaandam, Gorinchem, Venlo and Zwolle were targeted. Incidents included arson attacks, defaming of Islamic centres and mosques, vandalism (such as broken windows), but also bomb alerts. Islamic schools in the cities of Nijmegen, Uden, Almere and Ede were also targeted, as were individuals of Islamic backgrounds. Individual targeting included an attack on a 16-year-old Afghan boy by a group of skinheads in the city of Heerlen. Turkish families were also targeted in the city of Hengelo, with windows broken. In The Hague, Muslim girls wearing headscarves were insulted and spat on and in some cases their scarves were torn off.

Aside from these anti-Muslim attacks, violence was also reported against 'native Dutchmen' and Christian organizations. Arson attacks against churches in the cities of Utrecht, Amsterdam, Rijssen and Tegelen were reported (Van Donselaar and Rodrigues 2002: 25) with motives traced back to confessional tensions. Increasingly, therefore, interethnic and confessional friction appeared on the rise within the Netherlands.

Pim Fortuyn

Feelings of national and even international polarization were exacerbated three weeks prior to the 9/11 attacks with Pim Fortuyn's announcement that he intended to take part in the next Parliamentary elections, set for 15 May 2002. Fortuyn decided to stand for election even though he was not a member of any political party at the time, having had a long history of involvement with established parties whilst failing to become embedded in any of them. Rather than turning his back on politics, Fortuyn took an increasingly independent political position. In 1994, he published a book dedicated to 'his cabinet of non-politicians' (Fortuyn 1994). This position in opposition to the established political parties became increasingly important. In 1997, he published another book titled *Against the Islamisation of our Culture* (Fortuyn 1997) that provoked much debate.

In the latter, Fortuyn criticised so-called 'cultural relativism' that, so Fortuyn argued, characterised the Dutch situation. This 'cultural relativism' was allegedly behind perceived indifference concerning 'our own identity'. 'This threatens', Fortuyn argued, 'our original culture with total collapse' (Fortuyn 1997: 7). In this publication, Fortuyn compared the developments in the Western world, allegedly ignoring the essentials of its values as well as the boundaries of the permissive, with the developments leading to the 1938 Munich Pact. These developments prevented the nurturing of self-identity, which would be needed in order to prescribe behaviour for migrants. 'A classical example of this moral and the absence of a concept of the multicultural society is the fight against racist utterances. Up until today, only native white Dutchmen have been prosecuted [for racist slurs]...' (Fortuyn 1997: 41). Fortuyn referred to the anti-racism organizations as 'the mind police' (1997: 42), viewing Islam as 'a cultural threshold against economic and social integration in the Netherlands.' Increasingly, this Islamophobic perspective became embedded after the 9/11 attacks (see van der Valk in this volume).

In November 2001, Fortuyn found himself a political home with the new political party *Leefbaar Nederland* (Liveable Netherlands), a platform opposing the established parties, which made major electoral gains in various Dutch cities. The bond between *Leefbaar Nederland* and Fortuyn lasted for three months. The break-up occurred after a newspaper interview, in which Fortuyn portrayed Islam as 'retarded culture' and pledged to abolish the 'crazed first article of the constitution: you should not discriminate' (*de Volkskrant* 9 February 2002). The entire political establishment descended on Fortuyn in condemnation of these statements. *Leefbaar Nederland* decided, following extensive internal discussions, to expel its party leader. Various observers and commentators expected this to be the end of Fortuyn's role in the forthcoming elections, who declared to a group of waiting journalists as he left a meeting with his former LN colleagues: 'I will be the next prime minister' (*NOS-Journaal* 10 February 2002).

On 6 March 2002, Fortuyn added credence to these claims after a landslide electoral victory in the city of Rotterdam for his new party, the *Lijst Pim Fortuyn* (LPF). In a television program that election night, Fortuyn played the role of the victorious winner, whereas the party leaders of the established parties appeared beaten and flabbergasted. Subsequent polls showed enormous gains for Fortuyn's party, making his own prediction that he would become prime minister ever more realistic. These hopes were never to be realised as Pim Fortuyn was murdered on 6 May 2002.

After it became apparent that the murder of Fortuyn was not linked to immigrants but rather orchestrated internally from within the animal rights movement, the resulting outburst of anger in the aftermath of the shooting was directed primarily towards the established politicians. Party leaders were threatened and the election campaigns drew to a halt. In the elections themselves, ten days later, the coalition parties of Labour and VVD (People's Party for Freedom and Democracy) lost 33 of their 97 seats in Parliament and thus the majority within the chamber. The leaderless LPF won 26 (of the 150) seats and became the second party in Dutch Parliament. The successful Christian Democrats, being the only party not opposing the LPF during the campaigns, formed a new coalition government with the LPF (also including the defeated VVD party). The 2002 polls were the first elections for years without any participation of 'classical' far-right parties. The first months after the elections were marked by continued undermining of the established parties, in addition to the electoral losses they suffered. Nonetheless, the *Monitor on Racism and Extremism* (Van Donselaar and Rodrigues 2004) reported a decrease in the number of registered incidents in 2002, even though violent attacks on individuals were on the rise.

Hirschi Ali and Theo Van Gogh

The coalition government consisting of Christian Democrats, LPF and the VVD did not last long. As the government crumbled, new Parliamentary elections had to be held within a year, after which the LPF, established by Fortuyn, was reduced to eight seats. The liberal VVD saw its support increase slightly compared with the previous elections, as the outspoken critic of Islam, Hirschi Ali, became a Member of Parliament for the VVD. Since 2002

Ali had been known for her emotive criticism of Islam, especially of the prophet Mohammed, whom she labelled a 'perverted man according to Western standards' (*Trouw* 25 January 2003). As an MP, her criticism and outspoken comments became louder and sharper, increasingly focusing on the position of women within Islam. In 2004, Ali produced a short film, *Submission Part 1*, together with the film director Theo van Gogh, also a well-known columnist and television personality and a prominent critic of Islam. On 2 November 2004, Van Gogh was brutally murdered in the streets of Amsterdam by Mohamed Bouyeri, a radicalized Muslim youth of Moroccan origin. The murder provoked enormous upheaval in the Netherlands, leading to numerous arson attacks and acts of vandalism of Muslim buildings and further violent confrontations in the streets. During the month of November 2004 alone the Monitor Racism and Extremism (Van Donselaar and Rodrigues 2004) registered 174 violent incidents which included 36 arson attacks, 41 threats of violence, 23 cases of damaged property, 12 harassment cases and 18 incidents of violent confrontation. In 61 per cent of the violent incidents the Monitor detected anti-Muslim motivations, with 47 incidents involving the targeting of mosques (Witte et al. 2005). In 19 per cent of cases, however, the victims were autochthonous with 13 churches for instance being targeted. The Monitor traced 27 incidents back to the involvement of right-wing extremist outfits (Van Donselaar and Rodrigues 2004).

For Hirschi Ali, her initial critical and disparaging comments of Islam in general had prompted the authorities to offer personal protection. The murder of Van Gogh eventually drove her out of the Netherlands altogether. In 2006, she withdrew from Parliament and continued her career in the United States.

Youth gangs

As mentioned, the Van Gogh murder was followed by series of violent incidents. Of the cases where involvement of extreme right-wing groupings was detected, just over one out of every ten incidents were found to involve perpetrators belonging to a specific group of youths often identified by the distinctive branded sportswear that they wore, which attracted much of the media attention surrounding the violence. These youth gangs frequently adopted xenophobic attitudes and speech as collective defining features of the group. In 2005–6 various studies into this youth subculture were published (see also Van der Valk, in this volume), including a study by the Dutch Intelligence Service (AIVD 2005). In their report the AIVD stated that the youth gangs were wrongly portrayed as racist and right-wing extremist.

Their behaviour, AIVD argued, could not be traced to a race agenda and there were no signs of systematic recruitment by right-wing extremist organizations from within this youth group. This representation of these youth gangs as a distinct subculture, the largest of its kind within the Netherlands, went largely unnoticed by the media and authorities. The report's conclusion that many of these youths were xenophobic and often involved in violent confrontations was seen mainly within the context of physical security. This youth subculture was presented mainly as a public security threat rather than as a threat to the democratic legal order or linked to right-wing radicalization. One could argue, therefore, that the authorities had both criminalized and depoliticized right-wing extremist and racist radicalization among youth at the same time. By 2005 the number of physical attacks against individuals from minorities, especially Muslims, had increased dramatically. The Monitor Racism and Extremism registered 296 violent incidents (against 260 in 2003 and 173 in November 2004). Of these, only 19 were traced back to extreme right-wing sentiments and included clashes with anti-racist organizations and an attack on a building used by left-wing political activists. The other 277 violent incidents concerned cases of racist violence, filed separately, among which a large number involved confrontations between the aforementioned youth gangs and groups of youngsters from immigrant and minority backgrounds, as well as cases of harassment and assault against the latter (Van Donselaar and Rodrigues 2006).

The radicalisation of Geert Wilders

Another outspoken political figure that contributed to this discourse was Geert Wilders, a former colleague of Hirschi Ali before he left the VVD party in 2004 due to comments critical of Islam and his vocal opposition to Turkish entry into the EU. Wilders remained in Parliament within his one-man party, the Group Wilders, later reformed into the Freedom Party (PVV), which went on to win six parliamentary seats in the 2006 elections.

At the beginning of the decade, Wilders had added his input to the debate on Islam by responding to Fortuyn's call to fight the 'Islamisation of the Netherlands' by arguing the latter had placed too much emphasis on 'regular Muslims' rather than focusing on Islamist terrorism and extremism. 'I have made clear from the beginning, that I, that the VVD, does not have anything against Islam', Wilders proclaimed:

> Religion is not the issue here. Contrary to Fortuyn, who pleads for a crusade, or [...] a cold war against Islam – which is a condemnable remark

because it generalises for all Muslims, I have stated from the beginning: There is nothing wrong with Islam, it is a respectable religion. Most Muslims in the world, as well as in the Netherlands, are respectable citizens. What is of concern is the small fringe of Muslim extremism. (Fennema 2010: 55)

The deputy leader of PVV, Fleur Ageman, later declared that Wilders had made this statement as representative of the VVD, rather than the nascent Freedom Party, and that he had been seeking to reflect the official party position of the VVD rather than his own personal opinion (*24 uur met ...*, VPRO 24 January 2011).

Indeed, after his withdrawal from the VVD, Wilders became more explicit in his criticism of Islam, frequently adopting radical statements and standpoints. Fennema (2010) describes the radicalization of Wilders as a process of increasing political involvement as well as being caused by personal isolation. Events had also been fundamental in this radicalization process, such as the 9/11 attacks, his contacts with Hirschi Ali and the Van Gogh murder. Fennema, moreover, traces the undemocratic nature of PVV to the lessons learned from the implosion of Fortuyn's LPF. As the decade progressed, Wilders' political appearances seemed increasingly unparliamentary in style, relying on insults, generalizations and populist utterances.

Although security, welfare and a vehement anti-EU stance are important issues in Wilders' political orientation, Islam forms the central focus of his rhetoric. In his provocations, Wilders does not equate Islam with Islamist extremism but yet portrays the latter as a direct consequence of the former and true to the message and content of the Koran. Wilders repeatedly emphasises that he is not against Muslims, but against Islam, which he presents not as a religion but as a violent ideology. In an interview with the Austrian news magazine *Profil*, for instance, Wilders claimed to have no objections against Muslims. Responding to a question as to why his PVV fought to halt immigration from Islamic countries, Wilders affirmed his desire to halt immigration but argued this was:

not because we think they are bad people or because we fear them. That would be ludicrous. The vast majority of Muslims in the Netherlands are law-obeying citizens who want to live a good life. However, we believe that the culture and ideology, which they bring with them, are contrary to our values and identity. Therefore we want a halt to Islamisation and to mass immigration from Islamic countries. This, however, is not targeted against Muslims as persons, even if that is difficult to understand. (*Profil* 24 January 2010)

On 8 August 2007, the newspaper *de Volkskrant* published an article by Geert Wilders with the title 'Enough is enough: prohibit the Koran', in which Wilders portrayed the Koran as a fascist book justifying violence that ought to be banned in the same way as *Mein Kampf* was (again highlighting the distance the nascent far right has travelled from traditional extreme right-wing sentiments). On 27 March 2008, Wilders published his film *Fitna* (Wilders 2008), in which he tried to attract attention to the perceived violent character of Islam, according to his interpretation. The article and film, alongside other statements by Wilders, prompted a number of police investigations into alleged cases of discrimination. By late June 2008, however, the Public Prosecutor declared Wilders would not be prosecuted as these expressions were not judged to be offensive or punishable. This decision raised objections and on 21 June 2009, the Amsterdam Court of Appeal instituted its own legal proceedings against Wilders. On 23 June 2011, Wilders was cleared of all charges. Some of the utterances by Wilders were 'rude and disregarding', the Court found, but 'not inflammatory'. Where Wilders had insisted a battle was raging with Muslim influences and that the Dutch people had to defend themselves, the Court found the statements had 'reached the boundaries of the permissible', albeit not surpassed them (*NRC* 23 June 2011).

This Court of Appeal case has lead to widespread discussions about freedom of expression and especially the right of MPs to express their opinion. Meanwhile, the court case had not prevented Wilders from engaging in political debate. During the annual Parliamentary Debate on the Queen's speech for example (16 September 2009) Wilders stated the following:

> Individual efforts are required to improve our environment. Scores of Dutch people have been affected by the pollution of the public space by Islam. Our society looks increasingly like that of Mecca or Teheran. Headscarves, long beards, burkas, men in long dresses; Madam Speaker let us do something about this! Let us recapture our streets. Let us amend so that the Netherlands will finally resemble the Netherlands once again. Those headscarves surely are a symbol of the suppression of women: a sign of submission; a sign of conquest. They represent an ideology underpinning a quest to colonise us all. Therefore, Madam Speaker, it is time to clean up our streets. Whenever our fellow compatriots want to express their love for this seventh century ideology that has its origins in the desert, they should do so in an Islamic country, but not here, not in the Netherlands. Madam Speaker, the Netherlands have taxed petrol and diesel, we have taxes on parking permits, on dogs, we even have an air transportation tax and we still tax packaging materials, so why have we not, according to my proposal, introduced a headscarf tax, a head trash tax, as I would call it?

[It would be] Simple: renew the permit once a year and pay immediately. A thousand Euros would be a perfect amount. Then, finally, we would start to earn something back from what has cost us so much over the years. I would say: let the polluters pay themselves. (Wilders 16 September 2009)

Neither the prosecution nor subsequent statements by Wilders have reduced his political support. On the contrary, the PVV became the third-largest party in the Netherlands after Parliamentary elections on 9 June 2010, securing 24 seats. In the negotiations for a new coalition government the PVV held a central position. Finally, on 14 October 2010, a novelty in Dutch politics occurred when a minority government was established, which depended on support by the PVV to reach majority support in Parliament. Furthermore, although the PVV is not a member of the government itself, three months after the formation of the government, 16 per cent of the Dutch believed Wilders to be a cabinet minister and 22 per cent argued Wilders was the most influential person in terms of Dutch government policies (Synovate 2011). Three parties, Christian Democrats, the Liberal Party VVD and the PVV, have agreed to disagree on issues concerning Islam. On the one hand, through this arrangement, the PVV is able to introduce several political issues and impact policy on security, migration, asylum policies within the government framework. On the other, it has 'its hands free' to continue with its anti-Islamic policies and statements.

Wilders and Breivik

On 22 July 2011 Anders Behring Breivik attacked his fellow-citizens in Norway with a bomb attack in Oslo and a shooting rampage on Utøya island, inflicting 77 fatalities. Breivik posted a manifesto online to coincide with the attacks in which he spoke highly of Geert Wilders and his party. This triggered various debates within the Netherlands that centred on questions regarding the potential responsibility of Wilders in creating an atmosphere and discourse in which xenophobia and Islamophobia prevailed, provoking 'lone wolves' such as Breivik to surface.

As a result of this debate, Wilders published a declaration on behalf of his Freedom Party expressing deep shock over the brutal murders, arguing Breivik's Manifesto was clearly the work of a 'lonely lunatic'. Wilders accused Breivik of 'misusing' the 'struggle against Islamisation' in order to justify his own violence, whilst, in turn, undermining efforts to counter the spread of Islamisation. Wilders spoke of his profound regret that Breivik had referred to the Freedom Party in his Manifesto, dismissing allegations of responsibility regardless of how eager 'some people' were to find links between the two. 'We are democrats by heart', Wilders insisted, arguing the Freedom Party had never promoted violence and would never do so, preferring 'the power of the ballot box and the wisdom of the voter rather than bombs or guns' (Wilders 2011). Subsequent attempts by journalists or parliamentarians to provoke further discussion with the Freedom Party regarding the Breivik attacks have not borne fruit.

Conclusions

As this chapter demonstrates, a lot has changed within the Dutch social and political landscape in recent decades. First of all, it has been argued, the dominant self-image of the Dutch as a tolerant nation that has become embedded over the ages has now become more nuanced. The history of discrimination and racism, including incidents of racist violence, throughout the years since 1945 presents a rather different picture. If one indeed can and wishes to speak of a self-image of a people or nation, one would view this image of the Netherlands and the Dutch as reconstructed and morphed into a more haphazard and splintered image that includes examples of tolerance as well as intolerance, of anti-racist activity as well as racist abuse and violence.

Immediately after the Second World War, some small fractions of 'classical' right-wing extremism emerged, usually with direct links to more traditional movements of (neo-)Nazism, anti-Semitism and racism, in terms of personalities as well as ideology. During the 1970s and 1980s, this 'classical' type of right-wing, racist extremism was confronted, in an organizational sense, by the general public as well as by the state. Increasingly, however, right-wing extremist and racist thoughts, attitudes and behaviour within society at large became perceived not as extremist or racist in character, but rather as the utterances of people living under difficult circumstances, especially due to the impact of immigration or in relation to the presence of migrant populations.

In the 1990s, the dominant discourse on migration and integration and, by extension, on the status of migrant populations, changed rapidly. Discriminatory, racist (or culturist) thoughts and statements increasingly became included within this dominant public and political discourse. Various parts of the far-right and racist discourse became perceived as 'acceptable' within the academic and political elite. One can, therefore, speak of 'modern' right-wing extremism. (Neo-)Nazism, anti-Semitism and openly articulated support for violence was no longer part of this 'modern' extremist discourse, whereby 'classical' right-wing extremists no longer followed 'modern' radicals such as Wilders. Contrary to the position of the 'classical' right-wing extremists as 'outsiders' in relation to mainstream society and the established political arena, the 'modern' right-wing extremists have established themselves as 'insiders' within this arena, as established actors that include elements whose support is sought to sustain government majorities within Parliament.

More recently, the influence of this 'insider' position of the 'modern' right-wing extremist discourse has become increasingly noticeable as criticism becomes more vocal. For example, an annual speech by the historian Thomas von der Dunk was cancelled this year amid controversy, as he wanted to compare the Freedom Party with pre-war pro-Nazi-parties within the Netherlands (*Telegraaf.nl* 20 April 2011). During the same period the band 'Jos & Tosti's', which planned to play at the Liberty Festival, commemorating the liberation of the Netherlands from Nazi occupation, was asked to abandon plans to perform its song *Mussolini van de Lage Landen* ('Mussolini of the Nether Lands) in which band members equate the discourse emanating from Wilders with Nazi ideology (*Spitsnieuws.nl* 26 April 2011). What is troubling is that attempts to silence these voices are not being issued by the 'modern radical insiders' themselves but by members of established political elites, uncomfortable with outspoken criticism of the extremist elements.

Debates over the classification of the Freedom Party as a 'right-wing extremist' platform, however, are likely to continue over the coming years. Wilders himself, of course, does not present the party as such and has sought to distance himself and his party from 'classical' right-wing extremism within the Netherlands. In terms of core facets of such ideological dispositions, which include clear delineations of 'us' versus 'them', with positive orientations towards the former and hostility towards the latter and propensity for authoritarianism, these appear to feature in the Freedom Party despite attempts by the leadership to distance the party from such notions (Davidovic et al. 2008). In his review of the academic literature on the German far-right, Van Donselaar found distinctions between 'alte Rechte' and 'neue Rechte', whereby the 'old far-right' referred to relationships within traditional right-wing extremist formulations, such as National Socialism, and the 'new far-right' referred to the marginalization of these traditional forces. This distinction, however, can be problematic when elements of these 'old' relationships and manifestations are seen to persist within 'new' far-right platforms, especially behind a more mainstream political façade. Van Donselaar, in turn, argues that this distinction can inform perceptions of Dutch realities and separations between old and new. 'The Freedom Party', he argues, 'could be understood as part of the "new far-right" if understood as "national-democratic" in terms of ideological orientation but without the features of the "old far-right" relating to concepts of social genealogy and a "racial revolutionary" orientation' (Van Donselaar 2010).

The term 'national-democratic' refers to Bjørgo's (1997) distinction within right-wing extremism between 'national [nationalist] democrats' and 'racial revolutionaries'. This distinction coincides largely with the distinction between 'anti-immigration activists' and 'neo-Nazis'. Davidovic et al. (2008) discussed ways in which the different strands compare. Across strands there are broad similarities in terms of favoured forms of governance that rest on 'stringent' authority and rejection of existing political codes of conduct. 'National democrats', however, reject Nazism, whereas 'racial revolutionaries' embrace and identify with Nazism and Nazi Germany. 'Racial revolutionaries', moreover, condemn parliamentary democracy whereas 'national democrats' seek to operate within this system. Finally, the latter reject the use of violence as a matter of principle (at least as far as mainstream political activity is concerned), although some forms of violence are sometimes accepted as necessary expressions of self-defence. 'Racial revolutionaries', however, embrace and even glorify the use of violence in pursuit of their goals (Bjørgo 1997; Davidovic et al. 2008).

This chapter has presented the 'classical' right-wing extremists as overlapping substantially with what is referred to here as the 'racial revolutionary' movement. The right-wing extremist parties of the 1970s up to the 1990s, however, presented themselves (publicly at least) as 'national democrats.' Questions have been raised, though, as to whether parts of their activities did not constitute 'racial revolutionary' activity behind the scenes, especially when representatives had neo-Nazi sympathies or backgrounds. In terms of the rise of the 'national democrat' manifestation of these divergent strands within the right-wing extremist milieu, however, Geert Wilders and his Freedom Party provide a prominent and important example of this form of far-right political engagement.

Epilogue

On Sunday 30 September 1941, as my grandfather lay on the wooden slats that served as his bed in the Amersfoort concentration camp, he pondered over the members of the Dutch NSB (the Dutch National-Socialist Movement) torn by pity, rage and anger:

Their political thinking has been twisted by years of economic crisis and swept along by a fascist order and race theories. But to simply think of their guilt is too superficial. Shouldn't we look for this among those who incited them with their degenerate minds? (Bulten 1970)

Note

1 Parts of this chapter are based on Witte, 2011

References

Algemene Inlichtingen- en Veiligheidsdienst (AIVD) (2005). *'Lonsdale-jongeren' in Nederland. Feiten en fictie van een vermeend rechts-extremistische subcultuur*, Den Haag AIVD, 2005.

Alkmaarsche Courant, 27 January 1992.

Benz, W. and T. Pfeiffer (eds) (2011). *'Wir oder Scharia'? Islamfeindliche Kampagnen im Rechtsextremismus. Analysen und Projekte zut Prävention*, Schwalbach: Wochenschau Verlag.

Bjørgo, T. (1997). *Racist and right-wing violence in Scandinavia: patterns, perpetrators and responses*, Oslo: Tano Aschehoug.

Bulten, E. Joh. (1970). *Diary of E. Joh. Bulten, no. 230, Aaltense Gijzelaars*.

Buis, H. (1988). *Beter een verre buur. Racistische voorvallen in buurt en straat*, Amsterdam: SUA.

City of Amsterdam (1983). *Tussen Witkalk en Zwarthemden*, B&W gemeente Amsterdam, 22 February.

Davidovic, M., J. van Donselaar, P. R. Rodrigues and W. Wagenaar (2008) Het extreemrechtse en discriminatoire gehalte van de PVV, in Donselaar, J. van and Rodrigues, P. R. (eds) (2008). *Monitor Racisme en Extremisme, Achtste Rapportage*, Amsterdam/Leiden: Anne Frank Stichting/Universiteit Leiden.

Donselaar, J. van (1993). 'The Extreme Right and Racist Violence in the Netherlands' in T. Bjørgo and R.Witte (eds) *Racist Violence in Europe*, London: MacMillan, pp. 46–61.

—(1997). *Eerste Rapportage Monitor Racisme en Extreemrechts*, Leiden: LISWO.

—(2000). *Monitor Racisme en Extreemrechts. Derde Rapportage*, Leiden: Universiteit van Leiden Departement Bestuurskunde.

—(2010). Rechts Radicalisme, in H. Moors, L. Balogh, J. van Donselaar & B. de Graaff *Polarisatie en radicalisering in Nederland. Een verkenning van de stand van zaken in 2009*, IVA: Tilburg, pp. 77–98.

Donselaar, J. van and Rodrigues, P. R. (2001, 2002, 2004, 2006, 2008). Monitor Racisme en Extremisme, resp. Vierde, Vijfde, Zesde, Zevende en Achtste Rapportages, Amsterdam/Leiden: Anne Frank Stichting/Universiteit Leiden.

—(2004 December). *ANNEX Racism and Extreme Right Monitor: sixth report. Developments following the murder of Theo van Gogh*, Amsterdam/ Leiden: Anne Frank Stichting/ Leiden University.

Donselaar, J. van and Wagenaar, W. (2007). Monitor Racisme en Extremisme. Racistisch en extreemrechts geweld in 2006, Amsterdam/ Leiden: Anne Frank Stichting/Universiteit Leiden.
Fennema, M. (2010). Geert Wilders. Tovenaarsleering, Amsterdam: Bert Bakker.
Fortuyn, P. (1994). Het Zakenkabinet Fortuyn, Utrecht: Bruna.
—(1997). Tegen de islamisering van onze cultuur. Nederlandse identiteit als fundament, Utrecht: Bruna.
Holtrop, A. and U. den Tex (1984). 'Bij ons in Holland' in *Vrij Nederland Bijlage*, 30 June.
Lijphart, A. (1979). *Verzuiling, Pacificatie en Kentering in de Nederlandse Politiek*, 3rd edn, Amsterdam: DeBussy.
Moors, H., L. Balogh, J. van Donselaar and B. de Graaff (2010). *Polarisatie en radicalisering in Nederland. Een verkenning van de stand van zaken in 2009*, IVA: Tilburg.
NRC, 29 January 2000.
—23 June 2011.
NOS-Journaal, 10 February 2002.
Profil, 24 January 2010. (see www.profil.at/articles/1012/560/265086/man-islamfeind-geert-wilders-interview [accessed 2 October 2011].
Provincial Representative of the Province of Northern Holland, *Letter to the Mayors of the Cities in the Province of Northern Holland*, 29 January 1992.
Scheffer, P. (2000). *Het multiculturele drama*, in NRC, 29 January.
Schinkel, W. (2007). Denken in een tijd van sociale hypocrisie. Aanzet tot een theorie voorbij de maatschappij, Kampen: Klement.
—(2008). De gedroomde samenleving, Kampen: Klement.
Schnabel, P. (1991). De multiculturele illusie. Een pleidooi voor aanpassing en assimilatie, Utrecht: FORUM.
Spitsnieuws.nl, 26 April 2011. (see http://www.spitsnieuws.nl/archives/media/2011/04/bevrijdingsfestival_verbiedt_a.html [accessed 2 October 2011].
Synovate (2011). Beoordeling kabinet na 100 dagen, Utrecht: Synovate, 28 January.
Telegraaf.nl, 20 April 2011. See http://www.telegraaf.nl/binnenland/9590003/___Anti-PVV-lezing__geweigerd__.html [accessed 2 October 2011].
Trouw, 25 January 2003.
de Volkskrant, 9 May 1981.
—12 September 1991.
—28 January 1992.
—9 February 2002.
—8 August 2007.
VPRO broadcasting network, *24 uur met...*, 24 January 2011. http://programma.vpro.nl/24uurmet/afleveringen/2011/Fleur-Agema.html [accessed 2 October 2011].
Wagenaar, W. and J. van Donselaar, (2006). 'Racistisch en extreemrechts geweld in 2005' in J. van Donselaar and P. R. Rodrigues (eds) *Monitor Racisme & Extremisme. Zevende Rapportage*, Amsterdam/Leiden: Anne Frank Stichting/ Departement Bestuurskunde Universiteit Leiden, p. 15–37.
—(2008). 'Racistisch en extreemrechts geweld in 2007' in J. van Donselaar and P. R. Rodrigues (eds) *Monitor Racisme & Extremisme. Achtste Rapportage*,

Amsterdam/ Leiden: Anne Frank Stichting/Departement Bestuurskunde Universiteit Leiden, p. 17–42.
Wilders, G. (2008). *Fitna* (the film is available on: http://www.liveleak.com/view?i=18b_1207466634 as show on 2 October 2011).
—(2009). Algemene Beschouwingen, 16 September 2009. See www.youtube.com/watch?v=KbsewZuvvko [accessed 2 October 2011].
—(2011). Declaration on Norway. See http://www.pvv.nl/index.php/component/content/article/36-geert-wilders/4529-verklaring-geert-wilders-noorwegen.html as of [accessed 2 October 2011].
Witte, R. (1996). *Racist Violence and the State. A comparative analysis in Britain, France and the Netherlands,* London: Addison Wesley Longman.
—(2010). Al eeuwenlang een gastvrij volk. Racistisch geweld en overheidsreacties in Nederland 1950–2009, Amsterdam: Aksant.
—(2011). Blickpunkt Niederlande. Islamfeindschaft als wahlstrategisches Erfolgsmodell, in W. Benz & T. Pfeiffer (eds) (2011) *'Wir oder Scharia'? Islamfeindliche Kampagnen im Rechtsextremismus. Analysen und Projekte zut Prävention*, Schwalbach: Wochenschau Verlag, p. 16–30.
Witte, R., P. Brassé and K. Schram (2005). *Moskeebrand in Helden. Evaluatie van de aanpak en lessen voor de toekomst*, Utrecht: FORUM.
WRR, Wetenschappelijke Raad voor het Regeringsbeleid (1989). *Allochtonenbeleid Rapport 36*, Den Haag: SDU.

7

Youth Engagement in Right Wing Extremism: Comparative Cases from the Netherlands

Ineke van der Valk

Introduction

In the post-war period the traditional extreme right-wing movement in the Netherlands has for a long time been a rather marginal phenomenon. However, facilitated by greater access to information via the internet and through the focus of specific youth cultures, this movement has increased in prominence over the past two decades. The focus of this chapter is on research results relating to factors determining entry of these youngsters into the far-right extremist scene and factors contributing to their eventual disengagement from this movement. Special attention is given to the role of violence in joining and leaving the movement. Nowadays discrimination of ethnic minorities in the Netherlands is increasingly framed in terms of hostility against the Islamic religion. On the basis of research on radicalization and deradicalization of youngsters and on ongoing research into islamophobic ideologies and practices such as violent attacks on mosques, this chapter argues that the Dutch far-right extremist landscape may be transformed when radical groups are increasingly influenced by an Islamophobic ideology that is gradually gaining momentum. Ideological shifts are already visible in the discourse and practices of several right-wing extremist groups. The chapter also discusses what Islamist extremism and the extreme right wing have in common and in what respect they differ. Insight into factors determining entry and exit of extremist groups and organizations equally offers insight into the possibilities of intervention.

Right-wing extremism

Defining the concept of right-wing extremism has been a subject of debate among scholars investigating the extreme right for decades (see *inter alia* Backes & Moreau 1994; Betz 2003: 74–93; Eatwell 2003: 47–74; Hainsworth 2000; Husbands 2002: 38–59; Ignazi 2002: 23–37; Jaschke 2001; Kowalsky and Schroeder (eds) 1994; Pfahl-Traughber 1994; Pfahl-Traughber 1995). These continuing discussions are often inherent to the study of complex social phenomena, which – by their very nature – are always subject to change. Aside from this, however, there is something else about right-wing extremism that sets it apart from other socially complex phenomena: its emotionally charged history since the Second World War, by which it has come to be associated with mass murder, annihilation and conquest. That association brings with it two complicating aspects that make it more difficult to achieve a shared definition of right-wing extremism:

- Since 1945, right-wing extremist groups have been the object of political and social isolation, together with repressive measures of all kinds. That is why the extreme right has been following a survival strategy for decades that is intended to conceal its ideological views and to present a more moderate message, or one that is modified in some other way. This survival strategy involved divergent efforts of adaptation as well as mainstream and fringe political activity[1] (van Donselaar 1991: 16ff).

- After the Second World War, aside from being used as a concept within political sciences, right-wing extremism also became a label that was used to discredit groups, ideas or personalities.

In this context it should be noted, moreover, that the concept of right-wing extremism, at least in the Netherlands, did not feature in public discourse until after the Second World War.

On the basis of definitions and theories of right-wing extremism in the relevant literature I use the following working definition. Right-wing extremism is a catch-all concept for political opinions situated on the extreme right fringe of the conventional left/right spectrum and for those formations – political parties, social movements and media – that support and disseminate these opinions. Scholars engaged in the study of right-wing extremism and the ideas and convictions it espouses generally agree on the following common ideological characteristics:

1. A direct or indirect resistance to the principle of fundamental equality of all human beings as it is conceived in human rights treaties. This resistance is primarily expressed by giving primacy and great value in social and political relations to belonging to a 'race', ethnic group, nation, culture or religion. Human and civic rights in this vision are subordinated to the strife for ethnic homogeneity. A positive orientation to what is considered 'us and ours' and a negative orientation to what is considered 'alien' is a strong characteristic of right-wing extremism: nationalism, ethnocentrism and racism are strongly articulated. Contemporary right-wing extremism defines itself as a movement struggling for the protection of its own national or Western identity in a world that it considers fundamentally hostile to Western values and culture.

2. A direct or indirect resistance to the current political system of parliamentary democracy and the constitutional state, including daily political practices of governments, political parties and judicial authorities. This resistance is expressed by systematic practices of delegitimization of mainstream political practices. These are often combined with a populist claim of representing the common folk.

3. A tendency towards non-democratic, authoritarian and hierarchical forms of organization in which a strong leader dominates.

The extreme right-wing view is not clearly demarcated, theoretically founded and closed. Many variations, accents and different emphases occur. It is a dynamic phenomenon that varies in terms of expressions and changes according to time and social context. It includes social movements and partisan orientations alongside diffuse mentalities that may be found amongst youngsters and practices of signification constructed around everyday experiences of ordinary people. For the post-war period a distinction should be made between classical neo-Nazi parties and hard-line movements on the one hand and post-industrial right-wing radical movements that have developed since the 1980s on the other. The latter are generally more moderate than the former and do not reject the constitutional state as a matter of principle. On the contrary, they are often part and parcel of a political system which they try to delegitimize in the eyes of common people. To mark a clear distinction between different right-wing currents and the boundaries of extremism, the

Dutch Intelligence Service AIVD assesses the extent to which political goals are deemed antidemocratic or within the legal order and whether the means and instruments used are undemocratic or democratic (AIVD 2011: 5).

Comparative research has shown that in countries where modern populist radical right parties that operate within legal boundaries are strong, hard-line neo-Nazi right-wing extremist parties tend to be weak (Spöhr and Kolls 2010). This is also the case in the Netherlands. Indeed, a review of the Dutch extreme right-wing movement over the past 15 years reveals some striking patterns in this respect.[2] Compared to other European countries such as France or Germany, 'classic' right-wing extremism in the Netherlands has been weaker (see also Witte in this volume). This was already the case during the inter-war years. Politically organised classical right-wing extremist organizations have become less and less significant, particularly in recent periods. By contrast, by the mid-point of the past decade, expressions of radicalism on the internet, the formation of loosely organised extremist youth groups, as well as the gathering of some tougher, violence-prone neo-Nazi groups (all predominantly composed of adolescents) became all the more important. The number of underage perpetrators of racial violence increased. At the same time other subjects attracted attention: in the new millennium the Western world was brutally confronted with 'new' forms of extremism. Islamist extremists committed terrorist crimes inflicting many casualties. In the Netherlands the brutal killing of one person, the filmmaker Van Gogh, by a jihadi extremist shocked people locally and across the globe. Partially as a reaction to the phenomenon of Islamist extremism, the problem of Islamophobia has grown considerably in the past years, not only in terms of the increased verbal and physical violence directed at the Muslim community but also in terms of the growing tendency to turn a blind eye to crimes of expression and discriminating utterances aimed at them. Expressions that raised indignation some years ago are now passing unnoticed without provoking any public reaction at all. Most importantly, Islamophobia in the Netherlands has now become politically organised. A new phenomenon developed in the first decade of the new millennium: the rise and prospering of a populist Islamophobic party that is strongly supported by international opinion makers that shape Islamophobic viewpoints and consider the Netherlands the frontline in the war against Islam (Car 2005). The remainder of this chapter focuses on the author's research into these issues: radicalization and deradicalization of youngsters; Islamophobia and responses to Islamist extremism.

Entry and exit

To gain a deeper understanding of the mechanisms whereby young people become involved in the extreme right wing, a research team at the Anne Frank House initiated a study in which in-depth interviews were held with former extremists who had been hard-line activists of far-right groups and movements. The researchers studied in particular the determinants and phases of involvement and disengagement and the correlation between them. They also looked at the possibilities of effective interventions.[3] The majority of the persons they interviewed were male, as is typical of right extremist organizations. The respondents lived across the country and were between 12- and 18 years-old when they joined the extreme right and between 15 and 24 when they left the movement. Several had committed racist crimes and some of them had been in jail. Family circumstances differed widely: with complete families and single-parent families, working-class and better educated parents; apolitical parents or rightist and leftist voters amongst the parents; some parents had outspoken prejudices about ethnic minorities and others none at all. Most of the interviewees were secondary school students who lived at home with their parents; a few had part-time jobs in addition to school. Despite this varying picture, a common element for many of the respondents was that they experienced problems at home. This might have been a factor that made them vulnerable.

It is impossible to discuss all the findings of this research project, but some particular results are worth mentioning. First of all it is important to note that political ideas did not appear to play a prominent role for any of the respondents as a motivation to engage in the extreme right-wing movement. They felt at most a vague ideological identification. However, it was found that respondents often did have ethnic prejudices that were sometimes prompted by negative experiences with ethnic minority youth.

The experience of unjust treatment by the government and society, a factor contributing to radicalization as identified in Van der Pligt and Koomen (2009), especially with regard to radicalized Islamists, was not found to be a factor in this investigation. The research team did, however, detect a general negative attitude and mistrust towards the government and society. There sometimes was evidence of experiences of unjust treatment from peers, some of them from ethnic minority backgrounds. The interviewees had little trust in the police to protect them from such threats.

A more important motivating factor that was identified, however, was a search for social belonging, a wish to make friends. The youngsters were looking for a lifestyle that fitted them and felt a need for excitement, adventure and often violence. There was also an emotional need to rebel, to protest and to discuss social problems. Frustrations and feelings of hatred, sometimes vague and sometimes related to lived experiences, found in extreme right-wing groups an outlet for these emotions, which quite often led to violence. 'The extreme right offers an interpretive framework for these experiences and prejudices that strongly appeals to the experienced group threat of "us versus them"'(Van der Valk and Wagenaar 2010: 72). It is only in a later phase that more ideological elements such as anti-Semitism were introduced to the young recruits by more experienced leaders. It was also in this later phase that the use of violence increased and came to occupy a central position.

The study results suggest that young people are active in the movement for shorter or longer periods, and during that time they fulfill varying functional roles such as ideologues, organisers, implementers and followers. Some organise a group, arrange meetings and initiate actions. Others are more managerial and inspirational when it comes to vision and ideological issues. They educate members in right-wing extremist doctrine, dominate formally or informally organised debates and discussion sessions and practise politics. Yet another group, the implementers, is active in daily practices. They take part in secret or open actions and activities.

Sooner or later some of the young members decide to walk out of the group and leave the extreme right-wing movement behind. The study clearly shows that this decision to leave the scene and the implied processes of socio-cognitive deradicalization and physical disengagement do not follow a linear pattern that applies to all respondents. Some begin to doubt the ideology, others are disappointed in the behaviour of other members who, in their eyes, do not even live according to the norms and values of the group. Still others begin to have misgivings about the actions of the group or they are disappointed in the movement as 'a trustworthy social environment' (ibid: 73). Some activists leave but remain loyal to the ideas, but the obverse is also true. An obvious factor that stimulated people to leave the movement, according to the study, was the need for a more conventional, socially integrated existence: in short, work, partner and a house, a wish that was obviously related to their age.

A question that was identified as crucial to the process of leaving the movement is whether there is any perspective of a new social life when the right-extremist milieu is left behind. If not, and if the person is socially isolated from mainstream society and peers, then leaving the right-wing extremist scene turned out to be very hard.

Violence

The study found that violence played a multifaceted role in relation to both radicalization and deradicalization. Being victim of violence sometimes furthered the radicalization process at the onset but also in later phases. Reports of violence committed by youngsters of other ethnic groups not only stimulated racist prejudices but also the use of violence by the radicalized interviewees themselves. Once the youngsters were completely engaged in the movement, identified with it and had successfully been introduced into its ideology, the use of violence became self-evident: for many of them, to carry weapons became a normal way of life. Pre-organised street violence directed towards ethnic minorities in different cities across the Netherlands became an important activity for some groups, as one respondent described:

> Violence does take place in the streets. A number of people are really good at it. You're walking down the street and feel like a little violence and you start looking for a foreigner to bash. Sometimes it is just a few punches and the person runs away. Sometimes you really lay into the person and leave him lying on the ground. One of us got into a fight with a nigger once and beat him to pulp. (...) Some people pick a fight with Moroccans and get scared and try to calm things down, whilst they themselves provoked the fight.

Leftist, anti-racist young people who demonstrated against right-wing extremism were also confronted violently (and sometimes responded in kind). The researchers argue that the use of violence clearly enhanced the status of activists in the right-wing extremist milieu. Under pressure from the group people sometimes did what they would not do in a more normal context:

> Sometimes it was fun and sometimes it was fucking difficult, especially when you had to hit people you know. I forced myself to do this in order not to let down the group.

In the movements that were examined violence and threats of violence were also used internally as a means of applying pressure and intimidation. Officially, most formal organizations however rejected the use of violence whilst at the same time turning a blind eye when their members were involved in such violent incidents.

Violence was also found to be a factor that plays a role in deradicalization and disengagement processes. It was, however, seldom a decisive factor provoking someone to leave the movement. By contrast, violence may also induce individuals to stay within the movement, when perceived as an attractive characteristic of right-wing extremism. Those who leave may be confronted with yet another expression of violence as a form of revenge and reprisal. One interviewee voiced these concerns:

> I am afraid that people get nervous. If I meet them in the street it is the question who runs the fastest (...) It is a world of squaring accounts.

Quite often, however, it never goes beyond threats. Various respondents argued that this was different to other countries, where reprisals are more common and leaving the movement is more frequently seen as a betrayal.

Right-wing extremism is a dynamic and fluid phenomenon that is subject to ideological change. Racism towards foreigners and citizens with a migrant background, however, is a durable component. In the current climate in the Netherlands, Muslims, and especially Moroccan Muslim immigrants are the most common targets. This form of targeting has been termed 'Islamophobia' within academic circles and anti-discrimination movements – a concept initially defined as a set of feelings and expression of fear, enmity and hatred towards Islam and Muslims (Runnymede Trust 1997).

Islamophobia

The Netherlands has about 850,000 Muslims out of a total population of 16 million inhabitants. The majority of the Muslim population in the Netherlands can be traced back to the arrival of migrant workers during the 1960s primarily from Morocco and Turkey. Today the Netherlands has 475 registered centres of Islamic worship.

Although Islamophobia is a relatively recent concept, it is not a recent phenomenon. It has strong roots in (colonial) history but has undergone a revival due to international developments, in particular the end of the Cold War, the rise of transnational Islamist violent extremism, expressed so dramatically in the 9/11 attacks on the US, the ensuing war on terror, international migration and the evolution of ethnically diverse societies with related social problems. The Islamophobic discourse targets the Islamic religion – often understood or rather deliberately represented as ideology – as well as Muslim culture. The conception of Islamophobia as an expression of feelings of fear and hatred is too limited, however. It highlights the emotional component whilst underestimating its cognitive aspects. Think, for example, of conscious efforts to discredit certain groups of people in order to raise people's fear. Following theories of racism and the studies of Chris Allen (2010) on Islamophobia, this chapter adopts the following working definition of the concept: Islamophobia is an ideology that is historically and socially determined. It attaches a negative signification to Islam and Muslims with the help of images, symbols, texts, facts and interpretations. The perception, signification, attitudes and conduct of people towards Islam and Muslims thus underscore their exclusion as 'the Other' whilst favouring unequal and discriminatory treatment in the social, political, cultural and economic realm. These processes often also include people who are viewed as Muslims on phenotypic or other grounds such as clothing, but who in fact are non-believers. Islamophobia as a contemporary form of exclusion and discrimination has religious as well as gender and ethnic dimensions. These dimensions are closely intertwined. The complexity of the phenomenon is partly due to this intersectional character. Islamophobia may be considered as a new form of culturally orientated racism that has replaced more biologically orientated forms since the 1980s (Barker 1981).

A rise in Islamophobia within the Dutch context is in particular visible in terms of anti-Islamic discourse on the internet, in the political discourse of the Dutch Populist Party (PVV) which obtained 24 seats in the 2010 parliamentary elections, and in hate speech of extremist organizations. It is visible in widespread opinions that consider the Islamic faith as a backward ideology that hampers human and societal development and threatens civilization by throwing it back to the Middle Ages. It is also visible in negative attitudes in wider sections of the population towards Muslims. Almost seven years have passed since the murder of filmmaker Van Gogh in November 2004. Opinion polls show that high levels of hostility towards Islam have persisted ever since. On average, around 50 per cent of respondents in the Netherlands and Germany have expressed negative attitudes towards Muslims, according to the Pew Research Centre (2005), a far higher degree of animosity than has been detected in, for example, the UK (14 per cent) and the US (22 per cent). These are worrying signs not only from the perspective of equality and human rights but also because resulting polarization may foster radicalization on both sides, a fertile ground for both jihadi and Islamophobic extremism.

Islamophobic viewpoints are central to PVV politics (Fennema 2010; Kuitenbrouwer 2010; Van der Valk 2012; Willemsen 2010). The party characterises Islam as an ideology rather than a religion and no distinction is made between Islam and Islamist extremism. According to this interpretation, Islam is a global force for domination and conquest of the Western world. This vision is expressed in a political program that sets out to counter 'Islamisation' and violate the rights of Muslims. Although the Dutch criminal justice system has not condemned party leader Geert Wilders according to the penal law, judges have described some of his expressions as denigrating, shocking, hurtful, discriminatory and on the border of what could be tolerated. Wilders has made numerous references to Islam as an existential future threat:

> (...) I have good intentions. We tolerate something that totally changes our society. Of course I am aware that there will not be an Islamic majority in the next decennia. But it is growing. With aggressive elements, imperialism. Walk on the streets and see where it leads to. One feels that one does not live in one's own country any more. There is a struggle going on and we have to defend ourselves.[4]
>
> Islam is an ideology that is distinguished by murder and manslaughter and only produces societies that are backward and pauperised.[5]

According to the party leader, the demise of Western society and civilization is immanent due to 'the multicultural elites that fight an all out war against their populations' and protect 'an ideology that has been aiming at our destruction for fourteen centuries'.[6]

Despite the outspoken Islamophobic position of the PVV, the liberal and Christian-democratic coalition that forms the actual government officially cooperates with the PVV, thereby tolerating and legitimizing its anti-Islamic stance, as Witte discusses in this volume.

Traditionally hard-line neo-Nazi right-wing extremist organizations and groups (which are small both in number and size) are rather reluctant to follow the PVV in this respect. They are primarily anti-Semitic and have national socialist sympathies, although this is sometimes publicly denied. Their racism is not based on ethno-religious grounds. These groupings are not interested in Islam and explicitly reject PVV politics, not least because the PVV rejects anti-Semitism and strongly supports Israel. The anti-Semitic dispositions of these traditional neo-Nazi groupings have thus prevented mergers with more recent organizations focusing animosity towards Islam.

Nationalistic and patriotic movements, however, which form another current of traditional extreme right-wing politics distinct from the neo-Nazi elements and increasingly driven by Islamophobia, tend to support Wilders' PVV and have become ever more vocal against Islam and Muslims. This has, for example, been the case for one of the oldest post-war parties, the NVU (Dutch People's Union) since 1973. Close reading of their texts shows a combination of moderate viewpoints promoting collaboration with Muslims as well as vehement rejection of Islamist extremism. The NVU actively disseminates leaflets entitled 'Against the Islamisation of Europe' and was involved in a demonstration against a mosque in Aken in September 2010. In May 2011 German far-right activists joined an NVU-sponsored protest in Enschede near the German border, carrying a banner that read 'Kein Islam in Europe'. In September 2010 NVU party members were advised to vote for the PVV in the next elections.[7]

This development could provoke further growth of Islamophobia in the traditional right-wing extremist movement, spreading this ideology of enmity, hate and fear. In this respect it is also remarkable that some of the youngsters interviewed for the aforementioned Anne Frank House study warned about support for Islamophobia amongst the younger generation of extremists and the Dutch people in general:

> (…) If it were now it would have been Wilders. Why? That man says what you think, that is the danger of that man, why he has so many followers. Because there are now an awful lot of people who are against Moroccans or against Muslims more generally. That man says what people think. But those people don't know about politics, they follow blindly. (…) I think Wilders is dangerous, I am concerned. I think that Wilders is an obstacle for our beautiful society and that worries me, what will happen if that man comes to power. (…) And Wilders says that we have democracy but we can be clear: he presents a dictatorship (…).

Different manifestations of Islamophobic radical street groups, however, developed in recent years but have disappeared again following a lack of mobilizing support. This was the case, for instance, of Stop Islamisation of Europe (SIOE NI) that did not succeed in mobilizing more than forty people during 2008 demonstrations. In July 2011 the Dutch Defence League (DDL), related to the English Defence League (EDL), decided to disband too.

Violence against mosques

The rise in prominence of Islamophobic discourse within traditional and nascent far-right movements coincided with the proliferation of violent incidents directed against the Muslim community. Some youngsters who were interviewed as part of the study participated in organised actions against Islamic targets. The number of documented cases of Islamophobic violence in the Netherlands has been steadily increasing over the years, peaking in the aftermath of specific contextual events such as the 9/11 attacks and the murder of Van Gogh in November 2004 (Bovenkerk 2006: 95–7; Van der

Valk 2012; Van Donselaar and Rodrigues 2002: 23–6). Much of the violence against Islamic targets is directed at centres of worship, mostly mosques as the most visible symbol of Islam. As Lambert observed in this volume within the UK context, violent acts against mosques in the Netherlands mainly consist of arson (or arson attempts), targeted graffiti, vandalism and threats. This author's data on violence against mosques were collected from a variety of sources such as the Dutch National Police Services Agency, the National Anti-Discrimination Agencies, specialized research groups and the media. Despite this variety of sources there are good reasons to assume that the figures are an underestimation of the actual number of incidents of islamophobic violence. Underreporting is rather the rule than the exception: many incidents are not reported to the police or to other institutions. The reason is that victims sometimes do not know whom to report to or lack confidence in the advantages of reporting the attack. Sometimes the administrators of the mosques are asked by the police not to publish the incidents in order to prevent more problems. Most of the perpetrators of racial violence remain unknown. The resolution rate of racial violence cases in general is relatively low in the Netherlands: 12 per cent in, for instance, 2007 (Wagenaar and Van Donselaar 2008). This is also the case for violence against mosques. Almost all the perpetrators in the cases that have actually been resolved are young offenders. It is striking that far more acts of violence against mosques take place in small and medium-size municipalities than in large municipalities and big cities such as Rotterdam, Amsterdam and Utrecht, where of course migrant communities are larger and the number of mosques greater. This is obviously related to the fact that people in large municipalities and big cities have become used to the presence of citizens of ethnic minority backgrounds over the past decade. A review of mosque attacks from 2005 to 2010 reveals that a country as small as the Netherlands witnessed almost three times as many violent incidents against mosques compared to the United States, in terms of reported incidents (data of the American Civil Liberties Union, ACLU 2010): 42 in the US and 117 in the Netherlands. Altogether 239 acts of violence have been committed against Dutch mosques in the last decade (2000 to 2010), 62 of which were arson attacks (or attempts). The zenith was reached after the 9/11 attacks and the Van Gogh murder, with both years concluding with 45 to 50 incidents for each period, including 19 cases of arson for each period.[8]

Similarities in extremes

Despite the anti-Islamic slant of these traditional and nascent far-right groups, a number of similarities emerge when far-right and Islamist extremism are compared. To identify but a few comparative factors, on the ideological level, for instance, the rejection of democracy as historically the most acceptable and just system to rule the state is notable. A common practice of violence may equally be identified, or at least an extremely strong resistance against political opponents and a strong tendency to rely on conspiracy theories. Accounts implicating the West in conspiracies against Islam form a prominent feature of the Islamist extremist narrative, whilst the concept of 'Eurabia' is prominent in Islamophobic conspiracy theories.[9] In some cases, anti-Semitism would appear to be a common characteristic between the two forms of extremism, although it does not appear to be a feature of primarily Islamophobic movements. Whilst far-right extremism shows clear preferences for authoritarianism, moreover, Islamist extremist movements appear to rely more on networks bound by a common ideology rather than on structured forms of organization with authoritarian leaders. A network lacks such a formal (hierarchical) structure and has informal and flexible membership and fluctuating leadership, even though a core group might provide coordination (AIVD 2006: 13–18). Experiences have shown that tactics that differentiate between public and informal discourse and political activity – a characteristic of right extremism – also feature within Islamist extremism. But besides the common characteristics that can be identified between Islamist extremism and far-right extremism in terms of common interests, mutual contacts do, surprisingly, also exist (see Holbrook in this volume).

An important reason for studying similarities and differences between divergent forms of extremism is the need to hone possible forms of intervention that can address some of the underlying processes of engagement. This does not necessarily relate to ideological similarities, therefore, but rather similarities that emerge when the people who adhere to these extremist ideologies are compared. As far as young people, adolescents, are concerned the individuals in question would appear to have a number of things in common.

Islamist extremism was long seen as an exclusively imported problem that originated in Islamic world. The reality is quite different. Many violent extremist activists and their supporters were born and raised in European countries or lived their adult lives in Europe. Converts also play an important and sometimes even a leading role. Islamic networks often consist of a complex mixture of actors of various kinds: so-called 'heartland-orientated' actors, working together with 'reborn believers', and local activists (De Poot and Sonnenschein 2009).

The Islamist networks that have been the subject of research in the Netherlands (ibid) consisted mostly of men, although there were also a few women. They included young and old people, many did not have residence permits and some had criminal records or a history of substance abuse. Converts and second-generation youth were also involved. Only a section of these networks involved what could be regarded as idealistic political activists. Young people especially were rather looking for meaning and social relationships instead of being motivated on ideological grounds. Many second-generation migrants that were involved experienced feelings of alienation. They felt discriminated against and excluded by a majority society that, in their eyes, also oppressed Muslim people in the larger global world (Van der Valk 2010: 89). These youngsters sometimes consider radical Islamist views as a third way, an alternative to the values of their parents and to the values of the secular society. It serves their interests as they are already publicly positioned, and feel themselves, 'in between two societies': their own community of origin and the European societies in which they were born and raised.

Radicalization processes in different groups and different ideologies in this respect often have much in common and follow similar patterns. The psychological factors that lead to extremism are partly related to reactions of indignation to local situations that are experienced as unjust. Anger and frustration, a vague sentiment of rebellion against society equally emerged as important factors for right extremist radicalization in the aforementioned study on right-wing extremist youth. As we see developmental processes in adolescence work out in different ways, they may find a specific outlet through political radicalization. Adolescent thinking is often black-and-white, without nuances. The youth are often uncertain about themselves, their social identity and their future in a society that is characterised by social polarization along ethnic lines. This makes them particularly vulnerable to group threats, be they symbolic or real. At the same time this form of radicalization is often related to a quest for identity, to a desire for companionship and social belonging and to a drive for revenge or violence, fuelled by propaganda. By joining the radical group they join an 'imagined community' that is shaped by such propaganda and this gives them the sense of belonging that they are missing in their daily lives.[10] In this way different radical youth cultures, Islamist and right-wing extremist, have gradually developed in recent years (Van der Valk 2010; Van der Valk and Wagenaar 2010). The youngsters' radical speech, appearance and conduct, be it extreme right-wing or Islamist, are an attempt to belong and to shape their social identity, and it is in this respect that young Islamist extremists have much in common with young people who organise themselves into extreme right-wing groups.

Intervention policies – some suggestions

A salient outcome of the Anne Frank House study into determinants of involvement and disengagement were the possibilities of intervention. People disengaging from the right-wing extremist milieu in the Netherlands receive little or no support in the process, although they certainly are in need of it. Even in situations that lend themselves particularly well to such assistance, such as in prison, surprisingly, no such support or help is being made available. The study has shown that interventions are most likely to succeed if they are carried out when the person is still in an early phase of the process of involvement. But the results of this research also suggest that interventions can be successful when subjects begin to question their involvement too. In many cases, right-wing extremists are so isolated from the society around them that finding a way back to society is very hard. This often hampers the termination of a right-wing extremist career. The process of disengagement becomes unnecessarily difficult. Van der Valk and Wagenaar offer an outline for policy interventions to facilitate exit from these movements. Help from outsiders in such cases, they argue, is clearly important, as is a local approach in the communities where the young people live their lives. A helpdesk for formal and informal social support and support groups for parents are considered beneficial in this respect. The researchers also strongly recommend the use of former radicals with hands-on expertise. More than any other actor in the social domain they can contribute positively to the success of interventions.

Several of these former extremists have informed researchers that they feel guilty and consider participating in such a program in order to do something to pay their debt to society. Policies should enable them to do so and give these young people the opportunity to re-integrate into mainstream society.

Final remarks

This chapter has discussed some of the pathways young activists have followed as they become engaged in extreme right-wing organizations as well as their disengagement from these groups. For these youngsters the role of ideology was often less important than their search for adventure, belonging and friendship, although ethnic prejudices and indignation about the socio-political situation also featured. The new recruits were later introduced to extremist ideologies by more experienced members. Violence turned out to be an important and multifaceted factor in both entry and exit of these groups.

The Dutch cultural and political landscape is rapidly changing and an Islamophobic ideology is gaining ground, facilitated by the possibilities of the internet and the political expression of a populist party that has seen electoral success. This development may well induce a growth of Islamophobia in the traditional extreme right-wing milieu and more nascent extremist movements, leading to further dissemination of this intolerant discourse and heightening the risk of violent extremist attacks being carried out in pursuit of this agenda. Based on a comparison of youth engagement in Islamist and far-right extremism, it was argued that policy development designed to counter and prevent engagement in extremist activity should place attention on what the people who adhere to these extremist dispositions have in common. As far as young people are concerned, this highlights the importance of social needs in particular.

Notes

1 J. van Donselaar elaborated this pattern in extreme right-wing strategies in *Fout na de oorlog, fascistische en racistische organisaties in Nederland 1950–1990,* Amsterdam: Bert Bakker 1991, p. 16ff. Van Donselaar borrowed the theatrical metaphor from Goffman's analysis of everyday interaction processes.
2 For an overview see the two-yearly reports of the Monitor Racism and Extremism project of the Anne Frank House in cooperation with the University of Leiden. Right-wing extremism in the Netherlands has been the subject of research by this project for 15 years (1996–2011). Otto Frank, Anne's father wanted the Anne Frank House not only to encourage people to visit the secret hiding place and remember the past but also asked them to realise that still today people are persecuted because of their race, religion or political conviction. Against this background the Anne Frank House developed the Monitoring project. English versions of the Monitor reports and related publications may be found on the website of the Anne Frank House: www.Annefrank.org. See also Witte, in this volume.
3 For the full report and the English translation, see Van der Valk, I. and Wagenaar. W., 2010.
4 Rechtbank (Court of Justice) Amsterdam 23 June 2011, LJN BQ9001.
5 G. Wilders, speech at the Court of Justice 7 December 2011, http://drimble.nl/bericht/3466017.

6 Ibid.
7 For more data and analysis of Islamophobia in relation to traditional extreme right-wing and extremist formations see Van der Valk, 2012.
8 For a more detailed overview of violence against mosques in the Netherlands see Van der Valk, 2012.
9 This concept was first developed by Bat Ye'or, a Jewish-Egyptian female writer working in Switzerland, and refers to a process in which Europe is supposedly invaded and subjugated by Arabs and Muslims.
10 The concept of imagined community is from Benedict Anderson, Imagined Communities: Reflections on the origin and spread of nationalism, London: Verso 1991(rev. edn).

References

ACLU 2010 – Nationwide Anti-Mosque Activity on the website of the American Civil Liberties Union. (2010). http://www.aclu.org/print/map-nationwide-anti-mosque-activity.

AIVD (General Intelligence and Security Service) (2011). *Right wing extremism and the extreme right in the Netherlands* (p. 5). The Hague: Ministry of the Interior and Kingdom Relations. [www.aivd.nl].

—(2006). *De gewelddadige jihad in Nederland: actuele trends in de islamitisch-terroristische dreiging* (pp. 13–18). The Hague: Ministry of the Interior and Kingdom Relations. [www.aivd.nl].

Allen, C. (2010). *Islamophobia.* London: Ashgate.

Barker, M. (1981). *The New Racism: Conservatives and the ideology of the tribe.* London: Junction Books.

Backes, U. and Moreau, P. (1994). *Die Extreme Rechte in Deutschland : Geschichte – gegenwärtige Gefahren – Ursachen – Gegenmassnahmen.* München: Akademie-Verlag.

Betz, H-G. (2003). The Growing Threat of the Radical Right in P. H. Merkl and L. Weinberg (eds), *Right Wing Extremism in the Twenty-First Century* (pp. 74–93). London/Portland: Frank Cass.

Bovenkerk, F. (2006). Islamofobie in J. van Donselaar and P. Rodrigues, (eds), *Monitor Racisme and Extremisme: Zevende rapportage* (pp. 95–7). Amsterdam: Amsterdam University Press/Anne Frank Stichting/Universiteit Leiden.

Car, M. 'You are now entering Eurabië', in *Race & Class*, 48 (2006). 1, pp. 1–22. London: Sage Publications. [http://rac.sagepub.com].

Commission on British Muslims and Islamophobia (1997). *Islamophobia: A challenge for us all*, London: Runnymede Trust.

Eatwell, R. (2003). Ten theories of the extreme right in P. H. Merkl and L. Weinberg (eds.), *Right Wing Extremism in the Twenty-First Century* (pp. 47–74). London/Portland: Frank Cass.

Fennema, M. (2010). *Geert Wilders: Tovenaarsleerling.* Amsterdam: Bert Bakker.

Hainsworth, P. (2000). *The Politics of the Extreme Right: From the margins to the mainstream.* London: Pinter.

Husbands, C. (2002). How to tame the dragon, or what goes around comes around: a critical review of some major contemporary attempts to account for extreme-right racist politics in Eastern Europe. In M. Schain, A. Zolberg and P. Hossay (eds), *Shadows over Europe: the development and impact of the extreme right in Western Europe* (pp. 38–59). New York: Palgrave Macmillan.

Ignazi, P. The Extreme Right: Defining the object and assessing the causes. In M. Schain, A. Zolberg and P. Hossay (eds), *Shadows over Europe: The development and impact of the extreme right in Western Europe* (pp. 23–37). New York: Palgrave Macmillan.

Jaschke, H-G. (2001). *Rechtsextremismus und Fremdenfeindlichkeit: Begriffe – Positionen – Praxisfelder.* Wiesbaden: Westdeutscher Verlag.

Kowalsky, W. and Schroeder, W. (eds) (1994). *Rechtsextremismus: Einführung und Forschungsbilanz.* Opladen: Westdeutscher Verlag.

Kuitenbrouwer, J. (2010). *De Woorden van Wilders and Hoe ze Werken,* Amsterdam: De Bezige Bij.

Monitor Racism and Extremism (1996–2011). Anne Frank House/University of Leiden. [English translation of reports: www.Annefrank.org].

Pew Research Centre (2005). *Islamic Extremism: Common concern for Muslim and Western publics*: 17-nation Pew global attitudes survey, Washington, DC, [http://pewglobal.org/reports/pdf/248.pdf].

Pfahl-Traughber, A. (1994). *Volkes Stimme? Rechtspopulismus in Europa.* Bonn: Dietz.

—. (1995). *Rechtsextremismus: Eine kritische Bestandsaufnahme nach der Wiedervereinigung.* Bonn: Bouvier (2., erw. Aufl.).

Poot, de C. and Sonnenschein, A. (2009). *Jihadistisch Terrorisme in Nederland: een beschrijving op basis van afgesloten opsporingsonderzoeken,* Den Haag: Ministerie van Justitie, Wetenschappelijk Onderzoek en Documentatiecentrum. <http://www.wodc. nl/onderzoeksdatabase/inzicht-in-islamitische-terrorismebestrijding-obv-vanrecent-afgesloten-opsporingsonderzoek.aspx> [accessed 13 August 2010].

Spöhr, H. and Kolls, S. (Hrsg.) (2010). Rechtsextremismus in Deutschland und Europa, Actuelle Entwicklungstendenzen im Vergleich, Frankfurt am Main: Peter Lang.

Van Donselaar, J. (1991). *Fout na de oorlog, fascistische en racistische organisaties in Nederland 1950–1990,* (p. 16ff). Amsterdam: Bert Bakker.

Van Donselaar, J. and Rodrigues, P. (eds) (2002). *Monitor Racisme en extreemrechts: vijfde rapportage,* (pp. 23–26). Amsterdam Anne Frank Stichting/Universiteit Leiden.

Van der Pligt, J. and Koomen, W. (2009). *Achtergronden en determinanten van radicalisering en terrorisme.* Amsterdam: Universiteit van Amsterdam, Onderzoeksinstituut psychologie.

Van der Valk, I. (2010). Islamistisch extremisme, in P. Rodrigues and J. van Donselaar (eds), *Monitor Racisme & Extremisme: Negende rapportage.* (pp. 85–108). Amsterdam: Amsterdam University Press/Anne Frank Stichting/Universiteit Leiden. [English version: http://www.annefrank.org/en/Worldwide/Monitor-Homepage/Research/Fifteen-years-of-the-Racism–Extremism-Monitor/]

—. (2012). *Islamofobie en Discriminatie.* Amsterdam: Amsterdam University Press.

Van der Valk, I. and Wagenaar, W. (2010). *Monitor Racisme & Extremisme: In en uit extreemrechts*. Amsterdam: Amsterdam University Press/Anne Frank Stichting/Universiteit Leiden. [English version: http://www.annefrank.org/en/Worldwide/Monitor-Homepage/Research/With-help-rightwing-extremists-pull-out-sooner/].

Wagenaar, W. and van Donselaar, J. (2008). Racistisch en extreemrechts geweld in 2007, in J. van Donselaar & P. R. Rodrigues (eds), *Monitor Racisme & Extremisme: achtste rapportage*, (pp. 36) Amsterdam: Amsterdam University Press/Anne Frank Stichting/Universiteit Leiden.

Willemsen, C. (ed.) (2010). *Dossier Wilders: uitspraken van de meest besproken Nederlandse politicus van deze eeuw*, Schelluinen: House of Knowledge.

Ye'or, B. (2005) *Eurabia: The Euro-Arab Axis*. New Jersey: Farleigh Dickinson University Press.

8

Right Wing Political Violence in France: Stock Take and Perspectives

Michel Gandilhon

For the past 30 years or so, the French extreme right, in the form of the Front National, has occupied an important place in the political landscape of the Fifth Republic. It was actually in the early 1980s and especially around the time of the municipal elections at Dreux in 1983 that the first signs appeared of an upsurge which was to take it through to the second round of the Presidential elections in 2002. At the present time, polls carried out in connection with the coming Presidential elections, planned for 2012, continue to suggest it will achieve a high score, somewhere around 20 per cent of the vote. This unprecedented rise of the extreme right in France and the steady institutionalizing of the Front National have together brought about, on the fringes of the main party, the emergence of a small number of more radical groups who are critical of an organization which they often feel to be too timid. Does this development, and the accompanying radicalization, foreshadow a return to political violence, or even to terrorism, from the French extreme right?

By way of answer to this question, the first section considers, at the outset, the historical nature of the ground in France in which political violence did develop on the radical right. It will do this by showing how the nature of this violence was unusual, through being moulded by the quite specific historical circumstances created by the decolonizing that took place in the 1950s; it was also significant to the extent that this was the original source of those groupings that were to create the Front National in 1972. The second section draws up an assessment of the extreme right at the present time, as it has been formed by its main ideological groupings. A final section considers the specific risks which may emerge from the way that a large part of the radical right focuses its attention on the demographic changes experienced by France and the continent of Europe as a result of the arrival and permanent settlement in their midst of immigrants coming from the Maghreb and sub-Saharan Africa at the same time as the rise of radical Islam.

The OAS and the Algerian period

From the nineteenth century, when modern terrorism first appeared (Huyghe 2011) with the emergence of Russian terrorists rising up against the autocracy of the Romanovs, France has experienced three periods of terrorist violence that sprang from within its own borders[1]. Two of these had their roots in the extreme left; one in the 1890s with the 'propaganda through deeds' of the anarchists which specifically came to an end with the assassination of President Sadi Carnot in 1894 (Maitron 2007); second, in the 1980s with the armed struggle on the part of Action Directe which at that time formed part of the framework of terrorism which derived from violent communist groupings similar to the Red Brigades in Italy or to the Red Army Faction (RAF) in Germany.

The third emerged from the extreme right, and was interposed in time between the two others just mentioned. It made itself felt in practice in the early 1960s with the creation of the OAS (Secret Army Organization) but in the quite specific context of the war in Algeria, when the spectre of civil war threatened the Fifth Republic which had come into being as the result of the uprising of Europeans in Algeria. It is true that France, through the creation of OSARN (Secret Organization for National Revolutionary Action)[2], better known under its name 'La Cagoule' (Vial 2010), had already experienced a period of terrorist violence deriving from the extreme right, with the radicalization of politics which followed the coming to power of the Popular Front in 1936. But this failed to show that it could last, and was soon swallowed up through the defeat of the French left in 1938 and the rising threat of war.

On the other hand, the period involving the OAS and its Delta commandos is of absolutely capital importance, both on account of its wide range and of its duration. In practice, OAS terrorism was to cause around 2,000 deaths in metropolitan France and in Algeria. Despite the brevity of this organization's existence – two years at most – it was to create a lasting impact on the political landscape of the radical right in France (Dard 2011). The OAS thus provided a kind of mould from which there emerged the violent political groupings which were active in the 1970s and, also, elements of those who were to become leading figures in the Front National. So it can be said that it was the struggle for French Algeria which led to the greatest wave of terrorism that France has experienced throughout her history. It paralleled the violence being experienced by French society at that time, which took the form of a 'war with no name'; the authorities chose simply to speak of operations to maintain public order in the Departments to the south of the Mediterranean. Confronted by the rise of Algerian nationalism, which, from 1954, was represented by the FLN (Front de Libération Nationale), there developed a political trend which was hostile to independence; this drew its strength mainly from the populist social groups of those of European origin. The increasing trend towards extremism and the resort to terrorism amongst Europeans at this time developed extremely rapidly. To start with, this came about as a reaction to the violent terrorist activities by the Algerian FLN against the European civilian population in Algiers and in the area round Constantine[3]. Confronted by the criminal attacks which took place from June 1956 on the orders of the FLN, which enjoined the Mujahedin to strike down any European male aged over 18 (Monneret 2008), the first armed counter-terrorist group came into being in 1956 with the ORAF (Resistance Order of French Africa), which was the forerunner of the OAS.

This group, significantly, was the instigator of the violent episode in Algiers on 10 August 1956, in the Rue de Thèbes in the Kasbah (Muslim quarter), which caused several dozen deaths. At the time, the originators of this group plainly came from the extreme right; they were close to traditional catholic thinking based on a rejection of the French Revolution and of the Republic. The ORAF drew its inspiration from the supporters of Franco and Salazar[4], who hoped to take advantage of the Algerian civil war so as to overthrow the Republic and install a regime which would be corporatist and nationalist. It was, however, very quickly the case that, as the European population became more radicalized, European terrorist groups were to broaden their base to include groups which must be characterised as being on the left (the Communist party was very strong in Algeria at that time), and which included militants who had their origins in working-class trade unionism and in the former International Brigades of the war in Spain from 1936 to 1939. Furthermore, prompted by the fact that the French government's policy favoured self-determination, the 'ultras' no longer set their sights only on the FLN; they now included the Gaullists, the left, and, more widely, the Republic's forces of law and order both in Algeria and in metropolitan France.

The formation of the OAS in 1961, in the wake of the failed coup d'état of Generals Challe and Salan, strengthened the move towards terrorism, which had become radicalized through the French government's determination to rid itself of Algeria, which was seen as an economic burden that hindered the modernization of French capitalism (Lefeuvre 2006). From this time on, the OAS and its armed commandos gave themselves over to violence that covered a wide spectrum; this became all the more desperate once this group could no longer ignore the fact that the war was lost. As things were, at the time of the 1961 putsch which was the work of the supporters of Algérie Française, the army did not swing behind these factious elements among the population; at the same time, the Europeans in Algeria – although in many cases attracted by the idea of Algérie Française – did not rise en masse (as they had done in 1958 to support the coming to power of General de Gaulle) to support this coup d'état. Now cut off from people on the mainland, large numbers of whom were now attracted by the idea of independence, hard pressed by the army, hunted down by the forces of both the FLN and the Gaullists who had joined hands for the purpose, the OAS threw itself into desperate attempts to carry out murderous attacks that derived from a scorched earth policy. These gave some support to certain offshoots of the FLN by pursuing a policy of reprisal and massacre, such as happened in Oran in 1962, when they turned against the Europeans. This historic defeat of the OAS did not, however, leave it without any successors. For a very long time, the events in Algeria were, for the French extreme right, to continue as a myth which acted as a recruiting ground and which was to provide the leaders of those future legitimate groups and violently inclined elements which, though admittedly only marginal, were to appear in the 1970s.

After 1962, the kind of politically inspired violence that continued to be carried out was still largely determined by the scars of the Algerian war. It was thus that there came into being a mysterious group named after Charles Martel.[5] This was essentially made up of former OAS militants who gave themselves over chiefly to making violent attacks against the hostels of immigrant Algerian workers. Around this period, it was the assault made on the Algerian consulate in Marseilles in December 1973 which made the greatest impact on opinion, on account of the four deaths that were caused. The activist attitude adopted by some of the former partisans of Algérie Française forms part of the overall picture of powerful tensions that were to be found between different communities and ethnic groups that were apparent in the south of France at that time. Thus it came about that, in 1973, the city of Marseilles was the scene of a wave of racist crimes (known as 'ratonnades') which followed the murder of a tram-driver by an Algerian, which provoked many assassinations; these do not seem to have been the work of isolated individuals but of organised groups (Giudice 1992). This wave of violence, which was very localized, faded away until it found some kind of political outlet through the increased power of the Front National in the 1980s.

Thus it can be seen that, in the 1960s and 1970s, political violence on the part of the extreme right occurred in the very special context of decolonization and of 'the defence of the West' which was threatened by the emergence of the third world that was being supported by the USSR. Such violence, however, did not hinder the extreme right from adopting a lawful position in the Republic by taking part in the 1965 Presidential elections through the candidacy of Jean-Louis Tixier-Vignancourt, a champion of General Salan. This was important, for it characterised the ambivalence of the extreme right in France, split as it was between the appeal of activist violence and its hope of becoming integrated into traditional political manoeuvring. It was the latter which decisively predominated once the Front National became institutionalized.

Despite all this, the events of 1968 would allow the extreme right the chance to bring their ideas before the nation by making themselves once more part of the political interplay in metropolitan France. Militant activity was now carried forward by a new generation who were represented by a group calling itself 'Occident' and later on 'Ordre Nouveau'[6]. This group focused its attention on anti-communism and the struggle against left-wing ideas which were increasingly flourishing at that time (Charpier 2005). A few years later, confronted with the sight of the left attaining power, as was revealed when the Socialist party, the Communist party and the left-wing radicals signed up to a joint programme of government in 1972, the various right-wing trends in the country formed links with the Front National, even going so far, from 1978 onwards, as to integrate the traditional right in France, and, significantly, including the Union for French Democracy (UDF), the party of the then President of the Republic, Valéry Giscard d'Estaing, who was hostile to Gaullism and a one-time supporter of Algérie Française. The hour had come for legalism, and political violence virtually disappeared, appearing only in a residual way, still clung to by isolated groups of pieds-noirs, as a kind of concomitant of the war in Algeria.

The characteristics of present-day nationalism: Its integration into normal political life

This new law-abiding manifestation was to be strengthened when the Front National finally reached the end of its 'desert crossing' in the early years of the 1980s. Ten years after its creation, the party gained its first electoral successes and engaged in an ongoing process which today makes it an unshakeable element of French political life; above all, it has become an essential factor in the development of a more peaceable policy at the heart of the radical right. The birth, growth and eventual institutionalizing of the Front National indicates how the extreme right had become integrated into French political life, in a way that had scarcely ever been previously seen in France. In other respects, this situation was something of a paradox for a country thought by the historian Zeev Sternhell to be the wellspring of modern fascist ideology (Sternhell 2000).

Even if there had always been a vigorous and lively intellectual trend, seen especially in Charles Maurras' Action Française, the extreme right had throughout its history never managed to form a significant element of any organization that achieved lasting political and electoral success. The Vichy period, when its ideas could be put to work at the highest levels of the state, was no more than an exception that came about in quite unusual historical circumstances, which were, in Maurras' estimation, a 'divine surprise', and of which the main features were the defeat of 1940 and the German occupation.

Thus it is today that the Front National, despite being still ostracized in some quarters, provides a way of bringing together the various radical elements in nationalism, and of watering down the political violence that is still liable to emerge from the radical elements of the right. Furthermore, this party is in effect a front made up of the whole spread of the right, stretching from traditionally minded Catholics all the way to 'identitaire'[7] neo-pagans, and encompassing royalists and revolutionary nationalists.

The very fact that, at the present time, the organization holds – in the unsettling context of the world financial crisis and the prospect of a breakdown of the eurozone – genuine prospects of political success makes the emergence of political violence on the part of the extreme right in France barely credible. As things stand, the Front National does offer radical militants a credible alternative policy which provides realistic hopes of attaining a satisfactory outcome. Furthermore, a glance at the other organizations to be found among those with radical tendencies in France shows clearly that they, too, adopt a law-abiding position in the electoral struggles. This is notably the case with the Bloc Identitaire, the most significant organization on the extreme right after the Front National. Although it emerged in 2003 out of the dissolution of Unité Radicale, a tiny nationalist revolutionary group which was banned by the state after an attempt made on the life of the President, Jacques Chirac, by one of its members in 2002, the Bloc Identitaire, with a few hundred supporters, parades a form of militant activism[8] which does not prevent it from making local deals with the Front National. This is notably the case in Nice, where there is talk of adopting common candidates between the two groups for the legislative elections in 2012. After making all due allowances, one may say that the 'Identitaires' play the same role in relation to 'big brother', the Front National, as, on the left, do the NPA (New Anti-Capitalist Party), which developed from the LCR (Revolutionary Communist League), alongside the Socialist Party. This is a role where the young radicals can be seen criticizing the main party at the same time as they call on people to vote for it and even to adopt candidates in common, whilst still, in the words of a statement by their president, Fabrice Robert, expanding 'a proposal that is "identitaire", social and ecological which does not aim to compete with the Front National'. [9]

With such a state of affairs, it is hard to discern any sources from which, in either the short or the medium term, political violence might emanate from these circles. Furthermore – and this is a feature worth our attention – with the arrival of Marine le Pen as head of the Front National in 2011, we are witnessing a significant ideological shift on the French extreme right. This shift is clearly linked with the passing of older generations; former militants who were imbued with those trends of thought that were associated with those inspired by Maurras, Pétain or even by neo-fascism, or concerned with the defence of the colonial empire, and who had often provided the protagonists of politically orientated violence in the 1960s and 1970s, have all now disappeared from the political stage.

This change of viewpoint is typified by the arrival of Marine le Pen, a young woman born in 1968, at the head of the Front National in 2011 as an outcome of the party congress held at Tours and of the obliteration of the progressive policy of her father, who was the perfect embodiment of the archetypal militant from the French nationalist right that had been influenced by the wars arising from decolonization. At the present time, these lines of thought no longer attract the support of anyone. Furthermore, the Front National, like Gianfranco Fini's National Alliance in Italy, has been engaged in a strategy of 'de-demonizing' itself, leading it to give up sulphurous references to fascism and the period of the Second World War.

To all this we must add the impact of sociological factors. The first of these is linked with changes in behaviour and with a deep-seated 'de-Christianizing' by which French society has been influenced. These things affected the Front National, whose associated traditional-minded fundamentalist Catholics were in the process of being marginalized both ideologically and numerically.[10] At the present time, the Front National is in step with the developments in French society where abortion and homosexuality are concerned, something which would have been unthinkable ten years or so ago.

The other big factor in the modernization of the French extreme right is to be found in the development of its electorate, which has now little in common with the one which, 30 or 40 years ago, provided the foundations for the nationalist parties. Over the last few years, on the electoral level, the Front

National is in the process of becoming the workers' party for the early years of the twenty-first century. The start of this phenomenon was to be seen towards the latter years of the 1990s, when the party determined to give up its Reaganite character so as to turn to the working class by defining itself as 'the party of labourers and the workers in their struggle against poverty and social injustice' (Charpier 2005). The first advantages of this new approach were vividly to appear at the time of the presidential elections in 2002, when the party of Jean-Marie le Pen emerged a long way ahead of Lionel Jospin's Socialist party as the main party among the working-class elements in the electorate, and this is nowadays confirmed by every opinion poll. Thus we find that a recent opinion poll by IFOP showed that if the presidential election scheduled for 2012 were to take place at the time of writing, Marine le Pen, the Front National candidate, would garner nearly 40 per cent of the working-class vote and 32 per cent of the clerical classes.[11] Moreover, one of the electoral strongholds of the Front National is to be found in a town in the Pas de Calais, Hénin-Beaumont, which used to be communist and which is chiefly made up of former miners. It was in this district that Marine le Pen set herself to storm the party apparatus by attaining a powerful electoral legitimacy when she garnered over 47 per cent of the votes in the municipal elections of 2009 (Monnot and Mestre 2011).

The social basis of the extreme right is thus no longer the same as it was thirty years ago when the traditional middle classes (small traders, small employers) were disproportionately represented in its ranks. These elements are nowadays dwindling, their political causes – typified by the Poujadism of the 1950s – having been taken over by the extreme right. This gradual shift in the social make-up of its electors has clearly had a marked effect on the traditional notions of the extreme right, which has had to take account of the historical background of the French working classes, who are in the main deeply republican and in most cases hostile to the Catholic Church. Thus, the way that workers and the unemployed of European origin have given electoral support to the Front National does not indicate that they share the classic preoccupations of the radical right. In the 1990s, the important vote of the most underprivileged, at a time when electoral support for the Communist party had collapsed[12], mainly indicated a protest against the way the left was moving towards neo-liberalism, as well as anxiety caused by a rising tide of crime and violence in those suburbs that were densely populated by those of immigrant origins[13].

However that may be, the fact that the Front National's expressions of protest had an impact on those elements of society that had historically been unmoved by the attitudes of those on the extreme right has now, paradoxically, led these latter to abandon what, until now, had been their favourite lines of argument. At the present time this can be seen in the way that the Front National puts itself forward as the best defender of the Republic and of those ordinary elements of the population that are supposedly under threat from Islam. It can be seen too in connection with economic issues since, following a phase in the 1980s during which the Front National associated itself with the conservative and market-orientated changes brought about by Thatcher and Reagan, the right wing now defends protectionism and even de-globalization – ideas dear to the heart of French communists and of the left wing of the Socialist party. Even questions concerning the protection of French identity, threatened by massive immigration and by Islam, did not involve any break with the republican heritage of France, for ever since the French Revolution[14] and the Paris Commune, and later the Resistance, patriotism has exerted a strong influence among ordinary people.

All these changes (where the extreme right can be found taking credit for whole swathes of the legacy of the French left such as state interventionism, or the defence of the Republic and of the secular arm of society and even the credit for some aspects of Gaullism) influenced not only the Front National but virtually the whole of the radical right. One might have supposed that, in response to these ideological changes, some militant elements in the population might have reacted with a breakaway movement which, in the traditional manner of this trend, would have reasserted its ideological character. There was nothing, or almost nothing, of the kind. Apart from a few small elements that had developed from fundamentalist Catholicism or from the notion of Algérie Française, no significant groups broke away in an attempt to create a credible alternative to the policy changes that were taking place.

In the context of these developments, mention must be made of the quite fundamental part played by the Nouvelle Droite, best characterised in the influence of Alain de Benoist. This is now, and has been for nearly forty years, one of the main breeding-grounds for those who seek to update the ideology of the French radical right. It was, in fact, the creation of GRECE (Group for Research and Study of European Civilization) in 1969 that marked the beginning of the intellectual renewal of the radical right; this involved a break with the intellectual tradition that had hitherto been a marked feature of Action Française and which was influenced by royalism and by 'fundamentalist' Catholicism (Taguieff 1994). In the awkward circumstances that arose from the defeat of the OAS and of the notion of Algérie Française, and the preponderance of left-wing thinking in the universities, the aim of the young intellectuals forming the Nouvelle Droite was to fight their battle in the field of ideas and to abandon the activism that had characterised the years of struggle against de-colonization.

For those involved with GRECE, the task of renewal at the ideological and theoretical level would, by extolling a genuine 'gramscisme de droite'[15], enable them to prepare for future political success by striving to gain pre-eminence on the intellectual battleground. Today, the political balance-sheet has been modified. If it can be said that the Nouvelle Droite has not managed to make a decisive impact on the parliamentary right, it can on the other hand be argued that it does, at the present time, exercise a masterful ideological influence on that significant element of the extreme right known as 'identitaire'; at the same time, it has succeeded in bringing to the fore a number of underlying lines of thought, and especially in introducing a greater scepticism where the dreams of violent activism are concerned. Among these lines of thought, the predominance of ideas coming more from the left, or even the extreme left, becomes more and more apparent: criticism of globalization, and of the way the world is obliged to focus increasingly on trade; criticism of the concern with economic value; criticism of utilitarianism. For the last fifteen years or so, such criticisms are at the heart of the theoretical work of GRECE and have led it to draw closer, or to try to draw closer, to left-wing university groups such as MAUSS (Anti-Utilitarian Movement in Social Sciences).

Furthermore, a theoretical review like Krizis, established in 1988 by Alain de Benoist, by throwing open its columns to left-wing intellectuals such as Serge Latouche, Jean Baudrillard or Régis Debray, all critics of the neoliberal movement, has fostered the theoretical changes and the willingness to share ideas which have characterised the organizations formed by activist political thinkers. Among the more noteworthy of these developments is the abandonment of arguments deriving from a biology-based type of racism or the view of fascist regimes which saw them as the embodiment of modern ways of thought or of rule through technology (Vietta 1996). In this connection, Alain de Benoist has recently become involved in discussions about the ecological future of the planet by mounting a defence of ideas involving downsizing (Benoist 2007). All these developing ideas are being played out on the ground established by French right-wing radicalism, which now seems to have taken on board the importance of theoretical activity, and, in the great majority of cases, to have given up the violent forms of activism that were in vogue in the 1960s.

At the present time, younger generations of activists are turning away from the traditional radical right, and, in the wake of the Nouvelle Droite, are borrowing heavily from the theoretical arsenal of the extreme left (Bourseiller 2002). This phenomenon is not only to be found in France. Italy, as seen in the experiment of La Casa Pound[16], also provides evidence for this (see below). This experiment has become an undeviating reference-point for the radicals on the French right, especially those from the 'Bloc Identitaire' and 'Egalité et Réconciliation'[17]

The paradigm of La Casa Pound

Italy has always been a source of inspiration for radical political movements, whether of the extreme right or for that matter the extreme left. It is, in fact, the only country of Western Europe to have experienced, as it did in the 1970s, a period of significant armed struggle; in this, unlike what happened in Germany in connection with the RAF, the main participants can be found profiting from the support of significant elements of the population[18]. Thus it came about that for the French extreme right, and subsequent to Benito Mussolini's fascist *ventennio*, groups such as the MSI (Italian Social Movement) or *Ordine Nuevo* provided models that involved ideas concerning both policy and theory, most clearly to be seen in the person of Julius Evola. Nowadays, this continues to be the case, although in a quite different way from what was to be seen in 'les années de plomb'[19], with the foundation in Rome in 2008 of La Casa Pound by former activists on the Italian extreme right during the 1970s, whose position was close to the ideas of the 'third way' and of revolutionary nationalism. Deriving their thinking from the traditions to be found among social groups loyal to the extreme left, these militants – who, in the main, rejected the technique adopted by Gianfranco Fini of making themselves 'respectable' – turned abandoned buildings into places for communal living. Since that time the movement has spread to other Italian towns, and has given its support to mass activism (in forms such as supporters' clubs, free radio stations or rock 'identitaire'[20]) and has broken with the avant-garde notions of the 1970s. This movement has adopted certain left-wing lines of thought, such as the struggle against globalization, as a way of defending the individuality that was under threat from mercantile capitalism. The Casa Pound also played its part, through its involvement with the student body, in the great struggles against the university reforms of the Berlusconi government in October 2008. In 2010, as the result of the death of two immigrant workers in Calabria, the organization, whilst loudly proclaiming its antipathy to immigration, sprang to the defence of the migrants by deploring the exploitative behaviour of the bosses.

So in today's circumstances we find an ideology where traditional arguments about race have been abandoned: a thorough-going updating of ideas borrowed from the left and built up on a basis of involvement with a law-abiding attitude to policy-making; and some promising prospects for future policy, derived from the Front National. It is hard to see where in all this elements might emerge that would imply an upturn among those factions on the radical right that are inclined towards political violence and terrorism, unless perhaps (and this notion needs to be considered carefully) there is something which is felt to benefit the struggle against the 'Islamization' of France and of Europe, a struggle which is to be found at the heart of the propaganda put forward by a majority of those on the extreme right both in France and in Europe.

The question of Islam in France and Europe

In the last few years, the political campaigns linked with the struggle against Islam have become more and more vital to those on the extreme right. With the development of major immigration – felt more and more by significant elements of the population to be out of control (Tandonnet 2006) – coming from the Maghreb and sub-Saharan Africa, and taking place in a worldwide situation which is increasingly marked by the development of radical trends favouring Salafism, in just the same way as Islam has become more and more evident in Western society, all this has led to the increase in a trend of feeling that is markedly hostile in regard to the Muslim religion which is seen as a threat to European civilization (Caldwell 2011). It should, however, be noted that such an attitude is somewhat at odds with the traditions of that part of the French extreme right that was close to activist tendencies in the OAS. At that period, the latter were in fact in favour of the notion of an 'African' element in France, and of the integration of Muslims into the rest of the nation. It has nowadays been forgotten that several of the commanders in the OAS were themselves Muslims, and that some of those trends in Algerian nationalism that were most hostile to the FLN put forward the idea of joint action with the OAS. Thus it was that, on the mainland, one of the individuals who was most in favour of the idea of maintaining Algérie Française was the vice-president of the National Assembly, Pasha Boualem. And it was Jean-Marie le Pen, the future president of the Front National, who asserted in the National Assembly in 1958 when he was a Poujadist Deputy:

> I declare that, from the moral point of view, there is nothing in the Muslim religion which prevents a believing or practising Muslim from becoming a complete French citizen. Quite the contrary. Essentially, his precepts are the same as those of the Christian religion, and the basis of Christian civilisation and of Western civilisation. Furthermore, I do not believe that there any longer remains an Algerian race any more than there remains a French race. (Dard 2011)

In the 1970s, assassinations carried out, especially in Marseilles, by a few ultras favouring Algérie Française were not aimed at Islam as such, but at

Algerian immigrants, who, after the defeat, were turned into being expiatory victims.

At the present time, the radical right is not of one mind where Islam is concerned. One group, Egalité et Réconciliation, is led by a former member of the Front National who has broken away from the party; Alain Sorel extols, for example, the idea of dialogue, even alliances, with certain Muslim organizations in the name of the struggle against 'Zionist and American influence' in France. Alain de Benoist has declared himself hostile to all forms of Islamophobia, and even, at the time of the dispute about dress at Creil in 1989, came down on the side of the girls who wished to wear the Islamic veil whilst at school, defending their right to be different and asserting that the affirmation of community values was an antidote to market-led individualism. Here, then, was one part of the radical right joining those forces on the left which see Islam as a factor in the struggle against capitalist globalization and against American imperialism.

Nonetheless, it remains the case that this 'Islamophile' position is a long way from being shared by the majority. The Front National has adopted a very clear attitude against the 'Islamification' of France by putting itself forward as the defender of secularity in France and by a denunciation of open-air prayers in certain French cities such as Paris, Marseilles or Nice. The 'Bloc Identitaire' has followed in its footsteps, especially so when mobilizing their Nice section (Nissa rebella) in opposition to localized Islamic movements and against open-air prayers. Furthermore, in the name of this struggle, the 'identitaires' do not hesitate to proclaim the link formed with certain small left-wing groups which have worried about the threat posed by Islam to the traditional French republican model. Thus, as recently as in 2010, Assizes held in Paris to deal with 'Islamisation' have been seen to involve, equally well, militants coming from the left such as 'Riposte Laique'[21] and those from the 'Bloc Identitaire'. On top of that, on the web, where the radical right is very active, numerous sites have appeared such as 'L'Observatoire de l'Islamisation', 'François de Souche' or 'Polemia'; these all make resistance to Islamisation a main plank in their political reflections

Thus, despite the resistance of one part of the radical right, this is a theme which is probably destined to become a central feature of French political life in the years to come. On the one hand (and many opinion polls show this to be the case) anxiety on the score of Islam is shared by many French people. This anxiety, the manifestation of a growing cultural insecurity is, as has recently been shown by a French geographer, Christophe Guilluy, to be seen in the movement of populations of a separatist cast of mind: Europeans, especially through their refusal to live alongside Muslim immigrants, are leaving the outer suburbs of big, globalized cities to set themselves up in areas which are either rural or on the very fringes of cities (Guilluy 2010).

There is, in consequence, a social and a political redistribution, pregnant with significant risks, that is in the process of establishing itself in France. This cultural separatism is steadily shaping a landscape hitherto unknown in the history of the Republic, where communities are created which are more or less mutually hostile, and which are becoming more and more geographically separated, and all against a background of 'identitaire' radicalization amongst one part of the groups of those originating in the Maghreb and sub-Saharan Africa. In such circumstances, it is not impossible that radical groups might emerge that are dedicated to carrying out a violent struggle against the alleged Islamification of France. This scenario cannot be entirely excluded, since the most recent manifestations of right-wing terrorism were the work of neo-Nazis, nowadays moribund as a political force, by the PNFE (Nationalist French and European Party) which, in 1986 and 1989, made attacks on the meeting-places of immigrant Muslim workers[22], whilst in 2007, a few attempts by former members of Unité Radicale intending to blow up a mosque were thwarted by the security services (Leclercq 2010).

Conclusion

In the last ten years or so, the ideological and the human picture presented in France by the extreme right has evolved considerably. This is partly because the militant-minded generations of the post-Second World War era who had been influenced by the impact of the Vichy period, by anti-communism and especially by the war in Algeria have now given way to a new generation of men and women who have broken from this heritage. Furthermore, and despite persistent efforts to demonize their activities, which were prompted by their steadily growing place in the electoral system, the way that this trend has become progressively more important in the legitimate political life of the country has tended to create a barrier against any consequent temptation to violence, let alone terrorism, which might have shown itself. This phenomenon is also to be found in the context where the ideological landscape has been through a significant upheaval as a result of the near-disappearance of the traditional mould for the national right wing.

Nowadays, the old trends which had developed from Action Française and from the extreme right-wing elements of Vichy and Catholicism, which provided the leadership for political violence in the 1960s, are now in the process of disappearing from the scene, and survive only in marginal form. Equally, the most violent trends of neo-Nazism, located during the 1980s in such bodies as FANE or PNFE whose past had made recourse to terrorist violence a possibility, are now in the throes of extinction, surviving only in the virtual form of internet sites which get swallowed up in the great ebb and flow of the web. Today, also, the pages of that part of royalism that was minded to insurrection and anti-communist activism have been turned, in the same way as references to Marshal Pétain or Adolf Hitler as tutelary figures have disappeared. Following on the ideological studies carried out by Alain de Benoist's GRECE, the hour belongs to the defence of the regional and national sense of identity which had been built on the abandonment of old theories based on biological racism.

In this connection, the French extreme right (if so it can still properly be called) is now to be found forming part of that populist surge in Europe which, from Flanders to the north of Italy, taking in Holland and Switzerland en route, sees parties developing which do not seem to have much in common with the classic forms of fascism. What is more, the electoral successes that have been achieved by populist trends throughout Europe are a fundamental factor in the process where dreams of political and terrorist violence have been exploded through showing how keeping within the law, along with mass effort, can prove effective.

Does this mean that all prospects of political violence on the part of the extreme right should now be written off? Obviously not. There are, certainly, basic attitudes which do not argue for any such prospect in the short or medium term; but, in the much longer term, there is the possibility that the ever more substantial presence of Muslim immigrants on French and European soil might create the circumstances for more and more violent opposition. For the time being, peaceful denunciation of Islam, which in France brings together people from both the left and the right, has generally derived its intellectual baggage from the classical French political legacy, namely the Republic and the secular arm of the State. In these circumstances, and despite efforts to rule it out by terming it 'Islamophobia', opposition to Islam is to be found striking a familiar note, which at times recalls the years of anti-clericalism at the time of the struggles by the Republic against the Catholic Church at the start of the twentieth century. However, the trend which is hostile to Islam might become radicalized, and take on forms which tie in with the kinds of violence seen in the past, notably in the surge of racist crimes seen in Marseilles in the 1970s or in the series of attacks on the meeting-places of immigrant workers in the 1980s. Even if this possibility does not pose any immediate threat, the radicalization of the 'identitaires' now going on in France, and more broadly in Europe too, might make such a prospect credible at some point in the future which is difficult to pinpoint.

Notes

1 There will be no consideration here of those episodes of terrorism which had foreign origin, especially those linked with the Iran-Iraq war which caused the deaths of seven people in Paris in 1986, with around fifty wounded, or with the repercussions of the civil war in Algeria when assaults by the GIA (Armed Islamic Group) brought ten deaths and some 100 wounded during 1993.

2 OSARN (Secret Organisation for National Revolutionary Action) was formed in 1936 by former militant members of Action Française (a royalist group) who were critical of the softness of Charles Maurras' organisation. Once the Popular Front had come to power, OSARN, which saw itself linked to Italian fascism, sought to set up an atmosphere of political tension, not altogether unlike the situation found in Italy in the 1970s. Thus it was in September 1937 that this group organised an assault on the Paris headquarters of the French employers' association which led to two deaths. This action was intended to throw the blame on the French communists, and to prepare public opinion for a coup d'état to overthrow the discredited republican regime.

3 In the summer of 1955, the area round Philippeville (Skikda) was notable for the massacres of Europeans that were organised by FLN groups under the leadership of Zighout Youcef. The best known of these was in the village of El Halia.

4 At this time, Franco's Spain was the ultimate base for the activism of the pieds-noirs. With the defeat of the OAS, a number of militants took refuge in the Iberian Peninsula.

5 This 'Groupe Charles Martel' (the Frankish nobleman who halted the Arab invaders at the battle of Poitiers in 732) made sporadic appearances throughout the 1970s and 1980s with the murder of men of Arab origin and attacks which targeted organisations that were closely associated with those in power in Algeria. Its latest manifestation was to be seen in 2010, when threats were made against cinemas which were showing the film 'Hors La Loi' (Beyond the Law) which was held to be too sympathetic to the FLN.

6 Occident came into being in 1964, and was made illegal by the Ministry of the Interior in 1968. It was created by young militants belonging to the Federation of Nationalist Students in the context of the war in Algeria. This organisation was to leave its mark through having among its ranks several future Ministers in the Fifth Republic (Alain Madelin, Patrick Devedjian, Gérard Longuet). It quickly moved on from the period concerned with Algérie Française to set its sights on the extreme left. The group never had more than a few dozen militants and made its existence felt though confrontations in the streets, especially against Maoists.

7 'Identitaire', a trend on the extreme right which urges the defence of European identity when confronted by American hegemony or by 'Islamisation'. Its main characteristics include harking back to the

pre-Christian (pagan) past, and a vigorous hostility to a market-orientated society. [Translator's Note : Since an English equivalent of 'identitaire' is not widely used the word is left untranslated but in quotation marks, wherever it occurs in the original text.]

8 Militant activisism: demonstrations against Muslim open-air prayers, and against delinquent behaviour of the young offspring of immigrants, together with social activity aimed at the underprivileged (soup kitchens for example).

9 See Xavier Eman, 'Naissance d'un Nouveau Parti, Ni Droite ni Gauche: identitaires', *Le Choc du Mois*, 35, January 2010.

10 The Front's fundamentalist Catholic component typified by Bernard Antony, a former member of the OAS who had rejoined the Front National in 1984, condemned the way the party was developing over questions of moral behaviour, and seems now to have left the organisation.

11 See IFOP, 'Voting Intentions for the 2012 Presidential Elections,' *Le Journal du Dimanche*, 23 May 2011.

12 The fact that one part of the Front National would very much like to take over some of the ground left empty by the decline of the French Communist party is beyond question. Thus, the decision to hold the party's congress in December 2011 at Tours, the birthplace of the PCF, was unlikely to have been fortuitous.

13 For a criminological interpretation of the rise of the Front National in France, see the article by Xavier Raufer, Front National: sur les motifs d'une ascension, *Le Debat,* 63, January-February 1991.

14 In 2006, on the occasion of the anniversary of the battle of Valmy in September 1792, when revolutionary forces drove back the Prussian army, Jean-Marie Le Pen (who had emerged from a political background that was broadly hostile to the French Revolution) was to be found making a speech which celebrated the victory of the republican troops.

15 Antonio Gramsci, one of the founders of the Italian Communist party in 1921, used to stress the importance of ideological effort and of the need to ensure that intellectual dominance was successfully transferred to the heart of the masses, this being a necessary precondition for seizing power. See Pour un Gramscisme du Droite, *Proceedings of the 16th national assembly of GRECE,* Éditions du Labyrinthe, 1982.

16 Extreme left/extreme right: a stocktaking of the confusion. La Casa Pound. See *Ni Patrie, Ni Frontières*, 36–37 at http://www.mondialisme.org/spip.php?article1703

17 This is an association formed in 2007 by a former Communist party and Front National militant, Alain Sorel. Finding himself unable to accept the line taken by the FN, which he felt to be Islamophobe, he defended the idea of reconciliation between French Muslims and the rest of the country as part of the struggle against Zionism and the United States.

18 See the chapter by Guido Panvini, Black Terrorism and Red Terrorism during the 'Années de Plomb': War will not happen, in *L'Italie des Années de Plomb, le Terrorisme entre Histoire et Mémoire,* edited by *Marc Lazar* and *Marie-Anne Matard-Bonucci, Paris: Autrement 2011.*

19 Translator's Note: 'Les années de plomb' (literally 'the leaden years') is a term used in connection with Italy in the 1970s and 1980s when there was a significant amount of violence.
20 Rock groups which extol nationalist ideas in their songs.
21 Another association formed in 2007 by militants from the secular element of society which felt that the political left was too easy-going where the Muslim religion was concerned.
22 The only attack where blood was shed took place at a centre called Sonacotra at Cagnes-sur-Mer in December 1988, which led to one death and twelve wounded.

References

Benoist (de) A. (2007). *Demain la Décroissance! Penser l'Ecologie Jusqu'au Bout,* E-dite.
Bourseiller, C. (2002). *La Nouvelle Extrême-Droite,* Editions du Rocher.
Caldwell, C. (2011). *Une Révolution sous nos Yeux, Comment l'Islam va Transformer la France et l'Europe,* Editions du Toucan.
Charpier, F. (2005). *Génération Occident,* Editions du Seuil.
Dard, O. (2011). *Voyage au Cœur de l'OAS,* Perrin.
Eman, X. 'Naissance d'un Nouveau Parti, Ni Droite ni Gauche: Identitaires', *Le Choc du Mois,* 35, January 2010.
Institut Français d'Opinion Publique (IFOP), 'Voting Intentions for the 2012 Presidential Elections,' *Le Journal du Dimanche,* 23 May 2011.
Gautier, J.-P. (2009). *Les Extrêmes Droites en France, de la Traversée du Désert à l'Ascension du Front National (1945–2008),* Editions Syllepse.
Giudice, F. (1992). *Arabicides, une Chronique Française (1970–1991),* La Découverte.
Gramsci, A. (1982). Pour un Gramscisme du Droite, *Proceedings of the 16th National Assembly of GRECE,* Éditions du Labyrinthe.
Guilluy, C. (2010). *Fractures Françaises,* François Bourin éditeur.
Huyghe, F.-B. (2011). *Terrorismes, Violence et Propagande,* coll. Découvertes, Gallimard.
Leclercq, J. (2010). *Droites Conservatrices, Nationales et Ultras, Dictionnaire 2005–2010,* L'Harmattan.
Lefeuvre, D. (2006). *Pour en Finir avec la Repentance Coloniale,* Flammarion.
Maitron, J. (2007). *Le Mouvement Anarchiste en France, Des origines à 1914* (tome 1) coll. Tel, Gallimard.
Monneret, J. (2008). *La Guerre d'Algérie en Trente-Cinq Questions,* L'Harmattan.
Monnot, C., Mestre A. (2011). *Le Système Le Pen, Enquête sur les Réseaux du Front National,* Denoël.
Panvini, G. (2011). Black Terrorism and Red Terrorism during the 'Années de Plomb': War will not Happen, in *L'Italie des Années de Plomb, le Terrorisme entre Histoire et Mémoire,* Marc Lazar and Marie-Anne Matard-Bonucci (eds), Paris: Autrement.

Raufer, X. Front National: sur les Motifs d'une Ascension, *Le Debat,* 63, January-February 1991.
Sternhell Z. (2000). *Ni Droite ni Gauche, L'idéologie Fasciste en France*, Fayard.
Taguieff, P.-A. (1994). *Sur la Nouvelle Droite*, Descartes & Compagnie.
Tandonnet M. (2006). *Immigration, Sortir du Chaos*, Flammarion.
Vial, E. (2010). *La Cagoule a Encore Frappé*, Larousse.
Vietta S. (1996). *Heidegger, Critique du National-Socialisme et de la Technique*, Pardès.

9

Breivik's Mindset: The Counterjihad and the New Transatlantic Anti-Muslim Right

Toby Archer

Introduction: Breivik's manifesto

On 22 July 2011 a bombing in central Oslo followed rapidly by a mass shooting on the small island of Utøya, not far from the capital, shocked Norway and the wider world. When armed police reached Utøya, Anders Behring Breivik, a 32-year-old Norwegian man, surrendered to them. Breivik had shot dead 69 people on the island whilst an additional eight had been killed by the bomb in Oslo; 151 further people were injured in the attacks but survived. The fact that he targeted a youth camp on Utøya, and that therefore many of those killed were only teenagers, only added to the horror of the crime.

Less than two hours before the bomb exploded in Oslo, Breivik sent just over 1,000 people around the world who he felt would be sympathetic to his cause a copy of a document that has become known as his manifesto (*Guardian* 26/7/11). The manifesto is a rambling document, reaching a little over 1500 pages in PDF format, written all in English and entitled *2083: A European Declaration of Independence* (Breivik 2011). The title page states that it is 'by Andrew Berwick – London 2011' but it quickly became apparent that this Anglicised version of his name was merely a pen name and the document had been compiled and written in Norway (*Time* 24/7/11; BBC 25/7/11).

The document is more than just a manifesto. Alongside being a political treatise on how he sees Europe and the world, *2083* is also a diary of his preparations for the attacks including lengthy descriptions of his own mental state, a media pack – including staged photographs – in preparation for what he correctly predicted would be worldwide media attention, a technical manual on how to build bombs and select weapons for attacking one's enemies, and much else beside. It includes large amounts of material from other authors that he republishes, along with unacknowledged sections that he has plagiarized. At numerous points in the document, Breivik states that he believes his attack will be a 'martyrdom operation' that he will not survive[1]. In this light, the document can be seen as Breivik's preparation to attempt to posthumously explain what he seemed to realise would be inexplicable to many. The depth of political analysis and argument he goes into in the document would suggest that he wanted to be seen as politically motivated, and realised that in doing so he would be labelled a terrorist. Nevertheless, this did not seem to trouble him:

> Most people will today openly condemn us as terrorists. However, a hundred years from now we will be celebrated as pioneers, as heroes who gave their lives combating a tyrant oppressor. (Breivik 2011: 1350)

Expecting death, he wanted to make sure that his political motivation for committing such a heinous crime was understood. This essay is an attempt to do this – to treat Breivik as a politically or ideologically motivated terrorist, just as analysts do with others who commit political violence around the world. Of course there are valid questions for psychologists, psychiatrists and other mental health researchers to ask in terms of whether Anders Behring Breivik was suffering from some type of mental health disorder at the time of the attack, and indeed that he was was the initial conclusion of court-appointed experts, but this is not a question that is often asked of the Palestinian or Iraqi suicide bomber, of Jihadi terrorists around the world, or of ethno-nationalists radicals be they Basque, Corsican or Tamil. In these cases, most in the West are willing to take their justifications, explanations and ideological or theological exegesis at face value, even if they are morally abhorrent to us. We do not just call them mad and look no further; Breivik should be treated in the same way. This is not to say that we should trust Breivik's words; he has already been proven to be a liar on some points (on Breivik as an untrustworthy narrator, see Dalton 2011[1]) and much more in his tract appears to be fantasy rather than fact. Nevertheless, *2083* is what Breivik wants us to believe, and this is important even if none of it is true.

Central to Breivik's view of the world is a fear that Islam is taking over Europe, and that European elites – particularly those of liberal and left-wing traditions – are complicit in the supposed surrender of the continent to what he believes is an alien cultural and religious tradition. These beliefs, called by many who subcribe to them 'the Counterjihad', are by no means particular to Breivik. Indeed large portions of *2083* consist of reprinting the work of various writers who hold this world view. It is this intellectual milieu that Breivik overtly identifies which is the central focus of what follows. Many in Europe (and in other countries around the world) share his world view, even if they condemn his actions. The influences of the Counterjihad ideology are now visible in the electoral politics of many European countries and provide a rallying point for populist right-wing parties. There are also street movements and other political groups pushing the ideology both in Europe and beyond. In particular, the Counterjihad is reinvigorating anti-immigration politics by avoiding the racism of the far-right and instead providing a critical discourse on Islam and Muslims which claims to be a liberal critique, even if the outcome – the demonization of certain minority social groups – is not dissimilar.

A new right: The counterjihad – against Islam, 'cultural Marxists' and neo-Nazis

In the immediate aftermath of the attacks in Norway, the BBC published an article entitled 'Norway's far right not a spent force' (BBC 23/7/11). The writer noted that Breivik had described himself as a 'nationalist' and from this, described him in the context of the small neo-Nazi scene that existed in Norway in the 1990s and to a lesser extent in the 2000s. But in *2083: A European Declaration of Independence*, in outlining what Breivik calls the 'Vienna School' to which he subscribes, he argues that amongst the things that it opposes are racism, fascism, Nazism and totalitarianism (Breivik 2011: 1233). Indeed, in the section of his document where he interviews himself, he answers a question about how will it feel to be deemed by some to be 'just another Nazi fascist disguised with anti-Muslim rhetoric'? Breivik's answer is that this is ridiculous, because he will work with people of any race who oppose Islam and that 'The old definitions do not apply anymore. The current internationalist elites (cultural Marxists, suicidal humanists, globalists) are the Nazis of our age and deliberately collaborating with the Muslims' (Breivik 2011: 1354).

'The Vienna School' appears to be Breivik's own suggestion for a name for this new anti-Islam, anti-immigration school of thought that is now more commonly called the Counterjihad. 'Vienna' refers to the Battle of Vienna in 1683 (which is one explanation for why Breivik picked 2083, the 400th anniversary of the battle, as the title of his document). This battle broke the Ottoman siege of that city and ended Ottoman incursions into central Europe. It has become symbolic for many opposing Islam in contemporary Europe. Indeed one of the most prominent blogs of the Counterjihad school of thought, a blog listed by Breivik as a leading site for 'the Vienna School' (Breivik 2011: 1236) and cited numerous times elsewhere in his text, is called 'the Gates of Vienna'. Breivik's second argument for this name is that 'the Vienna School' would stand against 'the Frankfurt School' of Theodor Adorno and other left-wing German intellectuals of the inter-war period from which the idea of critical theory originated. Breivik writes much about the Frankfurt School in his text, but his interest in German interwar sociology has American roots. Investigative journalist and expert on the US far right, Chip Berlet, quickly realised that Breivik's manifesto had used large sections of text from a 2004 publication of the Free Congress Foundation, edited and in part authored by a William S. Lind. This leaflet argues that political correctness is 'cultural Marxism' and is the product of the Frankfurt School (Berlet 2011). Professor Martin Jay of Berkley, a historian of the Frankfurt School, has written previously about how the Frankfurt School, including a very incorrect reading of their position, has become an important meme in the conspiracy theory-drenched far right (and to some degree far left) (Jay 2010) and this helps us to understand the genesis of Breivik's interest in the issue, rather than the nature of the Frankfurt School itself.

Breivik believes the Frankfurt School to be the source of what he sees as the traitorous betrayal of Europe by its own leaders, continuously describing his non-Muslim enemies in his document as 'cultural Marxists' and arguing the term is interchangeable with 'multiculturalist'. When Breivik called the police from Utøya, moreover, he used his full name and introduced himself as the commander of the 'Norwegian anti-communist resistance' (*Telegraph* 24/11/11), clearly demonstrating who he sees as the threat to be resisted.

There is little that is brief about the 1,500 pages Breivik released, but his claims for his document do succinctly sum up his world view:

> It covers most topics related to historical events and aspects of past and current Islamic Imperialism, which is now removed or falsified by our academia by instruction of Western Europe's cultural relativist elites (cultural relativism=cultural Marxism). It offers [a] thorough analysis of Islam, which is unknown to a majority of Europeans. It documents how the political doctrines known as multiculturalism/cultural Marxism/cultural relativism was [sic.] created and implemented. Multiculturalists/cultural Marxists usually operate under the disguise of humanism. A majority are

anti-nationalists and want to deconstruct European identity, traditions, culture and even nation states. (Breivik 2011: 5)

Those writers and bloggers who Breivik cites extensively have never used his suggested label of 'the Vienna School'. As noted above, they call themselves 'the Counterjihad'. Counterjihad writers and activists have condemned Breivik's actions and have sought to distance themselves from him. Nevertheless, Breivik's own words show that he felt that his actions were the logical endpoint of a world view that he shared with such writers — of a threat to Western civilization and traditions from Islam and from its own left-wing elites — and this alone makes the Counterjihad worthy of study.

History

The Counterjihad is now describabable as a political movement with a defined programme and ideology. It has emerged in a relatively short period of time from a much wider discourse that includes many voices who were in some way critical of the religion of Islam, the cultural and/or political practices of some Muslims, or merely fearful of terrorism post–9/11. To appreciate where the movement is now, it is important to consider the recent historical development of anti-Islamic political thought and action on both sides of the Atlantic.

One of the leading bloggers of the Counterjihad, Edward 'Ned' May, who writes predominantly under the pseudonym of Baron Bodissey, has produced a history of the Counterjihad. May claims that, as a movement, it can trace its antecedents to those medieval European kings and knights who fought against Islamic armies that were bidding to take control of Europe (Gates of Vienna 24/11/11). All political movements have their heroes, but it is perhaps more useful to see the Counterjihad as a far more modern phenomenon. I argue that the Counterjihad is fundamentally a product of both the 9/11 attacks on the United States and the connectivity brought about by the internet over the last decade. Without these two factors its seems unlikely that the Counterjihad would exist now in form that it does. This is not to argue that tension arising from Muslim (and other) immigration did not exist in Europe prior to 9/11 — it clearly did, but access to the internet transnationalized the issue and the violence of 9/11 connected Islam to violence in the minds of some and hardened opinions.

As noted above, the two central themes of the Counterjihad are the belief that Islam threatens Western civilization and a distrust of domestic elites in the West. The latter not only includes elected politicians but also the opinion leaders, such as journalists and academics, and non-elected policy makers, such as senior police officers, civil servants and local authorities. Resistance to immigration and a populist distrust of the authorities is clearly nothing new; most of the western European democracies have political parties that hold ideologies that in some way accord with these two general themes. The same is also now true of most of the eastern European, post-Cold War democracies. Due to the two-party structure of the American political system, there is not a specifically anti-immigrant, populist party but there are long traditions of nativism and populism in both the Democratic and Republican parties. Currently these strains are most obvious with the Tea Party movement, mainly a faction of the Republicans. Populist and nativist parties have also been seen at different times in Australia, New Zealand and Canada. In recent years, particularly in Europe, such populist and anti-immigration parties have generally been identified as being on the right and often called 'far right'. This term is of course problematic; the populist radical parties in Scandinavia, for example, generally do not stand against the welfare state, rather they just hold that immigrants should have no access to it. Also politicians on the left sometimes use populist rhetoric criticizing immigration. Nevertheless, in the last five years, the Counterjihad ideas have most often been articulated by politicians from these populist right-wing parties, and Counterjihad bloggers have openly supported such parties (see below). It is therefore unsurprising if the Counterjihad is sometimes called 'far right', even if this label is not particularly helpful. Nevertheless, understanding how the Counterjihad differs from traditional European far-right politics is central to understanding it. In turn, this places Breivik's actions in a more accurate context.

The diverse origins of anti-Muslim sentiments

As argued above, concern over the impact Islam has on the West and over Muslims living in Europe is central to the Counterjihad. Many see the rise of 'Islamophobia'[2] in Europe and North America as a phenomenon resulting from 9/11 and the connections made after it between Muslims and terrorism. It is undoubtedly true that the media coverage of Jihadist terrorism and of social tension resulting from differences between Muslim and majority communities in Western countries has massively increased since 9/11 but these issues existed prior to that now-infamous day. In the UK, the fatwa against Salman Rushdie both politicized some British Muslims as well as created critics of Islam in wider British society who were horrified to see books being burnt and a writer being threatened. In the United States, fear of 'Islamic terrorism' predated 9/11, particularly in relation to the first World Trade Centre bombing in 1993, with researchers like Steven Emerson exposing radical activity within the United States but also being accused of scaremongering (see Ali et al. 2011: 47–51). Nevertheless, it was clearly the al-Qaeda terrorist attacks on Washington and New York in 2001 that really brought the subject of Islam to the fore of public debate.

Concerns that Islam somehow promoted violence and that Muslim communities in Western countries were living with parallel ethical standards was by no means solely an issue for the right or the far right. There were liberal, left and feminist critiques of Islam that predated 9/11. For example, when in the late 1990s the Clinton administration began some discussion with the Taliban, who were by then the de facto government of Afghanistan, the negotiations led nowhere in the main due to domestic pressure on the US administration over the status of women in Afghanistan, organised by the US feminist movement, Feminist Majority (Rashid 2001: 182). Atheists, secularists and humanists also were amongst the voices condemning Islamic fundamentalism, again often focusing on the position of women within Islam, or on prejudices expressed by some Muslims against religious minorities within Muslim countries, or against women, homosexuals and Jews more generally. Nevertheless, in Europe and the US there were also many left and liberal voices warning against scapegoating all Muslims for the crimes committed by terrorists who claimed to be acting in the name of religion.

The US decision to invade Iraq divided the left far more than the invasion of Afghanistan. Some in the US and UK in particular saw the Iraq war as a humanitarian intervention that would free Iraqis from totalitarianism, even if it was launched with questionable motives (see for example Cohen 2007: 7–8). Nevertheless, even in those two countries that led the invasion, most on the left opposed the war. In the UK what was called 'the pro-war left' by those who opposed it, but sometimes referred to itself by Michael Walzer's term 'the decent left' (Walzer 2002), was highly critical of British Muslim organizations over their attitudes to issues such as women, homosexuals and anti-semitism (Archer 2009: 338–9). On the other hand the 'anti-war left' created new alliances between peace organizations, radical left groups and British Islamist organizations. The apogee of this trend was when in 2004 former Labour MP George Galloway founded the Respect Party. He was elected to Parliament representing the party in 2005. Various prominent Muslim activists, such as Anas Altikriti, were party members and have stood for office in local or national elections (see Yaqoob 2007: 281–4).

Particularly the bombings in Madrid in 2004 and then in London in 2005 put a spotlight on the politics within European Muslim communities as they became seen as ever more threatening. Often it was not the threat of violence emanating from such communities that concerned some on the left, who were willing to see that as a fringe activity of just a handful of individuals. Rather it was wider political questions about the impact of socially conservative Muslim communities on wider society – be that the role of women, attitudes to homosexuality, anti-Semitism and anti-Israeli positions. Another strain within this criticism came from the anti-religious, from writers such as Richard Dawkins and Christopher Hitchens. At the same time other sections of the left were allying with Muslim organizations to protest against US, UK and their allies' policies in Iraq and in the wider Middle East. With accusations of Islamophobia going one way, and appeasement of tyranny the other, a 'civil war' developed within the left. Divisions over where to draw a line between criticizing *all* Muslims and *only* criticizing Jihadi violence and/or social oppression coming from conservative interpretations of Islam meant that, to a great extent, the left ceded the field on which the battles of multiculturalism were being fought to the right. Although those critical of Islam from a leftist or liberal position are sometimes accused of Islamophobia, there still seems to be an essential difference between them and the writers and activists of the Counterjihad. Those coming from the left are critical of Islam for what they see as the limits the religion puts on individuals, where, it is perceived, moral worth originates in a cosmopolitan normative position. Contrarily, the Counterjihad is a communitarian stance, seeing moral value in the collective – in this case the collective being an arguably romanticized image of European nation-states of the modern era.

The Counterjihad styles itself as being in the 'classical liberal tradition', standing up for universal human rights (Gates of Vienna 1/12/11) and it is from this position that it announces its anti-racism. Nevertheless, as an Islam-critical discourse has produced an actual movement (see below) it has become less ideologically diverse and many texts from Counterjihad writers are far from liberal. For the Counterjihad, a rejection of Islam in the West is no longer enough; other political positions have increasingly become part of the 'package'. Some of these could be identified with the right or far right, although their strong support of Israel is obviously not a historical feature of the European far right[3]. Indeed in Breivik's document, he lists the positions that he sees as going with the central resistance to Islam in the Counterjihad. Breivik lists 'anti-feminism', 'anti-pacifism', 'anti-EU(SSR)'[4], and 'anti-matriarchy' alongside resistance to Islam (Breivik 2011: 1234). One of the Counterjihad's leading essayists, Fjordman – the pseudonym of one Peder Jensen, a fellow Norwegian of Breivik – wrote in 2006 an article entitled *How the Feminists' 'War against Boys' paved the way for Islam* (Fjordman 2006). This essay, which Breivik republishes in full in his manifesto, is indicative of how these various ideas come together and the misogyny of Fjordman is a good example of why the Counterjihad's claims to the liberal tradition can be treated with scepticism. It also shows how critics of Islam from a left or liberal position are unlikely now to be comfortable within the movement which includes what have been described as such misogynist views (on the misogyny of Fjordman and Breivik, see Dalton 2011[2] and Repo 2011).

Geopolitical difference

The Counterjihad is very much a transatlantic phenomenon, with much sharing of ideas between Europeans and Americans and daily linking between blogs and websites on both sides of the Atlantic, but geo-politics still matter. Most Americans saw 9/11 very much as an attack on the homeland by foreign powers, hence the response – the invasion of Afghanistan and later Iraq – were foreign policy responses. There are many Muslim Americans, but they are diverse geographically, ethnically, religiously and politically. They are on average more likely to be better educated, wealthier and more integrated into majority society than European Muslims. There are also Arab-Americans who are not Muslim. American Muslims have faced prejudice, and considerable problems arising from counter-terrorism policing, but more generally the American 'war on terrorism' narrative looked overseas for an enemy, particularly whilst considerable numbers of troops were in Iraq and Afghanistan. George Bush directly made this link, justifiying the Iraq war saying: 'We are fighting these terrorists with our military in Afghanistan and Iraq and beyond so we do not have to face them in the streets of our own cities' (Bush 2004).

The situation in Europe was very different. Terrorism did come to European cities, first in Madrid and later in London, with the perpetrators coming from those societies, or at least having lived within them for many years, and there have been other notable attacks or attempted attacks such as the Stockholm suicide bombing in 2010 and the killing of American servicemen at Frankfurt airport in 2011. Additionally, security forces across Europe have disrupted many other plots. Secondly, and predating 9/11, there were already tensions in European societies between communities of immigrant descent and wider society. The religion of these minorities mattered less than their ethnicity before 9/11. In the summer of 2001, before the attacks in the US, the north of England saw serious rioting in number of towns and cities; this was seen generally as related to problems faced by the 'Asian' or 'Pakistani' community as opposed to Muslims (Archer 2009: 334). After 9/11 and with the sense that there was a threat of violence stemming from Muslims, the religious identity became central to European Muslims, in some cases as a self-selected identity and in others, an identity imposed upon them by media and wider society. Within Europe, the idea that Islam threatens the continent came to be seen predominantly in terms of immigration. Social change was seen as the threat, as reflected in the myriad of debates around Europe over symbolic issues such as burkhas and minarets. The Counterjihad, particularly as a network of bloggers on the internet, has played an important part in bringing these individual political debates or conflicts in different cities and countries of the continent together – to create a discourse claiming that this is the same conflict across Europe. Breivik's writings reflect this; although describing himself as a nationalist and expressing a loathing of the EU (of which, of course, Norway is not a member), the very title of his work is a 'European declaration of independence' and there is much within his manifesto about the need for 'European cultural conservatives' to work together – he lists most nationalist and culturally conservative political parties and organizations that he has discovered (Breivik 2011: sections 3.107, 3.108) and even goes as far as to estimate (with no obvious justification of where or why he suggests those numbers) 'Western European battle-ready cultural conservatives' who he believes are ready to join the fight (Breivik 2011: 1256).

It is noticeable that in recent years, activists in the Counterjihad in the United States – Pamela Geller of the blog 'Atlas Shrugs' and Robert Spencer of 'Jihad Watch' most notably – have been successful at introducing more 'European'-style societal tensions over a supposed threat presented by Muslim citizens into the US debate. This is particularly the case with what was to be called Park51, an Islamic cultural centre in Manhattan, but was successfully dubbed by its critics, led by Geller, as the 'Ground Zero mosque' (*NYT* 8/10/10). There were numerous protests against the building of the cultural centre. The keynote speaker at a rally against the project, held on the 11 September 2010, was Geert Wilders (*PressEurop* 13/10/10). Wilders is the controversial Dutch MP, widely known for his ardent anti-Islam positions and, as a result of those statements, his need for constant personal protection and a failed prosecution for inciting hatred and discrimination (see Witte in this volume). Many in the Counterjihad see Wilders as among their greatest heroes.

From a discourse to a movement

There were other Europeans at the New York anti-'Ground Zero mosque' protest in September 2010 besides Geert Wilders. A group of Englishmen were present, some holding a banner based on the Cross of St George, but with an Israeli flag making up one quarter, an American flag another quarter, the phrase 'no mosque at ground zero' in the third, and in the fourth the initials 'EDL' (*Guardian* 12/11/10). Indeed the English Defence League support for the protest was meant to be slightly larger but the EDL's leader Stephen Yaxley-Lennon, who uses the pseudonym 'Tommy Robinson', had been stopped from entering the US the previous day at JFK airport.

This 2010 protest against the mosque/cultural centre had become rather symbolic of the Counterjihad. It was organised by ardently anti-Muslim American bloggers whose websites have hundreds of thousands of readers a month, but also with a wider echo-chamber of other bloggers linking to those sites and regular coverage on various right-of-centre media channels such as Fox News. These activists have links to some well-known political figures on the American right – such as the former Bush administration UN ambassador John Bolton, who spoke at the protest via video link, and the former Speaker of the House of Representatives Newt Gingrich[5]. They also have the connections and funding[6] to bring a major European political leader to the States for the event – in this case Geert Wilders. Additionally, activists from an English street movement with well-publicized connections to the world of organised football hooliganism crossed the Atlantic to lend their support, perhaps to repay the support that they had received from those prominent US-based bloggers who championed the EDL as non-racist and the victim of a smear campaign on the part of the mainstream media.

The Counterjihad formed and has taken on a certain structure and shape in the years since 2001. Its origins are in what is perhaps best described as a the post–9/11 transatlantic critical discourse on Islam. That criticism was aimed at Jihadi terrorism but in many cases also at some aspects of wider Islamic politics and practice, particularly amongst Muslims living in the West, as well as at the policies of states that are Islamic. Yet, as argued above, this criticism came from diverse origins and not all would either join the Counterjihad as it formed into a movement, or be embraced by the movement's prime figures. Secondly, the medium through which the Counterjihad has formed, the 'blogosphere', has matured greatly over the last decade. Blogging was only beginning to achieve any real level of popularity and reach in the years following 9/11 and it was only during the 2004 presidential election in the United States that bloggers and the online non-traditional media were seen to be having significant and immediate impacts on electoral politics. Clearly the internet has been central in allowing people to form a community of interest, such as the Counterjihad, learn from each other and reinforce each others' views, and in negating older resource problems in communicating, particularly internationally. It has allowed instantaneous linkages between different countries and has understandably built a feeling of community as activists in one state relate their experiences and beliefs and find something similar is happening in other states; this has produced a hardening of views (on the process of group polarization via the internet, see Sunstein 2001: 69–73).

The more organised group self-identifying as the Counterjihad may have grown out of this wider discourse, but its start as an actual movement can be dated to when a group of activists and bloggers came together in Copenhagen in April 2007. As recorded at the time by Edward May of the Gates of Vienna blog, who was one of the organisers of this first meeting: 'The purpose of the meeting was to bring various groups into face-to-face acquaintance with one another, and to share information that would help them formulate strategies to oppose sharia and resist Islamisation in their various countries' (Gates of Vienna 25/11/11). This first event was called the UK and Scandinavia Counterjihad summit, but some attended from countries outside those countries showing wider interest and enthusiasm for the project. Later in the same year another conference was organised, this time in Brussels. This conference was addressed by Bat Ye'or (the pen name of Giselle Litmann), the author of *Eurabia*, arguably the most single influential work in shaping the world view of the Counterjihad. Robert Spencer of the influential Jihad Watch website in the US was another speaker, who along with Edward May of the Gates of Vienna showed the transatlantic dimension to the event. Perhaps the most interesting thing about the Brussels meeting, though, was the hosts, the Flemish nationalist party Vlaams Belang (VB). VB is considered as 'far right' by many Belgian political commentators. The conference used the facilities of both the Flemish regional parliament and the European Parliament, an irony that must have been enjoyed by those attending, considering that the central thesis of their main speaker is that the EU is the conduit for the betrayal of Europe by its own elites to Islam. The involvement of Vlaams Belang is important because it is indicative of the symbiotic relationship that has developed between the Counterjihad as predominantly blog-based phenomenon with political parties and other groups across Europe (see Archer 2008). Representatives of political parties and activist groups have continued to attend or speak at Counterjihad conferences. Those named on Counterjihad websites include the Sweden Democrats, UK Independence Party, UK Freedom Party, English Defence League, the Swiss People's Party, and Italy's Lega Nord, but attendees have also come from many other European countries (along with the US and Israel) with no listed political or institutional affiliation. And as noted previously, the most prominent US Counterjihad activists have attracted speakers to their demonstrations both from Europe and also from the Republican Party in the US.

Influence and results

As Edward May of the Gates of Vienna points out, the purpose of the Counterjihad has been in part to build alliances between different groups and activists, who would have been less likely to come into contact with each other before the internet, and to help share and spread information about what they see as the attempts to subjugate Europe to Islam. Whilst the political parties they have supported have had some successes, for example Sweden Democrats members were active in the Counterjihad movement before the party's electoral success in 2010 when they entered the Swedish parliament for the first time, no evidence suggests that connections to the Counterjihad has direct impact on success at the polls. Rather, the Counterjihad blogosphere has raised such parties' international profile and support, and shown them that there is network of people in other countries with similar concerns to them. Having said that, and to continue with the example of the Sweden Democrats, they clearly have had success using the discourse of Islam as threat to European countries that the Counterjihad has been central to shaping.

Considering activism beyond electoral politics, the Counterjihad as a movement has become the biggest international supporter of the EDL, indeed the successes and the problems of this street protest movement were one of the major issues discussed at the 2011 Counterjihad summit in London, with the leaders of the EDL in attendance. Due to the violence and heavy policing costs associated with EDL demonstrations in the UK, the group has had predominantly negative press coverage, even from the right of the British media (see further, Busher in this volume). It is notable that Counterjihad bloggers have worked hard to produce a brighter picture of themselves internationally.

Until the terrible events in Oslo and Utøya, the biggest impact of the Counterjihad appeared to be in providing a discourse for populist right-wing parties across Europe that gave them an enemy to blame (the multicultural elites and Muslims) and a way of criticizing immigrants and immigration to Europe without being easily denounced as straightforward racists. The idea that multiculturalism has failed has now been put forward by many politicians, even those from centre-left and-right parties who are fishing for votes in the populist pond. But the idea of the Islamization of Europe is now common currency for populist right political parties, from Italy to Norway, from France to Finland, from Holland to Hungary, and inevitably with it travels the idea of the treachery of the elites; the idea that, when pushed to its twisted extreme, gave Breivik his target list. The writers of the Counterjihad have protested vehemently that they are in no way responsible for his actions, just because he quoted them approvingly, but nevertheless, it remains to be seen whether the relentless logic of their position – that Europe is moving towards a civil war between Muslim and non-Muslim citizens and that European elites are guilty of betraying the nations of Europe – will be involved in the radicalization of others in the same way in which Breivik seems influenced by it, or at least willing to use it to justify his own murderous rage.

Conclusion

The manifesto left by Breivik provides a clear picture of a man convinced that Europe was at risk of Muslims taking control, and that it was the elites of Europe who were to blame for this situation. His bloody rampage was propaganda by deed, in the Bakunian sense, in an attempt to avoid that outcome. Whilst Breivik was the first terrorist to act in the name of this ideology, at least on such an extreme scale, he was far from the first proponent of it. As has been shown above, he took the ideas and indeed full articles from other writers and activists who have shaped the ideology over the last decade. Whilst some of the positions that this perspective leads to may look like the traditional European fascist and post-fascist far right, there are clear differences. Most notably the Counterjihad is vehemently against the anti-Semitism of the old far right. Islam and Muslims have become the replacement 'other' to be resisted. The Counterjihad holds that its position is a liberal one, based on a concept of universal human rights, yet the positions that it supports often seem to suggests that these rights are dependent on being part of a nation, and that those who are not of that nation – for example immigrants – or who are deemed to threaten the interests of that nation – for example women who have been influenced by 'feminists' – are seen as not having an equal claim on such rights.

For the outsider observing the development of the Counterjihad, the tension between its claims to liberalism and the arch-conservatism of many of its positions remains the central issue for it to resolve if it wants to become a wider movement. But the right-wing views of many of the Counterjihad's adherents make the movement intolerant, not only of Muslims and immigrants, but of many of the progressive policies – not just multiculturalism – that have made Europe what it is today.

Notes

1. Breivik actually surrendered on his first encounter with armed police, despite still having ammunition, suggesting that he was less brave or less prepared to die than he stated in his document.
2. 'Islamophobia' remains a contested concept, not the least by Counterjihad bloggers themselves who see it as a method for their opponents to demonize their views. The term is difficult in that it can be applied to very different critiques of the religion of Islam and of the social and political actions of some Muslims. Not all criticism of Islam and Muslims can be said to start from a 'phobia' – a fear; criticism can reflect valid political differences. Secondly, in liberal democracies, free speech remains an important principle with citizens having the right to criticize and disagree with other citizens within the limits set by legal systems of those countries. For further discussion on the problems of the concept of Islamophobia, see Maussen 2006: 100–3; Zúquete 2008: 323–4.
3. Although an unwavering support of Israel is an article of faith within the Counterjihad, it might be more accurate to describe it as supporting a particular strain within Israeli politics – those parties that believe that occupied territories are an undividable part of Israel. Leftist and moderate Israelis who believe in a two-state solution with the Palestinians tend to be described in similar terms, such as 'traitorous', to European leaders who are seen as surrendering Europe to Islam (on relations of the Counterjihad to Israel, see Archer 2008).
4. 'EUSSR' is a common term for the EU on Counterjihad blogs and in radical Eurosceptic circles. Although being an amusing play on words, it also reflect the very real sense of Counterjihad supporters who see the EU as a totalitarian Marxist institution no better than the USSR. It is also notable that within the UK, the Counterjihad has been supported by of a number of UKIP activists.
5. Gingrich, who at the time of writing is leading in the Republican primaries for the party's nomination to run for the US presidency, was also advertised as speaking at the protest against the Park51 mosque and cultural centre. Eventually he pulled out of the protest in confused circumstances, despite having previously made comments comparing a mosque at that site to putting Nazi signs next to the Holocaust museum in Washington DC (The Hill 21/8/10).
6. Geller's activities appear to be funded from donations and her personal wealth, but Spencer and Jihadwatch are predominantly funded via David Horowitz's Freedom Centre, having received USD 920,000 from there over the three years up to 2010. In turn Horowitz attracts donations from foundations and wealthy individuals (Politico 4/9/10; see also Ali et al. 2011: ch. 1).

References

(non-bylined news stories)
BBC (25/7/11). Profile: Anders Behring Breivik. http://www.bbc.co.uk/news/world-europe–14259989
—(23/7/11). Norway's far right not a spent force. http://www.bbc.co.uk/news/world-europe–14260195
Gates of Vienna (1/12/11). 'A Brief History of the Transatlantic Counterjihad, Part VII'. http://gatesofvienna.blogspot.com/2011/12/brief-history-of-transatlantic.html
– (24/11/11). 'A Brief History of the Transatlantic Counterjihad, Part I'. http://gatesofvienna.blogspot.com/2011/11/brief-history-of-transatlantic.html
—(25/11/11). 'A Brief History of the Transatlantic Counterjihad, Part II'. http://gatesofvienna.blogspot.com/2011/11/brief-history-of-transatlantic_25.html
Guardian (26/7/11). Breivik sent 'manifesto' to 250 UK contacts hours before Norway killings. http://www.guardian.co.uk/world/2011/jul/26/breivik-manifesto-email-uk-contacts
—(12/11/10). English Defence League members attend New York mosque protest. http://www.guardian.co.uk/uk/2010/sep/12/english-defence-league-mosque-protest
Time (24/7/11). Killer's Manifesto: The Politics Behind the Norway Slaughter. http://www.time.com/time/world/article/0,8599,2084901,00.html
The Hill (21/8/10). 'Gingrich not to address 9/11 rally against mosque project as had been advertised'. http://thehill.com/homenews/news/115247-mosque-protest-loses-gingrich
New York Times (8/10/10). 'Outraged, and Outrageous'. http://www.nytimes.com/2010/10/10/nyregion/10geller.html
Politico (4/9/10). Latest mosque issue: The money trail. http://www.politico.com/news/stories/0910/41767.html
PressEurop (13/9/10). 'Wilders makes Ground Zero speech'. http://www.presseurop.eu/en/content/news-brief-cover/336971-wilders-makes-ground-zero-speech
Telegraph (24/11/11). Tape of Anders Behring Breivik's phone call to police after mass murder on Utoya released. http://www.telegraph.co.uk/news/worldnews/europe/norway/8913536/Tape-of-Anders-Behring-Breiviks-phone-call-to-police-after-mass-murder-on-Utoya-released.html

References

Ali, Wajahat. Clifton, E. Duss, M. Fang, L. Keyes, S. and Shakir, F. (2011) *Fear, Inc. The Roots of the Islamophobia Network in America,* Washington, DC: Centre for American Progress.
—(2008a). 'Countering the Counterjihad' *Homeland Security and Resilience Monitor* September 2008. Vol.7 No.7, RUSI.
—(2008b). *Learning to love the Jews: the impact of the War on Terror and the counter-jihad blogosphere on European far right parties.* Paper prepared for

and present at the XV NOPSA conference, Tromsø, August 08. uit.no/getfile. php?PageId=1410&FileId=1337

Archer, T. (2009). 'Welcome to the Umma: The British State and its Muslim Citizens Since 9/11' *Cooperation and Conflict,* 2009; 44, 329.

Berlet, C. (2011). 'Updated: Breivik's Core Thesis is White Christian Nationalism v. Multiculturalism' 25 July 2011. Talk to Action website http://www.talk2action.org/story/2011/7/25/73510/6015

Breivik, A. B. (2011) *2083: A European Declaration of Independence,* available at: http://www.kevinislaughter.com/wp-content/uploads/2083+-+A+European+Declaration+of+Independence.pdf

Bush, G. W. (2004). Speech on Promoting Democracy. 25 October 2004, Colo Greeley: http://www.cfr.org/world/speech-promoting-democracy/p7472

Cohen, N. (2007). *What's Left? How Liberals Lost Their Way,* London: Fourth Estate.

Dalton, A. (2011a). [1] '2083 by Anders Behring Breivik, Part 3: Breivik' *I read odd books* 24/8/11. http://ireadoddbooks.com/2083-by-anders-behring-breivik-part-3/

—(2011b). [2] '2083 by Anders Behring Breivik, Fjordman: Part Two' *I read odd books* 24/8/11. http://ireadoddbooks.com/2083-by-anders-behring-breivik-fjordman-part-two/

Fjordman (2006). *How the Feminists' 'War against Boys' paved the way for Islam,* http://www.brusselsjournal.com/node/1300

Jay, Martin (2010). 'Dialectic of Counter-Enlightenment: The Frankfurt School as Scapegoat of the Lunatic Fringe' *Salmagundi,* 168–9 (Fall 2010-Winter 2011) http://cms.skidmore.edu/salmagundi/backissues/168–169/martin-jay-frankfurt-school-as-scapegoat.cfm

Maussen, Marcel (2006). 'The Netherlands Anti-Muslim sentiments and mobilization in the Netherlands. Discourse, policies and violence' in Cesari, Jocelyne (ed.) *Securitization and Religious Divides In Europe. Muslims In Western Europe After 9/11: why the term Islamophobia is more a predicament than an explanation.* Submission to the Changing Landscape of Citizenship and Security 6th PCRD of European Commission (available at: http://www.libertysecurity.org/IMG/pdf_Challenge_Project_report.pdf)

Rashid, Ahmed (2001). *Taliban: the storey of the Afghan Warlords* London: Pan Books.

Repo, Jemina (2011). 'Äärioikeiston rasismi kytkeytyy naisvihaan' [The far-right's racism links to hatred of women] *Helsingin Sanomat* 25.8.11

Sunstein, Cass (2001). *Republic.com* Princeton Univeristy Press: Woodstock.

Walzer, Michael (2002). 'Can There Be a Decent Left?' *Dissent* (Spring). Available at: http://www2.kenyon.edu/Depts/Religion/Fac/Adler/Politics/Waltzer.htm [accessed 15 August 2008].

Yaqoob, Salma (2007). 'British Islamic Political Radicalism', in Tahir Abbas (ed.) *Islamic Political Radicalism: A European Perspective.* Edinburgh University Press: Edinburgh.

Zúquete, José Pedro (2008). 'The European extreme-right and Islam: New directions?' *Journal of Political Ideologies*, 13:3, 321–44.

10

Still Blind in the Right Eye? A Comparison of German Responses to Political Violence from the Extreme Left and the Extreme Right

Peter Lehr

On the occasion of a workshop on extreme right-wing terrorism in May 2011, this author tentatively argued that when it comes to countering terrorism and political violence from the extreme right and the extreme left, certain European states still tend to be 'blind in the right eye', in the sense of seriously underestimating the threat for a variety of reasons. Two events later that year highlighted the threat posed by extreme right-wing terrorism, also supporting the author's argument on the blind-sighted right eye: first, the Breivik massacre in Norway, and second, the discovery of an extreme right-wing terrorist cell in Zwickau, Germany, responsible for a decade-long series of murders throughout the republic – all in all, ten murders (one Greek and eight Turkish immigrants plus one police woman) and a bombing in Cologne that injured 22 people, most of them of Turkish origin. The activities of the cell which called itself *National-Socialist Underground* (NSU) were originally attributed by police authorities to the Turkish mafia, under the assumption that they were connected to organised crime and a protection racket.[1] It also emerged that at least some of those murders were committed under the very noses of the authorities: members of the cell had been employed as 'contact persons' (informants) both by the German domestic intelligence service and the police. Thus, it seems that the leader of the German Green Party parliament fraction, Beate Künast, is quite right to argue that 'if one really had wanted to know more, one could have known more.'[2] However, complacency or even 'ignorance' towards the extreme right seemed to have been the order of the day within intelligence and police forces still biased against the extreme left. Retrospectively drawing parallels to the extreme-left RAF and calling the Zwickau-based cell a *Brown Army Fraction* sounds a bit like a knee-jerk reaction out of guilt.[3]

If one takes a look at the history of the Federal Republic of Germany, it seems to be fair to state that whilst the activities of the so-called *Fighting Communist Organizations* such as the German RAF or the June 2nd Movement triggered a flurry of legislative and administrative measures with the sole purpose to crush them, activities of extreme right-wing groups usually did not lead to such responses. Instead of effectively being 'othered' (i.e. declared enemies of the state) like the extreme left wing (XLW), extreme right-wing (XRW) groups seemed to have been tolerated to a certain degree, and (grudgingly) accepted as parts of society. And since they essentially stood for a 'strong state' and 'law and order', they even tended to be defined as belonging to 'us' – 'us' very narrowly defined here as state administration, especially police forces, and possibly the majority of the conservative mainstream of society.

Drawing on Paul Wilkinson's concept of *corrigible* and *incorrigible* terrorists, this chapter examines why German authorities still tend to be blind in their right eye, whilst being eagle-eyed in the left – even more than two decades after the Cold War ended. Essentially, it is argued that whilst extreme left-wing violence seems to directly target the political system as such, extreme right-wing violence usually does not – which may explain the absence of urgency when it comes to developing counter-measures. It is also briefly argued that as of today, Islamist groups suffer the same often-times ham-fisted treatment as the extreme left for very similar reasons: after the (temporary) demise of the 'red threat', they are seen as the 'new incorrigible terrorists' which have to be crushed – if need be even in a 'no holds barred' approach. However, drawing on the official and public perceptions to the activities of the Zwickau cell, an important caveat will be added: who is seen as a 'corrigible' or 'incorrigible' terrorist depends on perceptions – and they can change. Hence, simply offering the usual argument of 'blindness in the right eye' as explanation for the state's and the public's under-reaction to XRW activities is far too simplistic, and missing some essential points.

Concepts and definitions: radicalism, extremism, terrorism

As most readers know only too well, defining the term 'terrorism' is not exactly a straightforward task: even under the impression of the current wave of global terrorism, it is contested due to its sensitivity, and thus, ambiguity. Somehow, one cannot avoid the impression that more often than not, terrorists get lumped together with all sorts of other 'undesirables' as a matter of convenience, and that, essentially, 'terrorism is violence committed by those we disapprove of.'[4] However, as the life histories of individuals like Menachem Begin, Nelson Mandela or Gerry Adams show, this disapproval may not necessarily be set in stone; or at the very least, it may not prevent negotiations from taking place, and peace from eventually breaking out. Disapproval or approval of violence thus cannot be seen as overly helpful when it comes to explaining perceptions of, and state reactions to, terrorist violence, or the crucial question of why certain states tend to be blind in one eye whilst eagle-eyed in the other.

More helpful, especially with regard to perceptions, might be defining terrorism with a focus on its most visible part – the 'shocking' act of terrorist violence itself – because this is the part one's imagination usually latches on, more often than not helped or fuelled by widespread coverage of them in mass media. Peter Waldmann for example offers such a definition:

> 'Terrorism means premeditated, systematically planned, shocking acts of violence directed against a political order from the underground. They are designed to produce a general sense of insecurity and fear, but also sympathy and support.'[5]

The element of 'shock' is, as Waldmann further points out, not just a minor or random attribute of terrorist actions but a focal part of terrorist logic and strategy: the element of shock explicitly aims at generating widespread publicity, and is meant to guarantee that the act itself will come to the attention of the general public.[6] In this regard, Waldmann's definition mirrors the core characteristics of terrorism described by Wilkinson to set it apart from other forms of politically motivated violence:

1 Terrorism is premeditated and designed to create a climate of extreme fear;
2 Terrorism is directed at a wider target than the immediate victims;

3 Terrorism involves attacks on random or symbolic targets, including civilians;

4 Terrorism is considered as 'extra-normal', in the literal sense that it violates the norms regulating disputes, protest and dissent;

5 Terrorism is used primarily, though not exclusively, to influence the political behaviour of governments, communities or specific social groups.[7]

For our intent and purpose, Waldmann's definition and Wilkinson's elaborations are useful since they will offer us, at a later section of this contribution, a starting point for criticizing the current understanding of – and thus, discourses on – XRW extremism and terrorism.

Waldmann also offers a useful and interesting categorization of terrorism, distinguishing between social-revolutionary, ethnic-nationalistic, religious and vigilantist terrorism.[8] Like all other attempts to categorize terrorism, or waves of terrorism, his categories tend to overlap. For the purpose of discussing perceptions of XRW and XLW extremism and terrorism in Germany, this does not really matter. However, we would like to draw attention to Wilkinson's two categories of 'corrigible terrorists' and 'incorrigible terrorists':

- 'Corrigible terrorists' can be defined as those fighting for attainable, tangible goals which are negotiable in the end.

- 'Incorrigible terrorists' can be defined as those fighting for ideological and 'pure' causes which are not negotiable.[9]

Of course, whether a terrorist group is seen as 'corrigible' or 'incorrigible', and whether its aims are perceived as attainable, tangible and, hence, negotiable or not, depends on the actor defining them. State actors – in our German context defined as consisting of the 'five powers' (legislative, executive, judiciary, mass media, economy) – tend to define terrorist groups as incorrigible if they are perceived as going for the 'heart of the state'[10] itself, i.e. if they aim at changing the current political system, and as corrigible if they are not perceived as a threat to the seat of power itself.

For example, ethno-nationalist groups fighting either for an autonomous region within the motherland or for a new sovereign entity are usually perceived as corrigible since their aims and objectives are ultimately seen as rational and thus open for negotiation or mitigation. The talks between the various governments of the United Kingdom and the IRA, even during 'The Troubles', are a case in point. In that special case, a peace agreement could be reached in which the IRA essentially gave up their ultimate objective of a united Ireland – at least one created through the sheer force of arms – in favour of the 'ballot box' due to concessions offered by the British government. The cases of the ETA in Spain or the Corsican separatists are different though: many rounds of negotiations remained inconclusive, and, so far, an end of the struggle is not yet in sight. Nevertheless, this does not stop both sides agreeing new ceasefires and returning to the negotiation table.

In the case of the so-called *Fighting Communist Organizations* (FCO) fighting for the 'overthrow of capitalist circumstances'[11] however, the very survival of the political and economic system, and thus, the heart of the state itself, is at stake – which is why bringing 'them' to the negotiation table makes far less sense than in the cases above. Thus, Western liberal democracies based on a market economy – 'capitalist states' in FCO parlance – by their very nature tend to see all those ideologically driven socio-revolutionary terrorist groups aiming at a complete change of the political system as incorrigible, be they Anarchist, Marxist, Leninist, Maoist – or, nowadays, Jihadist-Islamist. For example, the threat posed by the anarchist terrorists to the seats of power in Europe and the United States sparked the first global war on terrorism in the time of US President Theodore Roosevelt, and even the largely rhetorical and imagined international threat posed by groups of the New Left of the 1970s/1980s – magnified by the lenses of Cold War logic – was matched by renewed international cooperation between various police forces to crush this second attack on the heart of the state launched by socio-revolutionary movements.

Terrorism, however, is not the only term in need of clarification. In our context, we also encounter 'radicals' and 'extremists' from both wings of the political spectrum. And since this contribution focuses on Germany, it is only appropriate to make use of an official definition of those terms, as offered by the Landesamt fuer Verfassungsschutz, Baden-Wuerttemberg (state office for the protection of the constitution, Baden-Wuerttemberg; LfVBW). With regard to the terms 'radical' and 'radicalism', LfVBW explains that 'radical' (from Latin = root, origin) should be seen as 'the description for political-ideological views or endeavours which attempt to solve societal issues and problems down to the most minute detail, i.e. with utmost zeal and single-minded uncompromizing attitude. However, radical movements do not necessarily violate the principles of the liberal-democratic constitution.'[12] On the other hand, 'extremists' (from Latin 'extremus' = utmost) do violate the principles of the German constitution, and are thus seen as being hostile to it. According to § 3 Bundesverfassungsschutzgesetz[13], extremist movements can therefore be defined as 'endeavours which contravene the constitution or are directed against the existence or security of the Federal Republic or one of its states or aim at illegally impairing the functions of the constitutional organs of the Federal Republic or one of its states (for example, *Bundestag*, state parliaments, federal government, state governments) or its members.'[14]

However, the authors of the report readily admit that the boundaries between radicalism and extremism usually are fluid – which also means that 'every-day language' does not always differentiate between 'radical' and 'extremist'.[15] And, as we shall see, this 'every-day language' also does not necessarily differentiate between radicalism, extremism, and terrorism, happily lumping them together when it suits a purpose – for example, excluding 'undesirables' and their opinions from public debate on the one hand, and 'mainstreaming' desirables and their opinions on the other.

Patterns: XLW and XRW extremism and terrorism in post-war (Western) Germany

The emergence of XLW extremism and terrorism in the Federal Republic of Germany in the late 1960s can be explained – at least in parts – by the perceived 'fascist' and 'imperialist' nature of the state on the one hand, and the brutal repression of anti-system demonstrations against the state by the police on the other. With regard to the perceived fascist nature of the state, the Federal Republic of the 1950s and 1960s was quite vulnerable to such attacks. For instance, the government of Federal Chancellor Konrad Adenauer included individuals with a rather dubious past.[16] Also, many judges, even those of higher courts, had started their careers during the 1930s and early 1940s, and some of them had passed equally dubious sentences, including some that had sent opponents of the regime straight to the concentration camps, or deserters to execution squads.[17] Thus, seeing the conservative Federal Republic as a continuation of the old regime by other means, as the extreme left did, was not that surprising. The perceived 'imperialist' nature of the West German state can be explained by its close alliance with the United States of America, and its membership in the North Atlantic Treaty Organization (NATO). Even though German troops were not deployed to Indochina, the logistical support offered to US activities in Vietnam, Laos and Cambodia were enough to justify this claim – at least in the opinion of the extreme left.

With regard to the perceived repressive nature of the state and the harsh treatment meted out to the extreme left as opposed to the much more lenient reaction to extreme right-wing violence, the police (over-)reaction to anti-Shah demonstrators in Berlin in August 1967 is a telling example. The brutal actions from the police as well as from Iranian Savak-agents (tolerated by the police) culminating in the death of student Benno Ohnesorg (shot by a detective inspector under dubious circumstances) were reported and sensationalized by the conservative German press in a blatantly distorted way, as we shall see later.

We do not intend to discuss the complete set of root causes of XLW extremism and terrorism in Germany at length and in detail in this contribution. Suffice it to say that whilst daily events in Vietnam such as the napalm-bombing of Vietnamese villages and one-off affairs such as the Shah's visit to Germany provided the motivational causes for extreme left-wing militant actions including terrorism, the death of Benno Ohnesorg could be seen as the triggering cause which 'led to the outbreak of latent conflicts'[18] and prompted many students who had been undecided to make up their minds to join anti-state XLW organizations and 'to actively participate in the resistance'[19]. From within the diffuse scene and concentric circles of XLW radical and extremist student movements, three groups with terrorist inclinations emerged, forming the tip – or the spearhead – of the XLW scene: first, the Red Army Faction (RAF) as the self-appointed avant-garde and embodiment of the idea of an internationalist struggle against imperialism and as the German ally of ethno-nationalist liberation movements in the Third World plus the Northern Irish as well as the IRA; second, the *Revolutionaeren Zellen* (Revolutionary Cells, RZ) espousing a social-revolutionary strategy focusing on current and local conflicts; and third, the *Movement 2nd June* which consisted of culture-revolutionary, anarchist groups hostile to what they saw as the 'elitist arrogance' of the RAF.[20]

The history of the 'elitist' RAF, which emerged in 1970 and was formally dissolved on 20 April 1998, can also be seen as a history of the rise and fall of XLW *terrorism* in Germany. XLW radicalism and extremism however survived – for example in the shape of the *Linke Autonome* (Autonomous Left) and so-called *Antifa* (anti-fascist) movement, followed later by anti-globalist and vaguely anarchist cells. The boundaries between (legal) radicalism and (illegal) extremism, however, are fluid indeed, as pointed out above: so-called 'militant actions' such as the daubing of graffiti on war memorials seem to slightly overstep the norms regulating protest and dissent – and so does the torching of police vehicles or the cars of known or suspected neo-Nazis.

Interestingly, during the 1970s and 1980s when the XLW scene boomed, Nazism was seen as on its way out. The Federal Republic had moved on from the conservative era of Adenauer and was about to move from the centre-right more to the centre-left, even trying to 'dare more democracy', as Chancellor Willy Brandt said. The so-called *Ewig Gestrigen* (those eternally living in the past, i.e. unreformed Nazis) were expected to pass away, and in the successful modern welfare state so dependent on export there was meant to be no need or room for the return of old-fashioned nationalist ideas. The emergence of a new generation of 'neo-Nazis' was thus initially seen as an embarrassing aberration, affecting only a few social misfits – probably just some misguided young males spoiling for a fight. However, against all expectations and predictions, the XRW scene grew, attracting more and more mostly young male followers in addition to the known circle of elderly radical right-wing party members.

The re-emergence of XRW extremism and terrorism can at least partly be explained as a consequence of problems of adaption and integration as a result of social change in West Germany. With regard to the rapid growth of the XRW scene during the 1990s, the negative side-effects of the reunification on 3 October 1990, especially for some East German rural regions, also need to be mentioned. Here, disproportionally high rates of unemployment and rising costs of living were matched by rapid social decline and a loss of confidence in the future. Not very surprisingly, the segments of (mostly East) German society that lost out in the reunification process and its aftermath, thus feeling excluded, were susceptible to a set of easy-to-understand explanations promising to make sense out of what was happening, and quite frequently also offering some easy-to-identify scapegoats. Examples of such crude explanations were (and still are) claims that 'they steal our jobs', with 'they' defined as immigrants, legal or not, and especially highly visible immigrants with a different culture. In the Federal Republic of Germany (West Germany) before reunification, these were mostly Turkish immigrants or 'guest workers', joined by Vietnamese and African immigrants to the former 'socialist' German Democratic Republic after reunification. Immigrants however do not form the only target group for XRW extremism and terrorism: anybody seen as 'not fitting in' can be a target, for example punks (also highly visible), left-wing intellectuals (journalists, teachers), gays, Sinti and Roma, foreigners in general and Jewish citizens.

After reunification, not only the number of XRW scene members grew but also the pace of XRW militant actions, as Mayer and Meyer-Rewerts point out:

> [XRW violence] still was of a rather spontaneous single-action nature, planned and carried out in a short-term fashion without any coherent strategy, but with the same motives and the same targets reappearing. However, the relentless series of attacks on facilities for asylum seekers made it difficult to analytically keep them apart: names of places such as Rostock-Lichtenhagen, Hoyerswerda or Mölln resurfaced again and again in this context.[21]

On the occasion of the football world championship in 2006, former speaker for the government Heye explicitly warned foreigners to stay away from certain regions of East Germany (for example Brandenburg) due to the high number of politically motivated acts of violence directed against them.[22] Indeed, although XRW activism has to be seen as a pan-German problem and not only an East German one, the percentage of those supporting extreme-right ideas tends to be noticeably higher in East Germany than in West Germany: a poll taken just prior to the world championship of 2006, for example, revealed that 53 per cent of East Germans agreed with anti-foreigner slogans, as compared to only 38 per cent of West Germans.[23]

In 2010, the Bundesamt fuer Verfassungsschutz (Federal Office for the Protection of the Constitution, BfV) reported 219 XRW organizations (2009: 195; 2008: 156) and 25,000 XRW individuals (2009: 26,000), 9,500 of whom were categorized as potentially violent.[24] The BfV also reported two trends: first, a tendency of at least parts of radical and extremist groups of the XRW scene, including neo-Nazis, to cooperate and form networks, the main objective being to coordinate parliamentarian and activist strategies. Secondly, the BfV highlighted the emergence of a loose extremist organization calling itself Nationale Autonome (nationalist autonomous groups, NA). The NA members' outfit does not match the usual appearance of members of the XRW scene but rather that of the extreme left-wing autonomous groups. And just like them, they make use of Anglicisms usually shunned by the extreme right, adopt similar slogans (for example, 'destroy the capitalist system'; 'fight the system, fuck the law') and demand a more aggressive stance towards the police and political opponents, including what they call 'militant actions'.[25] Their number still is rather small and estimated to be around 500, but the XRW scene seems to be getting more organised and, thus, more dangerous.

Quite remarkably, however, the fact that the XRW scene also includes terrorist cells as defined by Waldmann and described by Wilkinson largely escaped public attention. Hence, Mayer and Meyer-Rewerts speak of the 'forgotten terrorism' when it comes to XRW terrorist actions.[26] In August 1980 for example, members of a group called *Deutsche Aktionsgruppen* (German Action Groups) firebombed a home for immigrants in Hamburg, killing two Vietnamese asylum seekers. Just one month later, on 26 September 1980, a 'lone wolf' XRW activist carried out a bombing attack targeting the famous Munich Oktoberfest, killing 13 people and seriously injuring about 200 more. The perpetrator, Gundolf Köhler, allegedly had contacts with the notorious XRW Wehrsportgruppe Hoffmann. The same group was also mentioned with regard to the assassination of Jewish publisher Shlomo Lewin who was killed in front of his house in December of the same year.[27] In 2003, a planned bombing attack targeting the foundation-laying ceremony for a Jewish cultural centre in Munich was prevented at the very last moment[28] due to timely information from a V-Mann (informer)[29]: a group around neo-Nazi Martin Wiese, organised in the so-called Kameradschaft Süd, had already acquired the explosives necessary for the attack.[30]

Contrary to the terrorist actions of the RAF, however, the XRW terror acts did not leave much trace in the public memory – not even the devastating one on the Oktoberfest, for reasons we shall endeavour to explain later. Two possible explanations that can be offered here are that those acts were committed not by one group, as was the case with the RAF, but by different ones, seemingly without any coherent programme or strategy, and that they did not seem to meet the definitional element of 'shock' in the eyes of the German public as the wider audience.

Reactions: Knee-jerks and bouts of blindness

In the fight against extremism and terrorism 'there should be no over- or under-reaction by the police and the judiciary', as Heitmeyer points out. Instead, '[what] is required is a credible probability of sanctions, which, however, [in the case of extremists at least committing militant actions below the threshold of terrorism] do not destroy the chances of a normal career open to all citizens.'[31]

During the 1970s and 1980s, the Federal Republic of Germany witnessed a spate of terrorist attacks perpetrated by various groupings belonging to the extreme left, with the assassination of Rohwedder in April 1991 as the final act. Reeling under the impression of the Red Army Fraction's seemingly relentless attacks going right to the heart of the state, the German Bundestag passed a flurry of legal and institutional anti-terrorism measures aimed at improving the national intelligence and police forces' ability to cope with this unprecedented wave of terror, preferably in a pro-active way. In the haste to be seen to do something against the menace, the politicians tended to ride rough-shod over certain civil liberties, thus turning the state into an 'Ueberwachungsstaat' (surveillance state) – at least from the perspective of its critics, not all of whom were from the left.

The main triggers were the traumatic events of Germany's *Heisser Herbst* ('hot autumn') of September 1977: the kidnapping of industry representative Dr Hanns-Martin Schleyer on 5 September; the hijacking of Lufthansa flight LH181 (the *Landshut*) on its way from Palma de Mallorca to Frankfurt on 13 October; the elite GSG–9's recapture of the airliner in Mogadishu on the night of 17/18 October; the suicide of imprisoned leading RAF members in their cells in Stuttgart Stammheim prison on the same night; and the climactic murder of Dr Schleyer on the following day. The main thrust of the measures was to provide the police force with more powers for surveillance, search and arrest. Two surveillance measures stand out: *Rasterfahndung* (grid search or surveillance) and *Schleppnetzfahndung* (dragnet search or surveillance). The Rasterfahndung is a form of computer-based surveillance which filters information of certain groups of persons from public or private databases – which may be normal today but was still in its infancy during the late 1970s. The database had been devised by the head of the Bundeskriminalamt (Federal Criminal Office), Horst Herold, even before the traumatic events, but was now able to be fully exploited:

> Herold's data processing provided, for the first time, a system which simultaneously fulfilled two of a detective's dreams: the collection of as much information as possible, and the ability to fit the individual components together in the minimum time. In 1979, a review of the system […] listed thirty-seven data files containing 4.7 million names and some 3,100 organizations. Many of these occurred several times. The fingerprints collection contained the prints of 2.1 million people. The 'personal identification centre' set up after the murder of Federal Prosecutor General Siegfried Buback in 1977 contained the names of over 3,500 people, with a short personal description of each and a list of material available for their identification such as photographs, fingerprints and handwriting tests.[32]

Schleppnetzfahndung permitted the police 'to search all apartments in a block if they suspected that terrorists and hostages were there, and they were empowered to set up roadblocks to establish the identity of people passing through neighbourhoods in the vicinity of terrorist incidents'.[33] Such roadblocks could also be set up on major German motorways, for example by using one of the larger lay-bys of an Autobahn as a choke point through which all traffic had to pass.

Again, it should be pointed out that, with regard to the national-level anti-terrorism measures which found their equivalent in some Western European countries[34], all these measures came with a heavy price tag: making the state more secure also meant making it less liberal. It needs also to be pointed out that it would be too simplistic to conclude that the main reason behind these tougher laws was the German state's bid for more power. Rather, the terrorist events described above usually resulted in a call for tougher action from a variety of sources outside of the government – including, for example, the conservative tabloid press mirroring the opinion of the conservative mainstream of society. Anderson reminds us that such overwhelming pressure leads to a phenomenon named 'the politics of the last outrage'.[35] As soon as the impact of the trigger event starts to wane, the political system returns to normalcy. The tougher laws however tend to remain in force – unless they are passed with a so-called 'sunset clause', i.e. an expiry date.

On the other hand, extremist and terrorist actions committed from within the rather disorganised and far less tangible XRW scene seemed to have been insufficient to create a public outrage comparable to the actions committed by groups from the other side of the political spectrum: those actions were not met by a similar flurry of legal initiatives. Of course, from a legal point of view one can argue that the laws passed to combat one form of terrorism can also be used to combat yet another. Also, one has to admit that the odd XRW group or party was banned when they too obviously overstepped the blurry boundary between radicalism (legal) and extremism (illegal). Nevertheless, the bulk of actions against the extreme right usually were (and still are) closely related to specific incidents such as neo-Nazi marches or acts of XRW violence. Counter-demonstrations were (and still are) held, and acts of solidarity with the victims were (and still are) organised. However, such counter-actions were (and still are) mostly of a short-term, ad-hoc nature, whilst extreme right-wing activities beyond the highly visible marches are not.[36] The XRW scene kept organising itself in the background whilst the bulk of the population kept turning their eyes away.[37] One can even argue that many of the actions from the XRW scene met with tacit approval and acknowledgement – the author heard the argument that 'they only keep the streets clean from riff-raff' or 'they do what the police isn't allowed to do' quite often over the years. Even the acts of the Zwickau cell met with at least some approval, such as 'too much ado about some dead Turks' or the rather popular argument that 'in Germany, foreigners have already killed more Germans than vice-versa.'[38] Thus, Nicola Hieke from the Bavarian state's coordination office against right-wing extremism (LKS) is quite right to argue that the fight against the right could be characterised as an attempt to extinguish fires rather than to try to durably inoculate the population against the dangers emanating from the extreme right.[39] Seemingly, it is (still) all about treating the symptoms instead of curing the disease when it comes to the XRW scene.

Thus, despite the existence of XRW extremism, and even terrorism, at the same time as XLW extremism and terrorism, it is fair and accurate to say that the sole and near-exclusive driving factor behind all those rather draconian anti-terrorism laws passed in Germany were the acts of XLW terrorism – at least until very recently, when in November 2011 the spate of politically motivated murders originally ascribed to the Turkish mafia were finally correctly attributed to an XRW terror cell. Covering the news of these murders, one German journalist stated the glaringly obvious: whilst the German interior intelligence service (Verfassungsschutz; Office for the Protection of the Constitution) busily surveilled all critical democrats from the left, it completely ignored violent extreme right-wing activists, and even recruited some of them as informers.[40]

Comments: Distorted discourses

With regard to the extreme left, the process of 'othering' them actually started early in the Federal Republic – well before the birth of XRW extremism and terrorism. We already mentioned the ham-fisted treatment meted out to anti-Shah demonstrators in Berlin in August 1967, and the reception of the events by the conservative press in Berlin and in the Federal Republic itself. In his contribution to the famous *Analysen zum Terrorismus* (volume 4/2), Fritz Sack comments on the role of the 'Springer-Presse' as follows:

> The Springer press did not only manipulate through redactionary means and through leaving out, composing, rearranging of information, [rather] it composed, invented and lied – as long as one is prepared to already talk of 'lies' if pictures are used with the wrong text, information is presented as unassailable even in the face of massive challenges to it, [and] if information is presented with a degree of precision for which there is no official proof and which has been unofficially contradicted.[41]

To further illustrate this argument, he reminds readers of a headline of the German broadsheet *Bild Zeitung* of 3 June 1967 which read 'Bloody Riots: 1 Dead', followed by the comment: 'A young man died yesterday in Berlin. He is the victim of riots, stage-managed by political rowdies... Noise is no longer enough for them... they want to see blood... they wave the red flag, and they mean the red flag.'[42] In this short press comment, Sack already sees all necessary elements present which would determine the structure of future reporting, and which only needed some linguistic variation. For example, also on 3 June 1967, the *Berliner Zeitung* exclaims 'this is terror (...) who produces terror has to accept harsh counter-measures.'[43]

This 'othering' of essentially peaceful demonstrators – which at no point during the demonstrations went beyond the limits of the German constitution – in a sort of imaginative brilliance that would have made any playwright proud was at least initially echoed even by the then Governing Mayor of Berlin, the well-respected theologian Heinrich Albertz, ironically a social democrat and thus also from the left – but not the extreme one, the 'respectable' one.[44] On the night of 2/3 June, he stated:

> The patience of this city has come to an end. Several dozen demonstrators, among them students as well, acquired the sad merit of not only having offended and insulted a guest of the Federal Republic in the German capital, on their account also is one person dead and numerous persons injured – police officers and demonstrators. The police, provoked by rowdies, were forced to act forcefully and to make use of their batons […].[45]

Not surprisingly, the police of Berlin came up with a similar narrative of the events after having overreacted in a situation they helped to create[46], putting the entire blame for the events on the – supposedly extreme left-wing – demonstrators. With regard to the police force's chosen tactics, Sack even hints at a possible 'hidden curriculum' of the police planning around the visit of the Shah as a better explanation for the over-reaction than the alleged 'ineptitude of the Berlin police command' that the *Frankfurter Allgemeine Zeitung* saw behind the events in July 1967.[47] In that case, this may well have been a focus on 'efficiency' of police actions to the detriment of their legality. The element of 'efficiency' is notably absent in the context of acts of XRW political violence and terrorism committed by the Zwickau cell, as we have seen, and shall see again. At the moment, all we need to do is to reiterate that even in the prelude to German extreme left-wing terrorism, the 'Movement June 2nd' and the RAF, the 'othering' of the extreme left wing already was in full swing.

In the context of a divided Germany and the febrile and heated atmosphere of the Cold War, the danger posed by 'world communism' in general and the 'eastern bloc' in the shape of the socialist German Democratic Republic and the USSR in particular made this 'othering' an exercise in simplicity and rhetorical elegance: all it took was a couple of key words such as 'terrorists', 'political rowdies', 'blood-thirsty', 'red flags' in order to conjure up a menace from the extreme left and to brand them as 'Vaterlandsverraeter' (traitors of the fatherland), thus denying them any legitimate space in the public political discourse – the 'gate keeper' function of the press saw to that. However, by doing so they also fuelled the radicalization process within the extreme left in general and the student movement in particular. Hess explains the rationale behind this over-exaggeration of social-revolutionary extremism and terrorism:

[In] the usual discourse of terrorism it experiences a disproportionately high and exaggerated transformation to an enormous danger for state and society. whilst [this form of terrorism] carries out very selective actions, in the discourse 'we all' appear to be threatened. Although especially today the essential replaceability of leaders in the state and the general complexity of our modern system renders it less vulnerable than earlier ones, the discourse only too willingly follows the illusions of the social-revolutionary actors that they could 'attack the heart of the state', thus forcing it to collapse.[48]

Hess mentions two main reasons behind this overestimation of social-revolutionary terrorism. First of all, he opines that it is indeed a serious threat to many persons occupying leading roles in economy and state: 'Social-revolutionary terrorism turns them into prisoners of protective measures, thus ruining their private lives and that of their families as well. In such a situation it is understandable that they tend to generalise the danger. And since they have a huge influence on media, this interpretation is mirrored there as well.'[49] Thus, Hess argues that in a certain sense, 'social-revolutionary terrorism can be seen as a modern *crimen laesae maiestatis:* Even though today *maiestatis* is no longer tied in with the person but with the position, injuring a person in such a position still results in a wide-spread feeling of outrage within the population.'[50]

Secondly, Hess points out that the overestimation of social-revolutionary terrorism fulfils a series of important functions: 'For example, over-exaggeration of the problem of terrorism distracts from other and more pressing problems threatening the general population. Also, the general fear of terrorism can create a mass consensus. This fear translates into a general sense of insecurity, and as a consequence, into widespread demands for a stronger state, and a widespread acceptance and legitimization of more severe laws.'[51] At the same time, Hess argues, the all-pervading sense of fear opens the way for the growth of intelligence and law enforcement institutions: 'For example, the budget of the BKA rose from DM 22 million in 1969 to DM 199 million in 1978, and the budget of the Bundesamt fuer Verfassungsschutz (Federal Office for the Protection of the Constitution) from DM 17 million in 1968 to 110 million in 1978.'[52]

On the other hand, with regard to XRW activities, the element of *crimen laesae maiestatis* does not apply: only in a few exceptional cases were persons occupying leading roles in society targeted. Rather, the target groups were situated at the fringes of German society: legal and illegal immigrants, youth movements sporting a non-mainstream lifestyle (punks, for example), gays, Sinti and Roma. An all-pervading sense of fear thus failed to emerge, and neither was there a mass-consensus that the state should crush them as mercilessly as it had in the fight against XLW extremism and terrorism. As we already pointed out, the German conservative mainstream tended to have a rather dim view of these outsiders anyway, tacitly approving, or at least not condemning, XRW militant actions targeting them – which made 'othering' the XRW scene far more difficult even for interested parties than 'othering' the XLW scene.

More often than not it was (and still is) doubted whether even the most blatant and brutal of such acts could be classified as terrorism at all – as were similar acts from the XLW. This author used the minute of silence in Germany on Thursday 23 February 2012 in memory of the victims of the extreme right-wing terror cell of Zwickau, Thuringia, as an opportunity to discuss these activities with a group of Bundeswehr senior officers. Interestingly, the majority of the group did not think that the criteria Wilkinson developed to define terrorism could be applied to the series of murders that the Zwickau cell committed. For example, after having been introduced to Crelinsten's argument that 'the victims of terrorism function as signs in a propaganda war',[53] they remained unconvinced that the murders could be seen as directed at a wider target audience than the immediate victim – rather, they saw them as criminally motivated acts committed explicitly without the intention to be used as a kind of communication strategy within a propaganda war. Thus, they were also not prepared to accept that those acts were meant to create a climate of extreme fear, or that they were intended to influence the behaviour of a specific social group – in this context, immigrants of non-German ethnic origin: again, referring to Crelinsten[54], where was the 'symbolic and instrumental' character of those acts? If even the family members of the immediate victims were uncertain whether the murders were linked to organised crime, financial debts or matters of honour, how then could the wider community they belonged to feel terrorized under the assumption that they constituted the target audience, and that their behaviour was meant to be influenced?

The same line of reasoning also led them to dismiss the above-mentioned fear of a 'Brown Army Fraction' forming in Germany that needed the special attention of domestic intelligence services and police forces, arguing that Chancellor Angela Merkel's knee-jerk reaction in this regard could be explained by German history rather than a viable threat to the state's security, and the general safety of its citizens. Other participants in the discussion however disagreed, drawing attention to the possibility that immigrants could perceive themselves to be under permanent pressure and being terrorized by actors remaining in the dark 'in an unspectacular way such that [they] must, at any time (and now also in any place) expect to become victims of terror', thus experiencing 'a "loss of control" over their lives'.[55]

We do not intend to embark on a discussion of whether the positions of the participants of this interesting and thought-provoking discussion were right or wrong. Rather, we would like to highlight the perceptions of terrorism, reflecting the terrorism discourse as such: more often than not, and in a particular German context, terrorism is when terrorists attack highly symbolic and instrumental targets in a very public and widely reported manner, as the RAF did – unspectacular attacks targeting minorities do not seem to meet this criterion, and seem to remain below the radar screen of public attention. Here, the opinion of some of the group members is interesting: they opined that although the decades-long clandestine activities of XRW terrorists and extremists in certain regions resulted in 'nationally liberated zones' or 'no-go' areas for foreigners, they would still fall short of 'terrorism' in the absence of spectacular attacks against representatives of the state, and in the absence of a media strategy aiming at multiplying the effects of the attack. The activities of the Zwickau cell were therefore seen by some discussion group members as ultimately counterproductive for the XRW scene since they drew unwanted media attention to the activities of right-wing radicals and extremists in general.

In order to offer an explanation for this persistent under-reaction or blindness in the right eye, we need to return to the problem of defining terrorism. We already mentioned Wilkinson's core concepts of terrorism, which include the attack on random and symbolic targets, and also referred to Crelinsten who also emphasised the usually symbolic and instrumental character of terrorist acts. If we then close our eyes and think of any terrorist attack that readily comes into our mind, we would probably arrive at a definition of terrorism similar to Waldmann's we quoted in the introduction.

Heitmeyer, discussing Waldmann's definition in his contribution on right-wing terrorism to Bjørgo's volume, draws our attention to the definitional elements 'use of violence' and 'impact of shock'.[56] When it comes to public perceptions, and the impact of shock within the general population plus the creation of a general sense of insecurity and fear, this is clearly present in the 9/11 attacks, or London 7/7. Here, the feeling that 'it could have been me' is very visible. If we consider the reporting of the events in German and non-German mass media, it is also present, in the context of the German RAF, in the high-profile killings and assassinations of well-respected and well-known pinnacles of society such as Siegfried Buback (7 April 1977), Juergen Ponto (assassinated 30 July 1977), Hanns-Martin Schleyer (killed 18 October 1977 after having been abducted on 5 September), Alfred Herrhausen (assassinated 30 November 1989) or Detlef Karsten Rohwedder (assassinated 1 April 1991). Here, the element of general insecurity and fear consists of the perceived inability of the state to stop this wave of terrorist violence.

However, as already mentioned above, this is not necessarily the case when it comes to acts of violence directed against targets not commonly seen as symbolic and instrumental. Since it is neither the state itself nor the population at large that is targeted, be it directly or at least as 'wider audience', the elements of 'impact of shock' and 'general feeling of insecurity and fear' are either not present at all or are at least rather muted. This seems to be reflected by the reporting of such incidents in the press: if they are reported at all, media interest dies down rather quickly. But what is right for the general population and mass media does not necessarily need to apply to certain communities or specific social groups: they might feel terrorized by acts of violence that fall short of the 'shocking', highly visible, and more often than not spectacular nature of 'normal' acts of terrorism directed against symbolic and instrumental targets; and they might feel terrorized by acts of violence that do not attempt 'to exploit the media in order to achieve maximum attainable publicity as an amplifying force multiplier in order to influence the targeted audience(s) in order to reach short- and mid-term political goals and/or desired long-term end states.'[57]

We already referred to Heitmeyer's position on that: given a credible threat potential, terrorism can also occur in an unspectacular way – not necessarily reported by the national or international press, but nonetheless resulting in the victims' 'loss of control' over their own lives. Thus, Heitmeyer convincingly argues that

> the definitional framework, which primarily focuses on the spectacular act, and which can also be objectively identified, be extended to include the subjective side of the victims' groups in order to concentrate more on the political interactions. This also means looking at terror not only as an act, but seeing it as a process that is apt to change discourses, everyday life and public order in a society.[58]

Within the confines of terrorism studies, seeing terrorism as a process is not such a novelty any longer – here, the awareness is present that the violent act as such only represents the tip of the terrorist iceberg. It is doubtful whether this is also the case outside this rather small group of experts, and especially within the broader population. As Nicola Hieke from the Bavarian coordination office against right-wing extremism pointed out[59], people still need to be inoculated against the dangers emanating from this milieu – which can be framed in terms of a process aimed at changing discourses, everyday life and public order. The understanding that terrorism is actually a process might also lead to the realization that for certain communities or specific social groups, the 'climate of extreme fear' Wilkinson included in his core elements of terrorism may well be a permanent one – one that might not dissipate when the memories of the latest terrorist spectacular fade away. Heitmeyer explains why such a change in perceptions matters:

> If a central criterion of terror consists in placing people in a permanent state of fear so that they must expect an attack at any time, then the attacks by groups of right-wing youths should be included in the analysis. They use terrorist means, thereby severely limiting the freedom of movements of others. Certain urban neighbourhoods or locations are turned into 'zones of fear'. This is achieved by the simple numerical superiority of those who sometimes threaten and sometimes use violence against their victims who are clearly at a disadvantage. However, what distinguishes these groups from classical terrorist formations is that they do not act covertly and for this reason rarely use firearms or explosives.[60]

That conventional definitions of terrorism may not be suitable to cover current XRW manifestations of political violence is an interesting and compelling position. This position is also held by the *Spiegel* in an argument that deserves to be quoted at length:

> Until now, only two forms of political terrorism have existed, whether it was committed by people on the left or the right or by Islamists. One involved the 'propaganda of the deed,' as the 19th-century French anarchist Paul Brousse dubbed his concept, which was later perfected by Russian and Italian anarchists. According to Brousse, deeds were meant to speak for themselves and be self-explanatory for the masses. Words merely deprived deeds of their power. The second approach merely requires the deed as a template for the declarations, manifestos and claims of responsibility that follow. For each of its attacks, Germany's Red Army Faction wrote a long letter in which it explained why a particular high-ranking political or business figure supposedly deserved to die. Al-Qaida leader Osama bin Laden regularly explained himself in video messages and called for attacks on the West.[61]

In their decade-long killing spree, however, the Zwickau cell followed neither approach, as the *Spiegel* points out. First of all, since their acts obviously did not speak for themselves to the extent that they were attributed to the Turkish mafia, their acts were clearly not meant to be seen as self-explanatory propaganda of the deed in the hope of triggering a wave of copycat attacks from like-minded groups. And secondly, the absence of any written or other claims of responsibility or explanatory letters indicates that the deeds themselves were also not meant as vehicles for publicizing their political demands. Hence, no supporter base could emerge publicly justifying and defending their actions. And although it indeed guaranteed the survival of the cell for more than a decade, 'it came at the cost of no one understanding the racist motivations for their alleged deeds.'[62]

Why the Zwickau cell chose to go public and release a 15-minute video 'apparently intended to ignite the next stage, a propaganda campaign, after 13 years of silent terror'[63] remains uncertain, and we can only speculate with the *Spiegel* that they finally 'felt strong enough to take on all society'[64] as the RAF did from the start. Ironically, this move to the next stage would have finally ticked the remaining boxes of 'directed against a wider audience' and 'creating a climate of extreme fear' – crucial elements for discerning terrorism from other forms of political violence, according to Wilkinson. Supported by a suitable media strategy, we have no doubt that their acts would then have been readily attributed in the public perception with the other crucial element of terrorism that Waldmann mentioned: 'shocking violence'.

This brings us to what may be our most contentious argument: the underreaction of both state and the public to XRW terrorism as opposed to the overreaction to similar acts from XLW terrorism cannot and should not be explained in terms of 'being blind in the right eye' in the sense of tolerating it to a certain degree alone – that would seem to be too simplistic, convenient and ultimately reductionist. Rather, we contend that it is also a matter of state and public perceptions and understanding of terrorism. As the cases of Menachem Begin, Nelson Mandela or Gerry Adams demonstrated, the definition of who is a terrorist can change. After all, terrorism still is a label we attach or not to acts of violence depending on whether we approve or disapprove.

This being the case, and by logical extension, we can play the same game with the concept of 'corrigible' and 'incorrigible' terrorists. As we already argued with Hess, given the essential replaceability of leaders and the general complexity of our modern system, the very idea of attacking the heart of the state with any chance of success seems to be an illusion and a convenient construct used for creating a mass consensus rather than reality.[65] Hence, the notion of 'corrigible' and 'incorrigible' is also based on perception rather than being anchored in some measurable reality. The constructedness of the notions of 'corrigible' and 'incorrigible' also explains why the activities of the Zwickau cell caused the whole spectrum of the German XRW scene to be suddenly promoted to the status of 'incorrigible' after having been ignored for so long.

Conclusion: The 'politics of the last outrage' reloaded

So, what then explains the under-reaction of the German state and public to the activities of XRW extremists and terrorists for several decades? First of all, we would argue that prior to reunification, the XRW scene did not seem to pose a real threat: in general, they were seen as disorganised, somewhat dull, and of nuisance value rather than a real threat. The intellectually very articulate XLW scene, however, seemed to be of a completely different calibre, especially so in the context of the Cold War when all manifestations of XLW radicalism, extremism and terrorism could easily be seen as an existential threat. Thus, with regard to perceptions and discourses of terrorism during the Cold War, one could argue, somewhat ironically, that compared to the XRW scene, extreme left-wing extremists and terrorists suffered from the absence of what is called, in the context of asymmetric warfare, a 'level playing field': in the public eye, the global enemy was the Soviet Union and World Communism, not Fascism/Imperialism. Thus, the thematic issues used for 'othering' revolved around Communist themes, including 'fifth columns' fighting on behalf of the Eastern Bloc. Why, otherwise, would 'they' call themselves 'Red Army Fraction'? With regard to consensus building, this 'red threat' and the public branding of the whole Left as '(incorrigible) terrorist' was eminently useful for the state, and for the mainstream conservative mass media as well, since it helped to distract from other and more pressing problems threatening the general population, as Hess pointed out.[66]

When XLW terrorism finally bowed out in April 1998, a new threat had already appeared on the horizon: the threat of global and equally 'incorrigible' terrorism in the shape of Al Qaeda and Salafism-Jihadism. In the admittedly very different context of radicalization and de-radicalization, Githens-Mazar and Lambert argue rather convincingly that a similarly distorted terrorism discourse in the form of 'conventional wisdom' and assumptions again suited both the government and mainstream media: it enabled those interested parties to credibly demonstrate how even a 'good Muslim boy' can be led astray, morphing from 'good Muslim boy' to 'terrorist' rather quickly under the influence of blame factors such as ideology, alienation, lack of integration, personal influence of 'preachers of hate' or the internet – thus again avoiding having to discuss awkward issues such as the influence of foreign policy decisions.[67]

Above, we already referred to Anderson's concept of the 'politics of the last outrage'. In Germany, the last outrage related to global Islamist terrorism is in the distant past, and, whether for good or bad reasons, Islamist terrorism is not seen as a credible 'clear and present danger' any longer. For the purpose of consensus building, it has lost its allure. The XLW scene is largely dormant, except for the militant actions already mentioned, and the rather ritualistic clashes with the police, for example on Labour Day. When it comes to extremism and terrorism, the XRW scene is the only credible contender for domestic security consensus building at the moment. However, this might be a bit too cynical a view, especially against the backdrop of dwindling budgets even for intelligence and police services in the current climate of financial austerity: utilising an 'all-pervading sense of fear' to 'open the way for the growth of intelligence and law enforcement institutions' as Hess argued in the context of the fight against the RAF[68] is simply out of the question, which translates into fewer and fewer staff having to do more and more work. Also, the sense of moral outrage (and guilt) within the political elite across basically all German democratic parties seems to be genuine. One way or another, sight has been restored to the right eye at least for the moment, and that is not a bad thing at all.

Notes

1 See for example the coverage in Spiegel (2011). 'The Brown Army Faction: A Disturbing New Dimension of Far-Right Terror', *Der Spiegel,* November 14, at http://www.spiegel.de/international/germany/0,1518,797569,00.html [accessed 4 March 2012].
2 Sueddeutsche Zeitung (2011). 'Generaldebatte im Bundestag: Opposition attackiert Schroeders Extremismusklausel', *Sueddeutsche. de Politik*, November 22, at, http://www.sueddeutsche.de/politik/generaldebatte-im-bundestag-zum-nazi-terror-opposition-attackiert-schroeders-extremismusklausel–1.1196305 [accessed 6 March 2012].
3 See the Spiegel (2011), op.cit.
4 Whitaker, Brian (2001). 'The definition of terrorism', *The Guardian,* May 7, at www.guardian.co.uk/world/2001/may/07/terrorism [accessed 17 February 2012].
5 Waldmann, Peter (2002). 'Terrorismus als weltweites Phaenomen: Eine Einfuehrung', in Frank, Hans/Hirschmann, Kai (eds): *Die weltweite Gefahr. Terrorismus als internationale Herausforderung.* Berlin: Berlin Verlag Arno Spitz, pp. 11–26 (11) (translation PL).
6 Waldmann, Peter (2002), op. cit., p. 12 (translation PL).
7 Wilkinson, Paul (2001). *Terrorism Versus Democracy: The Liberal State Response* (1st edition). London: Frank Cass, pp. 12–14.
8 For example in Waldmann, Peter (1998). *Terrorismus: Provokation der Macht.* Munich: Gerling Verlag.

9 Wilkinson, Paul (2001), op. cit.
10 See the title of the two volumes of Hess, Henner et al. (1988). *Angriff auf das Herz des Staates*. Frankfurt am Main: Suhrkamp Verlag.
11 See for example rafinfo.de (undated). RAF-Aufloesungserklaerung, at http://www.rafinfo.de/archiv/raf/raf–20–4–98.php [accessed 6 March 2012].
12 Landesamt fuer Verfassungsschutz Baden-Wuerttemberg (2006). *Rechtsextremismus*. Stuttgart, March, p. 8 (translation PL).
13 Law regulating the powers and responsibilities of the office for the protection of the constitution (German federal domestic intelligence service).
14 Landesamt fuer Verfassungsschutz Baden-Wuerttemberg (2006), op. cit., pp. 8–9 (translation PL).
15 Since 1974, offices for the protection of the constitution (Verfassungsschutzbehoerden – both federal and state-level) only use the term 'extremist' for endeavours hostile to the constitution.
16 For example the director of the Federal Chancellory under Adenauer, Hans Globke, who was involved in the Office for Jewish Affairs during the 1930s, for example writing a commentary for the *Nuremberg Laws*.
17 See for example the *Filbinger Affair* of 1978, in which Baden-Wuerttemberg's First Minister Hans Filbinger was accused to having been involved in four death sentences as navy lawyer, and even sentencing an artillery soldier to six months imprisonment for disobedience on 29 May 1945 – i.e. after the surrender on 8 May.
18 Claessens, Dieter/de Ahna, Karen (1982). 'Das Milieu der Westberliner "scene" und die "Bewegung 2 Juni"', in Baeyer-Katte, Wanda et al. (eds) *Analysen zum Terrorismus Band 3, Gruppen Prozesse*. Opladen: Wesdeutscher Verlag, pp. 18–181 (72) (translation PL).
19 Claessens, Dieter/de Ahna, Karen (1982), op.cit. p. 77 (translation PL).
20 Scheerer, Sebastian (1984). 'Die Bundesrepublik Deutschland oder: die Gefahren der deutschen Empfindlichkeit', in Sack, Fritz/Steinert, Horst (eds): *Analysen zum Terrorismus Band 4/2: Protest und Reaktion*. Opladen: Westdeutscher Verlag, pp. 463–9 (463).
21 Mayer/Meyer-Rewerts (2011), op. cit. (translation PL).
22 Spiegel (2006). 'Rechtsextremismus: 'Grosses Problem wird kleingeredet'', *Der Spiegel,* 21. May, at http://www.spiegel.de/politik/deutschland/0,1518,417174,00.html [accessed 6 March 2012].
23 Ibid.
24 BfV (undated). *Zahlen und Fakten zum Rechtsextremismus: Rechtsextremistisches Personenpotenzial (Gesamtuebersicht)*. Bundesamt fuer Verfassungsschutz website, at http://verfassungsschutz.de/de/arbeitsfelder/af_rechtsextremismus/zahlen_und_fakten_2010/zuf_re_gesamtuebersicht_2010.html [accessed 6 March 2012].
25 BfV (2009). *'Autonome Nationalisten' – Rechtsextremistische Militanz*. Bundesamt fuer Verfassungsschutz, May, at http://verfassungsschutz.de/download/de/publikationen/pb_rechtsextremismus/

broschuere_2_0905_autonome_nationalisten/thema_0905_autonome_nationalisten.pdf [accessed 6 March 2012].

26 Mayer, Benjamin/Meyer-Rewerts, Ulf (2011). 'Der vergessene Terrorismus', Goettinger Institut fuer Demokratieforschung, November, at http://www.demokratie-goettingen.de/blog/der-vergessene-terrorismus–2 [accessed 3 March 2012].

27 See Mayer/Meyer-Rewerts (2011), op. cit.

28 Sueddeutsche Zeitung (2003). 'Anschlag in der Stadtmitte Muenchens geplant: Neonazis wollten juedisches Zentrum sprengen', *Sueddeutsche. de,* 11 November, at http://www.sueddeutsche.de/muenchen/anschlag-in-der-stadtmitte-muenchens-geplant-neonazis-wollten-juedisches-zentrum-sprengen–1.931901 [accessed 9 March 2012].

29 See Schallenberg, Joerg (2004). 'Fuer Sprengstoff ist gesorgt', *taz.de,* November 24, at http://www.taz.de/1/archiv/archiv/?dig=2004/11/24/a0162 [accessed 9 March 2012].

30 Mayer/Meyer-Rewerts (2011), op. cit.; Krug, Alexander (2005): 'Neonazis haben Material fuer Bombe gesammelt', *Sueddeutsche.de,* 20 January, at http://www.sueddeutsche.de/muenchen/lka-experte-neonazis-haben-material-fuer-bombe-gesammelt–1.672778 [accessed 9 March 2012].

31 Heitmeyer, Wilhelm (2005). 'Right-wing terrorism', in Bjørgo, Tore (ed.). Root Causes of Terrorism. Myths, reality and ways forward. London and New York: Routledge 2005, pp. 141–53 (144).

32 Aust, Stefan (2008). The Baader-Meinhof Complex. London: The Bodley Head, p. 141.

33 Anderson, Malcolm (2000). 'Counterterrorism as an Objective of European Police Cooperation', in Reinares, Fernando (ed.). European Democracies Against Terrorism. Governmental policies and intergovernmental cooperation. Aldershot et al.: Ashgate, pp. 227–43 (237).

34 For example in Italy, where laws of an equally sweeping nature were passed to combat XLW terrorism and, especially, the Red Brigades.

35 Anderson, Malcolm (2000), op. cit., p. 228.

36 See Kock, Felicitas (2012). 'Kein Bier fuer Nazis: Initiative von Wirten gegen Rechtsextremismus', *Sueddeutsche Zeitung,* 1 March, at http://www.sueddeutsche.de/bayern/initiative-von-wirten-gegen-rechtsextremismus-kein-bier-fuer-nazis–1.1296177 [accessed 1 March 2012].

37 Ibid.

38 See for example Prantl, Heribert (2012). 'Gedenken and die Nazi-Opfer: Wahlkaempfe leben von der angeblichen Ueberfremdung Deutschlands', *Sueddeutsche Zeitung,* 23 February, at http://www.sueddeutsche.de/politik/gedenken-an-die-neonazi-opfer-wie-integration-endlich-gelingen-kann–1.1292062–2 [accessed 4 March 2012].

39 As quoted in Kock, Felicitas (2012), op. cit. (translation PL).

40 Prantl, Heribert (2011). 'Rechter Terror und Verfassungsschutz: Wenn der Staat versagt', *Sueddeutsche Zeitung,* 17 November, at http://www.

sueddeutsche.de/politik/rechter-terror-und-verfassungsschutz-wenn-der-staat-versagt–1.1191241 [accessed 4 March 2012].

41 Sack, Fritz (1984), op. cit., p. 188 (translation PL).
42 Ibid.
43 Quoted in ibid.
44 Governing Mayor Albertz was later forced to resign when an investigation of the German Parliament of the events criticised his handling of them.
45 As quoted in Sack, Fritz (1984), op. cit., p. 182 (translation PL).
46 Sack, Fritz (1984), op. cit., p. 170.
47 Sack, Fritz (1984), op. cit., p. 179.
48 Hess, Henner (1988). 'Terrorismus und Terrorismus-Diskurs', in: Hess, Henner et al.: Angriff auf das Herz des Staates, Erster Band. Frankfurt am Main: Suhrkamp Verlag, pp. 55–74 (68) (translation PL).
49 Hess, Henner (1988), op. cit, p. 69 (translation PL).
50 Hess, Henner (1988), op. cit, p. 69 (translation PL).
51 Ibid. (translation PL).
52 Ibid. (translation PL).
53 Crelinsten, Ronald (2009). Counterterrorism. Cambridge: Polity Press, p. 1.
54 Ibid.
55 Heitmeyer, Wilhelm (2005). 'Right-wing terrorism', in Bjørgo, Tore (ed.). Root Causes of Terrorism. Myths, reality and ways forward. London and New York: Routledge 2005, pp. 141–53 (143–4).
56 Heitmeyer, Wilhelm, op. cit., p. 141.
57 Bockstette, Carsten: *Jihadist Terrorist Use of Strategic Communication Management Techniques*. George C. Marshall Centre for European Security Studies No 20, 2008, pp. 1–28.
58 Heitmeyer, Wilhelm 'Right-wing terrorism', in Bjørgo, Tore (ed.) (2005). Root Causes of Terrorism. Myths, reality and ways forward. London and New York: Routledge, pp. 141–53 (144).
59 As quoted in Kock, Felicitas 'Kein Bier fuer Nazis: Initiative von Wirten gegen Rechtsextremismus', *Sueddeutsche Zeitung,* 01 March 2012, at http://www.sueddeutsche.de/bayern/initiative-von-wirten-gegen-rechtsextremismus-kein-bier-fuer-nazis–1.1296177 [accessed 1 March 2012].
60 Heitmeyer, Wilhelm, op. cit., p. 144.
61 Spiegel (2011). 'The Brown Army Faction: A Disturbing New Dimension of Far-Right Terror', *Der Spiegel,* November 14, at http://www.spiegel.de/international/germany/0,1518,797569,00.html [accessed 4 March 2012].
62 Ibid.
63 Ibid.
64 Ibid.
65 Hess, Henner (1988), op. cit, p. 69.

66 Hess, Henner (1988), op. cit, p. 69 (translation PL).
67 Githens-Mazar, Jonathan/Lambert, Robert (2010). 'Why conventional wisdom on radicalization fails: the persistence of a failed discourse', *International Affairs* 86:4, pp. 889–901 .
68 Hess, Henner (1988), op. cit., p. 69 (translation PL).

References

Anderson, Malcolm (2000). 'Counterterrorism as an Objective of European Police Cooperation', in Reinares, Fernando (ed.). *European Democracies Against Terrorism. Governmental policies and intergovernmental cooperation.* Aldershot Ashgate, pp. 227–43.

Aust, Stefan (2008). *The Baader-Meinhof Complex.* London: The Bodley Head.

BfV (undated). *Zahlen und Fakten zum Rechtsextremismus: Rechtsextremistisches Personenpotenzial (Gesamtuebersicht).* Bundesamt fuer Verfassungsschutz website, at http://verfassungsschutz.de/de/arbeitsfelder/af_rechtsextremismus/zahlen_und_fakten_2010/zuf_re_gesamtuebersicht_2010.html [accessed 6 March 2012].

—(2009). *'Autonome Nationalisten' – Rechtsextremistische Militanz.* Bundesamt fuer Verfassungsschutz, May, at http://verfassungsschutz.de/download/de/publikationen/pb_rechtsextremismus/broschuere_2_0905_autonome_nationalisten/thema_0905_autonome_nationalisten.pdf [accessed 6 March 2012].

Bockstette, Carsten: *Jihadist Terrorist Use of Strategic Communication Management Techniques.* George C. Marshall Centre for European Security Studies No 20, 2008, pp. 1–28.

Claessens, Dieter/de Ahna, Karen (1982). 'Das Milieu der Westberliner "scene" und die "Bewegung 2 Juni"', in Baeyer-Katte, Wanda et al. (eds) *Analysen zum Terrorismus Band 3, Gruppen Prozesse.* Opladen: Wesdeutscher Verlag, pp. 18–181 (72) (translation PL).

Crelinsten, Ronald (2009). *Counterterrorism.* Cambridge: Polity Press.

Githens-Mazar, Jonathan/Lambert, Robert (2010): 'Why conventional wisdom on radicalization fails: the persistence of a failed discourse', *International Affairs* 86:4, pp. 889–901.

Heitmeyer, Wilhelm (2005). 'Right-wing terrorism', in Bjørgo, Tore (ed.). *Root Causes of Terrorism. Myths, reality and ways forward.* London and New York: Routledge, pp. 141–53.

Hess, Henner (2006). 'Die neue Herausforderung. Von der RAF zu Al Qaida', in Kraushaar, Wolfgang (ed.). *Die RAF und der linke Terrorismus.* Volume 1. Hamburg.

—(1988). 'Terrorismus und Terrorismus-Diskurs', in Hess, Henner et al. *Angriff auf das Herz des Staates, Erster Band.* Frankfurt am Main: Suhrkamp Verlag, pp. 55–74.

Kock, Felicitas (2012). 'Kein Bier fuer Nazis: Initiative von Wirten gegen Rechtsextremismus', *Sueddeutsche Zeitung*, 1 March, at http://www.

sueddeutsche.de/bayern/initiative-von-wirten-gegen-rechtsextremismus-kein-bier-fuer-nazis–1.1296177 [accessed 1 March 2012].
Krug, Alexander (2005). 'Neonazis haben Material fuer Bombe gesammelt', *Sueddeutsche.de*, January 20, at http://www.sueddeutsche.de/muenchen/lka-experte-neonazis-haben-material-fuer-bombe-gesammelt–1.672778 [accessed 9 March 2012].
Landesamt fuer Verfassungsschutz Baden-Wuerttemberg (2006). *Rechtsextremismus*. Stuttgart. March.
Mayer, Benjamin/Meyer-Rewerts, Ulf (2011). 'Der vergessene Terrorismus', Goettinger Institut fuer Demokratieforschung, November, at http://www.demokratie-goettingen.de/blog/der-vergessene-terrorismus–2 [accessed 3 March 2012].
Prantl, Heribert (2012). 'Gedenken und die Nazi-Opfer: Wahlkaempfe leben von der angeblichen Ueberfremdung Deutschlands', Sueddeutsche Zeitung, 23 February, at http://www.sueddeutsche.de/politik/gedenken-an-die-neonazi-opfer-wie-integration-endlich-gelingen-kann–1.1292062–2 [accessed 4 March 2012].
—(2011). 'Rechter Terror und Verfassungsschutz: Wenn der Staat versagt', *Sueddeutsche Zeitung*, 17 November, at http://www.sueddeutsche.de/politik/rechter-terror-und-verfassungsschutz-wenn-der-staat-versagt–1.1191241 [accessed 4 March 2012].
rafinfo.de (undated). RAF-Aufloesungserklaerung, *rafinfo.de: die Webressource zur Roten Armee Fraktion*, at http://www.rafinfo.de/archiv/raf/raf–20–4–98.php [accessed 6 March 2012].
Sack, Fritz (1984). 'Die Reaktion von Gesellschaft, Politik und Staat auf die Studentenbewegung', in Sack, Fritz/Steinert, Horst (eds). *Analysen zum Terrorismus Band 4/2: Protest und Reaktion*. Opladen: Westdeutscher Verlag, pp. 106–226.
Schallenberg, Joerg (2004). 'Fuer Sprengstoff ist gesorgt', *taz.de*, 24 November, at http://www.taz.de/1/archiv/archiv/?dig=2004/11/24/a0162 [accessed 9 March 2012].
Scheerer, Sebastian (1984). 'Die Bundesrepublik Deutschland oder: die Gefahren der 'deutschen Empfindlichkeit', in Sack, Fritz/Steinert, Horst (eds). *Analysen zum Terrorismus Band 4/2: Protest und Reaktion*. Opladen: Westdeutscher Verlag, pp. 463–9.
Schimel, Anne (1998). 'Justice "de plomb" en Italie', *Le Monde Diplomatique*, April 1998; at http://www.monde-diplomatique.fr/1998/04/SCHIMEL/10247 [accessed 18 January 2012].
Spiegel (2011). 'The Brown Army Faction: A Disturbing New Dimension of Far-Right Terror', *Der Spiegel*, 14 November, at http://www.spiegel.de/international/germany/0,1518,797569,00.html [accessed 4 March 2012].
—(2006). 'Rechtsextremismus: 'Grosses Problem wird kleingeredet'', *Der Spiegel*, May 21, at http://www.spiegel.de/politik/deutschland/0,1518,417174,00.html [accessed 6 March 2012].
Sueddeutsche Zeitung (2003). 'Anschlag in der Stadtmitte Muenchens geplant: Neonazis wollten juedisches Zentrum sprengen', *Sueddeutsche.de*, 11 November, at http://www.sueddeutsche.de/muenchen/anschlag-in-der-stadtmitte-muenchens-geplant-neonazis-wollten-juedisches-zentrum-sprengen–1.931901 [accessed 9 March 2012].

—(2011). 'Generaldebatte im Bundestag: Opposition attackiert Schroeders Extremismusklausel', *Sueddeutsche.de Politik*, 22 November, at http://www.sueddeutsche.de/politik/generaldebatte-im-bundestag-zum-nazi-terror-opposition-attackiert-schroeders-extremismusklausel–1.1196305 [accessed 6 March 2012].

Waldmann, Peter (2002). 'Terrorismus als weltweites Phaenomen: Eine Einfuehrung', in Frank, Hans/Hirschmann, Kai (eds). *Die weltweite Gefahr. Terrorismus als internationale Herausforderung*. Berlin: Berlin Verlag Arno Spitz, pp. 11–26.

—(1998). *Terrorismus: Provokation der Macht*. Munich: Gerling Verlag.

Whitaker, Brian: 'The definition of terrorism', *The Guardian*, 7 May, 2001, at www.guardian.co.uk/world/2001/may/07/terrorism [accessed 17 February 2012].

Wilkinson, Paul (2001). *Terrorism Versus Democracy: The Liberal State Response* (1st edn). London: Frank Cass.

11

Far Right and Islamist Extremist Discourses: Shifting Patterns of Enmity

Donald Holbrook

It is an obligation upon all Volunteers worldwide to defend their fellow Brothers and Sisters. Those who are capable must do so physically, and others according to their capability. This could be verbal, financial, and creating public opinion and awareness about the barbarism of the New World Order blueprint.

RACIAL VOLUNTEER FORCE

It is obligatory upon the Ummah with all its groups and sections and its men and women, young and old, to provide themselves, their wealth, their expertise, and all types of moral and material support what suffices to carry on the Jihad in the fields of Jihad

USAMA BIN LADIN (APRIL 2006)

Introduction

A range of groups, activities, agendas and platforms are included within the extremist fringe of right-wing political and ideological dispositions. Depending on level, purpose and scope of analysis the category can include numerous different (and conflicting) types of organizations. Hate groups, neo-Nazi gangs and established (but often proscribed) white-supremacist movements are normally included, but so can nationalist political platforms that operate within conventional and mainstream structures, espousing anti-immigrant agendas and, within Europe, opposition towards the EU. Additionally, more nascent quasi-social movements and single-issue groups risk fomenting tensions between different cultures and ethnic groups, the English Defence League being the most obvious case in point.

Within the lifespan of an individual group, moreover, substantial differences in terms of emphases and tactics can often be discerned. Groups engaged in legal political activism, as fringe movements on the conventional political scene, for instance, are often heavily dependent on the position of their populist leaders or founders. Change in leadership, therefore, can prompt significant changes in terms of direction and language. In some cases, a new generation of leaders is tempted by prospects of access to national or regional assemblies and elevated positions of political power through tapping into voters' concerns over issues such as immigration and security. In this sense, the hostile, exclusivist and nationalist agenda is reframed or packaged so as to appeal to a greater number of voters. The British National Party under Nick Griffin and the changes in emphasis and rhetoric from the days of John Tyndall appears to be illustrative of this trend.

For the more extreme far-right groups, however, engagement in the political, democratic, process is condemned or viewed as futile. This is partly due to the fact that party political competition of modern liberal democracies is so far removed from the ideal type of fascist and national socialist systems. Furthermore, extreme far-right groups invariably view mainstream media as being dominated by Jewish influence, thus creating an environment eminently hostile towards white-supremacist platforms. Such conspiracy theories inform perceptions of the wider political scene, which is thought to be biased towards fundamentally liberal values whilst ignoring the importance of race. In essence, therefore, extreme right-wing groups would not be operating on a level playing field if they embraced the democratic model. In light of this fundamental distrust of democracy the electoral successes of 'softer' nationalist right-wing platforms can cause a dilemma for these more extremist groupings: should the achievement be celebrated as a limited victory and recognition of at least some of the issues that are important to members, or would this present opposition to the democratic system as a whole as inconsistent and opportunistic?

As far as more extreme groups are concerned, therefore, goals can only be achieved and grievances addressed through popular uprising – even revolution – pitched against established powers and perceived societal ills and vices. It would be wrong to suggest, however, that these more extreme entities are necessarily all violent. Indeed, many emphasise publicly that violence is not an option often out of fear that explicit, or even implicit, support for aggression and militancy would prompt the authorities to intervene, thus threatening the group's existence.

Much of the extremist activity therefore has focused on propaganda generation, establishing and fomenting contacts with like-minded people, local meetings and lectures, the heavy-metal music scene and other activities that rely on and disseminate profoundly racist and hostile discourses without always prescribing or facilitating pathways leading to violence. In terms of proselytizing and networking, moreover, the internet has become increasingly important. This does not only apply to online 'fronts' for established groups and related virtual communities but also the ability of individuals to open or contribute to blogs and enter social networking sites and an increasing number of online forums where grievances and ideas can be shared.

Given the fluid and ambiguous boundaries of the far-right fringe, therefore, it is important to define the object of analysis in this chapter concretely. The focus is on *discourses* and the content of ideological material, rather than specific group structures, and attention is placed on more *extreme* arguments and platforms, especially those that favour *violent* tactics.

The objective of this chapter is to compare prominent extremist narratives of the far right with those of militant Islamism with the aim of assessing similarities and differences and the ways in which the former has reacted to the latter. This is important not least in light of the heightened profile of groups and movements, such as the EDL, that perceive the presence of Islamism and Islam within their countries as an existential threat, in a normative and cultural sense, if not in terms of racial purity. The findings suggest that the main body of the extreme right-wing discourse under review (see below) was often detached from real-life experiences, particularly when compared with output from militant Islamist groups. In terms of threat perceptions, moreover, it appears far-right activists have not traditionally highlighted militant Islamists as particularly dangerous, suggesting developments in this regard within far-right groupings are relatively recent and largely unprecedented. The 'traditional' extreme right-wing articles under review involve material from some of the most prominent far-right extremist groups, authors and activist networks operating within the United States and Britain. These are listed in Table 1.

Table 11.1. Sources under review representing core far-right extremist discourses

- David Lane & The Order
- Louis Beam
- George Lincoln Rockwell & The American Nazi Party
- William Pierce
- Ben Klassen/Church of the Creator/Creativity
- British People's Party, White Nationalist Party, Aryan Unity
- Blood & Honour
- Combat 18
- Racial Volunteer Force

Numerous books and papers have been written elucidating the core ideational features of extreme right-wing movements as an element of their identity and activities. Additionally, Kaplan and Weinberg (1998) produced a valuable volume on the interactivity between US and European movements. There would seem to be broad agreement among such writers about what these movements stand for, and often, more importantly, what they are against. Bjørgo (1995: 3), for example, identified the core issues as:

> Authoritarianism, anti-communism/-socialism, anti-liberalism, militant nationalism, racism/xenophobia/anti-Semitism, intolerance towards minorities, Golden Age myths, a particularist (as opposed to universalist) morality, and the notion of violence as a creative and cleansing force.

Bowman-Grieve (2009: 995) similarly emphasised the notion of siege mentality within the extreme right wing where conspiracies are seen as keeping the white race in a state of ignorance and 'unawakened' with an ambiguous belief in a form of racial holy warfare and revisionism to re-establish the 'correct' balance.

Mudde (2000), meanwhile, compiled and listed the principal 'ideological features and themes' (187) of extreme right-wing political parties, identifying different strands of the following components: nationalism; exclusionism; xenophobia; anti-democratic features; populism; anti-party sentiments; the strong state; environmental position; ethical outlook; and socio-economic policy (187–9).

Islamist and far-right discourses

David Lane, founder of the US white supremacist group 'The Order' declared, in one of his '88 precepts' that 'Propaganda is a legitimate and necessary weapon of any struggle. The elements of successful propaganda are: simplicity, emotion, repetition, and brevity' (n.d.). The need for any socio-political movement to generate and disseminate narratives that are targeted at a specific audience is widely recognised. These narratives are designed to correspond with the wider myths that are essential to the cultural context in which these movements operate. Social movement theorists and 'framing scholars' refer to this component as 'narrative fidelity' (e.g. Fisher 1984; Campbell 1988; Benford and Snow 1988).

Unsurprisingly, militant Islamist leaders have made similar public references to the importance of message generation and dissemination. The late Usama bin Ladin, for instance, famously argued (in private) that it was 'obvious that the media war in this century is one of the strongest methods [of jihad]; in fact, its ratio may reach 90 per cent of the total preparation for the battles' (n.d.). Dhiren Barot, who was sentenced in November 2006 for terrorism-related offences, expressed very similar sentiments to David Lane's 'precept' number 57, arguing in his book *The Army of Medinah in Kashmir*, 'it should be said first and foremost that both sides use propaganda; anyone who thinks not would be deluding himself for it is a justified art of warfare' (Al Hindi 1999: 54).

In this sense the production and distribution of ideational material is closely linked to operational activism and violence. The accompanying narrative appeals to core emotions of perceived constituents: to a feeling of collective belonging and duty; the anger caused by common grievances and desire for a better future, whilst channelling hostility towards specific targets.

The corpus of extreme right-wing material under review focuses hostility towards a range of communities for ethnic, racial and value-based reasons, including Jews and Israelis; non-white races and immigrants; governments, mainstream politicians and established authorities; mainstream media; homosexuals; whites who fail to support the racial cause; left-wing activists; feminists and those supporting abortion. Animosity towards Muslims, it will be argued below, appears to be a more recent phenomenon in this respect.

Prominent themes of the far-right narrative include denial of the Holocaust during the second world war with glorification of Nazism and a belief in an existential struggle for whites to retain their racial purity faced with a web of conspiracies maintained by Jews, who are seen as manipulating non-whites, mainstream media and governments in order to derail the 'awakening', or global mobilization of whites against these perceived ills, and prevent whites from enjoying their 'natural' superiority over others.

The solution is manifested in the creation of a 'new world order' normally following a vaguely defined but bloody confrontation or a cosmic and cleansing war that will rid the world of all corrupting forces or create an enclave for pure whites.

In addition to these core issues and sources of identity, which are generally universally recognised within the extremist right-wing realm, a number of more specific, local concerns also feature in the narrative. Local authors and outlets for extremist material thus seek to hone the narrative according to the more immediate concerns of fellow activists operating within the same regions, whereby the impact of these more holistic threats is assessed.

In terms of material disseminated and produced by extremist groups within the UK, for instance, prominent issues and topics include the following:

- Viewing continued immigration and presence of non-white communities within the UK as looming demographic catastrophe with some groups arguing immigrants should be forcibly 'repatriated' (see e.g. British People's Party, 2007)
- Condemning globalisation, pluralism and the EU.
- Speaking out against the 'surveillance society' and lack of freedom to discuss race issues.
- Warning against Asian and black gangs, especially as a threat towards white girls.
- Calls to defend Ulster as a permanent part of the United Kingdom.
- Vehement anger towards left-wing political and activist groups, *Searchlight* magazine and other such platforms.
- Accusations of government 'decay' and corruption within the police service, which is seen as unfair in its treatment of national socialists/white power groups.
- Infighting between leaders and groups and suspicion of Nick Griffin's leadership of the British Nationalist Party in comparison with John Tyndall's more hard-line stance.
- Increasing angst concerning Islamist fundamentalism or Islam more generally and the perceived threat from Islamist violent extremists.

Core features of traditional extreme right-wing discourses

Despite the ostensibly universal appeal of these fundamental concerns, however, when the most prominent extremist far-right discourses – that advocate illegal or fringe activism – are scrutinized, substantial variation emerges in terms of prescribed solutions, particularly as these relate to the use of violence.

Louis Beam's 'Leaderless Resistance', for example, a widely available pamphlet which encourages readers to adopt 'phantom cell' structures rather than tiered and hierarchical forms of resistance, sets out an activist framework with implicit violent connotations without elucidating the nature of violent tactics to be employed (1992: 4, see further below). Vagueness appears to be a prominent feature of many extreme right-wing discourses. The level of detail offered, however, differs substantially between groups and even within the same groups over time. George Lincoln Rockwell and the American Nazi Party is a case in point.

Rockwell's confusing tract 'How to get out or stay out of an insane asylum' expresses bitter animosity towards Jews but focuses on the ability of neo-Nazis to operate political platforms and pressure groups, rather than endorsing violent methods (Rockwell 1960).

By contrast, Rockwell's book *White Power* (1967), for instance, uses much starker terminology, referring to Jews as 'human parasites' (37) and black people as a 'plague' (57). Rockwell calls for enemies of whites to be 'annihilated', for Jews to be 'gassed' (12) and all dark-skinned people to be 'killed' (64). Only 'extreme' measures will suffice for the 'white revolution' to succeed (101). Even more ominously, Rockwell seeks to convey a hierarchy of targets to his readers, reminding them that the threat is not external (implying targets can be found with ease), and that Jewish presence in New York, for instance, is obvious. *White Power*, however, does appear to be more specific in its denunciation of perceived adversaries than is generally the norm in the material assessed.

Legal reasons and fear of arrest and prosecution no doubt explain elements of this cautious approach to tactical guidance. Another important factor appears to be the reliance on myth and fantasy. Several prominent extreme right-wing figures and articles under review, for example, rely on fictitious narratives when describing militancy and violent activism. In some cases, the reliance on novels will be partly linked to the legal concerns mentioned, whereby the mythical context provides a 'safer' environment for disseminators of the militant white supremacist message. These fantasies also express the excitement and anticipation activists feel for the advancement of their cause through confronting perceived oppression and the creation of the correct circumstances when mass mobilization and unification of whites can occur.

In addition to his '88 precepts' and other written works, for instance, David Lane's *KD Rebel* (2004) is a dystopian fiction, set in the near future. The book follows members of the 'Kinsland Defenders', part of a wider 'KD Odinist alliance' of a handful of US states, as they fight for the continued purity of the white race against the 'System', a powerful conglomeration of liberals, Jews, non-whites and immigrants seeking to destroy the white race and white culture.

The novel thus offers clear justifications for violence (including murder) against Jews, non-whites and homosexuals as the white supremacist protagonists undermine the 'System' that seeks to render the white race impure. No practical or operational details are conveyed, however, underlining the inspirational and aspirational role of the discourse. Jean Raspail's dystopian fiction *The Camp of the Saints* portrays a similar image.

These fantasies do seem to resonate with subjects engaged in terrorist violence. Timothy McVeigh, for instance, was famously inspired by William Pierce's *Turner Diaries*. When law enforcement officers searched his car, after the Oklahoma City Bombings on 19 April 1995, they found a sealed envelope containing photocopies of the section from the book where Pierce's fictional characters orchestrate an attack very similar to the bombing McVeigh himself carried out (United States District Court for the District of Colorado 1997; Macdonald [alias] 1978 [1st edn]).

Another of Pierce's novels, *Hunter*, tells the storey of Vietnam veteran Oscar Yeager as he fights the 'System' of liberal authoritarian regimes, Jewish conspiracies and uprisings and revolts of dark-skinned people, initially as a lone fighter but subsequently as a member of the white revolutionary 'National League.' On the surface, the storyline appears to be very similar to that of Lane's *KD Rebel*. The difference, however, lies in the extent to which the former adds intricate details in terms of production and placement of explosive devices and other tactical details that otherwise appear uncommon in the core literature. Thus, *Hunter* and *Turner Diaries* practically constitute a step-by-step guide to carrying out acts of terrorism against unarmed civilians. Some versions of the former book, moreover, include references to the Oklahoma City bombings in the publisher's preface and note that a copy was found when police officers searched the home of Terry Nichols, McVeigh's co-conspirator (Macdonald 1998: 2).

Developed further, the extreme right-wing fantasy constitutes the central myth of a quasi-religious racial creed. This is most prominently represented in material from the World Church of the Creator and the subsequent movement associated with Creativity. However, in terms of extremism and, especially, attitudes towards violence, Creativity-linked output differs according to the nature and purpose of the article. 'Softer' and slightly more measured representations of the otherwise starkly racist, anti-Semitic and hostile Creativity discourse, for instance, feature in pamphlets designed to introduce the creed and core doctrine to the wider public, such as 'Facts the Government and Media Don't Want you to Know' (Creativity Movement 2002) and '66 Questions and Answers on the "Holocaust"' (The Church of Ohio n.d.).

In the latter, Matt Hale, the leader of the Creativity Movement before being jailed in 2005, for example, argues that Creativity does not endorse violence. The two pamphlets urge white people to recognise the 'existential' threat allegedly emanating from a series of conspiracies controlled by Jews, seen as power-maximizing and calculating actors in control of politics and the media who rely on sympathy generated by their creation of a Holocaust 'myth'. Dark-skinned people are presented as lesser human beings, whose proliferation would be perilous for the white race, with the exception of Arabs and Palestinians, whose cause is supported. The pamphlets do not, however, prescribe any particular form of action, aside from securing and reading the core texts of the Creativity movement.

These, however, present an even more intolerant and hostile message. Established in the 1970s as the World Church of the Creator (a name which later had to be abandoned for legal reasons), the movement seeks to establish a religion for the white race based on social Darwinist notions of 'natural' progression and domination of the white race over others. The major treatises of Creativity warn that Jews globally, but primarily in the United States, have interrupted this balance and thus undermined the 'laws of nature', denying whites their right to reign over others and enjoy unity through the establishment of a vast empire.

Jews, according to this creed, managed to gain control over the main avenues of power, including media conglomerates, whilst fighting the white race by proxy through manipulating blacks, depicted as savage and subhuman, and immigrants to thin the ranks of pure whites through integration and race mixing. Christianity is portrayed as a Jewish conspiracy designed to keep the white race at bay.

Ben Klassen, a Ukrainian immigrant who settled in the United States, established the Church with the publication of his first in a series of books outlining the fundamentals of the creed. *Nature's Eternal Religion* was first published in 1973. In the first part of the book, 'The Unavenged Outrage', Klassen laments the perceived loss of superiority of the white race, the world's 'most outstanding and most advanced species' (1992: 5), identifying causes and culprits. The second part, 'Salvation', seeks to address this crisis, urging whites to unite in fierce resistance against blacks and Jews. This sets the scene for the rallying call of the movement for 'racial holy war' (RaHoWa) against Jews, blacks and non-whites, lackeys, traitors and other perceived forces of evil. The strategy involves the gradual expansion of the white race with the immediate expulsion of non-whites from the US. *Nature's Eternal Religion*, however, relies on inherently ambiguous terminology, conveying an extremist mindset without elucidating actionable prescriptions or even the intermediate parameters of success. Klassen calls on whites to unite and 'shrink' the ranks of Jews and blacks, in order to clear the way for the inevitable expansion of the white race, presumably through some form of 'cleansing' or 'cosmic' wars. No tactical detail is given, however, nor do references rely on existing or past experiences of force projection in this way (aside from inevitable glorification of the Third Reich and Roman Empire).

Indeed the only 'operational' advice contained within the treatise is for 'dedication, propaganda, and organization' (316). The emphasis is on further proselytizing, but no details concerning the application of the (seemingly indiscriminate) violence are communicated.

Klassen's subsequent core texts, *The White Man's Bible* and *Salubrious Living*, only address this lack of detail partially, focusing primarily on identifying bedrock normative principles and day-to-day behavioural guidelines for individual members or followers.

Two Creativity volumes compile issues from Klassen's journal *Racial Loyalty*. Although largely reiterating points made in earlier works, the first compilation, *Building a Whiter and Brighter World*, delves into some of the issues in more detail and considers the validity of other religious movements. Readers are warned of the coming cosmic clash with the righteous white race pitched against Jews, 'mud races' and white 'traitors' and liberals too. Echoing the anticipated climax of many extreme right-wing works of fiction, such as *KD Rebel* and the *Turner Diaries*, mentioned above, the *Racial Loyalty* articles predict the white race will emerge victorious from these racial wars, free to implement its 'final solution' (which is not explained in detail) and establish a state modelled on Nazi Germany, but recognizing the symbols and greatness of ancient Rome (Klassen 1986: e.g. Issue 13: 8).

Klassen highlights how Creativity was established as an activist framework, not a quietist or pacifist movement. It would channel the immense capacity of the white race to 'militant, meaningful action' (6). No discernable limitations can be detected in terms of the level of violence employed against Jews, non-whites, Christians, homosexuals and other identified foes. Indeed, the second part of this compilation, *Expanding Creativity*, notes explicitly that 'the end justifies the means – any means'. Nothing will interrupt the progression of whites to the pinnacle of world domination, but in order to achieve this goal, every white person will have to become 'a militant, aggressive White Partisan' for the cause. Despite the militant and aggressive narrative and stark dehumanization of identified enemies, however, no concrete guidelines are ever given for implementation (Klassen 1985: 21, 6).

A more recent Creativity publication seeks to address this apparent lack of practical detail. 'The Little White Book', a pamphlet summarizing the major works of the movement, goes much further in prescribing specific acts of violence against identified targets. The basic premise is that 'ideology without action is sterile'. Followers of Creativity should, therefore, establish legitimate political platforms and seek power through established means (as, the author notes, Hitler did in Germany). If Jews or others try to scuttle this process, however, by seeking to curtail the ability of whites to operate political platforms, the Creators should mobilise and fight against them. The desire for bloodshed is clear: 'for every one of ours they kill we will exact ten times their number, starting with the rabbis' (Hale, 2005: 22–3).

Although individuals linked to the Creativity movement have been convicted for violent offences, the ambiguous and hate-filled rhetoric that underpins this extremist creed does not, thankfully, rest on organizational experiences whereby desires for violent clashes have been implemented. Many advocates of Islamist militant groups, by contrast, have based their rhetoric on actual experiences from militancy, including the aforementioned Dhiren Barot.

Descriptions and celebrations of the coming 'racial holy war' form part of the underlying narrative and supporting myth. One senior Creativity figure even wrote a fantasy novel, *Klassen*, depicting the founder of the Church as a heroic leader of the 'Honour Brigade' fighting 'beasts' who made his land impure (Molyneaux n.d. [a]). Such mythologizing of the founder of the Church of the Creator (who committed suicide in 1993) appears paradoxical given Klassen's earlier condemnation of superstition and belief in 'myths' and 'fairy tales' (1992 [2nd edn]: 125).

Similarly, extreme right-wing outlets within the UK have sought to disseminate material intended to address the gap between aspirations of potential participants and those sympathetic with this extremist cause on the one hand and the lack of tangible details as presented in the discourse on the other.

The 'Blood and Honour Field Manual,' is, in many ways, similar to Creativity's 'Little White Book' in that it sets out to address the need to clarify the objectives and tactics that will lead to victory. Echoing Creativity's foundational philosophy, moreover, the national socialist model is presented as the only form of governance that respects 'Nature's eternal laws' and the need for the white race to rein supreme (n.d.: 4).

The booklet is split into six chapters: Ideology, Organization, Propaganda, Violence and Terror, The Activist, The Future. Intended as 'actual activist instructions' and an 'operational manual' for the 'B&H combatant', the booklet nonetheless is remarkably unclear on how activists eager to support the 'militant' campaign to reinstate the supremacy of the white race are supposed to proceed. The author endorses the activist stance of Combat 18 and its planned leaderless resistance within the UK (see further below), although the ongoing debate concerning the validity of more structured groups and organised strategies is also recognised, without endorsement for either model. The section on 'violence and terror', moreover, is cautious, ambiguous and mostly philosophical.

In another B&H pamphlet, 'The Way Forward', the rhetoric is less cautious, as white 'political soldiers' are urged to unite under the coordination of global B&H chapters and the pioneering force of a reinvigorated C18, spreading 'fear and terror among the enemy' (Hammer n.d.: 13). Pamphleteers and peaceful nationalists are condemned as they are seen as diverting attention away from the 'white power terror machine' (13). Although clearly endorsing militancy (with pictures of B&H combatants wearing balaclavas and brandishing rifles and shotguns, apparently training for combat), the scope and nature of targeting is not elaborated.

Diamond in the Dust, a book distributed by C18 celebrating the life of British white supremacist leader Ian Stuart Donaldson, similarly endorses equally extreme solutions, calling for the execution of gays and mixed-race couples, the incarceration of Jews before the implementation of their 'final solution', expulsion of immigrants ('alive or in body bags') and 'plunder' of raw materials from the developing world (Combat 18 2006: 87–8). How activists are supposed to advance towards such horrific end-goals, however, remains unclear.

This is in sharp contrast with much of the material disseminated by militant Islamists. Abdullah Azzam, for instance, whose works have been translated into English and disseminated by sympathetic distribution networks and groups, could refer, in his prescriptions for violent tactics, to his own experiences from fighting Soviet soldiers in Afghanistan during the 1980s. Material from or in support of Al-Qa'ida, moreover, also relies on references to and depictions of the 11 September attacks and other terrorist attacks carried out or inspired by the movement.

More recent manifestations of the global jihadist media campaign, such as the *Inspire* magazine, are sometimes dedicated solely to recent plots, detailing the way in which they were organised and carried out, urging followers and readers to adopt the same tactics, familiarise themselves with specific weapons and their functions, as well as detailing bomb making.

The core texts of the extreme right-wing narrative appear, according to this analysis, to be more abstract, more detached from reality, than equivalent output from militant Islamist activists.

Perhaps for this reason, Islam was even presented as a model followers were urged to emulate (according to the misinterpretations and false representations used) in material from Ben Klassen and the World Church of the Creator. In his first book, for instance, Klassen (1992) wrote:

We can learn from this Moslem surge of power what a tremendous influence an aggressive, well directed religion can have on a scattered and disorganised group of people, even though they be as backward as were the Arab tribes of North Africa and Arabia. Given a religion that united and rallied this amorphous mass of Arab and Bedouin tribes, it laid the foundations for the rise of an Arab Empire. [...] I cannot emphasise too strongly what a tremendous fountain of energy religion can create when it is matched properly to the people that embrace it. Let the White Race learn this lesson again, and learn it well (228).

Indeed, what is striking in much of the core literature of the extreme right wing is the absence of animosity and hostility towards Islam, given the intolerant and exclusivist nature of the narrative that dehumanizes practically everyone outside the realm of 'pure' white activists who have mobilised for the 'cause'.

Furthermore, when extremist discourses of the Islamist and far-right fringes are compared, interesting similarities emerge in terms of language, framing and the concepts addressed.

Far-right and Islamist militant discourses: a comparison

This correlation can be grouped into three distinct categories: (1) convergence of issues; (2) the nature of the emotive language employed; and (3) strategy and the use of force.

1 Convergence of Issues

Militant Islamist and far-right cohorts identify lists of enemies, societal ills, challenges and desired ends that are in many ways comparable. Most obviously, both communicate extreme hatred towards Jews, who are accused of orchestrating conspiracies in order to secure the state of Israel and maximise personal gain, ignoring or even cherishing the suffering of those they are seen to subjugate. Indeed, the common references in extreme right-wing discourses to the 'Zionist-Occupation Government' appear to echo Al-Qa'ida-inspired chants against the 'Zionist-Crusader alliance.' Admittedly, the latter targets Christianity too.

White-supremacist attitudes towards Christianity, however, appear to be problematic and a potential source of tension. Extremist networks espousing supposedly Bible-based messages of hate towards Jews, government control and other perceived ills do exist, but at the same time, however, other strands – notably the Creativity movement (itself presented as a religious alternative for whites) – denounce Christianity as a fraud.

Anger based on observed societal norms and allegedly 'corrupt' features of modernity are equally prominent in both sets of discourses. These relate to observed adverse effects of intoxicants, sexual liberation and proliferation of abortion.

Homosexuality is universally condemned, with both sides advocating a death penalty for those developing relationships with the same sex. David Lane, for example, describes homosexuality as a 'crime against nature' and 'treason' (n.d.). The aforementioned biography in honour of Ian S. Donaldson, *Diamond in the Dust*, calls for gays to be 'executed' (Epilogue in Combat 18 2006: 87). There are countless references expressing animosity towards gays in the militant Islamist discourse. Jamaican cleric Abdullah Faisal, for instance, called for all homosexuals to be killed in a lecture titled 'natural disasters' (n.d.).

Militant Islamist denunciation of democracy as rule by 'man-made laws' is well documented, as is the desire for the establishment of emirates or a Caliphate ruling according to God's law (see e.g. McCants et al. 2006: 9). Similarly anti-pluralist, far-right extremist discourses present the hierarchy of national socialism as practiced in the Third Reich as a model to emulate, denouncing democracy and demanding the establishment of what the Nationalist Front called a 'state based on leadership, authority and discipline' (Morrison n.d.).

In economic terms, the practice of usury or applying interest for profit is condemned by both camps. The British People's Party, for instance, endorses 'distributionism' as an alternative economic model to capitalism, arguing for 'the elimination therein of usury and similar percentage-based profiteering in trade' (BPP 2007). Countless militant Islamist arguments have denounced usury (as indeed have more moderate Islamist accounts based on Qur'anic interpretation) including numerous Al-Qa'ida communiqués from the very beginning of the group's public campaign. The late bin Ladin, for instance, warned in an open letter to Saudi Grand Mufti bin Baz that 'he who tolerates usury is committing one of the greatest of mortal sins' (1994: 7).

Unsurprisingly, distrust of government and mainstream media is expressed throughout the discourse of both cohorts. As a result, establishing nascent media production networks to disseminate the message is perceived as invaluable. Indeed this has often been the preoccupation of many groups and activists who highlight the importance of indigenous media efforts and propaganda, as noted above.

Furthermore, as with any clandestine or illicit activist networks, issues relating to survivability, security and the fate of colleagues is an equal concern of both. The Racial Volunteer Force website, for example, contains links to 'white prisoners of war', asking sympathizers to pledge their support. Helptheprisoners.org, meanwhile, is dedicated to incarcerated Muslims, including Islamist militants convicted for terrorist offences.

A final ideational commonality, which both extremist fringes share, is the representation of the Palestinian independence agenda. References to the Palestinian cause are ubiquitous throughout Islamist and Islamist extremist ideological material. For the extreme right wing, however, references to Palestinian independence and the current situation of Arabs in the region are used to vilify Israelis and Jews. The 2002 manifesto of the White Nationalist Party, for instance, expressed 'total opposition to Zionism and Israel and all their supporters [and] solidarity with the oppressed Arab world, who are our natural allies against the New World Order' (WNP 2002). Aside from the apparent contradiction of such statements with the racist principles of the WNP and similar platforms, such expressions of solidarity with pro-Palestinian activists would later cause some tensions in relation to the perceived threat of militant Islam in Europe and elsewhere.

2 Emotive language

Corresponding to the convergence of issues, the far-right and militant Islamist discourses, by extension, frequently rely on the same or similar language in their tracts and communiqués.

In terms of self-perception, both see themselves as armed and legitimate *vanguards* fighting for the greater good of the masses that in many cases have failed to recognise the nature of the existential threat they face. In this sense the masses are, as Bowman-Grieve noted above, '*unawakened*', or what the Islamist militants would refer to as a state of *Jahiliyyah* (a term made popular by Sayyid Qutb, in this context).

Many who fail to support 'their' vanguard are accused of sacrificing unity among the masses in favour of *material reward*. Ian Stuart Donaldson, for example, lamented in an article titled 'Faith in the Struggle' that people had 'sold out their race and nation for personal gain' (1986).

Similarly, the introduction to Abdullah Azzam's influential book *The Signs of Allah the Most Merciful Ar-Rahmaan in the Jihad of Afghanistan* (published by Maktabah al-Ansaar) condemned Muslims who followed 'materialistic convictions' which drove them 'far from the realities of Jihaad' (Azzam n.d.). Many other Islamist extremist figures, including Anwar al-Awlaki and the Al-Qa'ida leadership, have criticised and warned wealthy Muslims in particular of their failure to contribute to and support the struggle of the vanguard.

Fellow members of this vanguard are referred to as '*brothers*' or '*sisters*' and fallen comrades are seen as '*martyrs*'. Max Hammer's 'Blood & Honour Field Manual', for example, is dedicated to slain 'martyrs' Ian Stuart Donaldson and George Lincoln Rockwell (n.d.). Prominent fighters who have died facing the enemy or whose death is seen as a sacrifice intended to elevate the cause of the vanguard and its community are thus eulogized and revered in both sets of discourses and presented as examples for others to follow.

Even '*infidels*', an obvious target in the faith-based strategy of militant Islam, are also the focus of anger, for example, in some of the more obscure Creativity output (see especially the two novels by Molyneaux, *Klassen* and *White Empire*).

For those unrighteous, or those from within the community of potential participants who have failed to support the cause of the vanguard, both the Islamist and far-right extremist discourses warn of an inevitable and cataclysmic event whereby these individuals will be condemned by a higher authority. Militant Islamist discourses, of course, are replete with references to the Day of Judgement when the righteous will be separated from those who betrayed their religion in favour of personal gain and whose eternal abode thereafter will be Hellfire.

Several references to such a (sometimes ambiguously defined) climax that will instantly vindicate the white supremacist fringe are to be found in its supporting literature too.

Perhaps the most vivid is Ian S. Donaldson's warning of the 'Day of Reckoning' where those who do not rise up and fight for the white race will be condemned by the 'ghosts' of those who fell for the white supremacist cause (Combat 18 2006: 9). Such notions, of course, fit comfortably with visions of Ragnarok – the most cataclysmic event of Norse mythology – celebrated in some 'Odinist'-inspired extremist discourses that glorify the perceived Aryan purity supposedly promoted by Norse culture and myths.

Furthermore, these individual references are embedded within an extremist narrative that appeals to the emotions of potential followers and is based on a feeling of collective belonging and duty for members of the same perceived community, a sense of common grievances and a desire for a better future.

3 Strategy and the use of force

Aside from aspirational and emotive similarities, the extreme right wing and militant Islamist fringes both seek to address more immediate and practical concerns relating to implementation and strategy. These deliberations, however, also have expressive implications for followers as images portraying combat, weapons training and associated camaraderie are used in propaganda material in order to appeal to desires for adventure, excitement and a sense of belonging.

In terms of strategic debates, both cohorts have considered the value of 'leaderless resistance' as opposed to hierarchical or structured forms of militant activism. Leaderless resistance is, in many ways, a more helpful term in this context than those referring to lone offenders or actors. The concept encompasses, according to Garfinkel (2003):

> A strategy in which small groups (cells) and individuals fight an entrenched power through independent acts of violence and mayhem. The cells do not have any central coordination – they are leaderless – and they do not have explicit communications with one another. As a result, causes that employ Leaderless Resistance are themselves resistant to informers and traitors. (1)

As Cozzens notes, the term and concept was popularized by white nationalist Louis Beam in the 1980s with the aforementioned pamphlet *Leaderless Resistance* (2007: 139). Purportedly adapted from Col. Ulius Amoss's strategic guidance to fighting Communism, the document explains how 'leaderless', clandestine and self-starting cells and independent groups would be the most effective device when attacking the materially superior resources of the federal government. Such 'phantom cell' structures would work without any central command, which would be vulnerable to state manipulation and infiltration (Beam 1992).

Attractive in its simplicity and elevation of grass roots activism as fundamental for the common cause, the leaderless approach was apparently endorsed by Ian S. Donaldson and is celebrated in *Diamond in the Dust*, with spontaneous uprisings seen as a precursor to the mass mobilization of whites (Combat 18 2006).

For many extremist and militant far-right groups, however, the leaderless approach contradicts the celebrated ideal type of structured authoritarianism and disciplined ranks organised according to specific spheres and areas of responsibility. Eddy Morrison, for instance, proposed for the National Front an organization with strictly defined and regionally bound layers with competences and roles falling within a clear organizational hierarchy (Morrison 2000). Many other activists on the far right who advocate militancy appear to favour membership or establishment of more grounded organizations, developing specific group identities. The recent example of the 'Aryan Strike Force' in Britain would be a case in point.

The differences, strengths and weaknesses of the two approaches are debated in books, manuals and discussion threads dedicated to identifying a suitable strategic direction for those fighting for the extreme right-wing cause. One example is the 'Blood & Honour Field Manual' by 'Max Hammer', which argues that members and group leaders should assess the situation on the ground before deciding which strategy to adopt, as some scenarios are favourable to encouraging leaderless resistance, whilst a group hierarchy with operational nodes is more appropriate in other environments (n.d.).

Debates within Islamist militant circles concerning the role of organizations, structures and leadership initiatives in the broader violent resistance movement have also been widely reported.

As with far-right extremists, consensus in this regard remains elusive. Sayf al-Ansari, for instance, warns against the consequences of spontaneous individual jihad operations which would not be coordinated and could be counterproductive. Others, most notably Abu Mus'ab al-Suri, have developed a comprehensive doctrine making the case for leaderless cells and deconstructed resistance which would be harder for conventional forces to uncover and destroy (see e.g. Stout et al. 2008).

Conclusion: The danger of reciprocal radicalisation

Militant Islamist and far-right extremist discourses thus appear to be comparable in more ways than perhaps appears probable at first glance, at least in terms of the more prominent articles available to English-speaking audiences. Some have even argued these commonalities provide the basis for physical links to be established and for far-right and Islamist extremist groups to cooperate. Michael (2006), for example, contends: 'it is conceivable that increasingly some elements of the extreme right may come to identify with the anti-Zionist orientation of Islamism' (272). Indeed, the head of Aryan Nations was reported to have endorsed Al-Qa'ida and bin Ladin, its former leader (Schuster 2005). Chermak et al. (2010), meanwhile, found examples of 'direct collaborative exchanges' between Islamist and far-right extremist activists, mostly in relation to fundraising efforts (1032–3).

In contrast with these notions, however, extreme right-wing activists, within the UK and elsewhere, are increasingly vocal in their hostility towards what is variously termed Islam or Islamism and extremism, even though definitions in this regard appear hazy. The aforementioned Aryan Strike Force, for example, advocated violent action against Muslims, as well as the more 'traditional' set of enemies identified in extremist right-wing discourses (Wainwright 2010). A recent discussion thread on the white-supremacist forum 'Stormfront' argues Islam 'is the biggest threat to Europe', although not all forum members agree on strategy and priorities (Stormfront 2010). These perceived vulnerabilities also appear to have motivated Anders Behring Breivik to carry out his attacks.

Furthermore, Ian Davison, one of the main leaders of the Aryan Strike Force, published a video online (under the username 'sweaney', see e.g. *The Northern Echo* 2010) warning Britons against the perceived threat arising from Islamist extremists within the UK, Islam in general, as well as denouncing the Qur'an and the Prophet Mohammed (see 'DVD Project', 2011). The English Defence League has focused on the same points in its output, including videos warning against the proliferation of mosques within the UK (see e.g. YouTube user 'PatriotUK' 2011). Similar material has appeared on the Racial Volunteer Force website. Anti-Islamic far-right political platforms, comparable to the EDL, have also proliferated outside the UK, such as the 'Pro' movement in Germany, prompting concerns that more extreme and violent groups might try to outbid them, in this sense, out of fear of appearing out of touch (e.g. Brandt and Kleinhubbert 2008).

Featuring prominently in the media output from these groups are excerpts and clips from Islamist extremist protests and preachers whose fiery rhetoric is used to present the rise of Islamism and Islam in general, as depicted, as posing a clear danger to domestic stability and the cohesion and safety of white communities. It appears that elements of the far right within the UK and elsewhere have radicalized in response to the heightened prominence of radical Islamist voices domestically and internationally with propaganda tapping into these concerns.

For some groups, this appears to be somewhat problematic, given the traditional focus of animosity and hostility towards Jewish influence and Israel, which is also prominent within Islamist extremist discourses, as discussed above, and the issue of pro-Palestinian groups.

The first issue of *White Nationalist Report* (of the White Nationalist Party), for instance, announced that members of the National Front in the Leeds-Bradford area had distributed leaflets warning against the threat of 'militant Islam' within the UK (Morrison [ed.] 2002a). A latter issue of the same magazine, however, suggested suicide bombings against Israeli targets were justifiable as the last resort of 'oppressed Arab people' (Morrison [ed.] 2002b).

Another of Morrison's groups sought to address this apparent tension between condemning Islamism within the UK whilst endorsing it when directed against Israel. Thus, Issue 100 of the British People's Party newsletter *Nationalist Week* sought to clarify that even though the Palestinian cause was to be supported, this did not amount to endorsement of Islamist-inspired terrorist movements, especially when operating within the UK (BPP 2006).

Leaders of extreme right-wing groups, as well as grass-roots activists, are thus faced with a perceived threat to those values and identities they hold dear, which the established discourse that remains so ubiquitous and celebrated fails to address.

The perceived threat of Islamist groups and ideologies and, increasingly, Islam in general fits uncomfortably with this core narrative, prompting the need for existing priorities to be debated and redrafted, as well as providing opportunities for nascent groups and movements. Although there are no signs Islam or Islamism will replace Judaism, government conspiracies or other perceived threats to the cohesion and purity of the white race, the identification of Islamist extremist groups, with a record of violent activism, as adversaries may encourage some right-wing violent extremists to embrace similarly militant methods. The threat may appear more immediate and the stakes may appear higher than they did when far-right militants focused their animosity on the rather stagnant set of enemies highlighted in the discourse under review. Ironically, of course, militant Islamist groups also provide other extremist activists and violent fringe groups with examples of 'successful' strikes against desired targets that match the dehumanizing narrative they espouse. Ardent followers of white-supremacist movements that underline the perceived intelligence and superiority of members will be loath to admit their militancy is less effective than those on the extremist Islamist fringe.

This dynamic is dangerous. Established extremist and violent groups will be concerned that newer platforms focusing on an issue which has a higher media profile than the core grievances emphasised by the older groups will diminish their power to mobilise individuals sympathetic with far-right causes. Competition between groups in this regard can also encourage extremist positioning as groups and activists struggle to make their voice heard. Responses to Islamist violent extremism, moreover, could prompt (and increase support for) greater and more organised use of violence by far-right activists as individuals and groups seek to demonstrate their ability to respond to the perceived threat of Islamism through escalating the use of violence they themselves seek to display. The potential threat of such reciprocal radicalization, therefore, should not be ignored. In terms of the content of media output, far-right and Islamist extremists are already clashing.

References

Al Hindi, E. (Dhiren Barot) (1999) *The Army of Medinah in Kashmir*. Maktabah al Ansaar Productions.

Azzam, A. (date unknown). *The Signs of Allah the Most Merciful Ar-Rahmaan in the Jihad of Afghanistan*. Maktabah al Ansaar Publications.

Bjørgo, T. (1995). Introduction to 'Special issue on Terror From the Extreme Right' in *Terrorism & Political Violence* (vol. 7, iss. 1), p. 3.

Bowman-Grieve, L. (2009). 'Exploring 'Stormfront': A Virtual Community of the Radical Right' in *Studies in Conflict and Terrorism* (32:11, pp. 989–1007), p. 995.

Beam, Louis (1992). 'Leaderless Resistance' (2nd edn), see e.g. http://www.louisbeam.com/leaderless.htm [accessed 8 May 2011].

Bin Ladin, O. (date unknown) 'Letter to Mullah Umar', Harmony Database (AFGP–2002–600321, translated 5 June 2002), Department of Defense.

—(1994). 'Open Letter for Shaykh Bin Baz on the Invalidity of his Fatwa on Peace with the Jews' (29 December 1994 [27/7/1415 A.H.]) available on the CTC Harmony Database, under 'Letters from Bin Laden' [no. 2], http://www.ctc.usma.edu/harmony/harmony_docs.asp [accessed 4 May 2011].

BPP (British People's Party) (2006). *Nationalist Week* (no. 100, 23 September), available on http://www.bpp.org.uk/nw100.html [accessed 7 May 2011].

—(2007a). Distributionism: A Short Synopsis', available at http://www.bpp.org.uk/distributism2.html [accessed 4 May 2011].

—(2007b). 'The BPP Calls a Truce' available on http://bpp.org.uk/truce.html [last accessed 3 May 2011].

Brandt, A. & Kleinhubbert, G. (2008). 'New Front for the German Far-right: Anti-Islamic Party Is Playing With Fear' in *Der Spiegel Online* (1 March) http://www.spiegel.de/international/germany/0,1518,526225,00.html [accessed 8 May 2011].

Campbell J. (1988). *The Power of Myth*, New York: Doubleday.

Chermak, S., Freilich, J. D. & Simone, J. (2010). 'Surveying American State Police Agencies About LoneWolves, Far-Right Criminality, and Far-Right and Islamic Jihadist Criminal Collaboration' in *Studies in Conflict and Terrorism* (33:11, pp. 1019–41).

The Church of Ohio (date unknown). '66 Questions and Answers on the "Holocaust"', Lakewood, OH.

Combat 18 (2006). *Diamond in the Dust: The Ian Stuart Biography*. (Originally published in 2004, according to distributor).

Cozzens, J. B. (2007). 'Approaching al-Qaeda's Warfare: Function, Culture and Grand Strategy', in Ranstorp, M. (ed.) *Mapping Terrorism Research: State of the Art, Gaps and Future Direction*, Abingdon: Routledge, pp. 131–7.

Creativity Movement (2002). 'Facts the Government and Media Don't Want You to Know,' Riverton, WY: Creativity Movement World Headquarters.

Donaldson, I. S. (1986). 'Faith in the Struggle', available e.g. from Stormfront: http://www.stormfront.org/forum/t717742/ [accessed 6 May 2011].

'DVD Project' (2011). website distributing video made by 'sweaney' (a.k.a. Ian Davison), available on http://blogtext.org/sweaney/ [accessed 6 May 2011].

Eman, X. 'Naissance d'un Nouveau Parti, Ni Droite ni Gauche: identitaires', *Le Choc du Mois*, 35, January 2010.
Faisal, A. (date unknown). 'Natural Disasters' audio lecture, available e.g. from http://www.kalamullah.com/faisal.html [accessed 4 May 2011].
Fisher, W. R. (1984). 'Narration as a Human Communication Paradigm: The Case of Public Moral Argument' in *Communication Monographs* (vol. 51, pp. 1–23).
Garfinkel, S. (2003). 'Leaderless Resistance Today', in *First Monday* (vol. 8, no. 3).
Hale, M. (2005). (revised edition) 'The Little White Book: The Handbook of Dynamic White Racial Religion, Creativity,' East Peoria, IL: World Church of the Creator.
Hammer, M. (date unknown). 'Blood & Honour Field Manual', B&H, widely available for download online, also available in html from http://www.skrewdriver.org/fmintro.html [accessed 6 May 2011].
—(date unknown). *The Way Forward,* Blood & Honour. Widely available online for download and in html format, e.g. http://www.skrewdriver.org/twf1.html [accessed 9 May 2011].
Kaplan, J. and Weinberg, L. (1998). *The Emergence of a Euro-American Radical Right*, Piscataway, NJ: Rutgers University Press.
Klassen, B. (1992). *Nature's Eternal Religion* (2nd edn), East Peoria, IL: World Church of the Creator.
—(1986) *Building a Whiter and Brighter World*, Creativity Book Publisher.
—(1985) *Expanding Creativity*, Creativity Book Publisher.
Lane, D. (date unknown). '88 Precepts', widely available online, e.g. http://www.resist.com/Articles/literature/88PreceptsByDavidLane.htm [last accessed 27 April 2011].
—(2004) *KD Rebel*, available e.g. on http://www.archive.org/details/KdRebel [accessed 9 Many 2011].
Michael, G. (2006). *The Enemy of my Enemy: The Alarming Convergence of Militant Islam and the Extreme Right*, Lawrence: Kansas University Press.
Macdonald, A. [Pierce, W.] (1998). *Hunter*, National Vanguard Books.
McCants, W., Brachman, J. and Felter, J. (2006). *Militant Ideology Atlas: Executive Report* (November), West Point, NY: Combating Terrorism Centre.
Molyneaux, K. (date unknown). *Klassen: For the First Creator*, World Church of the Creator.
—(n.d.) *White Empire*, World Church of the Creator.
Morrison, E. (date unknown). 'The Eight Principals of White Nationalism: The Foundation Stones of NF Ideology', available on http://www.national-front.org.uk/eightprinciples.htm [accessed 4 May 2011].
—(2000). 'The Need to Restructure,' republished for the White Nationalist Party, available on http://www.aryanunity.com/WNP/reorganisation.html [as of 6 May 2011].
—(ed.) (2002a). *White Nationalist Report* (no. 1), available on http://www.aryanunity.com/wnr1.html [accessed 7 May 2011].
—(ed.) (2002b). *White Nationalist Report* (no. 8), available on http://www.aryanunity.com/wnr8.html [accessed 7 May 2011].
Mudde, C. (2000). *The Ideology of the Extreme Right*, Manchester: Manchester University Press.

The Northern Echo (2010). 'Pipe Bomb and the Ricin Found' (1st May) http://www.thenorthernecho.co.uk/news/8132260.Keyboard_warriors_or_threat per cent20_the_public_/ [accessed 6 May 2011].

'PatriotUK' (2011). user channel on YouTube with EDL videos, available on http://www.youtube.com/user/thePatriotuk [accessed 6 May 2011].

Rockwell, G. L. (1960). 'How to Get out or Stay out of an Insane Asylum,' Arlington, VA: American Nazi Party.

—(1967). *White Power: A Nationalist Perspective,* Arlington, VA: American Nazi Party.

Schuster, H. (2005). 'An Unholy Alliance,' *CNN* (29 March), http://edition.cnn.com/2005/US/03/29/schuster.column [accessed 8 May 2011].

Snow, D. & Benford, R. (1988). 'Ideology, Frame Resonance, and Mobilization', in *International Social Moevment Research* (vol. 1, pp. 197–217).

Stormfront (2010). 'Biggest threat to Europe – Islam,' available on http://www.stormfront.org/forum/t737518/ [as of 9 May 2011].

Stout, M. E., Huckabey, J. M., Schindler, J. R., Lacey, W. (2008). *The Terrorist Perspectives Project: Strategic and Operational Views of Al Qaida and Associated Movements.* Annapolis, MA: Naval Institute Press.

United States District Court for the District of Colorado (1997). Criminal Action No. 96-CR–68: UNITED STATES OF AMERICA, Plaintiff, vs. TIMOTHY JAMES McVEIGH, Defendant. Opening Statement for the Prosecution (24th April).

Wainwright, M. (2010). 'Neo-Nazi Ian Davison jailed for 10 years for making chemical weapon' *The Guardian* online (14 February) http://www.guardian.co.uk/uk/2010/may/14/neo-nazi-ian-davison-jailed-chemical-weapon [accessed 6 May 2011].

WNP (White Nationalist Party) (2002). 'A Nationalist Odyssey' available on http://www.aryanunity.com/WNP/nocompromise.html [accessed 6 May 2011].

12

Conclusion

PM Currie

This concluding chapter summarises key points made by the contributors to this volume in answer to the questions that we had set ourselves in advance of the workshop that took place in May 2011 and on which this volume is based. By way of a reminder, the questions in summary were:

- What elements make up the extreme right wing in the UK, Europe and US and what drives it?
- Are more people being drawn to these groups than before? In this respect, is there a risk of reciprocal radicalisation whereby extreme right-wing groups emerge in response to extreme Islamist movements?
- How and why does someone become radicalised and engaged with the extreme right wing?
- How big is the risk of violence, beyond rhetoric and assembly/collection of explosives or weapons, and is there an element of change in this respect within the UK or Europe?
- What does the historical record show about the nature and incidence of extreme right-wing violence?
- What are the strands, sources and foundations of extreme right-wing propaganda and how dynamic is the political narrative? How do these ideological foundations compare with those of militant Islamism?
- What do we know about disengagement from extreme right-wing groups and how do people disengage?

Recent developments in the extreme right wing

Contributors to this volume agree that the extreme right wing in the UK and Europe can be divided into two main categories: on the one hand 'classic' right-wing, politically organised extremist organizations that often see themselves in a direct line of descent from Nazism and fascist parties of the first part of the twentieth century; and on the other, populist extremist groups and movements that do not necessarily reject the constitutional state but increasingly gather around a fear of a perceived growing threat from militant Islamism. There is also general agreement in this volume that the latter part of the twentieth century and the beginning of the twenty-first saw a decline in the influence of the former and an increase in the latter, and it is on this change of focus and its recent consequences that this concluding chapter will concentrate.

In the UK the shift to a new form of right-wing threat has lately coincided with the rise of the English Defence League (EDL) which, according to Nigel Copsey, can best be understood 'as an Islamophobic, new social movement, born of a particularly unattractive and intolerant strand of English nationalism'. Although the longer history behind this development has been considered above, a critical event in this shift was the popular reaction to protests by a small number of apparently Muslim activists against Royal Anglian troops returning from Iraq in 2009, during which the soldiers were denounced as 'baby killers' and 'butchers'. A network of small and already existing street movements came together to form the EDL, bound by a narrative claiming an all-embracing existential threat posed by militant Islamism. Individuals from a variety of backgrounds were attracted, including those who had a history of support for right-wing parties such as the British National Party (BNP) and National Front (NF); campaigners from counter-jihad and anti-Zionist networks; people from the football casuals milieu; those disenchanted with the left wing; and campaigners against persecution of Christians in majority Muslim countries. EDL's leadership and activists sought 'to distance themselves from Britain's "traditional" far right such as the BNP and the NF' replacing race with culture 'as the core concept around which far right or populist social movements are able to construct identities and mobilise support' (Joel Busher).

This shift in the dynamics of the right includes an insistence by the EDL that they are not extremist. They claim not to be racist, thus enabling some support from activists who are proud of their immigrant status. They also claim to articulate the concerns of ordinary British people, not to be Islamophobe but merely concerned about the threat posed by extremist

Islamism. They explain that the left, in particular its politics of multiculturalism, has undermined the ability of Western states to take action against the threat from militant Islamism.

A similar shift in the far right from neo-Nazism, Nazism and anti-Semitism towards a more populist movement motivated by concerns about extremist Islamism (and migration) is also observed in continental Europe. Michel Gandilhon gives an account of how this has developed in France both among extreme right-wing groups and in electoral politics, with the Front National portraying itself as the defender of French values in the face of the Islamist threat. Robert Witte describes how during the 1990s in the Netherlands 'the dominant discourse on migration and integration and, by extension on the status of migrant populations, changed rapidly. Discriminatory, racist (or culturalist) thoughts and statements increasingly became included within this dominant public and political discourse. Various parts of the far-right and racist discourse became perceived as acceptable. One can, therefore, speak of 'modern' right-wing extremism … Contrary to the position of the 'classical' right-wing extremists as 'outsiders' in relation to mainstream society and the established political arena, the 'modern' right-wing extremists have established themselves as 'insiders' within this arena, as established actors that include elements whose support is sought to sustain government majorities within Parliament.'

Ineke van de Valk agrees that politically organised classical right-wing extremist organizations have become less and less significant in the Netherlands in recent times: 'Partially as a reaction to the phenomenon of Islamist extremism, the problem of Islamophobia has grown considerably in the past years, not only in terms of the increased verbal and physical violence directed at the Muslim community but also in terms of the growing tendency to turn a blind eye to crimes of expression and discriminating utterances aimed at them.'

Donald Holbrook explains how the development of extreme right-wing discourse in Europe has supported the above shift. Traditional extreme right-wing propaganda tended to focus hostility towards 'a range of communities for ethnic, racial and value-based reasons, including Jews and Israelis; non-white races and immigrants; governments; mainstream politicians and established authorities; mainstream media; homosexuals; whites who fail to support the racial cause; and left-wing activists, feminists and those supporting abortion.' This accords with Leo Weinberg's summary of the world view of the revolutionary right in the United States: 'Aryans or whites see themselves as a beleaguered race. Aryans are the exclusive source of human invention and creativity'. Inferior races 'have come to dominate the United States and will shortly come to dominate the remaining Aryan domains'. In response, 'the revolutionary right would like to spark a Racial Holy War which would restore white racial supremacy in the United States and perhaps beyond. Jews would be annihilated ... If possible 'mud people' would be returned to their countries of origin.' At this stage of the development of the extreme right narrative, Islamism was presented as a model followers were urged to emulate: not only were its followers viscerally anti-Semitic, but also, in contrast to many of the extreme right wing, they were prepared to carry out acts of violence, rather than merely generate propaganda. However, the promise of linkages between the extreme right wing and Islamists failed to materialize, as the former became increasingly vocal in its hostility to Islam and increasingly focused on countering the jihadi discourse.

Toby Archer sees the origins of this change in 'what is perhaps best described as a post–9/11 transatlantic critical discourse on Islam' which was enabled by the connectivity brought about by the internet and the development of the blogosphere which created instant communities of interest, the ability to learn from each other, rapid linkages between groups nationally and internationally, and an accompanying hardening of attitudes. The essence of the counter-jihadi position may, he argues, be found in two central themes – the belief that Islam threatens Western civilization, and the diagnosis that Western elites have failed to protect against this threat and indeed have become part of the problem, complicit in the supposed surrender of the continent to alien cultural and religious traditions.

Archer suggests that the counter-jihad discourse transformed itself into a movement when a group of activists and bloggers came together in Copenhagen in April 2007 for the UK and Scandinavian Counter-Jihad Summit. A further summit in Brussels during the same year strengthened the movement. Ironically, it enjoyed the facilities of both the Flemish regional parliament and the European parliament. Until the attacks by Anders Behring Breivik in Oslo and on Utøya in July 2011, 'the biggest impact of the Counterjihad appeared to be in providing a discourse for populist right-wing parties across Europe that gave them an enemy to blame (the multicultural elites and Muslims) and a way of criticizing immigrants and immigration to Europe without being easily denounced as straightforward racists ... The idea of the Islamisation of Europe is now common currency for populist right political parties, from Italy to Norway, from France to Finland, from Holland to Hungary, and inevitably with it travels the idea of the treachery of the elites; the idea that when pushed to its twisted extreme gave Breivik his target list.'

Radicalisation and the risks of reciprocal radicalisation

There is also general agreement in this volume that elements of the far right have been radicalized in response to the heightened prominence of radical Islamist voices, domestically and internationally. Extreme right-wing propaganda, drawing inter alia on material from extremist Islamist websites, has effectively tapped into these concerns. Such propaganda and attempts to mobilise support have often found fertile ground in areas of particular deprivation and social breakdown. A core organising principle has been the notion that extreme right groups represent the true local culture and exist to protect and promote indigenous identity. McAuley notes how racism and sectarianism can reflect the strength of communal values and can be used in the development of 'in-groups' which can be set in opposition to the construction of 'out-groups' and the notion of the 'Other.' McAuley observes that in Northern Ireland, the largest concentration of extreme right-wing activities is in areas that are 'amongst the most economically and socially deprived in the Province' with the highest concentration of migrant workers. Lehr notes the appeal of the extreme right wing in conditions of relative deprivation in the former German Democratic Republic after reunification, and, more generally, as a consequence of 'problems of adaption and integration as a result of social change' across all of Germany.

Van der Valk's research in the Netherlands suggests that a range of factors causes young people to become interested in manifestations of the far right: a search for social belonging; a wish to make friends; and an emotional need to revolt, to protest and to discuss social problems. A common element for many of her respondents was that they experienced problems at home; they felt the need for an outlet for feelings of frustration and hatred, had a generally negative attitude and mistrust of government and society, and little trust in the police to protect them from threats from peers, including those from other ethnic backgrounds. Being the victim of violence by a member of another ethnic group was often a factor in radicalization. Political ideas did not appear to play a prominent role for any of the respondents as a motivation to begin to engage in extreme right-wing groups. However, it was found that respondents often did have ethnic prejudices that had sometimes been prompted by negative experiences with ethnic minority youth. Ideological elements tended to be introduced later on in the process, and it was also in this latter phase that the use of violence increased and came to occupy a central position in the lives of activists, enhancing their status in the group. Busher observes that for some activists, EDL demonstrations 'provide an outlet for violence, and an opportunity for marginalized (often young) men to enact an aggressive masculinity directed towards (militant) Muslims as 'the dangerous Other'.

Van der Valk also draws out the similarities of motivation for those on the extreme right and militant Islamists: indignation, anger and frustration; a vague sense of the need to rebel against society; binary thought categories with little appetite for nuance; a strong tendency to rely on conspiracy theories; experiences of social polarization along ethnic lines; vulnerability to group threats, whether symbolic or real; radicalization often relating to a quest for identity, a desire for social belonging and companionship; the drive for revenge against perceived injustices.

This raises the risk of reciprocal radicalization. As van der Valk concludes, 'resulting polarization may foster radicalization on both sides'. Or, as Busher puts it: 'The rise of the EDL has prompted widespread fears both about a re-emergence of far right street violence, and about broader processes of "cumulative extremism" or "tit-for-tat radicalization" – a spiral of hostility between opposing social movements as groups associated with the "far right" and with "radical Islam" antagonize one another and stir up prejudice and hatred in the communities from which they draw their support.'

But, at this point, it would be helpful to remember that not all who sympathize with the extreme right and take part in its activities will become violent. Given the accessibility and the wide range of hate-filled propaganda, and its apparent resonance for many, it is worth pausing to consider why there is not more violence. Relevant here is the finding offered by van der Valk that 'comparative research has shown that in countries where modern populist radical right parties that operate within legal boundaries are strong, hard-line, neo-Nazi right-wing parties tend to be weak'. This relates to the thesis expounded by Ruud Koopmans that levels of violence from the extreme right tend to be lower in countries which have relatively strong far-right political parties engaged in the democratic system.[1] Extreme right protesters are more likely to resort to violence, he suggests, 'when other channels of access to the political system are closed'.[2] Gandilhon's account in this volume of far-right developments in France provides evidence to support this: the rise and eventual institutionalization of the Front National as a political entity was accompanied by a decline in violence from the traditional extreme right wing.

Furthermore, in his survey of the development of extreme right discourse, Holbrook points out that it would be incorrect to imply that more extreme right-wing 'entities are necessarily all violent. Indeed, many emphasise publicly that violence is not an option often out of fear that explicit, or even implicit, support for aggression and militancy would prompt the authorities to intervene, thus threatening the group's existence'. Whilst much extreme right-wing activity is devoted to generating propaganda, often profoundly racist and hostile, Holbrook explains that it quite often lacks any prescription about what the diagnosis should lead to in terms of action.

Thus, Louis Beam's Leaderless Resistance 'sets out an activist framework with implicit violent connotations without elucidating the nature of violent tactics to be employed'. Similarly, the publications of the Creativity Movement do not prescribe action beyond securing and reading its core texts. Whilst the World Church of the Creator calls for racial holy war against Jews and non-whites, 'its founder's principal text gives no tactical detail of how this should be achieved ... The only operational advice is for dedication, propaganda and organization'. The emphasis is on proselytizing. Holbrook suggests that 'legal reasons and fear of arrest and prosecution no doubt explain elements of this cautious approach to tactical guidance'. He goes on to posit that another important factor appears to be the reliance on myth and fantasy. This may suggest that the discourse itself, its creation and collection, the sense of belonging to an exclusive group that has for its members a compelling explanation of the world's ills, may offer sufficient satisfaction without the need for the majority to take the risks associated with the violence that is in general terms recommended.

Busher explains that, whilst violence is important for some in relation to the EDL protest experience, it represents only a small part of it. For a majority, EDL demonstrations represent 'an enjoyable day out, a chance to catch up with friends, and there are always activists who strive to ensure that EDL events reinforce ... claims that the EDL is a legitimate and peaceful movement'.

Furthermore, radicalization into extremists groups is not a one-way street. Van der Valk describes some of the factors that may persuade individuals to try to leave right-wing extremist groups: 'Some begin to doubt the ideology, others are disappointed in the behaviour of members who, in their eyes, do not live according to the norms and values of the group. Still others begin to have misgivings about the actions of the group, or they are disappointed in the movement as a "trustworthy social environment". Some activists leave but remain loyal to the ideas, but the obverse is also true. An obvious factor that stimulated people to leave the movement, according to the study, was the need for a more conventional, socially integrated existence: in short, work, partner and a house, a wish that was obviously related to their age.' Similar factors have been found at work amongst those who have left other sorts of extremist groups.[3]

Assessing the risk

This multiplicity of factors in determining the shape of extremist groups, their motivations and the careers of individual members, make an overall assessment of the risk of violence and its calibration remarkably complex and necessarily inexact. Nevertheless, the findings of this volume suggest a broad consensus that the risk of violence from counter-jihad discourse is not inconsiderable, and growing. According to his own testimony, this was the source of Breivik's determination to murder. As Archer says, Breivik's manifesto, *2083: A European Declaration of Independence*, clearly suggests 'that he wanted to be seen as politically motivated, and realised that in doing so he would be labelled as a terrorist'.

'Central to Breivik's view of the world is a fear that Islam is taking over Europe, and that European elites – particularly those of liberal and left-wing traditions – are complicit in the supposed surrender of the continent to what he believes is an alien cultural and religious tradition. These beliefs ... are by no means particular to Breivik ... Many in Europe (and in other countries around the world) share this world view, even if they condemn his actions' – which led to the murder of 77 individuals and injuries to a further 151 (Archer).

Directly or indirectly, the counter-jhadist world view has inspired the increase in violence targeted against Muslims that is found at least in the UK and the Netherlands, as documented in this volume. Robert Lambert describes how in the UK criminal damage, violence and intimidation against mosques, Islamic institutions and Muslim organizations have become commonplace since 9/11. His preliminary analysis establishes what he calls 'a prima facie case for both extremist nationalist involvement and influence' in such violence. He concludes that his research provides 'a clear indication that extremist nationalist organizations including the BNP and the EDL have played a key role in fostering a climate in which anti-Muslim or Islamophobic violence has become an established feature of British life since 9/11'. He is not saying that 'the leaders of the BNP or EDL have been involved in criminal conspiracies to attack Muslims or their places of workshop or congregation', but rather that 'their campaigning activities against Muslims have provided motivation and a rationale for many of the criminal attacks that have taken place. In consequence, it becomes clear that many Muslim communities have since 9/11 faced a double jeopardy of becoming victims of violence aimed at them because of their religion as well as by virtue of their ethnic origins'.

The seriousness of the potential threat in the UK is illustrated by the cases that Lambert instances: Robert Cottage was jailed in July 2007 for possession of what was described by the police at the time as the largest amount of chemical explosive of its type ever found in this country; Martin Gilleard, jailed for possession of weapons including nail bombs, explained that he 'was sick and tired of hearing nationalists talk of killing Muslims, of blowing up mosques, of fighting back … the time has come to stop the talk and start to act'; Neil MacGregor, who pleaded guilty to 'threatening to blow up Glasgow Central Mosque and behead a Muslim every week until every mosque in Scotland is closed'; Terence Gavan, who was convicted of manufacturing bombs, and whose arsenal was described by the judge in the case as the largest find of its kind in the UK in modern history. In total, there are seventeen people serving prison sentences in the UK for terrorism-related offences who are known to have been associated with extreme right-wing groups.[4]

Similarly in the Netherlands, Van der Valk observes that 'the rise in prominence of Islamophobic discourse within traditional and nascent far-right wing movements coincided with the proliferation of violent incidents directed against the Muslim community'. As in the UK, much of this violence against Islam is directed at centres of worship as the most visible symbol of Muslim communities.

In France, Gandilhon notes that anxieties about Islam and attendant cultural insecurity are leading to the movement of populations, with some Europeans refusing to live alongside Muslims, and moving as a result to rural areas or the outskirts of cities: 'This cultural separation is steadily shaping a landscape hitherto unknown in the history of the Republic, where communities are being created which are more or less mutually hostile, and which are becoming more and more geographically separated.' He sees this 'social and political redistribution as pregnant with risks. In such circumstances it is not impossible that radical groups might emerge that are dedicated to carrying out a violent struggle against the alleged Islamification of France.'

In Germany, the recent uncovering of an extreme right-wing terrorist cell in Zwickau that was responsible for a series of murders (one Greek victim, eight Turkish victims and one police-woman), as well as a bombing in Cologne that injured twenty-two people mostly of Turkish origin, provided a wake-up call to the risks of xenophobe terror. A parliamentary inquiry[5] has been established in Germany to examine the strength of extreme right-wing groups, which Peter Lehr argues has been consistently underestimated (see below).

The threats posed by Islamist terrorism as perceived by recent manifestations of the extreme right and counter-jihad movement are likely to seem more real, compelling and requiring of action to them than those posed by the Zionist Occupying Government and other such imagined enemies. But we should, perhaps, remember that even the latter aspect of the threat has not been something that could wisely be ignored. Leonard Weinberg notes that, aside from 9/11, the most lethal act of terrorism in American history was the attack on the Alfred P. Murrah Federal Building in Oklahoma City in April 1995. FBI figures on hate crimes, according to Weinberg, suggest that 'prior to Al Qaeda's attack on the World Trade Centre and Pentagon, terrorist violence in the United States was significantly a right-wing activity measured both in terms of the frequency of incidents and the fatalities inflicted'.

But now the stakes may be rather higher. The new enemy can be seen by the new extreme right to have proved itself competent in its chosen forms of attack (9/11, 7/7 and the Madrid bombings being particularly resonant in the US and Europe) and so to have moved beyond rhetoric to murderous action. As Holbrook writes, 'ardent followers of white-supremacist movements that underline the perceived intelligence and superiority of members will be loath to admit their militancy is less effective than those on the extremist Islamist fringe'.

To conclude this brief summing-up of the risks of reciprocal violence between the extreme right-counter jihadists and militant Islamists, I cannot do better than to return to Weinberg's elegant conclusion:

> I think it is fair to say that the emergent Euro-American revolutionary right – no matter how much attention it manages to attract and how enticing its message becomes to increasingly threatened, economically and socially, white populations – is unlikely to induce a race war, holy or otherwise. It does share a common hatred of Jews and the state of Israel with growing Muslim populations and their leadership(s) in Europe and elsewhere. The common hatred, though, seems unlikely to produce more than temporary cooperation. In this instance, the enemy of my enemy is not my friend. Because it is precisely the growing Muslim populations, in Western Europe especially, that are likely to be the targets of intensifying 'white power' backlash.

If not RAHOWA within one or more of the Western democracies, the potential certainly exists for a wave of terrorist activity. For revolutionary right terrorism to occur, the late Israeli political scientist Ehud Sprinzak identified two indispensable elements. First, a racial or religious minority group(s) must be present that appears to be making illegitimate demands for political and social equality with the dominant white population. Right-wing groups form to protect this population from the minorities' claims to legitimacy and recognition. In turn, these groups seek the assistance of governments to prevent the minorities from achieving their aims. If the governments are unresponsive or, worse, appear to side with the white population's racial or religious enemies, then the conditions are present for a terrorist campaign directed not only at members of the minority groups, but also at the governments that now appear to constitute the 'enemy' as well. It seems difficult to deny these elements are currently present in a number of the western democracies.

It remains to be seen whether others in significant numbers will follow the logic of the extreme right wing/counter-jihadist rhetoric and act in ways similar to Anders Behring Breivik. That he murdered so many and was not the first to try to do so, apparently for similar motives, suggests that a posture of intelligent vigilance would be an appropriate governmental response. Vigilance does not mean that governments and counter-terrorist authorities need share the judgement of the extreme right and counter jihadists that either their militant Islamist enemies or their own reactions could pose an existential threat to Western democratic civilization. That would be to underestimate the restorative properties of well-established democratic states and to ignore the lessons of recent counter-terrorist experience. The key point here is the need for proportionate, even-handed characterization of the problem and response to it, in order to enhance security and avoid making things worse.

Lehr gives an interesting explanation of how it was that the German authorities paid relatively little attention to the extreme right wing in contrast to its treatment of the extreme left wing. The latter directly targeted the political system and, in the context of the Cold War, could be seen as extension of an existential threat. 'More often than not, and in a particular German context, terrorism is when terrorists attack highly symbolic and instrumental targets in a very public and widely reported manner as the RAF did – unspectacular attacks targeting minorities do not seem to meet this criterion, and seem to remain below the radar screen of public attention.' Lehr concludes that 'in the fight against extremism and terrorism there should be no overreaction or under-reaction by the police and the judiciary'. Tore Bjørgo has made a similar point: 'The process of radicalization is a function of political interaction. The role of the state is crucial in those interactions because both under-reaction and overreaction may well accelerate this escalation process.'[6] But even-handedness and proportionate responses to violence will only be possible if there is an accurate, early diagnosis and presentation of the problem.

In the case of the extreme right this has been a challenge not only for Germany. Witte explains how the extreme right in the Netherlands was to some extent able convincingly to portray itself as responding understandably to social and socio-economic issues such as the increasing presence of migrants, unemployed and poor housing. In the UK, evidence presented to the Home Affairs Select Committee in 2011 also questioned whether the extreme right wing was being regarded with sufficient seriousness.[7]

Peter Knoope (2011) offers a helpful analysis of this problem in terms of 'cultural distance'. He argues that 'threat perception is highly influenced by the cultural distance between the terrorist and the target. When the cultural difference is limited, the acceptance is easier and therefore the public resilience is higher ... Cultural distance defines the alienation, which defines the collective ability to accept somebody's (temporary) wrongdoing.[8]' This analysis, Knoope suggests, has significant policy implications. The greater the cultural distance between terrorist and target, the greater the effect in terms of fear, the greater the difficulty in understanding motivation and the greater the demand for punitive reaction. This exacerbates the sense of exclusion for those who are associated in the majority community's mind with the sources of such terrorism. Post–9/11 political rhetoric in the West unfortunately often had the effect of increasing this sense of exclusion, rather than lessening cultural distance. Knoope continues by suggesting that 'if exclusion is the problem, then political or societal inclusion is the answer' and he offers some examples in the Netherlands where interventions at community level to assist with the processes of disengagement from extremist groups would seem to have had some success.[9]

This realization of the importance of even-handed response is behind some of the innovations in, for example, the UK's latest iteration of its counter-terrorist Prevent strategy. This recognised that 'our work to address the ideologies underpinning other forms of terrorism, such as extreme right-wing terrorism, is less developed than work on terrorism associated with Al Qai'da. We will address this as a priority'.[10] The Home Affairs select committee's subsequent report noted some progress in this direction: 'The revised Prevent strategy is designed to address all forms of terrorism, whereas the original focus of the strategy dealt only with Islamist terrorism and therefore almost exclusively focused on Muslim communities. Resources are to be allocated proportionate to the threat. To a certain extent Prevent has already begun to address other threats; for example, 8 per cent of those referred to the Government's Channel programme[11] as being potentially vulnerable to violent extremism were referred owing to concerns around right-wing violent extremism.'[12]

No doubt there is more to be done in the UK and elsewhere in terms of developing strategies to manage risks associated with the extreme right wing. There is clearly also room for further research to develop understanding of what motivates members of the extreme right wing and, in particular, what causes them to leave such activities behind. But, in spite of some inevitable gaps, we hope that the essays collected in this volume will be of assistance in providing context for the judgements that need to be made by counter-terrorist practitioners and policy professionals in their challenging and often thankless task of calibrating and managing risks from terrorism and political violence to protect us all.

Notes

1 Koopmans, R. (1996). Explaining the rise of racist and extreme right violence in Western Europe: Grievances or opportunities? *European Journal of Political Research*, 30, p.185.
2 Ibid., p.195.
3 Bjørgo, T. and Horgan, J. (2009). *Leaving Terrorism Behind*, London: Routledge.
4 UK's Prevent Strategy, (2011), paragraph 5.10.
5 http://www.bbc.co.uk/news/world-17519871
6 Bjørgo, T. Root Causes of Terrorism: Myths, reality and ways forward, London: Routledge, Introduction p.10.
7 Home Affairs Select Committee, 19th Report – Roots of Radicalisation, 6 February 2012, paragraphs 44–5.
8 Knoope, P. Right Wing Extremism: A spoiled identity perspective (unpublished).
9 Ibid.
10 Prevent Strategy, (2011), paragraph 8.7.
11 Channel programme – UK activities designed to help identify and help individuals vulnerable to radicalisation.
12 Home Affairs Select Committee, op.cit. paragraph 42.

Bibliography

ACLU 2010 – Nationwide Anti-Mosque Activity on the website of the American Civil Liberties Union. (2010). http://www.aclu.org/print/map-nationwide-anti-mosque-activity [accessed 2010]
Adair, J. and McKendry, G. (2007). *Mad Dog*, London: John Blake.
Adorno, T. W., Frenkel-Brunswik, E., Levinson, D. J., Sanford, R. N. (1950). *The Authoritarian Personality*, New York: Harper & Brothers.
—(2006) *De gewelddadige jihad in Nederland: actuele trends in de islamitisch-terroristische dreiging* (pp. 13–18). The Hague: Ministry of the Interior and Kingdom Relations [www.aivd.nl].
AIVD (General Intelligence and Security Service) (2011) *Right wing extremism and the extreme right in the Netherlands* (p. 5). The Hague: Ministry of the Interior and Kingdom Relations [www.aivd.nl].
Algemene Inlichtingen- en Veiligheidsdienst (AIVD) (2005). *'Lonsdale-jongeren' in Nederland. Feiten en fictie van een vermeend rechts-extremistische subcultuur*, Den Haag AIVD, 2005.
Al-Hindi, E. (Dhiren Barot) (1999). *The Army of Medinah in Kashmir*, Maktabah al-Ansaar Productions.
Ali, W., Clifton, E., Duss, M., Fang, L., Keyes, S., and Shakir, F. (2011). *Fear, Inc. The Roots of the Islamophobia Network in America*, Washington, DC: Centre for American Progress.
Allen, C. (2003). *Fair Justice: The Bradford Disturbances, the sentencing and impact*. London: FAIR.
—(2009). *The Rise of the British National Party: Anti-Muslim Policies and the Politics of Fear*. University of Birmingham: Institute of Applied Social Studies.
—(2010). *Islamophobia*. Aldershot: Ashgate.
Allen, C. and Jorgen, N. (2002). *Summary report on Islamophobia in the EU after 11 September 2001*, Vienna: European Monitoring Centre on Racism and Xenophobia (EUMC).
Amis, L. (2009, November). In league with the extreme right? *Standpoint*. Retrieved 18/3/2011 from http://www.standpointmag.co.uk/in-league-with-the-extreme-right-features-louis-amis-english-defence-league [accessed 18 March 2011]
Anderson, Malcolm (2000). 'Counterterrorism as an Objective of European Police Cooperation', in Reinares, Fernando (ed.). *European Democracies Against Terrorism. Governmental policies and intergovernmental cooperation*. Aldershot: Ashgate, pp. 227–43.
Archer, Toby (2009). Welcome to the Umma: The British State and its Muslim Citizens Since 9/11, *Cooperation and Conflict* 2009, 44, 329.

—(2008a) Countering the Counterjihad, *Homeland Security and Resilience Monitor*, September 2008. Vol.7 No.7, RUSI. [accessed August 2008]

—(2008b) Learning to love the Jews: the impact of the War on Terror and the counter-jihad blogosphere on European far right parties. Paper prepared for and presented at the XV NOPSA conference, Tromsø, August 08. uit.no/getfile.php?PageId=1410&FileId=1337 [accessed August 2008]

Athwal, H., Bourne, J., and Wood, R., (2010). *Racial Violence: The Buried Issue*, Briefing paper number 6, London: Institute of Race Relations.

Aust, Stefan (2008). *The Baader-Meinhof Complex*. London: The Bodley Head

Azzam, A. (n.d.). *The Signs of Allah the Most Merciful Ar-Rahmaan in the Jihad of Afghanistan*, Maktabah al-Ansaar Publications. [accessed May 2010]

Backes, U. and Moreau, P. (1994). *Die Extreme Rechte in Deutschland : Geschichte – gegenwärtige Gefahren – Ursachen – Gegenmassnahmen*. München: Akademie-Verlag.

Balent, M. (2011). 'Disquiet over Identity in Europe: Rising to the Challenge set by National Populism', *European Issue Policy Paper*, Number 205, Paris: Robert Schuman Foundation.

Barker, M. (1981). *The New Racism: Conservatives and the ideology of the tribe*. London: Junction Books.

Barkun, M. (1994). *Religion and the Racist Right*, Chapel Hill, NC: University of North Carolina Press.

Beam, Louis (1992). 'Leaderless Resistance' (2nd edn), see http://www.louisbeam.com/leaderless.htm [accessed 8 May 2011].

Bell, D. (1987). *Acts of Union: Youth Culture and Sectarianism in Northern Ireland*, Basingstoke: Macmillan.

Bell, K., Jarman, N. and Lefebvre, T. (2004). *Migrant Workers in Northern Ireland*, Belfast: Institute for Conflict Research.

Bennett, D. (1995). *The Party of Fear*, 2nd edn, New York: Vintage Books, 1995.

Benoist (de) A. (2007). *Demain la décroissance ! Penser l'écologie jusqu'au bout*, E-dite.

Benz, W. & T. Pfeiffer (eds) (2011). *'Wir oder Scharia'? Islamfeindliche Kampagnen im Rechtsextremismus. Analysen und Projekte zut Prävention*, Schwalbach: Wochenschau Verlag.

Berlet, C. (2011). Updated: Breivik's Core Thesis is White Christian Nationalism v. Multiculturalism, July 25 2011. Talk to Action website http://www.talk2action.org/story/2011/7/25/73510/6015 [accessed July 2011]

Berlet, C. and Lyons, M. (2000). *Right-Wing Populism in America*, New York: The Guilford Press.

Betz, H-G. (2003). 'The Growing Threat of the Radical Right', in P. H. Merkl and L. Weinberg (eds), *Right Wing Extremism in the Twenty-First Century* (pp. 74–93) London/Portland: Frank Cass.

BfV (2009). *'Autonome Nationalisten' – Rechtsextremistische Militanz*. Bundesamt fuer Verfassungsschutz, May, at http://verfassungsschutz.de/download/de/publikationen/pb_rechtsextremismus/broschuere_2_0905_autonome_nationalisten/thema_0905_autonome_nationalisten.pdf [accessed 6 March 2012]

—(2010). *Zahlen und Fakten zum Rechtsextremismus: Rechtsextremistisches Personenpotenzial (Gesamtuebersicht)*. Bundesamt fuer Verfassungsschutz website, at http://verfassungsschutz.de/de/arbeitsfelder/af_rechtsextremismus/zahlen_und_fakten_2010/zuf_re_gesamtuebersicht_2010.html [accessed 6 March 2012].

Bin Ladin, O. (n.d.). 'Letter to Mullah Umar', Harmony Database (AFGP–2002–600321, translated 5 June 2002), U.S. Department of Defence.

—(1994). 'Open Letter for Shaykh Bin Baz on the Invalidity of his Fatwa on Peace with the Jews' (29 December 1994 [27/7/1415 A.H.]) available on the CTC Harmony Database, under 'Letters from Bin Laden' [no. 2], http://www.ctc.usma.edu/harmony/harmony_docs.asp [accessed 4 May 2011].

Birt, Yahya (2009). Defining Islamophobia today: the state of the art. Musings on the Britannic Crescent blog. 15 September. http://www.yahyabirt.com/?p=175 [accessed 29 December 2009].

Biswas, K. (2011). 'Eyes to the far Right', *New Internationalist*, 443, June, pp. 14–17.

Bjørgo, T. (1995a). Introduction to 'Special issue on Terror from the Extreme Right' in *Terrorism & Political Violence* 7 1.

—(ed.) (1995b). *Terror from the Extreme Right,* London: Frank Cass.

—(1997). *Racist and right-wing violence in Scandinavia: patterns, perpetrators and responses*, Oslo: Tano Aschehoug.

—(ed.) (2005). *Root Causes of Terrorism: Myths, reality and ways forward*, London: Routledge.

Bjørgo, T. and Horgan, J. (2009). *Leaving Terrorism Behind*, London: Routledge.

Bjørgo, T. and Witte, R. (eds) (1993). *Racist Violence in Europe*, London: Macmillan.

Bockstette, Carsten. *Jihadist Terrorist Use of Strategic Communication Management Techniques,* George C. Marshall Centre for European Security Studies No 20, 2008, pp. 1–28.

Bonnett, A. (1993). *Radicalism, Anti-Racism and Representation*, London: Routledge.

Bourseiller, C. (2002). *La Nouvelle extrême-droite*, Editions du Rocher.

Bovenkerk, F. (2006). 'Islamofobie', in van Donselaar, J. and Rodrigues, P. (eds), *Monitor Racisme and Extremisme: Zevende rapportage* (pp. 95–97). Amsterdam: Amsterdam University Press/Anne Frank Stichting/Universiteit Leiden.

Bowman-Grieve, L. (2009). 'Exploring "Stormfront": A Virtual Community of the Radical Right', in *Studies in Conflict and Terrorism* (32:11, pp. 989–1007).

BPP (British People's Party) (2006). *Nationalist Week* (no. 100, 23 September), available on http://www.bpp.org.uk/nw100.html [accessed 7 May 2011].

—(2007a). Distributionism: A Short Synopsis', available at http://www.bpp.org.uk/distributism2.html [accessed 4 May 2011].

—(2007b). 'The BPP Calls a Truce' available on http://bpp.org.uk/truce.html [last accessed 3 May 2011].

Brandt, A. and Kleinhubbert, G. (2008). 'New Front for the German Far-right: Anti-Islamic Party Is Playing With Fear', in *Der Spiegel Online* (1 March) http://www.spiegel.de/international/germany/0,1518,526225,00.html [accessed 8 May 2011].

Breivik, Anders Behring (2011). *2083: A European Declaration of Independence* available at http://www.kevinislaughter.com/wp-content/uploads/2083+-+A+European+Declaration+of+Independence.pdf [accessed 2011 and 2012]

Brewer, J. (1991). 'The parallels between sectarianism and racism: the Northern Ireland experience', in *One small step toward racial justice,* London: Central Council for Education and Training in Social Work.
—(1992). 'Sectarianism and racism, and their parallels and differences', *Ethnic and Racial Studies,* Volume 15, Issue 3, pp. 352–64.
—(1994). *The Edge of the Union: The Ulster Loyalist Political Vision,* Oxford: Oxford University Press.
Bruce, S. (1986). *God Save Ulster: The Religion and Politics of Paisleyism,* Oxford: Oxford University Press.
Bulten, E. Joh. (1970). *Diary of E. Joh. Bulten, no. 230, Aaltense Gijzelaars.*
Buis, H. (1988). *Beter een verre buur. Racistische voorvallen in buurt en straat,* Amsterdam: SUA.
Bush, G. W. (2004). Speech on Promoting Democracy, October 25, 2004, Greeley, Colo. http://www.cfr.org/world/speech-promoting-democracy/p7472
Caiani, M. and della Porta, D. (2010). *Extreme Right and Populism. A Frame Analysis of Extreme Right Wing Discourses in Italy and Germany,* Vienna: Institute for Advanced Studies.
Caldwell, C. (2011). *Une révolution sous nos yeux, comment l'islam va transformer la France et l'Europe,* éditions du Toucan.
Caldwell, J. and Robinson, J. (2006). *In Love with a Mad Dog,* Dublin: Gill and Macmillan.
Campbell, J. (1988). *The Power of Myth,* New York: Doubleday.
Car, M. 'You are now entering Eurabië', in *Race & Class,* 48 (2006) 1, pp. 1–22, London: Sage Publications [http://rac.sagepub.com].
Carter (2005). *The Extreme Right in Western Europe – Success or Failure?* Manchester: Manchester University Press.
Catterall, P. (1994). *The Battle of Cable Street,* Contemporary British History. 8 (1), 105–32.
Charpier, F. (2005). *Génération Occident,* Editions du Seuil.
Chermak, S., Freilich, J. D. and Simone, J. (2010). 'Surveying American State Police Agencies About Lone Wolves, Far-Right Criminality, and Far-Right and Islamic Jihadist Criminal Collaboration', in *Studies in Conflict and Terrorism* (33:11, pp. 1019–41).
Church, C., Visser, A. amd Johnson, L. S. (2004). 'A path to peace or persistence? The "single identity" approach to conflict resolution in Northern Ireland', *Conflict Resolution Quarterly,* Volume 21, Issue 3, pp. 273–93.
The Church of Ohio (n.d.). 66 *Questions and Answers on the 'Holocaust',* Lakewood, OH.
City of Amsterdam (1983). *Tussen Witkalk en Zwarthemden,* B&W gemeente Amsterdam, 22 February 1983.
Clerkin, Major D.V. (1989). 'Who we really are' *The Talon,* pp. 2–3.
Coates, J. (1987). *Armed and Dangerous,* New York: Hill and Wang.
Cohen, Nick (2007). *What's Left? How Liberals Lost Their Way,* Fourth Estate: London.
Collins, M. (2011a). War breaks out between EDL and 'Infidels'. *Searchlight* 431 8–10.
—(2011b). *Hate: My Life in the British Far Right,* London: Biteback Publishing.

Combat 18 (2006). *Diamond in the Dust: The Ian Stuart Biography*. (Originally published in 2004, according to distributor).
Commission on British Muslims and Islamophobia (1997). *Islamophobia: A challenge for us all*, London: Runnymede Trust.
Connolly, P. (2002). "Race' and Racism in Northern Ireland: A Review of the Research Evidence', Belfast: Office of the First Minister and Deputy First Minister.
Copsey, N. (2010). *The English Defence League: Challenging our country and our values of social inclusion, fairness and equality*. London: Faith Matters.
Copsey, N. and Macklin, G. (eds) (2011). *The British National Party; contemporary perspectives*, Abingdon: Routledge.
COT Institute (2008) *'20th Century Right Wing Groups in Europe: Prone to extremism or terrorism?'* European Commission Sixth Framework Programme: Case Study, Work Package 3.
Coulter, J. (2003). ' Ireland – The Orange Swastika: The rise of new millennium Loyalist Nazism', *Searchlight*, November.
Coulter, M. (2004). 'From bigotry to racism', *Searchlight*, February.
Cozzens, J. B. (2007). 'Approaching al-Qaeda's Warfare: Function, Culture and Grand Strategy', in Ranstorp, M. (ed.) *Mapping Terrorism Research: State of the Art, Gaps and Future Direction*, Abingdon: Routledge pp. 131–137.
Creativity Movement (2002). *Facts the Government and Media Don't Want You to Know*, Riverton, WY. Creativity Movement World Headquarters.
Crelinsten, Ronald (2009). *Counterterrorism*. Cambridge: Polity Press
Cusack, J. and McDonald, H. (1997). *UVF*, Dublin: Poolbeg Press.
Dalton, Anita (2011). [1] '2083 by Anders Behring Breivik, Part 3: Breivik' *I read odd books* 24/8/2011 http://ireadoddbooks.com/2083-by-anders-behring-breivik-part-3/
—(2011). [2] '2083 by Anders Behring Breivik, Fjordman: Part Two' *I read odd books* 24/8/11 http://ireadoddbooks.com/2083-by-anders-behring-breivik-fjordman-part-two/
Dard, O. (2011). *Voyage au cœur de l'OAS*, Perrin.
Davidovic, M., J. van Donselaar, P. R. Rodrigues and W. Wagenaar (2008). 'Het extreemrechtse en discriminatoire gehalte van de PVV', in Donselaar, J. van and Rodrigues, P. R. (eds) (2008). *Monitor Racisme en Extremisme, Achtste Rapportage*, Amsterdam/Leiden: Anne Frank Stichting/Universiteit Leiden.
Dees, M. (1996). *Gathering Storm*, New York: Harper Collins.
Donaldson, I. S. (1986). 'Faith in the Struggle', available e.g. from Stormfront: http://www.stormfront.org/forum/t717742/ [accessed 6 May 2011].
Donselaar, J. van (1991). *Fout na de oorlog, fascistische en racistische organisaties in Nederland 1950–1990*, (p. 16ff). Amsterdam: Bert Bakker.
—(1993). 'The Extreme Right and Racist Violence in the Netherlands', in T. Bjørgo & R.Witte (eds) *Racist Violence in Europe*, London: MacMillan.
—(1997). *Eerste Rapportage Monitor Racisme en Extreemrechts*, Leiden: LISWO.
—(2000). *Monitor Racisme en Extreemrechts. Derde Rapportage*, Leiden: Universiteit van Leiden Departement Bestuurskunde.

BIBLIOGRAPHY

—(2010). 'Rechts Radicalisme', in H. Moors, L. Balogh, J. van Donselaar and B. de Graaff (2010). *Polarisatie en radicalisering in Nederland. Een verkenning van de stand van zaken in 2009*, IVA: Tilburg.

Donselaar, J. van and Rodrigues, P. R. (2001, 2002, 2004, 2006, 2008). Monitor Racisme en Extremisme, resp. Vierde, Vijfde, Zesde, Zevende en Achtste Rapportages, Amsterdam/Leiden: Anne Frank Stichting/Universiteit Leiden.

—(December 2004). *ANNEX Racism and Extreme Right Monitor : sixth report. Developments following the murder of Theo van Gogh*, Amsterdam/Leiden: Anne Frank Stichting/Leiden University.

Donselaar, J. van and Wagenaar, W. (2007). Monitor Racisme en Extremisme. Racistisch en extreemrechts geweld in 2006, Amsterdam/ Leiden: Anne Frank Stichting/Universiteit Leiden.

Douglas, M. (1984). *Purity and Danger*, Abingdon: Routledge.

'DVD Project' (2011). website distributing video made by 'sweaney' (a.k.a. Ian Davison), available on http://blogtext.org/sweaney/ [accessed 6 May 2011].

Eatwell, R. (2003). 'Ten theories of the extreme right', in P. H. Merkl and L. Weinberg (eds), *Right Wing Extremism in the Twenty-First Century* (pp. 47–74). London/Portland: Frank Cass.

—(2006). Community cohesion and cumulative extremism in contemporary Britain, *The Political Quarterly*, 77(2) 204–16.

EDL (2011). Mission Statement. http://englishdefenceleague.org/about-us/mission-statement/ [accessed 7 October 2011].

Eyesnck, H. J. (1954). The Psychology of Politics. London: Routledge & Kegan Paul.

Faisal, A. (n.d.). 'Natural Disasters' audio lecture, available e.g. from http://www.kalamullah.com/faisal.html [accessed of 4 May 2011].

Fekete, L. (2004). Anti-Muslim racism and the European security state, *Race and Class*, 46 (1), 3–29.

—(2008). *Integration, Islamophobia and Civil Rights in Europe*. London: Institute of Race Relations.

—(2009). *A Suitable Enemy: Racism, Migration and Islamophobia in Europe*. London: Pluto Press.

Fennema, M. (2010). *Geert Wilders: Tovenaarsleerling*. Amsterdam: Bert Bakker.

Fisher, W. R. (1984). 'Narration as a Human Communication Paradigm: The Case of Public Moral Argument', in *Communication Monographs* (vol. 51, pp. 1–23).

Fjordman (2006). *How the Feminists' 'War against Boys' paved the way for Islam* http://www.brusselsjournal.com/node/1300

Flynn, K. and Gerhardt, G. (1990). *The Silent Brotherhood*, New York: Signet.

Ford, R. and Goodwin, M. (2010). 'Angry White Men: Individual and contextual predictors of support for the British National Party', Political Studies, Volume 58, Number 1, pp. 1–26.

Fortuyn, P. (1994). Het Zakenkabinet Fortuyn, Utrecht: Bruna.

—(1997) Tegen de islamisering van onze cultuur. Nederlandse identiteit als fundament, Utrecht: Bruna.

Gable, G. and Jackson, P. (2011). *Lone Wolves: Myth or Reality?* London: Searchlight Publications.

Gardell, M. (2003). *Gods of the Blood*, Durham, NC: Duke University Press.

Garfinkel, S. (2003). 'Leaderless Resistance Today', in *First Monday* (vol. 8, no. 3).
Gautier, J.-P. (2009). *Les Extrêmes Droites en France, de la Traversée du Désert à l'Ascension du Front National (1945–2008),* Editions Syllepse.
Geoghegan, P. (2008a). 'Beyond Orange and Green? The awkwardness of negotiating difference in Northern Ireland', *Irish Studies Review,* Volume 16, Issue 2, pp. 173–94.
—(2008b). 'Multiculturalism and Sectarianism in Post-agreement Northern Ireland', *Scottish Geographical Journal,* Volume 124, Numbers 2 –3, pp. 185–91.
Geraghty, T., McStravick, C. and Mitchell, S. (2010). *New to Northern Ireland: A study of the issues faced by migrant, asylum seeking and refugee children in Northern Ireland,* London: NCBNI.
Gilligan, C. (2008). 'Migration and migrant workers in Northern Ireland', *ARK Research Update,* Number 53, February, pp. 1–4.
Gilligan, C., Hainsworth, P. and McGarry, A. (2011). 'Fractures, Foreigners and Fitting In: Exploring Attitudes towards Immigration and Integration in "Post-Conflict" Northern Ireland', *Ethnopolitics,* Volume 10, Number 2, pp.253–69.
Gilligan C. and Lloyd, K. (2006). 'Racial prejudice in Northern Ireland,' *ARK Research Update,* Belfast and Londonderry: ARK.
Githens-Mazer, J. and Lambert, R. (2010). *Islamophobia and Anti-Muslim Hate Crime: A London case study.* Exeter: University of Exeter, European Muslim Research Centre.
Giudice, F. (1992). *Arabicides, Une Chronique Française (1970–1991),* La Découverte.
Goffman, E. (1969). *Strategic Interaction,* Philadelphia, PA: University of Pennsylvania Press.
—(1986). *Stigma: Notes on the Management of Spoiled Identity,* Simon & Schuster.
Goodwin, M. (2011). 'Europe's Radical Right: Support and Potential', *Political Insight,* Volume 2, Number 3, pp. 4–7.
Graham, B. (2004). 'The Past in the Present: The Shaping of Identity in Loyalist Ulster', *Terrorism and Political Violence,* Volume 16, Number 3, pp. 483–500.
Gramsci, A. (1982). Pour un Gramscisme du Droite, *Proceedings of the 16th National Assembly of GRECE,* Éditions du Labyrinthe.
Grieve, J. and French, J. (2000). 'Does Institutional Racism Exist in the Metropolitan Police Service?', in D. G. Green (ed.) *Institutional Racism and the Police: Fact or Fiction?* London: Institute for the Study of Civil Society (Civitas).
Griffin, N. (2007). Islamisation of Europe, Clemson University, 24 October, Part 2, http://www.youtube.com/watch?v= 916qkfhT8DU [accessed 21 November 2009].
—(2008). By their fruits (or lack of them) shall you know them. BNP website. http://web.archive.org/web/20071014195717/ http://www.bnp.org.uk/columnists/chairman2.php?ngId=30 [accessed 3 April 2009].
Guilluy, C. (2010). *Fractures Françaises,* François Bourin éditeur.
Hainsworth, P. (ed.) (1998). *Divided Society: Ethnic Minorities and Racism in Northern Ireland,* London: Pluto Press.
—(2000). *The Politics of the Extreme Right: From the margins to the mainstream.* London: Pinter.

Hale, M. (2005) (revised edition). *The Little White Book: The Handbook of Dynamic White Racial Religion*, East Peoria, IL: Creativity, World Church of the Creator,

Hammer, M. (n.d.). 'Blood & Honour Field Manual', B&H, widely available for download online, also available in html from http://www.skrewdriver.org/fmintro.html [accessed 6 May 2011].

—(n.d.). *The Way Forward*, Blood & Honour. Widely available online for download and in html format, e.g. http://www.skrewdriver.org/twf1.html [accessed 9 May 2011].

Hayes, B. C. and Dowds, L. (2006). 'Social Contact, Cultural Marginality or Economic Self-Interest? Attitudes Towards Immigrants in Northern Ireland', *Journal of Ethnic and Migration Studies*, Volume 32, Number 3, pp. 455–76.

Heitmeyer, Wilhelm (2005). 'Right-wing terrorism', in Bjørgo, Tore (ed.) *Root Causes of Terrorism. Myths, reality and ways forward*. London and New York: Routledge, pp. 141–53.

Hess, Henner (1988). 'Terrorismus und Terrorismus-Diskurs', in Hess, Henner et al. *Angriff auf das Herz des Staates, Erster Band*. Frankfurt am Main: Suhrkamp Verlag, pp. 55–74.

—(2006). 'Die neue Herausforderung. Von der RAF zu Al Qaida', in Kraushaar, Wolfgang (ed.) *Die RAF und der linke Terrorismus*. Volume 1. Hamburg.

Hewitt, R. (2005). *White Backlash and the Politics of Multiculturalism*, Cambridge: Cambridge University Press.

Hickman, M. Crowley, H. and Mai, N. (2008). *Immigration and social cohesion in the UK. The rhythms and realities of everyday life*. York: Joseph Rowntree Foundation.

Holtrop, A. and U. den Tex (1984). 'Bijons in Holland' in *Vrij Nederland Bijlage* 30 June 1984.

Huntingdon, S. (1993). *The Clash of Civilizations and the Remaking of World Order*. London: Simon and Schuster.

Husbands, C. (2002). 'How to tame the dragon, or what goes around comes around: a critical review of some major contemporary attempts to account for extreme-right racist politics in Eastern Europe', in M. Schain, A. Zolberg and P. Hossay (eds), *Shadows over Europe: the development and impact of the extreme right in Western Europe* (pp. 38–59). New York: Palgrave Macmillan.

Huyghe, F.-B. (2011). *Terrorismes, Violence et propagande*, coll. Découvertes, Gallimard.

Ignazi, P. 'The Extreme Right: Defining the object and assessing the causes', in M. Schain, A. Zolberg and P. Hossay (eds), *Shadows over Europe: The development and impact of the extreme right in Western Europe* (pp. 23–37). New York: Palgrave Macmillan.

Institut Français d'Opinion Publique (IFOP), 'Voting Intentions for the 2012 Presidential Elections,' *Le Journal du Dimanche*, 23 May 2011.

Intelligence Project, (2009). *Terror from the Right*, Montgomery ALA: Southern Poverty Law Centre.

Jackson, P. (2011a). *The EDL: Britain's 'new far right' movement*, Northampton: RNM Publications.

—(2011b). 'English Defence League: Anti-Muslim politics online' in P. Jackson and G. Gable (eds) *Far-right.com: Nationalist extremism on the internet*, Northampton: RNM Publications.
Jarman, N. (2003). 'Victims and Perpetrators, Racism and Young People in Northern Ireland', *Child Care in Practice*, Volume 9, Number 2, pp. 129–39.
—and Monaghan, R. (2004). *Racist Harassment in Northern Ireland*, Belfast: Institute for Conflict Research.
Jaschke, H-G. (2001). *Rechtsextremismus und Fremdenfeindlichkeit: Begriffe – Positionen – Praxisfelder*. Wiesbaden: Westdeutscher Verlag.
Jasper, J. M. (2007). *The Art of Moral Protest: Culture, Biography and Creativity in Social Movements*. Chicago, IL: University of Chicago Press.
Jay, Martin (2010). Dialectic of Counter-Enlightenment: The Frankfurt School as Scapegoat of the Lunatic Fringe, *Salmagundi* 168–169 (Fall 2010-Winter 2011) http://cms.skidmore.edu/salmagundi/backissues/168–169/martin-jay-frankfurt-school-as-scapegoat.cfm
Kaplan, J. (ed.) (n.d.). *Encyclopedia of White Power*, Walnut Creek, CA: Alta Mira Press.
Kaplan, J. and Bjørgo, T. (eds) (1998). *Nation and Race* Boston: Northeastern University Press.
Kaplan, J. and Weinberg, L. (1998). *The Emergence of a Euro-American Radical Right*, Piscataway, NJ: Rutgers University Press.
King, S. (2011, July). The EDL's Supergrass, *Searchlight* 433.
Klassen, B. (1985). *Expanding Creativity*, Creativity Book Publisher.
—(1986). *Building a Whiter and Brighter World*, Creativity Book Publisher.
—(1992). *Nature's Eternal Religion* (2nd edn), World Church of the Creator.
Knoope, P. Right Wing Extremism: A spoiled identity perspective (unpublished).
Knox, C. (2011). 'Tackling Racism in Northern Ireland: "The Race Hate Capital of Europe"', *Journal of Social Policy*, Volume 40, Number 2, pp. 387–412.
Koopmans, R. (1996). Explaining the rise of racist and extreme right violence in Western Europe: Grievances or opportunities? *European Journal of Political Research*, 30, pp. 185–216.
Kopeček, L. (2007). 'The Far Right in Europe', *Central European Political Studies Review*, Volume IX, Part 4, pp. 280–93.
Kowalsky, W. and Schroeder, W. (eds) (1994). *Rechtsextremismus: Einführung und Forschungsbilanz*. Opladen: Westdeutscher Verlag.
Kriesi, H., R. Koopmans, J. W. Duyvendak, M. G. Giugni (eds) (1995). *New Social Movements in Western Europe: A comparative analysis*, London: UCL Press.
Kuitenbrouwer, J. (2010). *De Woorden van Wilders and Hoe ze Werken*, Amsterdam: De Bezige Bij.
Lambert, R. (2011). *Countering al-Qaeda in London: Police and Muslims in Partnership*. London: Hurst.
Lambert, R. and Githens-Mazer, J. (2010). *Islamophobia and Anti-Muslim Hate Crime: UK case studies*. Exeter: University of Exeter. http://centres.exeter.ac.uk/emrc/publications/Islamophobia_and_Anti-Muslim_Hate_Crime.pdf [accessed 12 August 2011].
Lane, D. (n.d.). '88 Precepts', widely available online, e.g. http://www.resist.com/Articles/literature/88PreceptsByDavidLane.htm [last accessed 27 April 2011].

—(2004). *KD Rebel*, available e.g. on http://www.archive.org/details/KdRebel [accessed 9 May 2011].
Leclercq, J. (2010). *Droites Conservatrices, Nationales et Ultras, Dictionnaire 2005–2010*, L'Harmattan.
Lefeuvre, D. (2006). *Pour en Finir avec la Repentance Coloniale*, Flammarion.
Lewis, H. (2010). 'Racism & Sectarianism: Two Sides of the Same Coin?: The Northern Ireland Experience', *International Journal of Diversity in Organisations, Communities and Nations*, Volume 6, Issue 3, pp. 27–36.
Landesamt fuer Verfassungsschutz Baden-Wuerttemberg (2006) *Rechtsextremismus*. Stuttgart.
Lijphart, A. (1979). *Verzuiling, Pacificatie en Kentering in de Nederlandse Politiek*, (3rd edn), Amsterdam: DeBussy.
Lipset, S. and Raab, E. (1970). *The Politics of Unreason*, New York: Harper and Row.
Lööw, H. 'White Power Rock 'n' Roll: A Growing Industry' in Kaplan, J. and Bjørgo, T. (eds) (1998). *Nation and Race* Boston: Northeastern University Press.
Lowles, N. (2011, August). It's Time to Act against the EDL, *Searchlight* 434, 14.
Loyalist Commission (c. 2005). '*Loyalist or Racist? You can't be both*', Belfast: Loyalist Commission.
Lubbers. M., Gijsberts, M. and Scheepers, P. (2002). 'Extreme Right-wing voting in Western Europe', European Journal of Political Research, Volume 41, pp. 345–78.
Macdonald, A. [Pierce, W.] (1998). *Hunter*, National Vanguard Books.
Macpherson, Lord (1999). *The Stephen Lawrence Inquiry*, Report, Cm. 4262-1.
Maitron, J. (2007). *Le Mouvement Anarchiste en France, Dès Origines à* 1914 (tome 1) coll. Tel, Gallimard.
Malek, M. (ed.) (2010). *Anti-Muslim Prejudice,* London: Routledge.
Marsdal, M. (2008). 'Underdog politics', *Red Pepper*, June.
Marsh, J. (2010). *From Seasiders to Casuals United*, Mashed Swede Project.
Martynowicz, A. and Jarman, N. (2009). *New Migration, Equality and Integration: Issues and Challenges for Northern Ireland*, Belfast: Equality Commission for Northern Ireland.
Maussen, Marcel (2006). 'The Netherlands Anti-Muslim sentiments and mobilization in the Netherlands. Discourse, policies and violence', in Cesari, Jocelyne (ed.) *Securitization and Religious Divides In Europe. Muslims In Western Europe After 9/11: why the term Islamophobia is more a predicament than an explanation.* Submission to the Changing Landscape of Citizenship and Security 6th PCRD of European Commission (available at: http://www.libertysecurity.org/IMG/pdf_Challenge_Project_report.pdf)
Mayer, Benjamin and Meyer-Rewerts, Ulf (2011). 'Der vergessene Terrorismus', Goettinger Institut fuer Demokratieforschung, November, at http://www.demokratie-goettingen.de/blog/der-vergessene-terrorismus–2 [accessed 3 March 2012]
McAuley, J. W. (2008). 'Conflict resolution in asymmetric and symmetric situations: Northern Ireland as a case study' (with Catherine McGlynn and Jonathan Tonge), *Dynamics of Asymmetric Conflict: Pathways toward Terrorism and Genocide,* Volume 1, Number 1, pp. 88–102.

—(2009). 'Conflict Transformation and Former Loyalist Paramilitary Prisoners in Northern Ireland' (with Jonathan Tonge and Peter Shirlow), *Terrorism and Political Violence*, Volume 22, Number 1, pp. 22–40.

—(2010a). *Ulster's Last Stand? (Re)Constructing Ulster Unionism After the Peace Process*, Dublin: Irish Academic Press.

—(2010b). 'Changing Senses of Britishness in Northern Ireland after the Good Friday Agreement' (with Jonathan Tonge), *Parliamentary Affairs*, Volume 63, Number 2, pp. 266–85.

McAuley, J. W. and Spencer, G. (eds) (2011). *Ulster Loyalism after the Good Friday Agreement: History, Identity and Change*, Basingstoke: Palgrave Macmillan.

McAuley, J. W., Tonge, J. and Mycock, A. (2011). *Loyal to the Core? Orangeism and Britishness in Northern Ireland*, Dublin: Irish Academic Press.

McCants, W., Brachman, J. and Felter, J. (2006). *Militant Ideology Atlas: Executive Report*, West Point, NY: Combating Terrorism Centre.

McGarry, A., Hainsworth, P. and Gilligan, C. (2009). 'Political Parties and Minority Ethnic Communities in Northern Ireland: Election Manifestos 1994–2007', *Translocations: The Irish Migration, Race and Social Transformation Review* http://www.translocations.ie, Number: 2009–0420.

McVeigh, R. (2002). *A Place of Refuge? Asylum Seekers and Refugees in Northern Ireland: A Needs Assessment*. Belfast: Refugee Action.

McVeigh, R. and Rolston, B. (2007). 'From Good Friday to Good Relations: sectarianism, racism and the Northern Ireland state', *Race and Class*, Volume 48, Number 4, pp. 1–23.

Meer, N. (2008). The Politics of Voluntary and Involuntary Identities: Are Muslims in Britain an ethnic, racial or religious minority? *Patterns of Prejudice*, 42 (1), pp. 61–81.

Meer, N. and Noorani, T. (2008). A sociological comparison of anti-Semitism and anti-Muslim sentiment in Britain, *The Sociological Review*, 56 (2), pp. 195–219.

Meleagrou-Hitchens, A. and Standing, E. (2010). *Blood & Honour: Britain's Far-Right Militants*, London: The Centre for Social Cohesion.

Melucci, A. (1980). The New Social Movements: A theoretical approach, *Social Science Information*, 19 (2) 199–226.

Merkl, P. H. (2003). 'Introduction', in P. H. Merkl and L. Weinberg (eds) *Right-wing Extremism in the Twenty-First Century*, Abingdon: Routledge.

Michael, G. (2006). *The Enemy of my Enemy: The Alarming Convergence of Militant Islam and the Extreme Right*, Lawrence, Kan: Kansas University Press.

Modood, T. (1988). 'Black', Racial Equality and Asian Identity, *New Community*, 14 (3), pp. 297–404.

Molyneaux, K. (date unknown). *Klassen: For the First Creator*, World Church of the Creator.

—(n.d.). *White Empire*, World Church of the Creator.

Monitor Racism and Extremism, Anne Frank House/University of Leiden, 1996–2011. [English translation of reports: www.Annefrank.org]

Monneret, J. (2008). *La Guerre d'Algérie en Trente-Cinq Questions*, L'Harmattan.

Monnot, C., Mestre A. (2011). *Le Système Le Pen, Enquête sur les Réseaux du Front National*, Denoël.

Moors, H., L. Balogh, J. van Donselaar and B. de Graaff (2010). *Polarisatie en radicalisering in Nederland. Een verkenning van de stand van zaken in 2009*, IVA: Tilburg.

Morrison, E. (date unknown). *The Eight Principals of White Nationalism: The Foundation Stones of NF Ideology*, available on http://www.national-front.org.uk/eightprinciples.htm [accessed 4 May 2011].

—(2000). *The Need to Restructure*, republished for the White Nationalist Party, available on http://www.aryanunity.com/WNP/reorganisation.html [accessed 6 May 2011].

—(ed.) (2002a). *White Nationalist Report* (no. 1), available on http://www.aryanunity.com/wnr1.html [accessed 7 May 2011].

—(ed.) (2002b). *White Nationalist Report* (no. 8), available on http://www.aryanunity.com/wnr8.html [accessed 7 May 2011].

Mudde, C. (2000). *The Ideology of the Extreme Right*, Manchester: Manchester University Press.

Muslim Safety Forum (2007). *Islamophobia: the Impact on London*. London: MSF. http://muslimsafetyforum.org/docs/Islamophobia&ImpactonLondon.pdf [accessed 3 November 2009].

National Children's Bureau and ARK Young Life and Times (2010). *Attitudes to Difference: Young people's attitudes to and experiences of contact with people from different ethnic and minority communities in Northern Ireland*, London: National Children's Bureau.

National Front (2011). Statement of Policy – Northern Ireland. Available at: http://www.national-front.org.uk/policy.html [accessed 4 July 2011].

Nelson, S. (1984). *Ulster's Uncertain Defenders*, Belfast: Appletree Press.

Norris, P. (2005). *Radical Right Voters and Parties in the Electoral Market*, Cambridge: Cambridge University Press.

Northern Ireland Council for Ethnic Minorities (2009). Annual Report, 2008/2009, Belfast: NICEM.

Northern Ireland Department of Enterprise Trade and Investment (2006). 'New Disadvantaged Area Maps Published', *Press Release*, 25 September.

Northern Ireland Housing Executive (2009). 'Migrant Workers and the Housing Market: A Case Study of Dungannon', Belfast: NIHE Research Unit.

Northern Ireland Statistics and Research Agency (2010). 'Migration Statistics for Northern Ireland, 2009', Belfast: NISRA.

Panvini, G. 'Black Terrorism and Red Terrorism during the "Années de Plomb": War will not Happen', in Lazar, M. and Matard-Bonucci, M-A. (eds), *L'Italie des Années de Plomb, le Terrorisme entre Histoire et Mémoire*, Paris: Autrement 2011.

'PatriotUK' (2011). user channel on YouTube with EDL videos, available on http://www.youtube.com/user/thePatriotuk [accessed 6 May 2011].

Pearson, G. (1976). '"Paki-Bashing" in a North East Lancashire Cotton Town: A case study and its history', in G. Mungham and G. Pearson (eds), *Working Class Youth Culture*, London: Routledge and Kegan Paul.

Pehrson, S., Gheorghiu, M. A. and Ireland, T. (2012). 'Cultural Threat and Anti-immigrant Prejudice: The Case of Protestants in Northern Ireland', *Journal of Community & Applied Social Psychology*, Volume 22, Issue 2, pp. 111–24.

Pew Research Centre (2005). *Islamic Extremism: Common concern for Muslim and Western publics*: 17-nation Pew global attitudes survey, Washington, DC, http://pewglobal.org/reports/pdf/248.pdf [accessed 2011]

Pfahl-Traughber, A. (1994). *Volkes Stimme? Rechtspopulismus in Europa*. Bonn: Dietz.

—(1995). *Rechtsextremismus: Eine kritische Bestandsaufnahme nach der Wiedervereinigung*. Bonn: Bouvier (2., erw. Aufl.).

Pligt, J. van der and Koomen, W. (2009). *Achtergronden en determinanten van radicalisering en terrorisme*. Amsterdam: Universiteit van Amsterdam, Onderzoeksinstituut psychologie.

Police Service of Northern Ireland (2006). 'Domestic incidents and crimes 2005–06'. Available at http://www.psni.police.uk/2._domestic_incidents_and_crimes–3.pdf [accessed 4 July 2011].

—(2011). 'Hate Incidents and Crimes 2005–06'. Available at: http://www.psni.police.uk/3._hate_incidents_and_crimes–4.pdf [accessed 4 July 2011].

Poole E. (2006). 'The Effects of September 11 and the War in Iraq on British Newspaper Coverage', in E. Poole and J. E. Richardson (eds) *Muslims and the News Media*. London: I.B. Taurus, pp. 96–97.

Poot, de C. and Sonnenschein, A. (2009). *Jihadistisch Terrorisme in Nederland: een beschrijving op basis van afgesloten opsporingsonderzoeken*, Den Haag: Ministerie van Justitie, Wetenschappelijk Onderzoek en Documentatiecentrum, Available at http://www.wodc.nl/onderzoeksdatabase/inzicht-in-islamitische-terrorismebestrijding-obv-vanrecent-afgesloten-opsporingsonderzoek.aspx [accessed 13 August 2010].

Pratt, J. (2003). *Class, Nation and Identity: The anthropology of political movements*, London: Pluto Press.

Profil, 24 January 2010 (see www.profil.at/articles/1012/560/265086/man-islamfeind-geert-wilders-interview as of 2 October 2011).

Provincial Representative of the Province of Northern Holland, *Letter to the Mayors of the Cities in the Province of Northern Holland*, 29 January 1992.

rafinfo.de (undated) RAF-Aufloesungserklaerung, *rafinfo.de: die Webressource zur Roten Armee Fraktion*, at http://www.rafinfo.de/archiv/raf/raf–20-4-98.php [accessed 6 March 2012].

Ranstorp, M. (ed.) (2007). *Mapping Terrorism Research: State of the Art, Gaps and Future Direction*, Abingdon: Routledge.

Rashid, Ahmed (2001). *Taliban: the storey of the Afghan Warlords*, Pan Books: London.

Raufer, X. Front National: sur les Motifs d'une Ascension, *Le Debat*, 63, January–February 1991.

Repo, Jemina (2011). Äärioikeiston rasismi kytkeytyy naisvihaan [The far-right's racism links to hatred of women], *Helsingin Sanomat* 25.8.2011.

Richardson, R. (ed.) (1997). *Commission on British Muslims and Islamophobia: a challenge for us all*. London: Runnymede Trust.

Rockwell, G. L. (1960). *How to Get out or Stay out of an Insane Asylum*, Arlington VA: American Nazi Party.

—(1967). *White Power: A Nationalist Perspective*, Arlington VA: American, Nazi Party.

Rokeach, M. (1960). *The Open and Closed Mind: Investigations into the nature of belief systems and personality systems,* New York: Basic Books.
Rolston, B. (2004). 'Legacy of intolerance: racism and Unionism in South Belfast'. Available at http://www.irr.org.uk/2004/february/ak000008.html [accessed 4 July 2011].
Rydgren, J. (2004). *The Populist Challenge, Political Protest and Ethno-Nationalist Mobilization in France,* Oxford: Berghanan Books.
—(2005). 'Is Extreme Right-Wing Populism Contagious?' Explaining the Emergence of a New Party Family', *European Journal of Political Research,* Volume 44, pp. 413–37.
Sack, Fritz (1984). 'Die Reaktion von Gesellschaft, Politik und Staat auf die Studentenbewegung', in Sack, F. and Steinert, H. (eds), *Analysen zum Terrorismus Band 4/2: Protest und Reaktion.* Opladen: Westdeutscher Verlag, pp. 106–226.
Scarman, Lord (1982). *The Scarman Report: The Brixton Disorders, 10–12 April, 1981.* London: Pelican.
Scheerer, Sebastian (1984). 'Die Bundesrepublik Deutschland oder: die Gefahren der "Deutschen Empfindlichkeit"', in Sack, F. and Steinert, H. (eds) *Analysen zum Terrorismus Band 4/2: Protest und Reaktion.* Opladen: Westdeutscher Verlag, pp. 463–9.
Scheffer, P. (2000). *Het multiculturele drama,* in NRC, 29 January 2000.
Schimel, Anne (1998). 'Justice 'de plomb' en Italie', *Le Monde Diplomatique,* April 1998; at http://www.monde-diplomatique.fr/1998/04/SCHIMEL/10247 [accessed 18 January 2012].
Schinkel, W. (2007). Denken in een tijd van sociale hypocrisie. Aanzet tot een theorie voorbij de maatschappij, Kampen: Klement.
—(2008). De gedroomde samenleving, Kampen: Klement.
Schmid, Alex P. (2004). Frameworks for Conceptualising Terrorism. *Terrorism and Political Violence.* 16 (2) pp. 197–221.
Schnabel, P. (1991). De multiculturele illusie. Een pleidooi voor aanpassing en assimilatie, Utrecht: FORUM.
Searchlight (1986). 'Front's "Fixer" with Paramilitaries Moves Full Time to Northern Ireland', Issue 137, pp. 3–4.
—(1989). 'Wales and Northern Ireland NF Heads "Where the Terror Is"', Issue 163, pp. 9–11.
Sharrock, D. (2009). 'Northern Ireland has "culture of intolerance"', *The Times,* 18 June.
Shirlow, P. and McGovern, M. (eds) (1997). *Who are 'The People'? Unionism, Protestantism and Loyalism in Northern Ireland,* London: Pluto.
Simi, P. and Futrell, R. (2010). *American Swastika,* Lanham: Rowman and Littlefield.
Snow, D. and Benford, R. (1988). 'Ideology, Frame Resonance, and Mobilization', in *International Social Movement Research* (vol. 1, pp. 197–217).
Souhami, A. (2007). Understanding Institutional Racism: the Stephen Lawrence Inquiry and the Police Service Reaction, in *Policing beyond Macpherson: Issues in policing, race and society,* Devon: Willan.
Southern, N. (2007). 'Protestant Alienation in Northern Ireland: A Political, Cultural and Geographical Examination', *Journal of Ethnic and Migration Studies,* Volume 33, Number 1, pp. 159–80.

Spitsnieuws.nl, 26 April 2011. See http://www.spitsnieuws.nl/archives/media/2011/04/bevrijdingsfestival_verbiedt_a.html as of [accessed 2 October 2011].

Spöhr, H. and Kolls, S. (Hrsg.) (2010). Rechtsextremismus in Deutschland und Europa, Actuelle Entwicklungstendenzen im Vergleich, Frankfurt am Main: Peter Lang.

Sprinzak, E. 'Right-Wing Terrorism in Comparative Perspective', in Bjørgo, T. (ed.) (1995). *Terror from the Extreme Right,* London: Frank Cass.

Steenkamp C. J. (2008). 'Loyalist paramilitary violence after the Belfast Agreement', Ethnopolitics, Volume 7, Number 1, pp. 159–76.

Stern, K. (1996). *A Force upon the Plain,* New York: Simon and Schuster.

Sternhell Z. (2000). *Ni Droite ni Gauche, L'Idéologie Fasciste en France*, Fayard.

Stout, M. E., Huckabey, J. M., Schindler, J. R., and Lacey, W. (2008). *The Terrorist Perspectives Project: Strategic and Operational Views of Al Qaida and Associated Movements*, Naval Institute Press.

Stormfront (2010). Biggest threat to Europe,-Islam, available on http://www.stormfront.org/forum/t737518/ [accessed 9 May 2011].

Straw, Jack (2009). Stephen Lawrence Inquiry: Ten years on. London: Ministry of Justice. http://www.justice.gov.uk/news/speech240209a.htm [accessed 10 September 2010].

Spencer, G. (2008). *The State of Loyalism in Northern Ireland*, Basingstoke: Palgrave Macmillan.

Suall, I. (1995). *The Skinhead International,* New York: Anti-Defamation League.

Suarez, A. (2002). *Relatório Sobre Trabalhadores*, Belfast: Multicultural Resource Centre.

Sunstein, Cass (2001). *Republic.com,* Woodstock: Princeton Univeristy Press.

Synovate (2011). Beoordeling kabinet na 100 dagen, Utrecht: Synovate (28 January).

Taguieff, P.-A. (1994). *Sur la Nouvelle Droite*, Descartes & Compagnie.

Tandonnet, M. (2006). *Immigration, Sortir du Chaos*, Flammarion.

Tilly, C. (2008). *Contentious Performances*, Cambridge: Cambridge University Press.

Treadwell, J. and Garland, J. (2011). Masculinity, Marginalization and Violence: A case study of the English Defence League, British Journal of Criminology 51, 621–634.

UAF (2011, February). EDL's links to BNP exposed as antifascists march in Barnsley. http://uaf.org.uk/2011/02/barnsley-antifascists-march-as-edls-links-to-bnp-exposed/ [accessed 13 October 2011].

United States District Court for the District of Colorado (1997). Criminal Action No. 96-CR-68: UNITED STATES OF AMERICA, Plaintiff, vs. TIMOTHY JAMES McVEIGH, Defendant. Opening Statement for the Prosecution (24th April).

U.S. Department of Justice, Federal Bureau of Investigation (2008). *Hate Crime Statistics, 2007*.

Van der Valk, I. (2010). Islamistisch extremisme in P. Rodrigues and J. van Donselaar (eds), *Monitor Racisme & Extremisme: Negende rapportage*. (pp. 85–108) Amsterdam: Amsterdam University Press/Anne Frank Stichting/Universiteit Leiden. English version: http://www.annefrank.org/en/Worldwide/Monitor-Homepage/Research/Fifteen-years-of-the-Racism-Extremism-Monitor/

—(2012). *Islamofobie en Discriminatie*. Amsterdam: Amsterdam University Press.
Van der Valk, I. and Wagenaar, W. (2010). *Monitor Racisme & Extremisme: In en uit extreemrechts*. Amsterdam: Amsterdam University Press/Anne Frank Stichting/Universiteit Leiden. English version: http://www.annefrank.org/en/Worldwide/Monitor-Homepage/Research/With-help-rightwing-extremists-pull-out-sooner/
Vial, E. (2010). *La Cagoule a Encore Frappé*, Larousse.
Vietta S. (1996). *Heidegger, Critique du National-Socialisme et de la Technique*, Pardès.
VPRO broadcasting network, *24 uur met...*, 24 January 2011. http://programma.vpro.nl/24uurmet/afleveringen/2011/Fleur-Agema.html as of [accessed 2 October 2011].
Wagenaar, W. and J. van Donselaar (2006). 'Racistisch en extreemrechts geweld in 2005', in J. van Donselaar and P. R. Rodrigues (eds) *Monitor Racisme & Extremisme. Zevende Rapportage*, Amsterdam/Leiden: Anne Frank Stichting/Departement Bestuurskunde Universiteit Leiden.
—(2008). 'Racistisch en extreemrechts geweld in 2007', in J. van Donselaar and P. R. Rodrigues (eds) *Monitor Racisme & Extremisme. Achtste Rapportage*, Amsterdam/Leiden: Anne Frank Stichting/Departement Bestuurskunde Universiteit Leiden.
Waldmann, Peter (1998). *Terrorismus: Provokation der Macht*. Munich: Gerling Verlag.
—(2002). 'Terrorismus als weltweites Phaenomen: Eine Einfuehrung', in Frank, H. and Hirschmann, K. (eds), *Die weltweite Gefahr. Terrorismus als internationale Herausforderung*. Berlin: Berlin Verlag Arno Spitz, pp. 11–26.
Walzer, Michael (2002). Can There Be a Decent Left? *Dissent* (Spring). Available at: http://www2.kenyon.edu/Depts/Religion/Fac/Adler/Politics/Waltzer.htm [accessed 15 August 2008].
Werbner, Pnina, 2005. Islamophobia: Incitement to religious hatred – legislating for a new fear? *Anthropology Today*, 21 (1) pp. 5–9.
Wilders, G. (2008). *Fitna*. The film is available on: http://www.liveleak.com/view?i=18b_1207466634 as show on [accessed 2 October 2011].
—(2009). Algemene Beschouwingen, 16 September 2009. See www.youtube.com/watch?v=KbsewZuvvko as of [accessed 2 October 2011].
—(2011). Declaration on Norway. See http://www.pvv.nl/index.php/component/content/article/36-geert-wilders/4529-verklaring-geert-wilders-noorwegen.html as of [accessed 2 October 2011].
Wilkinson, Paul (2001). *Terrorism Versus Democracy: The Liberal State Response* (1st edn). London: Frank Cass.
Willems, H. (1995). 'Development, Patterns and Causes of Violence against Foreigners in Germany: Social and Biographical Characteristics of Perpetrators and the Process of Escalation,' in *Terrorism and Political Violence* (vol. 7, issue 1, pp. 162–81).
Willemsen, C. (ed.) (2010). *Dossier Wilders: uitspraken van de meest besproken Nederlandse politicus van deze eeuw*, Schelluinen: House of Knowledge.
Witte, R. (1996). *Racist Violence and the State. A comparative analysis in Britain, France and the Netherlands*, London: Addison Wesley Longman.

—(2010). Al eeuwenlang een gastvrij volk. Racistisch geweld en overheidsreacties in Nederland 1950–2009, Amsterdam: Aksant.

—(2011). Blickpunkt Niederlande. Islamfeindschaft als wahlstrategisches Erfolgsmodell, in W. Benz & T. Pfeiffer (eds) (2011) *'Wir oder Scharia'? Islamfeindliche Kampagnen im Rechtsextremismus. Analysen und Projekte zut Prävention*, Schwalbach: Wochenschau Verlag.

Witte, R., P. Brassé and K. Schram (2005). *Moskeebrand in Helden. Evaluatie van de aanpak en lessen voor de toekomst*, Utrecht: FORUM.

WNP (White Nationalist Party) (2002). 'A Nationalist Odyssey'. Available on http://www.aryanunity.com/WNP/nocompromise.html [accessed 6 May 2011].

WRR, Wetenschappelijke Raad voor het Regeringsbeleid (1989). Allochtonenbeleid *Rapport 36*, Den Haag: SDU.

Yaqoob, Salma (2007). British Islamic Political Radicalism, in Tahir Abbas (ed.) *Islamic Political Radicalism: A European Perspective*. Edinburgh: Edinburgh University Press.

Ye'or, B. (2005). *Eurabia: The Euro-Arab Axis*. New Jersey: Farleigh Dickinson University Press.

Zúquete, José Pedro (2008). The European extreme-right and Islam: New directions? *Journal of Political Ideologies*, 13:3, 321–44.

Index

7/7 34, 39, 42, 46, 203, 248
9/11 5, 10, 21–2, 31–2, 36, 38, 40–2, 45, 47, 49–50, 53, 55, 70, 114–15, 119, 136, 140, 173–5, 177, 179, 203, 242, 246, 248, 250
2083: A European Declaration of Independence (manifesto of Breivik, Anders B.) 169, 171

Action Française 157, 162, 164
Adams, Gerry 189, 206
Adorno, T. W. 4, 172
Afghanistan 175, 177, 226, 229
Ageman, Fleur (deputy leader of PVV, Netherlands) 119
Algeria 11, 150, 151–3
Al-Qa'ida 10, 175, 205, 226–8
Al-Ansari, Sayf 232
Alleanza Nazionale 87
Al-Suri, Abu Mu'sab 232
Ali, Hirschi 116–19
American Nazi Party 27, 218, 221
Amis, Martin 35
Amoss, Colonel Ulius 231
Anti-Defamation League 21
Antifa 193
anti-Semitism 35, 106, 122, 134, 138, 141, 175–6, 182, 241
Aryan Brotherhood 24
Aryan Nations 20–2, 24–5, 232
Aryan Republican Party 23
Aryan Strike Force 231–3
Aryan Warriors 24
Asatru 19
Austria 16, 87
Austria First 88
Austrian Freedom Party 87

Australia 18, 25, 97, 174
Azzam, Abdullah 226, 229

Baksh, Abdul Qadir (spokesman for Luton mosque) 47–8
Balin, Hirsch (Netherlands Minister of Justice) 109
Bangladesh 40, 46, 53–4
Barnbrooke, Richard (BNP) 68
Beam, Louis (member of US revolutionary right) 20, 218, 221
Begin, Menachem 189, 206
Bennett, David (historian) 16
Bennett, Ronan (novelist) 34–5
Berg, Alan (assassinated Denver talk-show host) 23
Benoist, Alan de, French (radical right thinker) 157–8, 161
Berlet, Chip (co-author of *Right-Wing Populism in America*) 172
Berlin 4, 9, 192, 199–200
Berwick, Andrew (pen name of Anders Breivik) 169
Bjorgo, Tore 9, 249
Black, Don (former Grand Dragon, KKK) 25–6
Blood and Honour Field Manual 225
Bloc Identitaire (French right-wing group) 154, 158, 161
Bolkestein, Frits 110–13
Book of Numbers 19
Bradford 42, 50, 233
Brandt, Willy (former Chancellor of the Federal Republic of Germany) 193
Breivik, Anders Behring 3, 10–12, 66, 71, 121–2, 169–74, 176–7, 181–3, 233, 242, 246, 249

INDEX

manifesto of 3, 121, 169, 171, 175, 177, 233
  see also *2083: A European Declaration of Independence*
British Israelism 19
British National Party (BNP) 32, 37–9, 41, 50–3, 55, 66–8, 80, 88, 89, 240, 246
British People's Party (BPP) 218, 220, 228, 233
Brixton, riots in 107
Brown Army Faction 208
Brussels 180, 242
Burnley, riots in 42
Bush, President George W. 177
Butt, Kamal Raza, murder of 39
Butler, 'Reverend' Richard 20, 24

Cagoule, La 150
California Nazi Low Riders 24
Calvert-Smith, Mr Justice 52
Carroll, Kevin, English Defence League 68, 78
Casa Pound, La 158–9
Choudhury, Emdadur 72
Church of Creativity 19
Church of Jesus Christian 25
Christianity 19, 110, 112, 223, 228
clash of civilizations 56, 70
Clerkin, Donald (head of Euro-American Alliance) 26
Cochrane, Kelso, murder of 39
Cold War 136, 174, 188, 191, 200, 207, 249
Combat 18 91, 218, 226, 228
Commander Pedro *see also* Langan, Peter Kevin 23
Community Security Trust 37
Condell, Pat 70
Copeland, David (nail bomber) 38
Copenhagen 180, 242
Copsey, Nigel (analyst of UK right-wing) 51, 65–6, 68, 80, 88, 240
Corsican radicals 170, 191
Cosmotheism Community Church 25
Cotswold Agreement 27
Cottage, Robert (jailed member of BNP) 51, 246

Counterjihad 3, 6, 12, 171–4, 179–9, 180–2, 242
Counter-jihad *see* Counterjihad
Covington, Harold (former of National White People's Party) 24
Cozzens, J. B. 231
Creativity Movement 223, 225, 228, 245
Cunningham, Jason (imprisoned member of UK extreme right) 51

Delta commandos 150
Deutsche Aktionsgruppen 195
Donaldson, Ian Stuart (British white supremacist) 226, 228, 229, 230–1
Duke, David (US Klansman) 24
Dutch Defence League (DDL) 139

East London Mosque 33–4
Egalité Reconciliation 158, 161
Engage (group monitoring right wing in UK) 32
English Defence League (EDL) 2, 3, 5–6, 11, 32, 46, 65, 139, 179–80, 216, 233, 240
ETA 191
Eurabia (seminal Counterjihad text) 70, 141, 180
Euro-American Alliance 26
European Kindred 24
European Liberation Front 26
Eysenck, H. J. 4

Fabrice, Robert (president of Bloc Identitaire) 155
Faisal, Abdullah, Jamaican cleric 228
Falwell, Jerry 16
FBI 17, 20, 23, 25, 248
Fighting Communist Organizations 185, 191
Fini, Gianfranco (former head of Italian National Alliance, current leader of Future and Freedom) 155
Finland 181, 242
Fortuyn, Pim 115–18
Four Freedoms (website) 70
France 2, 11, 66, 87, 90, 132, 149, 150, 241–2, 244, 247

INDEX

and Algeria 11, 150, 152–4
and Catholicism 157, 162
and decolonisation 156, 158
groups, movements and political parties in
  Action Française 154, 157, 162
  Anti-Utilitarian Movement in Social Sciences (MAUSS) 158
  Bloc Identitaire 154, 158, 161
  Cagoule, La 158
  Delta Commandos 150
  Egalité Reconciliation 158, 161
  Front de Libération Nationale (FLN) 151, 160
  Front National 149, 151–7, 159, 160–1, 241, 244
  Groupe Charles Martel 152, 164
  Group for Research and Study of European Civilization (GRECE) 157, 158, 163
  Nationalist French and European Party (PNFE) 162–3
  Nouvelle Droite 157–8
  Ordre Nouveau 153
  OAS (Secret Army Organisation) 150–2, 157, 160
  ORAF (Resistance Order of French Africa) 151
  OSARN (Secret Organisation for National Revolutionary Action) 150
  Union for French Democracy (UDF) 153
  Unité Radicale 154, 162
and Islam 157, 160–3
in the Vichy period 154
Frankfurt School 172

Gates of Vienna, blog 1172–3
Gavan, Terence (former BNP member) 53, 247
Germany 12, 27–8, 66, 87, 88, 124, 132, 137, 150, 159, 187, 188, 190, 191–6, 224, 233, 243
  attacks on
    Buback, Siegried 197, 203
    Herrhausen, Alfred 203
    Munich Oktoberfest 195
    Ponto, Juergen 203
    Rohwedder, Detlef Karsten 196, 203
    Schleyer, Hans-Martin 196, 203
    Shlomo, Lewin 195
  counter-terrorist legislation in 196–8
  left-wing groups in
    Antifa 193
    Fighting Communist Organizations 188, 191
    June 2nd Movement 188
    Linke Autonome 193
    racist confrontation in 109
    Red Army Faction (RAF) 150, 159, 188, 193, 196–7
    Revolutionary Cells 193
  right-wing groups in
    Brown Army Fraction 208
    Deutsche Aktionsgruppen (German Action Groups) 195
    Germany First 88
    Nationale Autonome (National Autonomous Groups) 195
    National Socialist Underground 187
    Wehrsportgruppe Hoffmann 195
    Zwickau cell 187–8, 198–200, 202–3, 205–6, 247
  right-wing targeting 194–201
  security services in
    Bundesamt fuer Verfassungsshutz (BfV) 194–5, 201
    Bundeskriminalamt (BKA) 194, 201
    Landesamt fuer Verfassungschutz (LfV) 191
  Turkish mafia in 187, 199, 205
Germany First 84
Gilleard, Martyn, (jailed British Nazi sympathiser) 51, 247
Gillespie, Sean (US neo-Nazi skinhead) 23
Gilligan, Andrew (commentator) 70, 91–4
Green, Reverend Alan (chair of Tower Hamlets Interfaith Forum) 33–4
Griffin, Nick (leader of BNP) 42, 216

INDEX

Hale, Matt (leader of Creativity Movement) 223
Hammer, Max (Blood and Honour writer) 230, 232
Hasan, Mehdi (editor of *New Statesman*) 51
hate groups 17, 216
hate music 25
   Hate Train 25
   Max Resist 25
   Skrewdriver 25
   White Power 25, 28
hate speech 27, 137
Hayden Lake, Idaho 20
Heitmeyer, Wilhelm 196, 203–4
helptheprisoners.org 229
Hess, Henner 200–1, 206–8
Hewitt, Christopher: *Understanding Terrorism in North America* 21–2, 71, 80
Hitler, Adolf 15, 20, 27, 163, 225
Hizb-ut Tahrir 70
Hofstadter, Richard 15
Holocaust 18, 219, 223
   denial of 18, 27

Identity Christianity 19, 25
Identity theology 25
Inspire magazine 226
Institute of Race Relations 54
Internet and recruitment to extreme right 25–6, 129, 132, 137, 145, 161, 171, 175, 177–8, 207, 230
IRA 85, 90, 190, 193
Islam4UK 70, 72
Islamic Forum of Europe (IFE) 34
Islamism 7, 8, 217, 232, 240
Islamists 5, 133, 205, 217, 226, 242
Islamization (Islamisation) 115, 118, 121, 137, 140, 181, 161, 242
Islamophobia 174, 176, 241
Islamophobia Watch 32
Italy 8, 87, 106, 150, 155, 158–9, 163, 242

Jameson, Neil (director of London Citizens) 34
Jay, Professor Martin 172

Jensen, Peder (Norwegian counterjihadist essayist) 176
Jews, as targets of extreme right-wing hostility 2, 16, 19–21, 23, 28, 216, 219, 221, 222, 226, 241
John Birch Society 16
Jordan, Colin, British Nazi 26
Justiciar Knights 3

Kaplan, Jeff 26, 218
Klu Klux Klan (KKK) 26, 51
Klansman 20, 234
Klansmen 3
Klassen, Ben (founder of Church of the Creator (also known as the Creativity Movement)) 19, 223–5, 227
Koran, extreme right-wing criticism of 119–20
Knoope, Peter: *Right-Wing Extremism: A Spoiled Identity Perspective* 1, 4, 250
Koopmans, Ruud 244
Kunast, Beate (leader of German Green Party) 188

Ladin, Usama bin 215, 219, 228, 232
Lane, David (US white supremacist and founder of The Order) 18, 218–9, 222
Langan, Peter Kevin (leader of US Aryan Republican Party) 23
Lauck, Gary Rex (US revolutionary rightist) 27
Leaderless Resistance (pamphlet by Louis Beam) 20, 221, 231
leaderless resistance, idea of 226, 231–2
Le Pen, Jean-Marie (founder of Front National) 156, 160
Le Pen, Marine (current leader of Front National) 155
Liddle, Rod 35
Lind, William S. 172
Lipset, Seymour 15
Litmann, Giselle: *Eurabia* 180
London citizens 34
London Muslim Centre (LMC) 33–4

INDEX

lone wolves 20, 23, 25, 38, 55, 121
Lööw, Helené (Swedish social scientist) 27
loyalism 94–5
loyalist paramilitaries 91, 96
loyalists 11, 85–6, 89–90, 96–8

MacGregor, Neil (threatened to blow up Glasgow Central Mosque) 51, 247
Macpherson, Lord: *The Stephen Lawrence Inquiry* 36
Mandela, Nelson 189, 206
Marseilles 152, 160, 163
Mattress, Serta 24
Maurras, Charles (leader of Action Française) 154
May, Edward (counterjihad blogger) 180, 181
McVeigh, Timothy 9, 20–1, 25, 92, 222
Mein Kampf 120
Merkel, Angela (Chancellor of the Federal Republic of Germany) 202
Molyneaux, K.: *Klassen; White Empire* 230, 234
Monitor on Racism and Extremism 112, 114, 116
Morrison, Eddy: White Nationalist Report 231, 233
MSI (Italian Social Movement) 87, 159
mud people 19–20, 242
mud races 19, 224
Mullins, Peter (BNP spokesman) 50
Murray, Douglas 70
Muslim Council of Britain (MCB) 34, 37
Muslims against Crusades (MAC) 70
Muslims, as targets 2, 6–7, 10, 12, 16, 18, 37–52, 53, 73–4, 80, 110, 115, 118–19, 132, 135–6, 139–40, 151, 232–3
Muslim Safety Forum (MSF) 37, 39

National Alliance (Italian political party) 155
National Front (NF) (right-wing party in UK) 52, 55, 66, 67, 80, 240
National White People's Party 24

Nationalist Week (newsletter of BNP) 233–4
Nazism 19, 106, 171, 193, 219
Neo-Nazis/Neo-Nazism 19, 25, 99, 109, 122, 162, 171, 193, 221, 241
Netherlands political
  parties in
    Centrum Democraten 109
    Centrum Party 108–9
    Christian Democrats 111, 116, 121
    Dutch People's Union (NVU) 138
    Freedom Party (PVV) 105, 118, 124
    Lijst Pim Fortuyn (LPF) 116
    Liveable Netherlands (*Leefbaar Nederland*) 115
    People's Party for Freedom and Democracy (VVD) 110, 116
  right-wing activity in
    anti-Semitism 133, 138, 140
    'classical outsiders' 11, 105
    deradicalization 129, 132, 134, 135
    migrants 106–7, 110–11, 113, 119–20
    'modern insiders' 11, 105, 123
    murder of Duinmeijer, Kerwin 108
    murder of Van Gogh, Theo 117, 119, 132, 137, 139–40
    racism 106, 108–9, 112–13, 115, 131, 135–6, 140
    radicalization 106, 117–119, 129, 131–3, 142–4
    riots 106–7
    targeting of mosques and Islamic schools 114, 139–40
New Christian Right 16
New World Order 17, 215, 220, 229
New Zealand 18, 97, 174
Nichols, Terry (McVeigh's co-conspirator) 21, 222
Nordland 20
Norse gods 19
Norse mythology 230
North America 18, 174
Northern Ireland and British National Party 89
  Combat 18 91
  Democratic Unionist Party (DUP) 95
  Life and Times Survey 94

INDEX

Loyalist Commission 96–7
migrant populations 87, 91–2
National Front 89–90, 93
Orange Order 97
Police Service of Northern Ireland (PSNI) 93, 102
Progressive Unionist Party (PUP) 95
racist violence 91–7
Ulster Defence Association (UDA) 89
Ulster Freedom Fighters (UFF) 90
Ulster Volunteer Force (UVF) 90, 95
Northern League 16
Norway 87, 171, 174
　Breivik's attacks in 10–12, 71, 121, 169, 187, 233, 242

Odin 19
Oklahoma City, attack in 9, 20–3, 222, 248
Oldham riots 42
Ordine Nuevo *see* Italian Social Movement

Paganism 19
Pentagon 22, 248
Philips, Melanie 70
Phineas Priesthood 19, 25
Pierce, William (former head of neo-Nazi Alliance) 20, 24, 27, 218
Pontifex Maximus (self-styled title of Ben Klassen) 19

Qutb, Sayyid 229

Rabb, Earl 15
Racial Holy War 20, 28, 218, 224, 225, 242, 245
Racial Volunteer Force 215, 218, 229, 233
RAHOWA *see* Racial Holy War
Raspail, Jean: *The Camp of Saints* 222
Robertson, Pat (leader of New Christian Right) 16
Robinson, Tommy (EDL spokesperson) 75, 76, 179
Rockwell, George Lincoln (founder of American Nazi party) 27, 218, 221, 230

Rokeach, M. 4
Roosevelt, President Theodore 191
Ruby Ridge, Idaho 21
Rudolph, Erick (attack in Alabama) 22
Rudolf Hess Day 20
Runnymede Trust 36, 55, 136
Rushdie, Salman 174
Russia 7, 27

Sack, Fritz (German commentator) 199
Salafism 160, 207
Scandinavia 66, 174
Scandinavian Counter-Jihad Summit 242
Searchlight magazine 66, 71, 90, 220
Schnabel, Paul 113–14
Silent Brotherhood 23–5
skinheads 18, 23, 27–8, 114
Sorel, Alain (French rightist) 161
Southern Poverty Law Centre 17–8
Spain 106, 151, 164, 191
spoiled identity 4–5
Spencer, Robert (Jihad Watch) 178, 180, 183
Sprinzak, Ehud (political scientist) 28, 248
Stephen Lawrence Inquiry 39–42
Sternhell, Zeev (historian) 154
Stormfront (white supremacist forum) 26, 233, 235
Sweden 25, 27, 88
Swedish Democrats 87

Tea Party 16, 174
Temple B'nai Israel, attack on 23
The Camp of Saints see Raspail, Jean
The Truth about Islam (BNP recording) 42, 50
Tobias, Rabbi Pete 35
Tower Hamlets, London 33–44, 40, 57, 75, 77, 79
Turner Diaries: William Pierce 20, 220, 224

United against Fascism (UAF) 66, 74
United Kingdom *see also separate entry* for Northern Ireland
　right-wing
　　attacks 31–55, 74–6, 246

INDEX

demonstrations 76–8, 181, 241, 243
hate crimes 36–7
motivation 54–5
racism 38–41
right-wing groups and parties
British National Party (BNP) 32, 37–9, 41, 50, 51–3, 55, 56, 80, 88, 89, 240, 246
British People's Party (BPP) 218, 220, 228, 233
Combat 18 91, 218, 226, 228
English Defence League (EDL) 2, 3, 5–6, 11, 32, 46, 65, 139, 179–80, 216, 233, 240
National Front (NF) 52, 55, 66, 67, 80, 240
riots in 50, 58, 107
United States of America 66, 175, 177–8, 183, 191–2, 218–19, 222–3, 244
attacks on
Berg, Alan 23
health clinic, Alabama 22
immigrants 23
Jewish community centre, Los Angeles 21
Murrah Federal Building, Oklahoma City 9, 20–2, 248
Olympic Games, Atlanta 22
Temple B'nai Israel, synagogue, Oklahoma 23
compounds of 19, 25
distinctive attributes of 15–20
international links of 26–8
and KKK 3, 20, 25 51, 234
and lone wolves 23–5
membership 24–6
and music 24–5, 27
and Nazism 20–1
and paganism 19
and prisons 24
and purpose 20
and Racial Holy War (RAHOWA) 20, 28
and skinheads 27–8
threat from 22, 28, 244
world view of 18–20, 237
and Zionist Occupation Government (ZOG) 23, 28
militia movements 16–17
revolutionary right groups
American Nazi Party 26, 218, 221
Aryan Brotherhood 24
Aryan Republican Party 23
Aryan Warriors 24
Californian Nazi Low Riders 24
Church of Creativity 19
Church of Jesus Christians 24
European Kindred 24
Identity Christianity 19, 25
Phineas Priesthood 19, 25
Silent Brotherhood 22–5
right-wing populist groups 15–6
US, USA see United States of America
US Justice Department 21
Unmasked: The Welsh Defence League (BBC documentary) 71

Van Gogh, Theo 116–17, 119, 125, 132, 137, 139
Vienna School 3, 171,–3
Viguerie, Richard (US New Right member) 16
Vlaams Belang (VB) (Flemish political party) 83, 168

Waco, Texas 21
Waldmann, Peter, historian 189–90, 195, 203
Weaver family, right-wing extremists at Ruby Ridge 21
White Aryan Resistance (WAR) 24
White Defence League (WDF) 39
White Nationalist Party (WNP) 89, 90, 229
White Nationalist Report 233
Wilders, Geert 5, 11, 70, 105, 118–24, 138–9, 178–9
Wilkinson, Paul 188, 190, 195, 20–3
World Church of the Creator 222–3, 227, 245
World Trade Centre 22, 248
World Union of National Socialists (WUNS) 26
Worrell, Nathan (neo-Nazi in UK) 52

Wotan 19
WOTANSVOLK 25

Yarborough, Gary (member of Silent Brotherhood) 24
Yaxley-Lennon, Stephen *see* Robinson, Tommy

Yockey, Francis Parker (founder of European Liberation Front) 26

Zionist Crusader-alliance 227
Zionist Occupation Government (ZOG) 2, 7, 23, 28, 227